DATE DUE

Texas
in the
CONFEDERACY

Shades of Blue and Gray Series

EDITED BY HERMAN HATTAWAY AND JON L. WAKELYN

The Shades of Blue and Gray Series offers Civil War studies for the modern reader—Civil War buff and scholar alike. Military history today addresses the relationship between society and warfare. Thus biographies and thematic studies that deal with civilians, soldiers, and political leaders are increasingly important to a larger public. This series includes books that will appeal to Civil War Roundtable groups, individuals, libraries, and academics with a special interest in this era of American history.

Texas
in the
CONFEDERACY

An Experiment in Nation Building

CLAYTON E. JEWETT

University of Missouri Press
COLUMBIA AND LONDON

Library of Congress Cataloging-in-Publication Data

Jewett, Clayton E.
    Texas in the Confederacy : an experiment in nation building / Clayton
E. Jewett.
        p.   cm.—(Shades of blue and gray series)
    Includes bibliographical references (p.) and index.
    ISBN 0-8262-1390-1
    1. Texas—History—Civil War, 1861–1865. 2. Texas—Politics and
government—1861–1865. 3. Texas—History—Civil War, 1861–1865—
Social aspects. 4. Group identity—Texas—History—19th century.
I. Title. II. Series.
E580 .J49 2002
973.7'13'09764—dc21   2002023836

Jacket designer: Susan Ferber
Text designer: Elizabeth K. Young
Typesetter: Bookcomp, Inc.
Printer and Binder: Thomson-Shore, Inc.
Typefaces: Times, Chestnut

Contents

Acknowledgments

This project would not have been possible without the help of many colleagues and friends. Rosemarie Zagarri, John O. Allen, and Mike Connally gave each chapter a thorough reading, offered much advice, and saved me from numerous mistakes. Emory Thomas, Mike Campbell, and Dale Baum offered many useful comments on various sections of this work presented at conferences. Larry Poos spent countless hours training me in the art of geographical and statistical analysis. Staff members at the Texas State Library and the Eugene Barker Center for American History made numerous searches and offered much useful information, and their patience is greatly appreciated. My parents' unconditional support pushed me to attain my goals. I am especially grateful to my editors, Beverly Jarrett and Jane Lago, for their continual support and patience throughout this process. Most of all, this would not have been possible without the guidance of my mentor and friend Jon L. Wakelyn, who shaped my ideas, challenged me at every turn, and offered his unyielding support. To him, I dedicate this work.

Texas
in the
CONFEDERACY

Introduction

Hath not the morning dawned with added light?
And shall not evening call another star
Out of the infinite regions of the night,
To mark this day in heaven? At last we are
A nation among nations; and the world
Shall soon behold in many a distant port
Another flag unfurled.
                            —*Henry Timrod, "Ethnogenesis"*

With these words, poet Henry Timrod hailed the first Confederate Congress's meeting at Montgomery, Alabama, and what many exclaimed as the creation of a Southern nation. To what extent a true nation existed, however, is debatable.[1]

In the 1960s, historian David Potter wrote that the idea that "the people of the world fall naturally into a series of national groups is one of the dominating pre-suppositions of our time." Potter revealed that historians use the framework of nationhood for two purposes. One is to discover the "degree of cohesiveness or group unity" of a people. Studies in this vein focus on nationalism and the prerequisites of nationhood, such as a common language, religion, traditions, and institutions. Potter, though, chided historians who are quick to equate culture with nationhood. To be sure, studies in this line of inquiry generally do not reveal the extent to which ordinary people claimed the same cultural or national loyalty, and provide only a top-down view of Southern nationhood and the Confederacy. The second purpose of the nationhood framework addresses the validity of "exercising autonomous powers." This route of study is concerned with the relationship between individuals and the appropriateness of exercising regulatory or punitive power over them. "It is axiomatic," Potter asserted, "that people tend to give their loyalty to institutions which protect them—that is, safeguard their interests—and political allegiance throughout history has been regarded as something given reciprocally in return for protection." Employing the framework in

---

1. Rollin G. Osterweis, *Romanticism and Nationalism in the Old South,* 154.

1

this context has led historians to concentrate on the development of central state authority and the extent to which a new Southern nation existed.[2]

Frank Vandiver argues, in *Their Tattered Flags: The Epic of the Confederacy,* that the Confederate constitution "smacked strongly of nationalism" and provided the framework for a strong central government. By the summer of 1862, he contends, the Confederacy "existed in its armies, in its emissaries, and in the hearts of its people—there was a Confederate nation." Furthermore, he claims that proof of a nation existed in the government's ability to control the white labor supply through conscription and exemption, and the government's ability to control the products of war through the supply departments that "shared the pattern of increasing nationalism." Emory Thomas extends this argument in his work *The Confederate Nation, 1861–1865.* Thomas argues that by establishing a framework for central state authority, the delegates at Montgomery, Alabama, created the Southern nation. Evidence for this contention emerged in the structures created to maintain central state authority: financing the government through bonds, agricultural gifts that were turned into specie, the creation of a national army, and the skeletal organizations of supply and service for the armed forces. Richard Bensel takes this line of inquiry an additional step in his monograph, *Yankee Leviathan: The Origins of Central State Authority in America, 1859–1877.* In his attempt to find "the true foundational moment in American political development," Bensel claims that the development of a strong central state followed as a result of Southern secession and Northern repression. Bensel argues that war mobilization for the South outstripped the region's productive capability and economy, and consequentially, "the southern mobilization was far more state-centered and coordinated than its northern counterpart." To support his argument, Bensel examines the centralization of Confederate authority, administrative capacity, the role of citizenship, control of property, the extraction of resources, and the conscription and exemption acts that were by far "the most important source of central state influence."[3]

These studies focusing on the establishment of central state authority assume political loyalty on the states' behalf, and have pointed to the downfall of the Southern nation due to cultural factors, military defeat, and poor governmental leadership. These studies also assume that individuals in the new Confederacy relied on the national government for the protection of individual rights. Whereas previous historians have pointed out the critical

2. Potter, *The South and the Sectional Conflict,* 35–39, 54–55.
3. Vandiver, *Their Tattered Flags,* 7, 23–24, 157; Thomas, *Confederate Nation,* 35–44, 57, 105, 117; Bensel, *Yankee Leviathan,* 10, 93, 97–98, 137.

issue of states' rights and the failure of the Davis administration to address the problems of the common individual, still there exists few studies that actually test the relationship between the state and the Confederate government.[4]

This study endeavors to fill this gap by employing an original theory of nation building. The process of nation building is intricate. It involves the definition, establishment, securement, and implementation of a political and economic identity. The responsibility for defining a political and economic identity partially rests on the elected political leaders who represent their constituents. In addition, the actions of the citizenry that mirror political rhetoric and action are an integral part of defining an identity. The extent to which this identity becomes established finds its expression in the actions of both the government and the people, and the magnitude to which they uphold and abide by this identity through the decisions that affect life, liberty, and property. Once defined and established, the securement of this identity is tested in the nation's relationship with other official bodies and the degree to which the nation, through political action, strives to promote the economic security of the citizenry. Finally, for a nation to exist and function in its fullest sense, government must implement this identity by working to promote and protect the economic and social welfare of the citizenry. This work uses the state of Texas as a case study to explicate this process of nation building. It examines how Texas, during the Civil War, defined, established, secured, and implemented an identity separate from that of other Southern states.[5]

Historians of Texas have gone far in revealing the contrasting loyalties and intricate relationships that existed in the Lone Star State during the Civil War.[6] Nevertheless, historians have paid little attention to testing these relationships on a larger scale. This gap is rather surprising because Charles W. Ramsdell and Frank Vandiver pointed out long ago the importance of state affairs as reactions to national politics.[7] Building on the suggestion

4. Frank Owsley, *State Rights in the Confederacy;* Paul Escott, *After Secession: Jefferson Davis and the Failure of Confederate Nationalism.*

5. Invaluable works that deal with the concept of nationalism and nationhood include Karl Deutsch, *Nationalism and Social Communication: An Inquiry into the Foundations of Nationality;* Ernest Gellner, *Nations and Nationalism;* Anthony D. Smith, *Theories of Nationalism;* Hans Kohn, *American Nationalism: An Interpretive Essay;* and Eric Hobsbawm, *Nations and Nationalism since 1780: Programme, Myth, Reality.*

6. Walter Buenger, *Secession and the Union in Texas;* James Marten, *Texas Divided: Loyalty and Dissent in the Lone Star State, 1856–1874;* Randolph Campbell, *An Empire for Slavery: The Peculiar Institution in Texas, 1821–1865.*

7. Charles W. Ramsdell, "Some Problems Involved in Writing the History of the Confederacy"; Frank E. Vandiver, "Some Problems Involved in Writing Confederate History"; Vandiver, *Rebel Brass: The Confederate Command System.*

of Ramsdell and Vandiver, the purpose of this study is to understand the function of state politics and the political relationship between Texas and the Confederate government during the American Civil War. The primary focus throughout much of the monograph is on the Texas legislature, a virtually neglected topic.[8] It examines political activity in Texas, seeking to discern how Texans related to secession and the formation of a new nation while simultaneously exhibiting a desire to safeguard their own economic well-being. In addition, it explores the role of leadership and how statesmen understood and handled the paradox between Confederate national interests of war and the protection of property and individual liberty. Furthermore, it illuminates the impetus behind and actions of state legislators as related not only to Texas and the Southwest, but also to the Confederacy as a whole.

The Civil War was more than a military battle over slavery; it was a struggle for the survival of all citizens, a battle for the future. It was there in the state legislatures that a conflict ensued. Politicians had a balancing act to perform as they struggled between the national interests of war and more localized concerns. For Texas politicians, the scales favored the interests of the state and its citizens over the Confederacy. Although most Texans were concerned about war and indeed divisions did exist to the degree of support for secession and a Southern nation, one thing rose above that to unite Texans: a desire for economic security. The effort of state politicians, rather than the Confederate government, to strive for economic security in the interest of the citizens did not bode well for the existence and success of the Southern Confederacy. Whether Texas politicians fully succeeded in their immediate endeavor to provide economic security and development is to some extent irrelevant. The fact that citizens were aware of their representatives' efforts and relied on the state, and that the state legislature responded in a time of crisis, is the critical issue.[9]

The definition of a political and economic identity for Texas emerged in the secession crisis. Secession from the Union represented a political move to

8. Studying under Frank Vandiver, Nancy Bowen sought to find "patterns of factionalism and to assess the impact of war on the State's political system." Although Bowen's work is an excellent study of the Texas governorship and state legislature, there is little attention given to Texas's political and economic relationship with the Confederate government. See Nancy Head Bowen, "A Political Labyrinth: Texas in the Civil War—Questions in Continuity."

9. For interpretations on the demise of a Southern nation and Confederate defeat, see Gabor S. Boritt, ed., *Why the Confederacy Lost;* Richard Beringer, *The Elements of Confederate Defeat: Nationalism, War Aims, and Religion;* Thomas, *Confederate Nation;* and Escott, *After Secession.*

define the economic interests of the South. Jon L. Wakelyn has shown in his recent work *Southern Pamphlets on Secession, November 1860–April 1861* that arguments for secession varied throughout the South. Though Southerners disagreed over what action to take, a consensus remained that the Republican Party's control of the federal government threatened the Southern way of life. Through an analysis of political pamphlets and speeches by Texas politicians, Chapter 1 examines the arguments for and against secession. Politicians offered constitutional, economic, and social justifications for and against secession. In addition, politicians vocalized their concern about the situation of Texas in this crisis. As with the rest of the South, Texans had many interests and many fears, but one element united Texans and all people: a defense of their material world. This defense found expression in the sociopolitical action of the citizenry. Thus, Chapter 2 examines the popular vote on secession, the economic factors associated with the popular vote, and organizations that emerged that represented citizens' desire for economic security and spurred Texans to embrace secession. The political speeches and sociopolitical actions of Texas citizens clearly defined a separate political and economic identity based upon the desire for economic security.

Chapter 3 reveals that it was the defense of their economic concerns and a desire for economic security that led Texans to conduct an offensive war, not against Union threat, but against civilized and uncivilized Indian tribes. An examination of Confederate-Indian treaties and the Indian problem in Texas sheds light on the precarious relationships among Texas, the Indians, and the Confederate government. Deep tensions existed among these groups as each sought to protect and promote their own material interests. The conflict that Texans faced with the Indians fostered the establishment of a separate identity from that of other Southern states. The establishment of a separate identity developed further and found expression through military service. Texans volunteered for and were drafted into both the state militia and the Confederate army. Chapter 4, a geographical and statistical analysis of military enlistment, sheds light on the extent to which Texans militarily supported the Confederate cause and reveals the county economic characteristics related to military enlistment. A thorough investigation of the muster rolls reveals that throughout the Civil War, a higher number and percentage of Texans chose to defend their material concerns by serving in the state militia instead of the Confederate army.

When Union forces gained control of the Mississippi River, the Confederate government reacted by strengthening the Trans-Mississippi Department, placing Gen. Edmund Kirby Smith in control of western states. Texans, though, viewed this as an assault upon their economic interests because the Trans-Mississippi Department relied heavily upon Texas to meet the necessities of war. Because Texans believed that Richmond had neglected them, especially in terms of frontier protection, state politicians were unwilling to cooperate fully with Kirby Smith. Thus, building on a separate identity that was defined and established through the initial stages of the Civil War, Chapter 5 reveals how Texas politicians secured this identity while confronting the necessities of war and encroachment from the Confederate government. Through a thorough investigation of the Texas State Penitentiary's production and supply of cloth, this chapter uncovers the pattern of Texas politics that sought to secure the economic interests of Texas citizens ahead of the Confederacy. Chapter 6 discloses that the conflict between Texas and the Trans-Mississippi Department fully erupted in the battle over cotton. The Confederate government desperately needed cotton to trade for the necessities of war. Consequently, Kirby Smith attempted to control the entire Texas cotton trade. Texas politicians, however, responded by establishing their own plan for the purchase and sale of cotton, creating conflict in the trans-Mississippi region. A detailed examination of Texas and Confederate legislative activity regarding cotton reveals that through the political process, Texas secured a separate identity by protecting and promoting the economic interests of the state and citizens.

Finally, Chapter 7 examines the political effort to promote economic security and social welfare through the legislature's support of railroads, education, mutual-aid societies, and state institutions—the implementation of a separate identity throughout the Civil War. The process and actions by which Texans defined, established, secured, and implemented a separate identity were intricately interwoven throughout the Civil War and did not necessarily take place in organized stages. Therefore, this work utilizes a topical approach, through the lens of the state legislature, to help explicate the understanding of Texas existing on its own in the Confederacy.

The focus on state legislative activity is a virtually neglected topic, an effect of the "Lost Cause." Before the Civil War ended, Southerners began writing their history of it, bringing a romantic interpretation to the battle over slavery. Scores of white Southerners took serious the immediate postwar effort to perpetuate the memory of the Confederacy, known as the "Lost Cause." Writings and institutions appeared, venerating the old and the new South. Organizations such as the Confederate Relief and Historical Association of Memphis, the Confederate Survivors' Association of South Carolina, and the Southern Historical Society based in New Orleans existed as the primary vehicles for promoting writings, rituals, and celebrations. The Southern Historical Society made a practice of inviting prominent ex-Confederates to speak about their wartime recollections and postwar solutions at its annual convention. Such societies went far in catapulting military leaders to historic fame, such as Robert E. Lee, Braxston Bragg, Albert Sidney Johnston, and Stonewall Jackson. Much of this transpired from the effort of a Virginia coalition under the leadership of Jubal Early who took over the presidency of the Southern Historical Society in 1873. Under Early's leadership, the society invited Texas politician Louis Trezevant Wigfall to address its convention in Dallas, Texas, in 1874. Wigfall, though, had been ill for quite some time and died in February, one month before the gathering. His appearance there and association with the organization no doubt would have secured him a more prominent place in Southern memory. Many of his contemporaries, after all, counted Wigfall as a great Southern leader. To an extent, though, Civil War historians have relegated political leaders to the back shelf of history, a result of the Lost Cause's effect on historical research. This enduring scholarly trend has darkened our understanding of leadership, the function of the government, and the crisis of the Southern Confederacy.[10]

Furthermore, because historians have often found it problematic to defend the existence of a Southern nation, they often point to the military defeat and failure of the Confederacy. Potter explains, "[I]t is difficult for the historian to attribute nationality to movements of which he morally disapproves, since the attribution itself would imply that the movement has a kind of validity." The continual focus on loss reveals an unwillingness to accept the possibility of an enduring Southern nationalism or nation in any form for fear it would be equated with a present-day acceptance of slavery. By examining the intricate process of nation building itself, however, we finally uncover the extent to which a Southern nation existed. In this manner, we finally put an end to striving for the answer to that century-old question of "why the South lost," and enter a new phase of inquiry regarding nationhood—one that not only helps bring a deeper understanding of the past and how the

10. Roman J. Heleniak and Lawrence L. Hewitt, eds., *Leadership during the Civil War: Themes in Honor of T. Harry Williams.* Initial works perpetuating the "Lost Cause" include Edward Pollard, *The Lost Cause: A New Southern History of the War of the Confederates;* Albert Taylor Bledsoe, *Is Davis a Traitor?* Robert L. Dabney, *A Defense of Virginia;* and Alexander Stephens, *A Constitutional View of the Late War between the States.* See Gaines M. Foster, *Ghosts of the Confederacy: Defeat, the Lost Cause, and the Emergence of the New South, 1865–1913,* 49.

South functioned, but also addresses the critical issue of the relationship among nationhood, individual rights, leadership, government relations, and government responsibility that holds implications for the present.[11]

This monograph employs not only the traditional method of studying textual sources, but also the technique of geographical and statistical analysis. The Borland Database 5.5 was used to create databases for statistical analysis. Databases were constructed according to counties. Counties were chosen as the primary field because Texas Senate districts contained several counties and House politicians often represented more than one county. In this manner, it becomes possible to analyze the voting behavior of politicians representing specific counties. Roll-call votes of state legislators were analyzed and assigned numbers according to support and nonsupport for an issue. Yea and nay votes did not necessarily correspond to support and nonsupport. In performing statistical analysis on legislative voting behavior, abstaining votes were counted as nonsupport for an issue. Through this method, voting participation and support were calculated using Minitab Release 10 for Windows. In addition, regression analysis was performed between roll-call votes and census data to determine the relationship between voting behavior and characteristics of the counties that politicians represented. Results of the statistical analysis are located in the appendixes. These results, transferred back into the Borland Database 5.5, along with general census data, were mapped using MapInfo Release 3.0 for Windows for the purpose of geographical analysis. Historians have generally shunned such analytical tools, "often regarding the time and effort involved in acquiring statistical, computer and analytical expertise as forbidding or antithetical to their main focus."[12] Regression analysis, though, is a means to making predictions about two or more related variables. Likewise, map production is not an end to itself but rather a means to provoke further questions and analysis, and explicate textual sources.

11. Potter, *South and Sectional Conflict,* 63.
12. Larry R. Poos and Clayton E. Jewett, "Digitizing History: GIS Aids Historical Research," 48.

PART I

Defining a Separate Identity

CHAPTER 1

"The Cold Sweat of Death"

Texas Prosecession and
Antisecession Politics

In September 1860, Texas politician Louis Trezevant Wigfall spoke in Tyler, Texas, where he outlined the pending political crisis.[1] With the importance of slavery to the political and economic life of Texans increasing, Texas's interest in the sectional conflict heightened. Southern political leaders such as Wigfall believed that if Abraham Lincoln won the upcoming presidential election, it would be a direct threat to the Southern way of life. A little more than two months after Wigfall spoke to the Tyler crowd, Abraham Lincoln's election victory in November 1860 heightened the fears of Southerners and Texans. They believed that Lincoln and the Republican Party would trample on individual rights by preventing the spread of slavery, and possibly worse—the full abolition of slavery. Consequently, politicians began to speak out about the state of the Union and the concern of individual states in this crisis. They spoke not only to clarify their interests and the interests of their constituents, but also to either support or refute the secession of Southern states.

Over the years, arguments have appeared attempting to explain the complexity of Texas's secession from the Union. The first thesis emerged during the Civil War when many individuals viewed secession as the work of radical fire-eaters and conspirators, leaders who were antidemocratic, who led the people to believe that only secession could guarantee the preservation of Southern rights and Southern institutions. In Texas, these sentiments sprang mainly from Union supporters who fled north once hostilities began to erupt.[2]

In the early twentieth century with the need for a "new South" argument,

---

1. See Louis T. Wigfall, *Speech of Louis T. Wigfall on the Pending Political Issues, Delivered at Tyler, Smith County, Texas, September 3, 1860.*

2. James P. Newcomb, *Sketch of Secession Times in Texas and Journal of Travel from Texas through Mexico to California, Including a History of the "Box Colony";* John T. Sprague, *The Treachery in Texas, the Secession in Texas, and the Arrest of the United States Officers and Soldiers Serving in Texas.* For more detailed attention to

Charles Ramsdell asserts, in "The Frontier and Secession," that local concern provided the impetus to accepting secession. The desire to protect slavery and the disgust over inadequate frontier protection, claims Ramsdell, moved Texans to embrace disunion.[3]

In the 1940s and 1950s, historians viewed secession in terms of the growth of Southern nationalism. This school of thought stressed the commonality of institutions, customs, and ideology as the motivating force behind disunion. Consequently, many historians began to see the South as a monolithic entity.[4]

Due to the nation's racial crisis in the 1950s and 1960s, however, slavery again became the driving force behind secession. Billy D. Ledbetter argues in his dissertation, "Slavery, Fear, and Disunion in the Lone Star State: Texans' Attitudes toward Secession and the Union, 1846–1861," that the desire to maintain slavery was the impulse behind secession. The fear of Republican ascendancy and potential slave insurrections brought on by the party's support of abolition, he asserts, motivated Texans to defend the *peculiar institution* through secession.[5]

In the past decade, historians have placed more emphasis on social and cultural differences. Walter L. Buenger argues in his work *Secession and the Union in Texas* that three distinct cultural groups existed in Texas that encompassed specific geographical regions. The process of settlement, Buenger claims, created distinct clusters of Texans separated by geographic bounds, reinforcing cultural attachments and diversity that influenced one's stance on secession. In a later article, "Texas and the Riddle of Secession," Buenger claims that the similarities and differences between the forces behind Unionism and secession, which were based on ethnocultural ties, accounted for the success of the secession movement in Texas. Other historians examining Texas secession, however, have revealed that religious affiliations, protection from abolitionist violence, and race unity also played significant parts in the secession crisis.[6]

---

the historiography of Texas secession, see Walter Buenger, "Texas and the Riddle of Secession," 151–82.

3. Charles W. Ramsdell, "The Frontier and Secession," 63–79.

4. Avery O. Craven, *The Growth of Southern Nationalism, 1848–1861.*

5. For other works in this historiographical line, see Steven A. Channing, *Crisis of Fear: Secession in South Carolina;* William L. Barney, *The Secession Impulse: Alabama and Mississippi in 1860;* J. Mills Thornton III, *Politics and Power in a Slave Society: Alabama, 1800–1860;* and Michael P. Johnson, *Toward a Patriarchal Republic: The Secession of Georgia.*

6. See Robin E. Baker and Dale Baum, "The Texas Voter and the Crisis of the Union, 1859–1861."

Even though historians have gone far in revealing the intricacies of Texas secession, less attention has been given to the politics of secession itself, specifically the arguments that political leaders proffered to support their course of action. Jon L. Wakelyn's monograph *Southern Pamphlets on Secession, November 1860–April 1861,* however, raises notice of this critical aspect of the Civil War and the need to study such discourse and sources. Using political pamphlets of Southern leaders, Wakelyn reveals the centrality of slavery to political arguments supporting Southern secession.

Texas politicians also made their opinions on secession known through political speeches that were printed in newspapers, and published and sold in pamphlet form to the public. Political pamphlets, as Wakelyn uncovers, not only reveal much about political pressures, but also were an effective tool to influencing constituents. Moreover, pamphlets disclose a great deal about society's values and anxieties. Texas politicians at the state and national levels held different ideas concerning the benefit and process of secession. Nevertheless, their arguments, in conjunction with political activity at the state level, shed light on the general and unique concerns of Texans. At the onset of the crisis, then, Texas politicians clearly articulated and defined a political and economic identity for the Lone Star State. They did so by presenting constitutional, economic, and social arguments for secession. In addition, political speeches railed against the Republican Party and its endorsement of abolition. Furthermore, politicians made a specific point of including Texas's position on the Civil War crisis. These arguments are essential to an understanding of Texas's worldview and reveal that the root of political crisis lay in the conflict to secure commercial interests. By exploring political rhetoric, one begins to understand that the political move to provide economic security emerged as the defining characteristic of Texas during the move for secession and through the Civil War, and provided the basis for defining a political and economic identity separate from that of other Southern states.[7]

Texas politicians relied on a constitutional defense to support their prosecession views and the necessity of a state convention to decide the issue of secession. A constitutional defense laid the groundwork for their opposition to the Republican Party and abolition. It also provided a framework to support slavery, commercial interests, and the protection of property. On the eve of secession, Texas was the fastest-growing state and was enjoying a period

---

7. The most current scholarship on secession pamphlets is Wakelyn, *Southern Pamphlets on Secession.* For a treatment on the importance of pamphlets in history and as current source material for historical research, see xiii–xxix.

of economic prosperity. Politicians sought to safeguard Texas's commercial fertility at all costs, and at the state and national levels they spoke fervently about such matters.[8]

On December 1, 1860, Judge Oran Milo Roberts spoke at the Texas state capitol on the impending crisis. Roberts was born in Laurens District, South Carolina, on July 9, 1815. He received his education at home until attending the University of Alabama in 1832. After college, he was admitted to the bar and served a term in the Alabama legislature. Roberts moved to Texas in 1841 and opened a law practice in San Augustine. Before the Civil War, he served as district attorney and district judge, and won appointment to the Texas Supreme Court. At the time of his speech, the Southern states had received word of the Republican victory only three weeks prior. The Texas legislature was not in session, yet was scheduled to convene in January. The United States Congress was set to convene in two short days. Oran M. Roberts started his speech by providing a constitutional argument for secession. He believed that the Constitution of the United States existed as a compact among independent sovereign states that formed a federal government with limited powers. He argued that if this compact were so broken as to take away the important rights of a state, then that state held the right to judge for itself, in its sovereign capacity, the proper course to preserve those rights, even if it meant seceding and joining another confederacy. He believed that the "inherent right" of the people to make and unmake governments, and to alter governments for the protection of their rights, existed as one of the reserved rights of the Constitution. He discounted the argument offered by Unionists that the government was "national" in all respects. It was, he claimed, national only in that it affected all people by its actions. Nationality in its actions, he said, was not inconsistent with the separate sovereignty of the states.[9]

Roberts further argued that states held the reserved right of power and authority over domestic institutions. He claimed that states had the power to reside over their domestic institutions and defend them to the fullest. He did not mean to support nullification in this argument, for he believed nullification was unconstitutional. However, he did believe that if state sovereignty

8. Ralph Wooster, *Texas and Texans in the Civil War*, 2.

9. O. M. Roberts, "Speech of Judge Oran Milo Roberts of the Supreme Court of Texas, at the Capitol, on the 1st December, 1860, upon the 'Impending Crisis,' " 8–10. For works on O. M. Roberts, see Lelia Bailey, "The Life and Public Career of O. M. Roberts, 1815–1883"; and Ford Dixon, "Oran Milo Roberts," in *Ten More Texans in Gray*, ed. W. C. Nunn.

were violated in this context, then a state held the right to end its loyalty, completely, to the federal government.[10]

The Constitution, he argued, thus served as a tool to balance the interests of the nation. To support this view, he drew upon the personal correspondence of James Madison. Roberts quoted Madison's letter to Edward Everett in which he wrote, "Free constitutions will rarely if ever be formed without re-ciprocal concessions—*without articles conditioned on, and balancing each other.*" Therefore, the main thrust of the Constitution, he argued, served to bind together states that had inherently different interests. Roberts clearly articulated, and people understood, that the Constitution therefore provided for and protected various political and economic interests.[11]

Similar constitutional arguments also provided the foundation for Louis Trezevant Wigfall's speech before the United States Senate, one week before the South Carolina convention planned to meet to decide on secession. Wig-fall was born in Edgefield, South Carolina, on April 21, 1816. He received his education at South Carolina College and the University of Virginia. He moved to Texas in 1846 and established a law practice in Nacogdoches with William B. Ochiltree. Wigfall was active in Texas politics from the moment he arrived in the state. In 1850, he was named to the Texas House of Representatives, was elected to the Texas Senate in 1857, and won elec-tion to the United States Senate in 1859. Wigfall's speech was a response to Senator Douglas from Illinois. Northern senators, specifically Douglas, were supposed to investigate the grievances of the South. Wigfall had asked Douglas if he intended to look into the specific charge that the federal gov-ernment denied that slaves were property. Douglas did not give him a direct answer, and Wigfall assumed that he would never receive one. Therefore, on December 11 and 12, 1860, Wigfall addressed the pending political crisis and the possible secession of Southern states.[12]

Wigfall likened the prospect of secession to the colonial break with Great Britain. Once gaining their freedom, he declared, states "retained their sovereignty, freedom, and independence." Citizens pledged loyalty to their states, state governments passed laws for the protection of liberty and prop-erty, and they joined in the Constitution on the premise that these rights were not abandoned. He claimed that the ratification of the Constitution did not relinquish states from their sovereignty. The Constitution instead served as a

10. O. M. Roberts, "Speech of Judge Oran Milo Roberts," 10–11.
11. Ibid., 14–15, 17; emphasis in the original.
12. For works on Wigfall, see Alvy L. King, *Louis T. Wigfall: Southern Fire-Eater;* Billy D. Ledbetter, "The Election of Louis T. Wigfall"; Clyde W. Lord, "Ante-Bellum Career of Louis Trezevant Wigfall"; and Clayton E. Jewett, "Louis T. Wigfall."

compact among the states, and its ratification did not cause the states to cease to exist. The Constitution did not create one nation without state boundaries. The United States, therefore, did not operate as one political body, but existed as a union of separate and sovereign political communities. The Union, he claimed, did not emerge from "any silly notion" of divine origin or "any absurd idea that blood was ever shed for it." The Union, he claimed, as such a compact, was similar to a treaty. Independent and sovereign states agreed to this "treaty" to "secure domestic peace and tranquility." He believed that each state held the responsibility to preserve and protect "the liberty and well-being and happiness of the citizens at home."[13]

Wigfall supported his constitutional argument with a lengthy discussion of the crimes of treason. He pointed out that if a person were charged in any state with the crime of treason or any felony, then that person is to be held in the state that holds jurisdiction over him. Therefore, reasoned Wigfall, the Constitution proved that treason could be committed against a state, thus confirming that states are sovereignties.[14]

Similar to Oran M. Roberts's argument, Wigfall claimed that the Constitution existed and functioned to bind together states with inherently different interests. If the nation consisted of a homogenous people, he argued, there would be no need for a Union or a Constitution, that the natural evolution of the country would be to create one giant nation with no state boundaries and no state governments. The North, he told fellow senators, erroneously viewed and administered the government upon the idea that there is "but one single State or nation." This view, he argued, gave Northern politicians the impression that they were responsible for the domestic institutions of other states.[15]

By January 28, 1861, South Carolina, Mississippi, Alabama, Florida, and Louisiana had already seceded from the Union, and Georgia seceded that day. On this day, John Hemphill stood before the United States Senate and launched immediately into an argument supporting the legality of secession. Hemphill was born in Blackstock, Chester District, South Carolina, on December 18, 1803. He attended Jefferson College in Pennsylvania, taught school in South Carolina, and began to study law in 1829, setting up practice in Sumter District, South Carolina. Hemphill moved to Texas in 1838 and established a law practice at Washington-on-the-Brazos. In 1840, Hemphill

13. Louis T. Wigfall, *Speech of Louis T. Wigfall of Texas, in Reply to Mr. Douglas, and on Mr. Powell's Resolution. Delivered in the Senate of the United States, December 11th and 12th, 1860,* 13, 24–25.

14. Ibid., 26.

15. Ibid., 14.

was elected chief justice of the Texas Supreme Court, a position he held until 1858. In 1859, Hemphill won election to the United States Senate. He told fellow congressmen that the whole issue of secession as a legal or rebellious move centered on the notion of sovereignty. He rhetorically asked politicians where sovereignty resided. In America, he said, "it is an undisputed political axiom that sovereignty resides in the people." He did not mean that sovereignty resided in the people as a whole mass of the United States, but in the people "as a political body or community." The question then becomes, he argued, whether this sovereignty resided in the United States as a political community or the individual states. For Hemphill, the notion was clear: individual states formed distinct and separate political communities that resided together for the purpose of the federal government. He relied on the colonial break with Great Britain to sustain his argument. He pointed out that when the colonists separated, they declared that they were free and independent states, not a free and independent nation. He punctuated his argument by pointing out that when the colonies united under the Articles of Confederation, each state expressly retained its sovereignty and independence and every power not specifically delegated to the United States. The "political communities," therefore, were communities of the colonies and then of the states, and not a whole political community of the United States. The adoption of the Constitution further reinforced this process. Each state chose under its own volition whether to adopt the Constitution. If any state had not acceded to the Constitution, Hemphill argued, then the Constitution could not be forced upon that state, and it would remain as free as France or England. Hemphill did not believe that the adoption of the Constitution and the granting of powers to the federal government affected "the sovereignty which remains in the political body, namely, the people, who can alter, modify, and revoke such constitution." Though states delegated a portion of their powers to the federal government, this action did not negate the states' existence as distinct political communities. The states, he argued, retained independent legislatures and the right to protect social and economic institutions and provide for the protection of property.[16]

16. Hemphill, *Speech of Hon. John Hemphill, of Texas on the State of the Union, Delivered in the Senate of the United States, January 28, 1861,* 1–3. Hemphill also represented Texas at the Montgomery convention and served in the Provisional Confederate Congress. For works on Hemphill, see Jon L. Wakelyn, *Biographical Dictionary of the Confederacy;* Arthur Beckwith, "Texas Letter from John Hemphill to his Brother, James, in Tennessee"; and C. W. Rains, ed., *Six Decades in Texas; or, Memoirs of Francis Richard Lubbock, Governor of Texas in War-Time, 1861–1863.*

The Constitution, Hemphill argued further, became binding upon the people of each state, by an act of the state, and not by the Constitution's ratification by other states. The people of individual states acted as separate political bodies. There never existed, he persisted, an independent political body of the people of the United States. Although ratifying the Constitution resulted in delegating important powers, states conferred only crucial powers and not their own sovereignty. This is proved, he claimed, by the fact that each state, as a political body, has the power to modify, control, and subvert their state governments and even revoke and adopt a new constitution. The principle of sovereignty, he claimed, is well recognized. Because the states exist and operate as sovereign powers, Hemphill concluded that they hold the right at any time to renounce and withdraw from the federation. If the states are sovereign, then the act of secession is legal and not an act of rebellion.[17]

Each of these politicians centered their constitutional arguments on the belief that through the process of separation from Great Britain, the adoption of the Articles of Confederation and the Constitution, the people always claimed the right to sovereignty of the state. State sovereignty included the inherent right of the people to make and unmake governments. They supported the notion that the United States consisted of separate political communities. Furthermore, sovereignty also extended to the right of each state to control its domestic institutions and the right to protect the lives and property of the people. This was more than a states' right argument; it was a firm belief that each state had the explicit responsibility to maintain their own political and economic institutions as a separate political community. The Constitution existed, therefore, to bind together these states that inherently held different political and economic interests. The United States was not a homogenous nation, but rather a confederation of sovereign political bodies united under the Constitution.

The constitutional arguments provided politicians supporting secession with the framework by which to criticize the Republican Party and its ties with abolitionist forces. These prosecessionist politicians believed that the presidential election of Abraham Lincoln threatened to subvert not only the very operation of government, but also the existence of slavery and commercial interests beyond the *peculiar institution*.[18] The Republican Party,

17. Hemphill, *Speech of Hon. John Hemphill,* 6–7.
18. Wayne K. Durrill claims, in *War of Another Kind: A Southern Community in the Great Rebellion,* that it was not until the Emancipation Proclamation that a threat to interests beyond slavery existed. For Texas, this threat existed at the time of Lincoln's election.

claimed Oran M. Roberts, intended to change the very designs of the government. The Northern states, he argued, "have determined to change the government on this subject, at all hazards, by construction, perversion and evasion of its powers, so as to discourage and destroy slavery, rather than to protect it." Their aim, from his perspective, was to promote "universal *freedom.*" By doing so, the Republican Party intended to neglect the constitutional right to the protection of property. As proof, Roberts pointed out the Republican Party's abolitionist activity. The party supported abolition by sending ministers abroad to arouse international support against slavery, by giving a premium to free labor and capital through protective tariffs, by pushing for the abolition of slavery in the District of Columbia, and by employing emigration aid societies to move more individuals into the border states and territories. The socioeconomic platform aimed at subverting the government and nation by creating a homogenous population throughout the United States, upon the basis of "universal freedom." For Roberts, this represented a clear indictment against the protection of individual rights and property ownership. Roberts did not believe that the South should await overt action by Lincoln. He claimed that the party platform provided enough proof that the Republicans intended to undermine the very object of government and destroy the Constitution and therefore the South should secede.[19]

Louis T. Wigfall also believed that the Union could not survive the recent election of Abraham Lincoln. Wigfall and Texas citizens viewed the election of a "Black Republican President" as an overt act of aggression that threatened the liberty and property of all citizens. It revealed an indication that Northerners would subvert the Union and run the government not according to the Constitution but rather per the Republican platforms of 1856 and 1860.[20]

The only way that the Union might survive, he argued, is if the North abrogated abolitionist societies and suppressed abolitionist presses. Wigfall railed against the abolitionists' depiction of Southerners as "cut-throats and pirates and murderers." If the North would end its abolitionist assault on the South, then hope might exist. Republicans only laughed at Wigfall, but he expected this sort of reaction.[21]

---

19. O. M. Roberts, "Speech of Judge Oran Milo Roberts," 22–25.

20. Wigfall, *Speech of Hon. Louis T. Wigfall,* 14. For the Republican Party platform, see Eric Foner, *Free Soil, Free Labor, Free Men: The Ideology of the Republican Party before the Civil War;* and William Gienapp, *The Origins of the Republican Party, 1852–1856.*

21. Wigfall, *Speech of Hon. Louis T. Wigfall,* 9–10.

Wigfall blamed not only abolitionists in general, but also Lincoln. Wigfall believed that Lincoln was a strong supporter of abolition. He recounted that Lincoln, before the election, had served as an abolitionist lecturer and received one hundred dollars per speech. Lincoln, therefore, held the responsibility for arousing the passions of the people against the South. He blamed Lincoln and abolitionists for exciting the passions of citizens and encouraging them to make "John Brown raids." He blamed the newspapers for causing conflict between the slaveholders and nonslaveholders. Wigfall demanded an end to this activity and demanded peace. "We will have peace," he told fellow politicians, "and if you do not offer it to us, we will quietly, and as we have the right under the constitutional compact to do, withdraw from the Union and establish a government for ourselves." He also warned Northern politicians not to underestimate the importance of economic interests in this conflict. Cotton was king, he declared, and the South would defend it in battle if pushed to that extreme.[22] Upon this assertion, the galleries erupted in a loud applause.

Wigfall's remarks expose the complexity of the crisis. The abolitionist attacks were, he decried, the result of the preaching and teaching of "Black Republican leaders," the "pretended followers of Christ," and the Northern education system that fostered abolitionist thought in schools. Wigfall's arguments revealed clearly that abolitionism threatened more than the institution of slavery. Their cause, he believed, threatened all property, assaulted the moral foundation of society, and corrupted national politics. It threatened the economic interests of the South and the nation, and their activities were responsible for class conflict in the South. At the very heart of the crisis, Abraham Lincoln, the Republican Party, and abolitionists threatened individual liberty and property ownership. The only way to secure the Southern way of life, argued Wigfall, rested in the path of secession from the Union.[23]

John Henniger Reagan also believed that Abraham Lincoln and the Republican Party held a commitment to the "ultimate extinction" of slavery. Reagan was born in Sevier County, Tennessee, on October 8, 1818. He moved to Texas in 1838 and worked as a surveyor, frontier scout, justice of the peace, and captain of a militia company in Nacogdoches. Reagan also studied to be an attorney and opened a law office in 1846. Shortly thereafter, he won election as county judge of Henderson County, and became a member of the second Texas legislature. A Democrat, he won election to the

22. Ibid., 11.
23. Ibid., 17–18.

United States Congress in 1857.[24] Speaking before the United States House of Representatives on January 15, 1861, Reagan argued that the strength of antislavery sentiment in the United States had been growing in the past twenty years and become very aggressive. He believed that the Republican Party stood committed to abolition and would pursue this course until it abolished all slavery in the South.[25]

John H. Reagan and other Texas politicians used their condemnation of the Republican Party and abolitionist forces to launch a defense of slavery, relying on constitutional, economic, and racial arguments. Reagan believed in the constitutional right to slavery. He pointed out to fellow representatives that slavery existed when the Founding Fathers framed the Constitution. More important, the slave trade had continued to exist for another twenty years. The mere fact that some states decided to dispose of their slaves did not give them the right to demand that slavery be abolished everywhere. The Southern states, he said, respected the constitutional right of Northern states to terminate slavery, and asked only that they continue to respect the constitutional right to retain slaves.[26]

Oran Milo Roberts also defended slavery on constitutional grounds. He believed that the great question before the American people was "shall the institution of slavery be put upon a sure basis of gradual extinction." He claimed that slavery was a Southern institution, that it was part of their political government, social organization, and industrial pursuits.[27]

In addition, Reagan defended slavery on a racial basis. He did not believe that the African race of people held the capability of maintaining a separate government in peace. He questioned their ability to frame a government and provide peace, security, and repose to society. He blamed Northern politicians for not considering this fact, for ignoring "the relative condition and capacities of the races." Reagan relied on the abolition of slavery in the West Indies to bolster his argument. He claimed that when Great Britain freed the slaves there, utter chaos resulted. Freedmen, he exclaimed, exterminated

24. Although Reagan was known more as a pro-Union man, he was elected as one of the seven Texas delegates to the Montgomery convention and served as postmaster general of the Confederacy. For more information on Reagan, see Ben Proctor, *Not without Honor: The Life of John H. Reagan.*

25. John H. Reagan, *State of the Union Speech of the Hon. John H. Reagan of Texas, Delivered in the House of Representatives, January 15, 1861*, 2. For a complete printing of the Reagan speech, see Wakelyn, *Southern Pamphlets on Secession*, 143–56.

26. Reagan, *State of the Union*, 3.

27. O. M. Roberts, "Speech of Judge Oran Milo Roberts," 6.

the white race. The once vibrant fields returned to jungles. Grass grew in the streets, and ships departed from ports. Carnage succeeded carnage, he claimed, "until at this time they have relapsed into and present a spectacle of savage African barbarism." Reagan believed that the abolition of slavery would lead to the same scenario in the United States and defended the institution on the grounds that abolition would lead to social, economic, political, and racial upheaval.[28]

Roberts further argued that the institution of slavery served to perpetuate republican institutions "by establishing an inferior class, fixed by law, and known by color, and by promoting the equality of the superior white race." He believed that the African race was intellectually inferior and therefore suited for servitude. Servitude, he claimed, "is a necessary consequence of any social organization, elevated above barbarism, by its wealth and refinement." He believed that the enslavement of the African race was both a moral and a political right.[29]

Roberts also supported slavery on the basis that it was in the best social interest of the country. What, he asked, were they to propose otherwise? That they turn the slaves loose? Where would they go? He believed that if the slaves were set free, they would "descend into the vilest barbarism" and that a race war would be the result.[30]

Reagan also defended the institution on the grounds that slaves were in a better condition under Southern rule than at any place in the world, at any time in history. He claimed that the slaves enjoyed more peace, more blessing, and more happiness than at any time or place. Reagan also asked Republican representatives what they would have the South do with the slaves. If the South voluntarily freed the slaves, and at their own expense sent them to the North to live as freemen and citizens, he asked if the North would accept them into that part of the country. In response, the Republican side of the House cried out, "No! No!"[31]

An economic argument was also essential to the political defense of slavery. John H. Reagan argued that the abolition of slavery would be a detriment to both northern and foreign manufacturing. He pointed out to representatives from the North that cotton was responsible for the capital success of

28. Reagan, *State of the Union,* 4–5.
29. O. M. Roberts, "Speech of Judge Oran Milo Roberts," 6.
30. Ibid., 7. Wigfall did not defend slavery to the extent that other politicians did. He did ask Northern politicians, though, if they would be willing to provide amendments to the Constitution that would protect the individual right of property ownership in slavery. See Wigfall, *Speech of Hon. Louis T. Wigfall,* 5.
31. Reagan, *State of the Union,* 4.

northern manufacturing. That staple made it possible for labor to work and was responsible for the success of northern shipping and commerce. This also held true for the English economy. The abolition of slavery, he claimed, would lead to economic ruin and starvation both in the United States and in England.[32]

Oran M. Roberts also argued that slavery accounted for a great deal of the capital in the South. Roberts asserted that the institution of slavery remained vital to both races and that it served to prevent any conflict between capital and labor.[33]

Louis T. Wigfall also warned Northern politicians of the economic consequences of abolition. If the Southern states were to secede, their commerce would be "cut up." Their merchants would go bankrupt, their manufacturers would stop, their shipping would suffer, and their sailors would be "turned loose to starve." Wigfall's indictment of Northern politicians reveals clearly that more was at stake than merely protecting the institution of slavery, that abolition and secession carried with them the potential for widespread economic calamity for the North. Wigfall also believed this held true for England. Great Britain depended upon cotton, he told politicians. If one exhausted the supply of cotton for one week, he claimed, all of England would be left to starve. For Wigfall, economic interests in cotton were paramount. He threatened Northern senators that if they proceeded with their course and secession did occur, then he would be the first to discuss a war tariff against the North, and he expected to do so "in another Chamber."[34]

These politicians, in their defense of slavery, revealed that more was at stake than merely protecting the right to hold slaves. Slavery, in their view, existed as a political, economic, social, and moral necessity. Their arguments supporting the *peculiar institution* also reveal that commercial interests beyond slavery existed as a major concern. Moreover, many of these politicians pursued this line of argument because they feared the prospect of war.

To avert the course of war, John H. Reagan appealed to the economic interests of the North. He reassured Northern politicians that Southern secession would not interfere with or terminate the North's navigation of the Mississippi River. He understood the necessity of the river to their commercial pursuits and reassured them that the South would not impede those interests. It was clear to Reagan and other politicians that commercial interests in the

32. Ibid., 6–7.
33. O. M. Roberts, "Speech of Judge Oran Milo Roberts," 6.
34. Wigfall, *Speech of Hon. Louis T. Wigfall,* 15, 12–13.

North were also at stake in this crisis, and the Texas representative attempted to reassure Northern colleagues that no harm would come to them. He asked only that the North give the South the same economic consideration. The South had no cause for war. War, he claimed, was a Northern pursuit that he sought to end.[35]

Whereas Reagan concentrated on an economic argument to avoid war, John Hemphill turned to the constitutionality of war. Hemphill's constitutional arguments supporting the legality of secession stressed that secession did not denote an act of rebellion and therefore did not present a just cause for war. The only exception, he pointed out, was if the process of secession menaced the safety or existence of other states. He feared, though, that the federal authorities who denounced secession as unlawful might deceive many individuals. Therefore, they might use a force of arms to maintain the Union. This fear of war forced Hemphill to make painstakingly clear his belief in the legality of secession. He hoped that Northern citizens would not be deceived into a false fidelity for the federal government, but that they too would realize that their loyalty and sovereignty resided in the state.[36]

Hemphill also did not believe that the federal government held the power to use military force to subdue a seceding state or its citizens. Hemphill relied on the writings of James Madison to support his argument. Madison doubted the practicability of war and believed that the use of armed force against a state signified a declaration of war. This, Madison wrote, dissolved all previous contracts between the state and the federal government. Hemphill also relied on the words of Alexander Hamilton, who believed that the coercion of states "is one of the maddest projects that was ever devised." Hemphill further pointed out that Hamilton, in *Federalist no. 16,* denounced "the use of military force against the sovereign States of a Confederacy." The framers of the Constitution, argued Hemphill, proved that they did not believe in the right to coerce a state by armed force. Any notion of the federal government, therefore, to support armed conflict against the South would represent a subversion of the Constitution. Hemphill used his arguments against war to reinforce the issue of state sovereignty. He argued that the real objection to armed aggression against an individual state was based upon the notion that each state was truly sovereign.[37]

35. Reagan, *State of the Union,* 12.
36. Hemphill, *Speech of Hon. John Hemphill,* 7–8.
37. Ibid., 8–10. For further arguments by Alexander Hamilton on this issue, see *Federalist no. 28.*

Hemphill admonished Northern politicians against the course of war. He warned them that they underestimated the strength of the South and the sympathy that would arise if the North pursued this course. Moreover, he threatened that blood would be spilled in cities in the North as well as the South if war broke out. He asked fellow politicians: "If for peace we are to have desolation, the butchery of our finest youths, the mangled limbs of men, the shrieks of virgins, the smoke and ashes of consumed habitations, think you that these scenes of horror will not be enacted in your opulent and magnificent cities, your great towns, and beautiful hamlets?" Hemphill cautioned against and feared war. He believed that such a course would devastate the entire country. Nevertheless, the South, if war came, would take the offensive and "redden" Northern streets. He pointed out to Northern senators that the conquering nations of antiquity were slaveholders, and the South too would take its place among the great nations of time.[38]

Among Texas politicians, only Louis T. Wigfall embraced the prospect of war. He seemed to expect it. He notified Northern senators that when South Carolina seceded, the United States should cede the federal forts to the state, for the land itself was a voluntary gift to the United States for federal purposes. He cautioned that if there emerged an attempt to strengthen these forts, clearly a reference to Fort Sumter, then "those forts will be taken, cost it the life of every man in the State."[39]

Texas politicians appealed to northern commercial interests, stressed the legality of secession, and threatened retaliation to prevent civil war. These politicians, with the exception of Louis T. Wigfall, feared war. They feared the economic, social, and political results of such a course. They wanted peace and pursued it. War, they claimed, was a Northern pursuit that threatened the entire South. Texas politicians, however, not only discussed the sectional crisis from a Southern perspective, but also explained in detail the position of Texas in the conflict. These politicians railed against abolitionist activity, complained of border hostilities, and supported the necessity of a secession convention to determine Texas's course of action.

"What," asked Oran M. Roberts, "shall Texas do?" Roberts stood for state action through the constituted authorities. He believed that Texas should make its own course, but also confide in other Southern states. He believed in calm deliberation on the part of all states. In addition, he supported a secession convention in Texas where the people could express their voices.

38. Hemphill, *Speech of Hon. John Hemphill,* 11.
39. Wigfall, *Speech of Hon. Louis T. Wigfall,* 29.

He also sustained that the people, through the ballot box, should have the final say on this matter. He preferred that the legislature sanction it, but argued that doing so was not fully necessary.[40]

Roberts, though, did theorize that the legislature had the responsibility to ascertain the will of its constituents and that it should recognize a secession convention "as competent to represent the sovereign power of the State." A secession convention, he declared, held the power and authority to rule on the violations of the federal compact. If the convention decided that these violations were flagrant enough, then it could declare the people absolved from their fealty to the federal government, and enact measures to take the state out of the Union. Roberts supported the proposed election of delegates to a convention and popular voting on the matter.[41]

Alluding to the specific situation of Texas, Wigfall chose to focus on the abolitionist activity in the state. He blamed abolitionists for the burning of at least eighteen towns. He condemned them for giving strychnine to the slaves to poison slaveholders. He denounced a secret group called the Mystic Red, which had roots in the Methodist Church North, for carrying out these assaults in Texas. He blamed them for trying to destroy the economic interests of the state by bringing free-soil Northern capital in, and thus attempting to gain possession of Texas and make it a free state. He claimed that Northern abolitionists aimed "to starve us out or cause us, like poisoned rats, to die in our holes." He told senators that even he had to stand guard at night against abolitionist incursions. He retorted to fellow politicians, "[T]his is what you call Union and fraternal affection."[42]

John H. Reagan, like Wigfall, also blamed abolitionist forces for the trouble in Texas the previous August. Members of the Methodist Church North, he claimed, organized a society called the Mystic Red, bent on causing disaffection among slaves, burning towns, and poisoning citizens. These crimes were the result of abolitionist teachings, "a part of the legitimate fruits of Republicanism." Reagan also pointed out Texas's frontier situation with the Indians and claimed that the federal government failed to defend citizens against the "hostile savages." Reagan further noted that Texans had already fought once, against Mexico, to defend their lives and liberty against a military despot. Texans, he claimed, would again defend their liberty if threatened in a similar fashion.[43]

40. O. M. Roberts, "Speech of Judge Oran Milo Roberts," 2–3.
41. Ibid., 4, 32.
42. Wigfall, *Speech of Hon. Louis T. Wigfall,* 18.
43. Reagan, *State of the Union,* 14–15.

Of all Texas politicians, John Hemphill provided the most comprehensive view of Texas's interests in this crisis. Texas, he pointed out, once existed as a sovereign and independent republic. At the time of annexation, it delegated several of its powers to the federal government. This act, he claimed, did not represent an abandonment of Texas's sovereignty. The federal government operated merely as a trustee of the designated powers. Texas, he argued, "is still a State, a political body, with control over the lives, liberties, and property of her people."[44]

Hemphill reminded fellow senators that Texas had agreed to annexation out of fear that the diplomacy of Great Britain would hazard the *peculiar institution*. Texas, he exclaimed, had not found peace or security for slavery, but experienced only peril. It should not surprise them, therefore, that Texas would secure itself against the threat to slavery by supporting secession from the Union.[45]

Hemphill further argued that the United States had not paid for Texas with the blood of its citizens. The annexation of Texas, he asserted, was not the reason for war with Mexico. Hemphill relied on an 1846 message in which James K. Polk declared that Mexico, "by her own act, forced the war upon us." Hemphill also complained that the United States had not adequately protected the frontier. As a result, it had been "desolated by the savage." The inadequate protection had cost more than one hundred Texas lives in the past year.[46]

Texas politicians pleading the case of the Lone Star State relied on constitutional arguments supporting state sovereignty and responsibility. They declared that Texas's annexation to the United States was not a relinquishment of state sovereignty. They protested abolitionist activity in the state that threatened the lives and property of Texas citizens. Furthermore, their arguments reveal that more was at stake than simply protecting slavery— economic interests beyond the *peculiar institution* also concerned them. Texas's situation in the crisis, therefore, was profoundly complex, and these politicians sought to safeguard the state's commercial interests through secession from the Union. Their support for secession was grounded upon constitutional, economic, and social arguments and helped to define a separate political and economic identity.

44. Hemphill, *Speech of Hon. John Hemphill*, 4.
45. Ibid., 8. For British activity in Texas, see Thomas R. Hietala, *Manifest Design: Anxious Aggrandizement in Late Jacksonian America*, chap. 2.
46. Hemphill, *Speech of Hon. John Hemphill*, 12, 15. In this section of his speech, Hemphill discussed at length the terms of annexation; boundary disputes among Texas, Mexico, and the United States; and the title of Texas.

Not all politicians in Texas, however, supported the move for secession. Some politicians believed that Texas's commercial interests would best be protected in the Union. Speaking to politicians and Texas citizens, these antisecessionist politicians also provided their views on the crisis. Likewise, their speeches were printed in newspapers and in pamphlets that were sold to the general public. Surprisingly, though, a systematic study of the political arguments that Texas antisecessionists offered during this critical period does not exist. Older studies of Texas Unionism concentrate on political-party alignment, the ethnocultural configuration of antisecession, and the religious affiliations associated with antisecession sentiment. Recent studies on Texas Unionism focus on the social and demographic patterns of voting support against secession. These works contribute greatly to our understanding of *who* the antisecessionists were, but there is still a gap in understanding *what* they argued.[47]

Just as prosecessionists proffered their views on the crisis, prominent Texas antisecessionist politicians also waxed eloquent about the dire straits, further revealing the deep complexity of Texas's situation in the Civil War crisis. Similar to the prosecessionists, a constitutional defense of the Union provided the fundamental base for many of their arguments. At a union meeting in Austin, Governor Sam Houston spoke about his devotion to the Union and how he placed his life, goals, and future with its destiny. If it fell, he said, he would rather end his career than continue in politics. Houston reminded the citizens of Austin that their liberties and properties had not yet been violated, and that they were still safe under the Constitution and in the Union. At this point in the debate, Houston believed that the proposed secession of Southern states would only hurt the individual states and not the nation at large. "Deprived of the protection of the Union, of the aegis of the Constitution," Houston argued, "they would soon dwindle into petty States, to be again rent into twain by dissension, or through the ambition of selfish chieftains, and would become a prey to foreign powers."[48]

At a meeting before the people of Bexar County in San Antonio on November 24, 1860, Charles Anderson railed against the constitutional arguments for secession. Anderson was born on June 1, 1814, in Louisville,

47. Buenger, *Secession and the Union;* Frank H. Smyrl, "Unionism in Texas, 1861–1865"; Claude Elliott, "Union Sentiment in Texas, 1861–1865"; Ralph Wooster, *Texas and Texans;* Dale Baum, *The Shattering of Texas Unionism: Politics in the Lone Star State during the Civil War Era.* The exception to this is Jon L. Wakelyn, *Southern Unionist Pamphlets and the Civil War.*

48. Houston, "Speech of General Sam Houston at the Union Mass Meeting, Austin, September 22, 1860," *Harrison Flag,* Sept. 23, 1860.

Kentucky. He graduated from Miami University in 1833, was admitted to the bar in 1843, and served in the Ohio legislature in 1844. He moved to San Antonio, Texas, in 1844. Anderson relied upon the United States operating under the Articles of Confederation to prove his argument. He pointed out that there had already existed an experiment of "being purely *sovereign States* and *independent of each other* in a mere confederacy." This, he claimed, proved "a dead, out-and-out failure!" He drew a sharp distinction between the Articles of Confederation and the Constitution as evidence for his argument. "Wherefore," he said, "we are solemnly assured in the very preamble to our noble Constitution, in its very first words,—'We, the *people*' (not the colonies, nor the States by name, but overlooking them,)—'We, the people of the United States, in order to form a more PERFECT Union, &c., &c.,' do ordain and establish this *Constitution,* (not enter into articles of confederation merely)."[49] For Anderson, prosecessionists looked backward with ignorance. The failed attempt to create a sovereign and independent confederacy should have proved to them the futility of secession.

Not only did antisecessionists seek to prove the futility of secession, but they also tackled head-on the constitutional arguments of the prosecessionists. On February 1, 1861, Andrew Jackson Hamilton stood before the United States House of Representatives to address the state of the Union. Hamilton was born on January 28, 1815, in Huntsville, Alabama. He studied law and was admitted to the bar in 1841. He moved to LaGrange, Texas, in 1846, to practice law. He represented Travis County in the Texas House of Representatives in 1851 and 1853. Rebutting prosecessionists, Hamilton's first remarks pertained to the question of the legal or constitutional secession of sovereign states. For Hamilton, the central question was whether the Constitution "was a *compact* merely between the different States, in contradistinction to a *constitution of the people of the United States.*" Hamilton believed that it was both; that it was a constitution and a compact. He argued that all constitutions are compacts, but that not all compacts are constitutions.[50]

49. Anderson, *Speech of Charles Anderson, ESQ., on the State of the Country, at a Meeting of the People of Bexar County, at San Antonia, Texas, November 24, 1860,* 14–15; emphasis in original. Anderson was a well-known Union sympathizer and was arrested by Col. Henry McCulloch in 1861. He escaped, however, and made his way back to Ohio where he served in the Union army and later served briefly as governor of Ohio in 1865.

50. Hamilton, *Speech of Hon. Andrew J. Hamilton, of Texas, on the State of the Union, Delivered in the House of Representatives of the United States, February 1, 1861,* 4; emphasis in original. After the Civil War, Hamilton was appointed provisional governor of Texas in July 1865.

Hamilton further disputed the prosecessionist view, pointing out its error of not recognizing the limited power of the federal government. Hamilton claimed that every constitutional government, which is not a despotism, is limited in power. The U.S. government, therefore, does not possess all the rights and interests of the citizenry, but leaves to the states all powers not specifically granted to the federal government. Hamilton reasoned that because a voluntary act of the people created the government, there is no sound argument in favor of their power to destroy the government, regardless of whether the citizens were of different sovereignties or the same state. Hamilton theorized, and asked fellow politicians, where does the sovereignty of the state lay? He argued that sovereignty resided in the people. "If in the people—as I have always supposed—then the people," he claimed, "by their act of acceptance, committed themselves to the contract; if in the legislature, still the people of every government are legally bound by the act of the sovereign power." To sum up his constitutional view, Hamilton stated simply that in the contract there did not exist a limitation by which the government ceased to exist. The organic law that creates government, he claimed, confers perpetuity unless otherwise established.[51]

Antisecessionist politicians parlayed their constitutional defense of the Union into a justification of slavery to support their position further. Texas antisecessionist politicians did not oppose the *peculiar institution,* but rather believed that the Union could best preserve slavery. One of the most zealous antisecessionists was Governor Sam Houston. Houston's antisecessionism, though, was not an abandonment of Southern ideals or Texas's commercial interests. In a speech before the Texas Senate in February 1859, Houston argued that all states had equal rights. The North could abolish slavery if it so desired, but by the same token, the South maintained the right to continue that institution. The Constitution, he claimed, guaranteed their right to do so.[52]

James Hall Bell, speaking at the Texas Capitol on December 1, 1860, also defended the *peculiar institution.* Bell was born on January 2, 1825, in Columbia, Texas. He attended Centre College in Kentucky, served in the Mexican War, and later attended Harvard University in 1845. He returned to Brazoria, Texas, to practice law in 1847. He served as district judge from 1852 to 1856, and later served as associate justice of the Texas Supreme Court from 1858 to 1864. Bell did not accept the premise that the existence of slavery was the primary cause of the agitation. He instead believed in the moral right to hold slaves. Furthermore, he maintained that the institution

51. Ibid., 6.
52. Houston, quoted in *Southern Intelligencer,* Feb. 16, 1859.

of slavery as it existed in the Southern states was of paramount necessity not only to the social welfare and prosperity of the South and all states, but also to the prosperity and happiness of the civilized world. Slavery, he said, had always been a sensitive subject, especially in the South. Nevertheless, he stood by the economic and political interests of the South and Texas and defended the institution.[53]

Like many politicians, Andrew J. Hamilton upheld the sanctity of property rights, even slaves as property. He argued against Northerners who attacked the Southern right of slave property. "We have a right to insist that you should treat us with justice," he argued, and "that you should respect our rights of property." Although the Constitution did not mention slavery specifically, it did uphold the sanctity of property and therefore slavery by default. Hamilton claimed that the Constitution supported the right to own slaves, and said "it will not do to say that the Constitution does not recognize it." For Hamilton, as for many Texans, slavery was simply a matter of property ownership.[54]

The antisecessionists' defense of the *peculiar institution* revealed their concession that slavery was the central problem of the nation. Robert H. Taylor, speaking before the Texas House of Representatives on January 28, 1861, acknowledged slavery as the crux of the problem, the "Pandora Box out of which all the evils are now upon us." Taylor was born on July 5, 1825, in Columbia, South Carolina. He studied law and moved to Texas in 1845, serving as justice of the peace in Bonham. He served in the Mexican War, won election to the Texas House of Representatives in 1851 and 1853, and served in the Texas Senate in 1859. Taylor, though, argued that Congress had not yet overtly acted to threaten the institution of slavery and therefore the South should avoid radical action. He specifically addressed the radical proponents of secession. He railed against their use of the press to stir the hearts of men and directly accused them of distorting all truth. He warned them that their actions would be the downfall of slavery. He told fellow politicians that "this disunion movement will doom slavery!" He blamed prosecessionist politicians for throwing the citizens into confusion over this issue without considering the consequences.[55]

Despite the staunch support of slavery by Houston, Hamilton, and Taylor,

53. Bell, *Speech of Hon. James H. Bell, of the Texas Supreme Court, Delivered at the Capitol on Saturday, Dec. 1st, 1860,* 4. After the Civil War, Bell served as secretary of the state under Texas governor Andrew Jackson Hamilton (Harbert Davenport, *History of the Supreme Court of Texas*).

54. Hamilton, *Speech of Hon. Andrew J. Hamilton,* 10.

55. Robert H. Taylor, "Speech of Robert H. Taylor, Delivered in the House of Representatives, of the Texas Legislature, upon the Joint Resolutions to 'Recognize' or

there existed slight disagreement among Texas antisecessionists on the slavery issue. For example, James H. Bell believed that the Founding Fathers had not wholeheartedly supported the institution of slavery in the long term. Instead, he claimed that when the Constitution was adopted, there existed little diversity on the matter. Most people at that time, he claimed, generally conceded slavery was evil. It was regarded as a temporary institution that would eventually pass away.[56]

The antisecessionists' discussion of slavery involved more than the Southern right to slaves as property. The position of slavery in the West also existed as a fundamental concern of antisecessionists. Charles Anderson argued that the course of the South, especially in terms of demanding the right to slavery in the West, threatened all slavery. He questioned, as a slave owner, whether it was worth the risk. "Shall we wholly forget the millions of slaves, worth thousands of millions of dollars, held legally, safely, *unquestioned* in the States," he postulated, "to go full moon mad after a black wet-nurse in Kansas, or a Kentucky runaway at Niagara?" For Anderson, the South's insistence on perpetuating slavery westward only agitated the nation and moved sentiment against the institution, revealing that more was at stake than merely the issue of property rights.[57]

The issue, according to Hamilton, centered on the power of the federal government and the extent to which it could regulate private-property interests. Not only did he believe that Southerners had a right to slaves as property under the Constitution, but he also believed that Congress did not have the right to exercise power upon the subject of slavery among the states, especially when it came to the matter of trading slaves. Hamilton agreed with the South in this matter, and denied the power of Congress to act upon the issue of property in the territories. He believed that each territory should guide its own desires in the matter of slavery. If, however, this was not to be the case, a solution to the crisis did exist: extend the Missouri line of 36°30' to the west and guarantee this solution in constitutional form. Although he proposed this resolution, Hamilton did not wholeheartedly endorse it. It was an attempt at compromise. His true beliefs stood with the right of each state and territory to decide the matter for itself; he believed that popular sovereignty should

---

Approve the Convention to Assemble the 28th of January, 1861," *Southern Intelligencer,* Feb. 13, 1861. Sam Houston commissioned Taylor to investigate the activities of Juan Cortina in 1860. After the Civil War, Taylor was a member of the 1866 Constitutional Convention, served briefly as judge of the Eighth Judicial District, and won election to the Texas House of Representatives in 1879.

56. Bell, *Speech of Hon. James H. Bell,* 9.

57. Anderson, *Speech of Charles Anderson,* 14.

rule. Hamilton claimed that the institution should take care of itself in the territories as it had taken care of itself in every Southern slave state that had been admitted into the Union since the adoption of the federal Constitution. Hamilton, as a Texan and Southerner, was willing to risk the chance that New Mexico would enter the Union as a free state. That, he asserted, was a gamble that people must be willing to risk. Nevertheless, this did not mean that the government held the authority to take away the right of people to travel there with their slaves. Hamilton also opposed deciding upon the issue of slavery from any territory gained from Mexico. In his opinion, it was presumptuous to determine the issue beforehand. This decision should be in the hands of future leaders, upon the actual acquisition of land.[58]

Although secessionists and antisecessionists stood on common ground in their defense of the *peculiar institution,* they differed on their views of Abraham Lincoln and the Republican Party. Texas antisecessionist politicians upheld moderate support for Lincoln and the Republicans. They did not believe that Lincoln or the Republican Party aimed at the abolition of slavery. Robert H. Taylor counseled patience on the part of Southerners based upon the reality that no harm had yet occurred from Lincoln or his party. He argued that radical secessionists worked to form public opinion into what they wanted and hence stirred much of the citizenry into unnecessary agitation.[59]

James H. Bell extended the argument further and concluded that the president himself, due to the sovereignty of the people, could not trample upon the rights of citizens. "No portion of the American people will ever submit to oppression, not even to the little finger of tyranny. Let insult and oppression come," he chided, "and the people will not need to be told of it by the politicians and orators, nor will they need to be told what they ought to do." To corroborate his assertion, he pointed out that the federal judiciary would uphold the Constitution against any tyranny. Furthermore, a majority of politicians in the House of Representatives stood opposed to the Lincoln administration, and the Senate existed as an effectual check upon the president. Bell relied upon the structure of the government to eradicate the unwarranted Southern fear of Abraham Lincoln and the "Black Republicans."[60]

Responding to the accusation that the Republican Party intended to abolish slavery, Charles Anderson replied that the Republican Party did not assert the right, through any of the governmental branches or the people, to abolish

58. Hamilton, *Speech of Hon. Andrew J. Hamilton,* 11–13.
59. Taylor, "Speech of Robert H. Taylor."
60. Bell, *Speech of Hon. James H. Bell,* 13–14.

or interfere with the institution of slavery in the states. Although Lincoln morally opposed slavery, he did not seek to abolish the institution where it existed. Nor is it true, continued Anderson, that Lincoln ever claimed, in word or print, the power or duty of the government to undertake this type of action. For a second time, the crowd interrupted Anderson's speech. A prosecessionist voice cried out: "We want no more of these Black Republican arguments." Anderson calmly retorted that these were not "Black Republican" arguments, but rather the simple truths of the situation.[61]

Anderson went on to use the presidential election of Abraham Lincoln as an argument against dissolving the Union. He pointed out that not all Northerners had elected Lincoln to the White House. He claimed that in the North, nearly four hundred thousand individuals voted against Abraham Lincoln. He told Texans that they suffered from "the figments of a heated or diseased imagination" to believe that the North stood united against the South. He argued that it was "insanity" for the South to throw away "such a tremendous army of allies" and march toward a bloody and endless civil war.[62]

Despite their moderate defense of Abraham Lincoln and the Republican Party, antisecessionists did acknowledge that there existed serious problems in the country perpetuating sectionalism. Sam Houston viewed the radical threats of disunion as "child's play and folly" that would hold no benefit for the South or the nation. Houston stressed that the South needed to reach a peaceful solution to the crisis by working within the Union. The great error that the South had made was meeting sectionalism with sectionalism. He did not view the prospect of Lincoln's election worth dissolving the Union, for the Union was more valuable than Lincoln. Should Lincoln and his party attempt to subvert the Constitution and the rights of Southerners, Houston remarked, "his party will scatter like chaff before the storm of popular indignation." Houston argued further that secession and revolution could be justified only once all legal and constitutional means of redress had failed. Given the history of the United States and the structure of government, he did not believe that this would ever occur. Houston then went on to deride the formation of a Southern constitutional party whose intent, he believed, was to destroy the Constitution. Houston put the blame for such radical action on the shoulders of Louis T. Wigfall, whom he regarded as "beyond the pale of National Democracy." Houston viewed Wigfall as one of the "transplants

---

61. Anderson, *Speech of Charles Anderson,* 6–7.
62. Ibid., 7.

from the South Carolina nursery of disunion" who failed to realize that the institution of slavery was safe and secure in the Union and that the North had nothing to do with slavery. Slavery, argued Houston, was a Southern institution and would remain so.[63]

James H. Bell further believed that the current crisis was the result of Southern politicians who did not allow the people to speak or follow their wishes. Likewise, though, the people were to blame, for they permitted the politicians to make issues for them and pledge them to a particular line of action. Bell questioned what the nation was to do in the wake of electing a "Black Republican President." Was the nation going to be preserved? Alternatively, would the country and its prosperity be "sacrificed upon the altar of sectional jealousy?"[64] He placed this question and the responsibility of preserving the Union before the people, believing it their ability and obligation to save the country from destruction.

In part, though, Bell did acknowledge that Northerners carried some responsibility for the crisis. Bell argued that the men who had made the most noise about slavery were those who had recently emigrated from the North. Because of their Northern heritage, they took great pains to proclaim an admiration of the institution of slavery. This laudation in turn forced men to revere slavery more adamantly, as their honor depended upon it. Consequently, there existed a constant agitation of slavery in the South and Texas. The need to prove their support of the institution to Southerners, he claimed, constantly drove them to defend slavery. Only when a man lived in the South for quite some time and became identified with slavery, claimed Bell, would he cease the clamoring over slavery, thus proving his friendship with the institution.[65]

In the interim, however, passions and tension arose over the *peculiar institution,* forcing Texans to defend it with the utmost vigor. Bell believed that the arousal of such feeling also resulted from party politics. He concluded that the crisis was due not to slavery specifically, but rather to the "spirit of party" that prevailed in all free governments. Party spirit is not inherently

63. Ibid. Col. John A. Wharton, who delivered a speech that found favorable review from the *Austin Texas State Gazette,* countered Houston's speech. Wharton railed against politicians supporting the Union and lashed out at abolitionist sympathizers and the recent troubles that abolitionists had caused in the state (*Austin Texas State Gazette,* Sept. 29, 1860).

64. Bell, *Speech of Hon. James H. Bell,* 3–4.

65. Ibid., 4. For Southern honor, see Bertram Wyatt-Brown, *Southern Honor: Ethics and Behavior in the Old South.*

dangerous. In this case, however, party spirit not only centered on sectional economic interests, but also reinforced economic sectionalism—with slavery at the center of this perpetual cycle.[66]

Party spirit perpetuated not just economic sectionalism, but political sectionalism as well. Bell argued that Northerners were apprehensive about Southern politicians and that there existed in the North a real fear of a slave power. He did not believe that slavery as a system of servitude or form of labor was the crux of the problem, but rather that opposition rested against the political power and influence of slavery in government. Bell did admit, though, that there was much to deplore, especially regarding abolitionist activity. He abhorred the "ceaseless belchings of their fury." Bell stressed, however, that the strife of party spirit was not the result of Lincoln or the Republican Party, both of which Southerners claimed were heavily influenced by the forces of abolitionism. Bell was careful to distinguish between the two. He looked with great abhorrence upon the abolitionists. Nevertheless, abolitionism itself was not to blame. Although they "have been proclaiming their designs and vomiting forth their rage for the last twenty-five years," Bell questioned whether all the "Black Republicans" were abolitionists. He did not think so.[67]

Bell reiterated that the hoopla of the current presidential canvass was partly responsible for the present crisis, not the Republican Party itself. He pointed to the platform of the party and declared that no evidence existed that proved the Republican Party claimed war on the institution of slavery. He urged individuals to examine the platform for themselves. Upon doing so, he believed they would find that the worst plank in it was the one declaring that slavery should not be extended. In Bell's opinion, the Republican Party platform distinctly acknowledged the right of each state to regulate its own institutions.[68]

Similar to the prosecessionists, these antisecessionist politicians argued their case because, in part, they feared the outbreak of civil war in the country. Sam Houston feared that departing from the Constitution would bring "civil

---

66. Bell, *Speech of Hon. James H. Bell,* 5.

67. Ibid., 6, 12; Gienapp, *Origins of the Republican Party,* 76.

68. Bell, *Speech of Hon. James H. Bell,* 12. Anderson believed that preachers in Texas also stirred public sentiment. He blamed part of the problem of the crisis on the ministers themselves, such as Dr. Boring, who was raised only in the South. Many preachers, he claimed, had "extraordinary mental abilities and moral influence" that they used on their audiences to sway them toward accepting the Southern way of life and a defense of slavery (*Speech of Charles Anderson,* 4). For specific examples, see Wakelyn, *Southern Pamphlets on Secession.*

war without end." He believed that union and liberty were synonymous: if one preserves union, then one also preserves liberty.[69]

Charles Anderson counseled patience and calm deliberation. He accused the South of traveling down a perilous path ultimately leading to war. He feared this outcome and beseeched the crowd to think through the ramifications of secession. He asked Texans who would fight in this war. Moreover, he questioned the wisdom and security of the matter. He pondered whether Texans were willing to risk going to battle if it meant leaving wives and children at home in the presence of slaves. He asked the San Antonio crowd if Texans could "*then* hold three millions of our slaves in their proper bondage and subjection with our left hands, whilst we should smite their pale faced allies with our right." He did not believe that the crisis warranted armed conflict. He urged Texans to remain calm and to realize that it was simply untrue that the people of the North were willing to march to the South as allies of the slaves.[70]

The fear of war also led Andrew J. Hamilton to argue against secession. Hamilton believed that secession represented an act of revolution. He further argued that a universal law governed civil society and well-regulated governments. Men, states, and nations, he maintained, were free to choose their own course. Nevertheless, natural law dictated that whatever course of policy was pursued, this approach should not infract the interests and rights of other citizens and governments. Hamilton reasoned that no European power—not Russia, France, or England—would ever exercise its own policy or interests without deference to the interests and rights of other governments whose rights might be affected. He argued that the seceding states did not abide by this organic law; they did not consult any interests. Instead, they were consumed with their own interests and rights. The South, he proclaimed, held grandiose ideas regarding its place among the mightiest nations of the earth. Yet, the South was unwilling to take the responsibility that came with this belief and failed to consult the interests of states that might be affected by secession. Hamilton used his own state, Texas, as a primary example of this neglect. At the time of his speech, Louisiana had recently seceded from the Union, and there existed much speculation about Texas's course. Due to Louisiana's secession, Texas lost direct communication between itself and the United States. Hamilton further conjectured that if Arkansas were to secede the next day, then Texas would be severed from the Union without

69. Houston, quoted in *Southern Intelligencer,* July 27, 1859. For a review on the scholarship of Sam Houston, see Greg Cantrell, "Whither Sam Houston?"
70. Anderson, *Speech of Charles Anderson,* 11–12.

any act of its own. Was this part of the agreement under which Texas had entered the Union? He did not think so. Thus, Hamilton strove to nail the point that secession in and of itself was more than just a legal or constitutional matter. At the very heart of the crisis was an issue of natural law—a rule that governed the entire world. Secession represented a flagrant violation of the natural law that governed all peoples and nations.[71]

Hailing from Texas, though, Hamilton expressed sympathy for the grievances of the South and the Lone Star State. He did agree that the Republican Party had caused hardship for Southerners. Nevertheless, these indictments were not enough to tear apart the Union. He believed that whatever malady did exist among the sections, between the parties, could be settled in the Union. He believed further that eventually the North would realize the error of its course and the potential for armed conflict that threatened not only Southern but also Northern interests.[72]

The prospect of war was merely one of many issues that weighed heavily on the political mind of antisecessionists. The sanctity of property also concerned them greatly. Like their prosecessionist counterparts, they strongly desired to protect commercial interests beyond the institution of slavery. Sam Houston was concerned not only with Texas's interest in slavery, but with protecting its borders as well. More than a full year before the presidential election, Houston remarked that "the regular troops have never protected us, and they never will be able to do so." Houston long sought to remove the Indians away from the Texas border to new reservations where they would not come into contact with Texas citizens. His attitude toward the Indian problem and his concern over the extension of slavery reveal him to be more of a Texas nationalist than a "Union" man, and reveal Texas's concern over the threat of both Indians and abolition.[73]

Not only did the Lone Star State's unique border situation create anxiety for these politicians, but economic interests beyond the *peculiar institution* also aroused their trepidation. Robert H. Taylor, speaking before the Texas House of Representatives, feared that disunion would destroy agricultural, commercial, and industrial pursuits. Deeply interested in the welfare and future of Texas, Taylor warned that "the hand that writes the declaration of disunion shall feel the blood curdle in its veins, and the tongue that speaks it to the world shall stiffen in the act;—thenceforward shall the American eagle drop the olive branch of peace and grasp only the arrow of war." After railing against secessionists, Taylor appealed to reason by discussing the

71. Hamilton, *Speech of Hon. Andrew J. Hamilton,* 7–8.
72. Ibid., 10.
73. Houston, quoted in *Southern Intelligencer,* July 27, 1859.

practical consequences of secession. He reminded politicians of the empty treasury, that Texas had a large frontier and water border to protect, that the state would have to carry its own mail, and above all that taxes would be raised. Taylor did not trust a new confederacy with "South Carolina as its head and Texas as its tail."[74]

In order to quell Texans' fears and deal with secession head-on, pro-secessionists called for a secession convention in Texas. Antisecessionists, however, railed against this proposal. On the same day that Oran M. Roberts prepared the call for a convention, December 3, 1860, Sam Houston wrote the "Address to the People of Texas." He warned them against fanatical action in the wake of the presidential election. He called for Southern unity and a commitment to the border states threatened by abolitionist forces. Houston believed that the "calamity of disunion" called for united Southern action. He warned that a radical response on the part of several Southern states would serve only to undermine the border states' interest in slavery by driving slavery from them and ruining their citizens. The border states, by standing as the "bulwark[s] against abolitionism" had a right to expect their sister states to stand by them.[75]

In the midst of the heated debate over secession and the path of Texas, the Texas legislature convened in January 1861. One of its first acts was to repeal Sam Houston's joint resolution to send delegates to a Southern convention. After repealing the resolution, the legislature entertained propositions to acknowledge the secession convention. The Honorable Benjamin Holland Epperson stood before his colleagues in the Texas House of Representatives and railed against the proposal. Epperson was born in 1826, in Amite County, Mississippi. He briefly attended Princeton University and moved to Texas in 1846, where he studied law in Clarksville. He was an unsuccessful Whig candidate for Texas governor in 1851. Epperson served in the Texas House of Representatives in 1859–1860, and was a staunch supporter of Sam Houston. Epperson could not give consent to a convention that he believed was called without authority of law. "Men treat it as a God," exhorted Epperson, "and demand that all shall bow in humble submission and adoration to its decrees." Epperson argued, though, that even supporters of the convention knew that something was amiss in this whole process—otherwise there would not have existed such a strenuous effort to build up the necessity of a secession convention. Recognizing the caucus, argued Epperson, would set a precedent

74. Taylor, "Speech of Robert H. Taylor."
75. Amelia Williams and Eugene C. Barker, eds., *The Writings of Sam Houston,* 8:206–7. For comment on secession's effect on the border states, see *La Grange True Issue,* Oct. 4, 1860.

never seen in the history of the United States. The convention should not be taken as a legal expression of the people. Epperson also opposed the process of electing delegates to the convention. He argued that in every area of the state, the mode of election was different, and some counties did not even hold elections. Endorsing a convention assembled in such a haphazard way would subvert the powers of the state authorities.[76]

Robert H. Taylor also chided the Texas House on the matter of turning over control of the government to a group of men who did not represent more than one-third of the state. He raised questions over the legitimacy of the entire delegate election process, from the holding of elections and the counting of votes to the calling of delegates. Taylor roared that those politicians who would turn control over to the secessionists were "as dumb as sheep in the hands of the sheerer."[77]

Like their prosecessionist colleagues, these antisecessionists also discussed at length Texas's course of action. They warned against Texas secession and independent action by the state. Based upon his theory of the Constitution, Andrew J. Hamilton did not accept the prosecessionist position that Texas, in annexing herself to the United States, had parted with none of her sovereignty.[78]

James Bell questioned the course that the people of Texas ought to pursue. He did not want Texas to sit idly in the midst of this crisis. Instead, he supported the concerted action of all Southern states. He believed that Texas should move with calmness and patience and not rush hastily into revolution. He believed in the sanctity of democratic politics and that the people of Texas should decide the fate of the Lone Star State.[79]

Charles Anderson, more pointed in his appeal to citizens, railed against independent action on the part of Texas. He believed that many citizens in the area already supported this course, and he warned against this experiment. Speaking boldly and defiantly before the crowd, he pointed to the American flag waving over the Menger Hotel and yelled, "*Our* flag is still there!"

---

76. Epperson, "Speech of Hon B. H. Epperson of Red River, Delivered in the House of Representatives, at the Capital, January 25, 1861," *Southern Intelligencer,* Feb. 6, 1861. During the Civil War, Epperson served on a frontier vigilance committee and practiced law. After the Civil War, he was a financial agent and legal representative for Texas under Governor Throckmorton. See Claude Elliott, *Leathercoat: The Life History of a Texas Patriot;* and Ralph Wooster, "Ben H. Epperson: East Texas Lawyer, Legislator, and Civic Leader."

77. Taylor, "Speech of Robert H. Taylor."

78. Hamilton, *Speech of Hon. Andrew J. Hamilton,* 4.

79. Bell, *Speech of Hon. James H. Bell,* 11.

However, he questioned, "your Lone Star—where is it?" The Lone Star flag stood for "truth, courage, fidelity, honor, not treason." Anderson exclaimed, however, that in nature there are no lone stars. He used vivid imagery to punctuate his argument and, he hoped, to arouse public sentiment against independent action.

> The historic Lone Star of Texas paused not in her dark solitude, but yielding to the life-like, divine impulse within her, towards the great central luminary— our Constitution—she darted upwards with the speed of a comet and the power and brightness of the imperial Jupiter, to unite with that—our constellation— no more a *lone* star—but one of the celestial flock, smoothly and sublimely wheeling and rolling her bright orb in her proper sphere of use and of glory.[80]

In the middle of his speech, a voice in the crowd yelled out that Texas, if left alone, would have died from starvation. Anderson replied that "her carcass would have been so poor and thin, that these *Mexican* buzzards would have scorned the pickings!" Anderson worried that independent action on the part of Texas would leave the state ripe for continued turmoil with Mexico and cause the state to fall back into financial ruin.[81]

James Bell also believed that independent action on the part of Texas and the possibility of war would hurt the economic and social welfare of the state. War, he concluded, was not in the best social or economic interest of the country. "It erects no asylums for the insane, the blind, the dumb and deaf. It does not spread the sail of commerce to the wind. It brings no respect for seed time and harvest. It brings not plenty to the board, nor cheerfulness to the fireside." Bell's remarks reveal that the antisecessionists were just as concerned with the economic security and social welfare of the state as the prosecessionists. He did not believe, though, that secession and war would benefit Texas economically or socially. Texas, however, would prove these antisecessionists wrong. After secession, Texas defended its economic interests against the Indians and against an encroaching Confederate government. Moreover, Texas proved that it was committed to the social and economic welfare of its citizenry. The state not only erected welfare institutions in the midst of war but also maintained them as part of its commitment to its own future and progress.[82]

Robert H. Taylor also worried about the economic interests of the state. He was concerned that the supporters of slavery would abandon his section of the country and that the slave issue would rise above all other economic

80. Anderson, *Speech of Charles Anderson,* 5–6.
81. Ibid., 6.
82. Bell, *Speech of Hon. James H. Bell,* 16.

interests. He asked his fellow politicians, "[I]n this new *Cotton Confederacy what will become of my section, the wheat growers and the stock raisers?*" Taylor also raised the important issue of representation in the new confederacy and asked on what basis, white or black, representation would be based. He worried that if it were based upon slavery, then Texas would have the least voice and representation in politics. "She will be the tail end of the concern," he told the House.[83] Despite his concerns and valid questioning of the ramifications of secession, Taylor was willing to submit to the results of popular sovereignty and cast his lot with the citizens of Texas through good or evil report. His speech reveals that the fear over economic security ran deeper than the threat to slavery. Texans, with a personal stake in ranching and agriculture production other than cotton, also worried about the future and the uncertainty of secession's consequences. For Taylor and other antisecessionists, the prospect of secession and the further possibility of independent action threatened the political and economic foundation of the Lone Star State.

Both secessionists and antisecessionists used their speeches to affect fellow politicians and the public in the midst of crisis. Both groups stood strong in their beliefs and spoke sternly about the troubled times. Though these politicians disagreed on the fundamental element of secession, common threads existed in their discourse. Both used constitutional arguments as the foundation to defend their political and economic world. They discussed the practicality of secession and the fear of war, and debated at length the course Texas should take. In all, both pro- and antisecessionist speeches revealed a deep concern for the political and economic welfare of Texas and the citizenry. This concern transcended a desire to maintain the institution of slavery. Politicians worried about the sanctity of democratic politics, fretted over the extension of border hostilities with the Indians, and sought to safeguard the economic interests in wheat and cattle. More than anything, these speeches defined the interests of the Lone Star State and reveal that Texas's identity in the crisis was based upon the desire for commercial security. To protect their political and economic world, Texas would hold its secession convention, and Texans would march to the ballot box to endorse secession as a means to protect their interests. These actions reveal, in the words of Louis T. Wigfall, that "so far as this Union is concerned, the cold sweat of death is upon it."[84]

83. Taylor, "Speech of Robert H. Taylor," 16; emphasis in original.
84. Wigfall, *Speech of Hon. Louis T. Wigfall,* 21.

CHAPTER 2

In Defense of Liberty
and Property

The Secession Movement

On February 1, 1861, the Texas secession convention voted to secede
from the Union. Immediately after the Ordinance on Secession passed, Gen.
George M. Flournoy escorted a group of Travis County ladies into the convention chamber. Amid cheers of jubilation, the ladies placed the Lone Star
flag in the center of the room, turned, and departed. The act was simple,
yet profound. Most Texans identified with the Lone Star flag, and the act of
placing it in the center of the room symbolized the unifying force that guided
Texas politicians to consider secession from the Union: loyalty to the state
and a deep concern for the welfare of the citizenry.[1]

As shown, political rhetoric reveals that politicians supporting secession
and antisecession shared the concern of protecting Texas's material well-
being. Texas had a diverse commercial economy that politicians sought to
safeguard at all cost. The citizens of Texas, through their words and actions,
expressed this same desire in the move toward secession. However, behind
this seeming act of unity lurked deep division over what Texans hoped to
achieve by their actions, and the road to secession was laden with difficulty as
citizens throughout Texas held pro- and antisecession meetings. At the end of
this road, however, Texans overwhelmingly voted to support secession from
the Union. Their defense of secession at the ballot box not only reflected their
political and economic interests, but also provided another step in defining
Texas's political and economic identity in this crisis.

Texas was a geographically and economically diverse state. Map 2.1
shows a division of four geographical regions: the Gulf Coast, east Texas,
central Texas, and the frontier. Geographical location in the state of Texas
determines these regions. They are not the outgrowth of some relative or

1. *Journal of the Secession Convention of Texas, 1861,* 65; Ralph Wooster, *The Secession Conventions of the South,* 125, 129–30; Francis White Johnson, *A History of
Texas and Texans,* 536.

germane process. In economic terms, Texas was just as diverse. Slavery and cotton production were the primary vital elements of Texas's black-belt economic system. Map 2.2, "Slave Population," reveals that the black-belt region stretched from the northeastern frontier region of the state to the Gulf Coast counties. Slaveholding per county ranged from 0 to 8,784 slaves, with a mean slaveholding of 1,373. Cotton production per county ranged from 0 to 12,536,800 pounds of cotton, with a mean cotton production of 1,392,000 pounds. Map 2.3, "Ginned Cotton x 400 Pounds," reveals that cotton production extended throughout the state with the greatest concentration in the south-central and Gulf Coast regions.[2]

Texas's agricultural interests, though, extended beyond cotton production. Wheat and corn production also made up essential aspects of the state's economic investment. Wheat production per county ranged from 0 to 194,264 bushels, with a mean wheat production of 11,921 bushels. Corn production per county ranged from 0 to 660,043 bushels, with a mean corn production of 133,556 bushels. Map 2.4, "Wheat Production—Bushels," reveals that only six counties produced in excess of 50,000 bushels of wheat. The majority of production was less than 50,000 bushels per county, with the least amount of wheat produced in both the black-belt and western frontier regions. The majority of counties in those regions produced less than 10,000 bushels of wheat. Map 2.5, "Corn Production—Bushels," reveals that the black-belt region produced the greatest amount of corn, whereas the western frontier region along with several Gulf Coast counties produced the least amount of corn.[3]

Texas's economy extended beyond agricultural concerns. A vast majority of Texans held an important investment in ranching. Livestock holding primarily consisted of cattle, horses, and sheep. Ranchers in Texas owned both beef and milch cattle. Beef cattle holding per county ranged from 0 to 153,758 head of cattle, with a mean holding of 22,296 head (see Map 2.6). Milch cow holding per county ranged from 0 to 19,922 head of cattle, with a mean holding of 4,851 head (see Map 2.7). Ranchers also held a personal stake in horses, both for personal use and for sale at market. Horse holding per county ranged from 2 to 12,932 horses, with a mean holding of 2,626 horses. Map 2.8, "Horse Holding," reveals that the majority of horse holding ran from north to south Texas along the western frontier section of the state.[4]

2. Campbell, *Empire for Slavery,* 68–69; *Population of the United States in 1860, Compiled from the Original Returns of the Eighth Census; Agriculture of the United States in 1860, Compiled from the Original Returns of the Eighth Census.*

3. *Population in 1860; Agriculture in 1860.*

4. *Agriculture in 1860.*

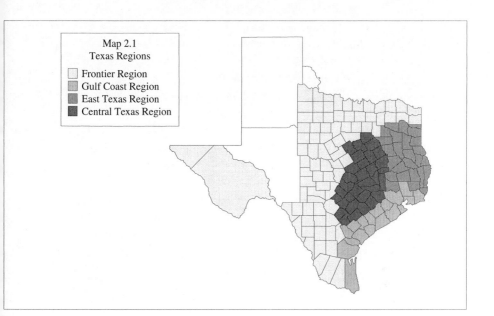

Map 2.1
Texas Regions

Frontier Region
Gulf Coast Region
East Texas Region
Central Texas Region

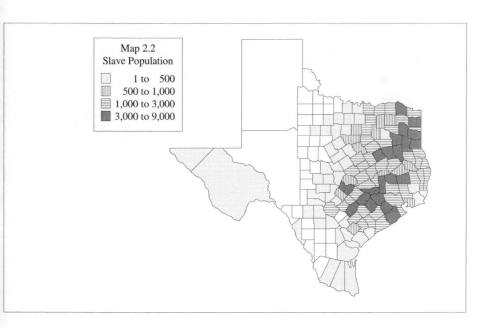

Map 2.2
Slave Population

1 to   500
500 to 1,000
1,000 to 3,000
3,000 to 9,000

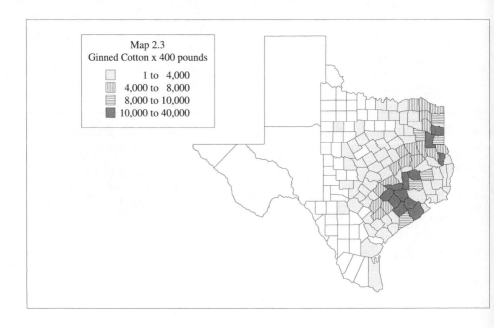

Map 2.3
Ginned Cotton x 400 pounds
1 to   4,000
4,000 to   8,000
8,000 to 10,000
10,000 to 40,000

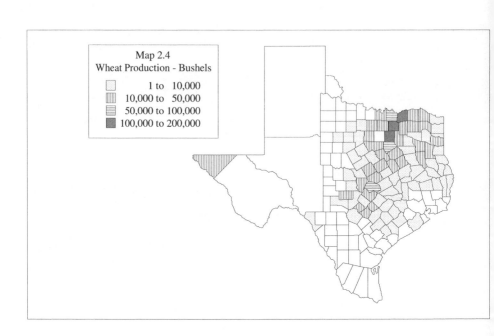

Map 2.4
Wheat Production - Bushels
1 to   10,000
10,000 to   50,000
50,000 to 100,000
100,000 to 200,000

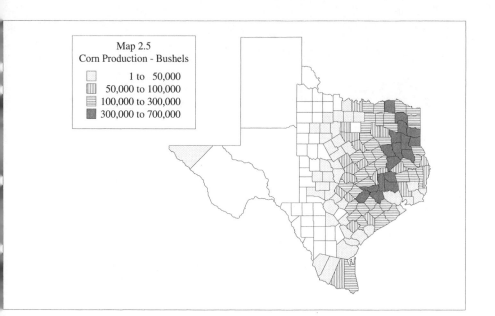

Map 2.5
Corn Production - Bushels

1 to 50,000
50,000 to 100,000
100,000 to 300,000
300,000 to 700,000

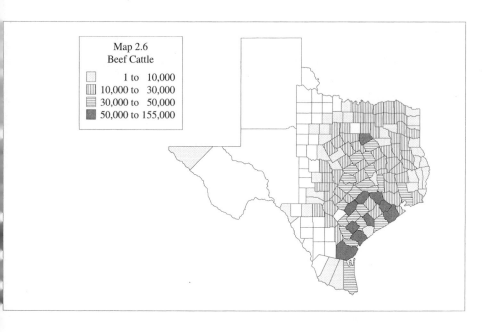

Map 2.6
Beef Cattle

1 to 10,000
10,000 to 30,000
30,000 to 50,000
50,000 to 155,000

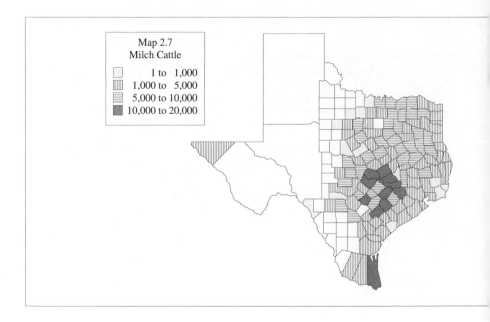

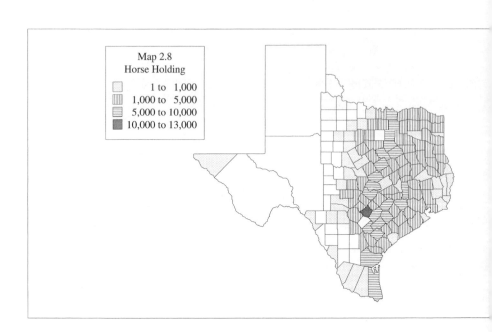

These economic interests would weigh on citizens' minds as they traveled the road of secession, especially in light of the fact that Texas's multifaceted commercial system faced several threats. Texas farmers and ranchers, especially in the frontier region, faced a dual threat from both Indian tribes and Mexican bandits. Indian raids were conducted by both the reserve and the nonreserve Indians. Indian attacks ensued for a number of reasons, primarily their economic desires and second the U.S. uprooting of Indian tribes from one reserve to another in the 1850s, which created instability and hostility between the Indian nations and the United States. Texas citizens complained to politicians that, across the state, the Indians committed numerous murders and were becoming much bolder in their attacks than in previous years.[5]

The central and southern frontier regions not only faced Indian attacks, but the proximity of the Mexican border fostered multiple problems for Texans as well. Mexico never abandoned its designs on Texas. It hoped to reannex part if not all of the Lone Star State. Consequently, Mexico did little to hinder vandal activity affecting Texans. Throughout the 1850s and early 1860s, the infamous frontier pirate Juan Cortina harassed the citizenry of south Texas with his cattle raids.[6] Cortina had a band of men between two hundred and five hundred in number. He had tremendous influence among the Mexican citizens to the point that politicians courted his favor at election time. Owning a ranch a few miles across the border from Brownsville, Cortina easily escaped arrest after his raids. Not only did Mexican politicians look the other way regarding Cortina's hostilities, but Mexico also did little to control the Indian population within its borders, resulting in numerous Mexico-based cattle raids into Texas. Texas ranchers constantly safeguarded their lives and property as a result of this dual threat. The problems with Mexico, though, extended beyond Mexican and Indian hostilities. The proximity of Mexico provided a means of escape for slaves, and Mexico made little to no effort

5. F. W. Johnson, *History of Texas,* 511–12; Sandra L. Myres, "The Ranching Frontier: Spanish Institutional Backgrounds of the Plains Cattle Industry"; J. W. Throckmorton to John H. Reagan, Mar. 17, 1860, John H. Reagan Papers, Barker Center for American History, University of Texas at Austin (hereafter Barker Center); Benjamin H. Good Papers, Barker Center. For insight into the tenuous relationship between the reserve Indians and Texas, see Commissioner of Indian Affairs Charles E. Mix to Secretary of Interior Jacob Thompson, Sept. 11, 1860, Washington Daniel Miller Papers, Barker Center; Governor's Papers: Sam Houston, Sept. 1860, Texas State Library, Archives Division (hereafter TSL); James M. Day, ed., *The Indian Papers of Texas and the Southwest, 1825–1916,* 4:24–25, 5:156, 246, 249, 281–83, 307–8, 326–29, 335–38, 343–44, 347–50, 354–57, 361–66, 374–84; and Executive Record Book: Sam Houston, 158, TSL.

6. Although today Juan Cortina is viewed as a folk hero of the oppressed Tejanos, nineteenth-century Texans held a different perspective.

to return slaveholders' property, undermining the institution of slavery. The proximity of the border and Mexico's unwillingness to recognize slaveholders' rights deeply concerned many Texas citizens.[7]

Not only did slave owners have to contend with the border situation, but they also remained intimately aware of the abolitionist threat that potentially served to undermine their wealth and property. Abolitionists made their presence known in many Texas counties. Most notable was a group known as the Mystic Red that was notorious for stirring up trouble among slaves and fostering tension between secessionists and antisecessionists. Furthermore, Northern abolitionists worked among the citizens of Mexico and various Indian tribes in hopes of gaining favorable sentiment for their cause. Abolitionist activity across Texas's border compounded the difficult relationship that Texas had with Mexico and the Indian tribes.[8]

Though many individuals were not guilty of embracing abolitionism, especially in north Texas, Texas politicians and plain folk still feared a threat to their economic security.[9] The pro- and antisecession speeches clearly articulated this apprehension. This trepidation manifested itself in many ways, most notably in the formation of fraternal associations such as the Knights of the Golden Circle (KGC), an organization with roots in the Southern Rights Clubs of the 1830s. William Lamb Bickley, a Cincinnati physician, officially organized the Knights of the Golden Circle in 1854. Through the months of October and November 1860, groups of this organization formed across Texas and much of the South.[10] Many known national and state leaders, such as Louis T. Wigfall, Sam Houston, William L. Yancy, Robert A. Toombs,

7. Official Report of Major Heintzelman, Davenport Collection, Barker Center; communication between Capt. William G. Tobin and Governor H. R. Runnels, Oct. 1859, Davenport Collection, Barker Center; Military Papers, TSL; John S. Ford to Sam Houston, Mar. 25, 1860, Governor's Papers: Sam Houston, TSL; Day, *Indian Papers,* 5:94–97, 128–29; Jerry D. Thompson, ed., *Juan Cortina and the Texas-Mexico Frontier, 1859–1877,* 11–28.

8. F. W. Johnson, *History of Texas,* 515; Campbell, *Empire for Slavery,* 68–69. For remarks on abolitionist activity and the Mystic Red, see Wigfall, *Speech of Hon. Louis T. Wigfall;* and Reagan, *State of the Union.* For abolitionist activity in Mexico and among Indians, see various issues of the *Columbus Colorado Citizen* and the *Galveston Weekly News.* For actions of the Methodist Church, to which the Mystic Red was tied, see David Pickering and Judy Falls, *Brush Men and Vigilantes: Civil War Dissent in Texas.*

9. Richard McCaslin, *Tainted Breeze: The Great Hanging at Gainesville, Texas, 1862,* 1.

10. Member of the Order, *An Authentic Exposition of the "K. G. C." "Knights of the Golden Circle"; or, A History of Secession from 1834 to 1861,* 5; Jimmie Hicks, "Some Letters Concerning the Knights of the Golden Circle in Texas, 1860–1861." Groups

John C. Breckinridge, Jefferson Davis, Pryor Lea, and Ben McCulloch, either held membership in the organization or knowingly approved of the group.[11]

The Knights of the Golden Circle operated with a distinct military, political, and economic agenda. It offered a voice for expansionists, nativists, and defenders of slavery. Members desired the acquisition of Mexico, Cuba, and Nicaragua; were sworn to uphold and promote southern interests; and committed themselves to forming a "free Southern Government" in case of encroachment by the U.S. government. Individual groups of the organization, known as Castles, formed in almost every southern state. The most pronounced participation in and activity of this group existed in Texas. The KGC first appeared in Texas in February 1860, establishing a Castle in McKinney; one month later, a Castle formed in San Antonio. During the secession crisis, the San Antonio Castle served as Bickley's headquarters. When Bickley moved the Knights' headquarters to San Antonio, the group no longer rested in the hands of the South, but "in the hands of Texans," and Bickley boasted loudly of that fact.[12] Gen. Elkhannah Greer, an established planter and merchant who served in the Mexican War under Jefferson Davis, joined the KGC in 1859, and served as Bickley's right-hand man, commanding the Texas Castles. Map 2.9, "Knights of the Golden Circle," reveals that thirty-seven Castles existed in thirty-three counties across the state. The formation and expansion of the KGC in Texas represented an embodiment of Texans' economic fears, and its widespread acceptance further revealed the efforts of many Texans to ensure their economic well-being.[13]

----

of this organization were not limited to the South; the KGC was extremely active in Indiana and California as well.

11. Member of the Order, *Authentic Exposition,* 8–10.

12. John Niven, ed., *The Salmon P. Chase Papers,* 374–75; Roy Sylvan Dunn, "The K.G.C. in Texas, 1860–1861," 543, 548–50; Ollinger Crenshaw, "The Knights of the Golden Circle: The Career of George Bickley," 43. For Reagan's condemnation of the KGC as a rumored secret political party, see Reagan to Oran M. Roberts, Nov. 1, 1860, Good Papers, Barker Center; and *By-Laws of the San Antonio Castle, "K.G.C.,"* approved June 15, 1861. Officers of the San Antonio Castle were: J. M. Carolan, captain; Albert Wood, secretary; J. H. Beck Jr., inspector; George Cupples, lieutenant; J. A. G. Navarro, treasurer; J. M. Smith, guide; and J. Marshall, sergeant. See also Donald S. Frazier, *Blood and Treasure: Confederate Empire in the Southwest,* 14.

13. C. A. Bridges, "The Knights of the Golden Circle: A Filibustering Fantasy," 288, 292, 294, 300; KGC, *A Full Exposure of the Southern Traitors: The Knights of the Golden Circle, Their Startling Schemes Frustrated,* 6–7; and A. Williams and Barker, *Writings of Sam Houston,* 7:495–96. When war broke out, Greer commanded the Third Texas Cavalry. In Oct. 1862, he was appointed brigadier general and soon after appointed head of the Trans-Mississippi's Bureau of Conscription. Texas newspapers, especially the

The KGC also contributed to the political crisis of the nation through its antiparty stance. According to the Knights, a breakdown in the nation's political system lay at the heart of the country's troubles. The political crisis, they held, had its roots in the Kansas-Nebraska Bill, which brought slavery to the fore in Americans' minds and gave rise to sectional politics. Members railed against the Kansas-Nebraska Bill and the destruction of the Missouri Compromise line, which threatened their hold over property. "Before one Southern man can get ready to migrate with his property, (niggers)," the order claimed, "they send a whole legion of Yankee Abolitionists to Kansas to cut his throat and steal his negroes."[14]

From the Knights' perspective, though, abolitionist activity manifested itself beyond the Republican Party. There existed a general sentiment among KGC members that fault for the political crisis also lay with the Democratic Party. The Knights believed that the rights of the South could be secured only in the Southern Confederacy because even the Democratic Party was becoming a vehicle for abolition. Members of the KGC believed that the Pierce administration did little to carry out the principles of the Kansas-Nebraska Act and furthermore failed to prohibit emigrant aid societies in Massachusetts from sending "their pauper cutthroats to disturb and endanger our people in the common territory of the United States." The situation of the country represented a political crisis and failure of the largest magnitude. "The whole American Government," the Knights held, "is really becoming a GRAND ABOLITION MACHINE, WHICH, EVEN IN THE HANDS OF DEMOCRATS, IS DESTINED TO CRUSH OUT EVERY VESTIGE OF SOUTHERN LIBERTY." The Knights' antiabolitionist position was so strong that some contemporaries, such as the Honorable Archie Dixon of Kentucky, believed that if it had not

---

Seguin Southern Confederacy and the *La Grange True Issue,* have numerous articles on Bickley and the KGC. See Dunn, "K.G.C. in Texas," 556. As secession loomed greater in the Southern mind, the Knights attempted to popularize and expand their initiation process by admitting members on a probationary basis. Only those individuals who were staunch secessionists and firmly decided on the question of slavery could join and rise in the ranks of the society. The Knights attempted to make the organization attractive by creating regalia and emblems (Maj. J. T. Sprague, "The Texas Treason: A Paper Read before the New York Historical Society, June 25, 1861," *War of the Rebellion: Official Records of the Union and Confederate Armies,* supp. 1, doc. 21, p. 110). For nineteenth-century fraternal organizations, see Mark Carnes, *Secret Ritual and Manhood in Victorian America,* 8; Frank Klement, *Dark Lanterns,* 14; and Member of the Order, *Authentic Exposition,* 12–14 (for a detailed account of the rituals, regalia, and emblems, see 27–29, 49; for women's role in the KGC, see 53–54).

14. Member of the Order, *Authentic Exposition,* 9–10. For Southern antipartyism, see George C. Rable, *The Confederate Republic: A Revolution against Politics.*

been for the group's forcible doctrine that stirred up public sentiment, then abolitionist forces would have died their own death.[15]

Prior to secession, Castles continually formed across the state. Support for the KGC was so strong that the Texas Castles outdistanced other Gulf states in the promotion of the organization's goals. Military buildup and political control were critical facets of the group's primary objective of economic dominance. This aim extended beyond the issue of slavery. They intended to monopolize the world's supply of tobacco, cotton, sugar, and a good portion of rice and coffee. They desired ascendance over the commerce of the Gulf of Mexico, the Mississippi River, and Latin America. The expansionist sentiments of the Knights coincided with Texas's motives to gain a western port in California and annex the territories of New Mexico to diversify its economy further. The activity of the Knights not only expressed the general economic sentiment of most Texans, but also served to foster the political debate over secession. Many members, especially Greer, outwardly supported the call for a secession convention to protect the commercial interests and property of Texas citizens. The KGC's cry for a secession convention became louder after the election of Abraham Lincoln.[16]

Abraham Lincoln's election reinforced Texans' fears of the threat to property of all kinds, and exasperated the political situation in Texas. For example, in Calhoun and DeWitt Counties, resolutions passed that communicated the residents' unwillingness to submit to "Black Republicanism," and argued for the right of Southern states to defend life and property, by force if necessary. Furthermore, the KGC rallied the citizenry and aided politicians in protest

15. Member of the Order, *Authentic Exposition,* 9–10, 69. The Knights were so distraught over the political condition of the country that two plans emerged to save the South. The first plan was an attempt to help break up the 1860 Democratic Party Convention by railing against Stephen Douglas and his supporters and encouraging John C. Breckinridge. The second plan involved the takeover of Washington and inauguration of Breckinridge as president. See ibid., 17–19, 32, 35; Niven, *Chase Papers,* 374–75; and Crenshaw, "Knights of the Golden Circle," 43. The Knights were also suspected in the assassination of Lincoln. A government agent visited Bickley in his Fort Warren jail cell and asked him directly whether the Knights were involved (see Klement, *Dark Lanterns,* 33 n. 98).

16. Bridges, "The Knights of the Golden Circle," 288. For Texas's western schemes, see Frazier, *Blood and Treasure.* Nativism served as part of the driving force behind the goal of economic dominance and the invasion of Mexico. See Executive Record Book: Sam Houston, Mar. 21, 1860; and George Bickley Papers, National Archives. For nativism and racial attitudes in Texas, see David Montejano, *Anglos and Mexicans in the Making of Texas, 1836–1986;* Arnoldo DeLeon, *The Tejano Community, 1836–1900;* and DeLeon, *They Called Them Greasers: Anglo Attitudes toward Mexicans in Texas, 1821–1900.*

of Lincoln's election. Across the state, KGC members organized political rallies favoring a secession convention. At these torchlight parades, citizens often waved the Lone Star flag, and hung "old Abe" in effigy to show their support for secession.[17]

Texas politicians and citizens reacted to Lincoln's election by pressing for a secession convention. For example, Louis T. Wigfall's printed speech stirred great excitement in Texas. Four days afterward, Chief Justice Royal T. Wheeler sent a letter to the press advocating the right of the people to defend their liberties through a state convention. Wheeler was born in Vermont in 1800 and raised in Ohio. He practiced law with Williamson S. Oldham, in Arkansas, in 1837. Shortly thereafter, in 1839, he moved to Nacogdoches, Texas, to practice law. He served on the Texas Supreme Court in 1844 and 1845, and later served as the court's chief justice from 1857 to 1864. Wheeler's letter reflected county action occurring in the state, and coincided with politicians' call for state action. In Brazoria County, for example, a mass meeting called for a statewide secession convention to be held in Galveston on January 8, 1861, for the purpose of deciding Texas's course of action. Similar action followed when a group of secessionists met in Austin on December 3 and called for a general election of delegates to a convention.[18]

On December 3, 1860, Oran M. Roberts, William Peleg Rogers, George M. Flournoy, and John Salmon Ford prepared the call for a secession convention. "We have no remedy for this evil but for the people of the Southern States, singly and conjointly, acting in their sovereign capacity, to take the defense of their rights and liberties in their own hands." These leading politicians believed that the inauguration of Lincoln would further the sectional crisis. Therefore, Texas should protect itself through the election of delegates to a convention. The call set January 8, 1861, as the election date for delegates and January 28 as the first meeting date. Copies of the call were sent to different parts of the state, published in local newspapers, and adopted in mass meetings.[19]

17. Dunn, "K.G.C. in Texas," 558–59.

18. Dudley G. Wooten, ed., *A Comprehensive History of Texas, 1685–1897,* 92; James A. Creighton, *A Narrative History of Brazoria County,* 229. For public sentiment in favor of a convention, see issues of the *Harrison Flag* beginning with Dec. 1, 1860. For citizens' move to call a convention, see Oran M. Roberts to John H. Reagan, Nov. 25, 1860; and Good Papers, Barker Center. For a speech by Royal T. Wheeler, see *Austin Texas State Gazette,* Dec. 22, 1860.

19. *Journal of the Secession Convention,* 9–10 n. 2; Wooten, *Comprehensive History,* 87–88.

The call for an election of delegates to a convention, however, caused much reaction among antisecessionists in the state. They did what they could to thwart the move toward secession. On December 17, 1860, Sam Houston acquiesced to the will of the people and political pressure by calling for an extra session of the legislature. His doing so was a result of the "great excitement existing in the public mind, arising from various causes," which affected Texas's relationship with the federal government. Houston said that the invasion of the frontier by Indians, where "the lives of our Citizens have been taken and their property destroyed," and the dire straits of the treasury that left Texas defenseless against any incursion, not to mention the inability to carry on ordinary activity, were the primary factors in his decision to call the legislature. The summons, though, was really an attempt to subvert the calling of a secession convention. Any step toward state action, without directly moving toward secession, furthered Houston's design to reconcile sectional differences.[20]

Houston even went a step further. On December 27, 1860, operating under the authority of legislative approval, he ordered a February 4, 1861, election for seven delegates to represent Texas in a convention of Southern states, even though politicians had yet to establish any agreement for the meeting. Again, Houston's action revealed his strong antisecession position. By calling for delegates and a Southern convention, Houston sought to impede more radical action at the state level.[21]

Many citizens across the state supported Governor Houston's actions. For example, a Unionist meeting in Austin adopted several resolutions against secession. The crowd deplored "the election of a candidate to the Presidency of the United States by a sectional party, based on geographical distinctions." Furthermore, these antisecessionists held that they would not submit to a federal government based upon principles that were hostile to the Southern states. Underlying their devotion to the Union, then, existed a determination to uphold Southern ideals, including a peaceful solution to the slave issue. Not only did these politicians oppose secession, but they also outwardly stated their objection to a secession convention and the establishment of a provisional government. The antisecessionists made it clear they refused to participate in the January election of delegates to the convention. They, however, supported Houston's call for the legislature and his move to elect

20. A. Williams and Barker, *Writings of Sam Houston,* 8:220–21; *Austin Texas State Gazette,* Dec. 20, 1860; *Harrison Flag,* Dec. 23, 1860; *Houston Telegraph,* Dec. 24, 1860; *Marshall Texas Republican,* Jan. 5, 1861; John H. Reagan to Oran M. Roberts, Nov. 20, 1860, Good Papers, Barker Center.

21. A. Williams and Barker, *Writings of Sam Houston,* 8:225–26.

delegates to a convention of Southern states. According to some reports, this Unionist meeting revealed to prosecessionists that the people remained divided over the issue of secession and that "it was not an easy game they had undertaken to play with such high stakes."[22]

While Houston made efforts to foil secession, other antisecessionists continued to meet across the state. On January 2, 1861, citizens in Montgomery County held a Unionist meeting that supported the joint effort of all Southern states to work for a peaceful solution to the crisis. They opposed any move toward the calling of a secession convention. Furthermore, on January 1861, a Union meeting in Jack County assembled a committee of leading citizens and adopted a series of resolutions. They renewed their devotion to Texas and to Texas in the Union. Nevertheless, they deplored the personal-liberty bills designed to nullify the fugitive-slave law. They viewed these acts "as a fearful remedy that should not be resorted to until every remedy under the constitution shall have been tried in vain." Although some outwardly supported compromise in the Union, they did not completely rule out the virtue of secession. For secession to be the proper course of action, President Lincoln would have to first perpetrate "some act of commission or omission on his part before secession could be esteemed a virtue." Antisecessionists across the state appeared united in deploring the potential threat to liberty and property, but there did appear to be a degree of difference in terms of their leaning toward eventual support of secession. More important, they continued to reveal the fear of many Texans concerned about economic security, and the existing division over the proper course to obtain that protection.[23]

On January 8, 1861, despite antisecessionist sentiment and efforts, an election of delegates to the secession convention took place. Opponents of the convention, though, claimed that these elections were a farce because many polls across the state were under the influence of the KGC. The Knights quite possibly did hold some influence in the election of delegates and the calling of a secession convention. Of the thirty-three counties where Castles existed, only five had a vote of less than 50 percent for secession. The other twenty-eight were scattered across the state, though the overwhelming majority of Castles were located in those counties that had an above-average holding of slaves and cattle. Previous studies argue that the KGC was most prominent in east Texas. Geographical analysis suggests, however, that the

22. *Southern Intelligencer,* Dec. 26, 1860. For other Unionist meetings, see Sept.–Dec. 1860 issues of the *La Grange True Issue.* See also "Resolutions of San Patricio County," Miller Papers, Barker Center.

23. *Southern Intelligencer,* Feb. 6, 1861.

KGC represented not only black-belt, proslavery radicals' interests, but also a broader class of citizens with diversified economic interests, all of whom feared a threat to their liberty and property.[24]

Despite the overwhelming political support for secession, antisecessionists such as Sam Houston remained actively opposed to this course. Houston addressed the Texas legislature on its first day of meeting, January 21. He engaged in a long discourse where he tackled the issue of Indian hostilities, which by that point extended to counties within fifty miles of the capital. He confronted the difficult conditions of the frontier counties and the offensive measures needed to resolve diligently the Indian problem. Furthermore, he addressed the failure of the U.S. government to reimburse Texas for its frontier expenses and the poor condition of the treasury, which was drained significantly due to the Cortina wars. Houston ended his address before the legislature with a reminder that in Texas's past time of trouble, other states had come to its aid, and now it should return the favor by uniting with other states in calm deliberation. Houston's words, though, fell on deaf ears. The Texas legislature repealed the joint resolution authorizing the sending of delegates to a convention of Southern states.[25]

On January 28, the secession convention of Texas held its first meeting, brought to order by prayer offered by the Right Reverend Alexander Gregg, bishop of the Protestant Episcopal Church of the Diocese of Texas. By this point, South Carolina, Florida, Georgia, Alabama, Mississippi, and Louisiana had already seceded, with Texas the only exception among the Gulf states. The convention spent the first day in the business of electing officials. Both Oran M. Roberts and William Ochiltree received nominations for the position of president, but Ochiltree declined the nomination and insisted that Roberts be declared the president of the convention. Ochiltree's motion carried, and Roberts took his seat. At once, he claimed that the convention represented the will of the people who had commissioned it to deal with the immediate crisis. More specifically, Roberts referred to the "right of self government" and "the immemorial recognition of the institution of slavery." It was their duty, as a sovereignty, to deal head-on with this crisis for the people's best interest.[26]

24. Irene Sandbo, "The First Session of the Secession Convention of Texas," 173; Dunn, "K.G.C. in Texas," 564; Baum, *Shattering of Texas Unionism,* 58–59.

25. A. Williams and Barker, *Writings of Sam Houston,* 8:236–52; *Journal of the Secession Convention,* 7.

26. *Journal of the Secession Convention,* 15–17. In its first two days, the convention also dealt with the credentials of the delegates, ensuring that the proper number from each district had been elected.

On the second day of the meeting, the convention set the tone early and established its intention to take Texas out of the Union. The Committee on Federal Relations was selected, and the assembly adopted by a vote of 152 to 6 a resolution "that without determining now the manner in which this result should be effected, it is the deliberate sense of this Convention that the State of Texas should separately secede from the Federal Union."[27]

The following day, January 30, Roberts selected the fifteen-member Committee on Public Safety, whose primary task would be to draft the Ordinance on Secession. Map 2.10, "Committee on Public Safety," reveals that the committee represented twenty-one counties containing the full range of Texas's commercial interests, and included three counties whose representatives had voted against the intent of secession. Roberts's appointment of those delegates represented a shrewd political move to guarantee that even antisecessionists had a voice in charting Texas's course.[28]

On January 30, the Committee on Federal Relations presented the Ordinance on Secession to Roberts and the convention. The entire committee unanimously agreed to the first section of the resolution: taking Texas out of the Union. The committee justified secession on the grounds that the "Federal Government has failed . . . in giving protection either to the persons of our people upon an exposed frontier or to the property of our citizens." For the committee, the crisis involved more than the simple matter of protecting slavery. It also charged the federal government with failure to protect both the welfare and the property of Texas citizens.[29]

Now that it was obvious Texas would secede from the Union, the issue of popular sovereignty remained the final question. The Committee on Federal Relations was divided on whether it was beneficial to submit this resolution to popular will by a vote of the people. Therefore, politicians debated the second section of the resolution, in secret session and before the general convention. Several substitutes were offered, even one by John Gregg to strike out the second section, but all were either laid on the table or defeated.[30]

Amid the debate over popular sovereignty, and aware of the possibility

27. Ibid., 25, 28; Ralph Wooster, *Secession Conventions,* 129. New members joined the convention the next day, and the final vote on the resolution rested at 157 to 8.

28. *Journal of the Secession Convention,* 28. The Committee on Public Safety comprised the following members: John C. Robertson, John Henry Brown, James H. Rogers, James R. Armstrong, A. T. Rainey, John S. Ford, William P. Rogers, James M. Norris, John A. Wilcox, James G. Thompson, William G. Miller, John Alexander Green, Charles L. Cleveland, James Hooker, and Philip Noland Luckett.

29. Ibid., 35–36.

30. Ibid., 40, 42–44.

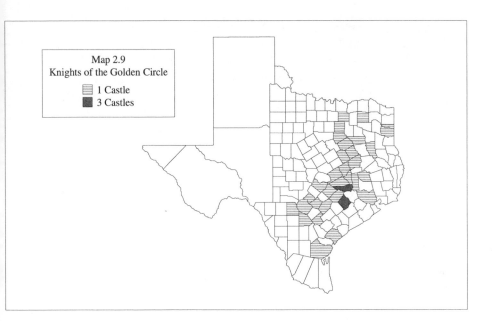

Map 2.9
Knights of the Golden Circle
1 Castle
3 Castles

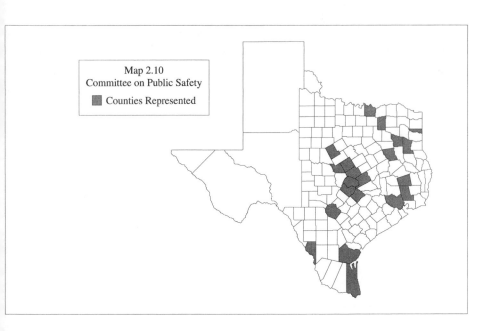

Map 2.10
Committee on Public Safety
Counties Represented

that delegates could eliminate the second section of the ordinance, Sam Houston wrote to the secession convention, acknowledging its right to convene. Furthermore, he conveyed to the delegates his support for popular sovereignty. He assured the convention that the citizenry of Texas had his "warmest and most fervent wishes" and that once the people spoke through the ballot box, he would yield to their will. "Their fate is my fate, their fortune is my fortune, their destiny is my destiny, be it prosperity or gloom, as of old, I am with my country." Although Houston was a Texas nationalist and supported the will of the people along with Southern ideals, he could not publicly support secession. His endorsement of popular sovereignty was yet another ploy to prolong further the convention and put off secession. Houston hoped that the citizenry of Texas would provide the last obstacle to Texas leaving the Union.[31]

On January 31, the secession convention took a general vote on whether to strike out the second section of the Ordinance on Secession. By a vote of 145 to 28, the convention adopted the measure to submit the issue of secession to a popular vote. Map 2.11, "Ordinance on Secession," reveals that those staunch secessionist delegates who voted to omit the second section represented twenty-nine counties across the state that had a high interest in both slavery and livestock. With south Texas, El Paso, and east Texas representatives voting to abolish the section, it is clear that Texas's interest in secession ran deeper than the east-west, slave-Indian dichotomy that earlier historians have highlighted. Furthermore, the move to subvert popular sovereignty in the name of stability did not appear to be purely the work of politicians representing slaveholding interests, but a general concern of many Texas politicians who represented a variety of commercial endeavors. Nevertheless, the majority of convention delegates, bolstered by the belief that the general population supported secession, upheld the sanctity of democratic politics by allowing the people to voice their opinion at the ballot box.[32]

On February 1, 1861, the secession convention met in quorum to address the issue of submitting the decision for secession to a popular vote. The convention established February 23, 1861, as the voting date. It established March 2, the twenty-fifth anniversary of Texas's declared independence from Mexico, as the day for secession—assuming the citizens of Texas passed the

---

31. Ibid., 47; A. Williams and Barker, *Writings of Sam Houston,* 8:253–54; Wilfred Buck Yearns, ed., *The Confederate Governors,* 195.

32. *Journal of the Secession Convention,* 44. For the argument of an east-west political division, see Ramsdell, "The Frontier and Secession."

Ordinance on Secession. After some minor committee business and admitting Governor Houston, Lieutenant Governor Edward Clark, and judges of the supreme and district courts to the convention, delegates took up and read for a third time the Ordinance on Secession. By a vote of 166 to 8, the convention adopted both sections of the Ordinance on Secession. The convention then resolved to have Oran M. Roberts send copies of the ordinance to Governor Houston and the state legislature. Furthermore, on a motion from Pryor Lea, the convention resolved to have the Committee on Federal Relations draft an ordinance for the mode of popular vote on secession.[33]

After adopting the Ordinance on Secession, the Committee on Federal Relations drew up a declaration of causes for secession. Map 2.12, "Committee on Federal Relations," reveals that this committee comprised twenty politicians who represented approximately thirty-six counties from every economic and geographical region of the state.[34] The concern facing these representatives was the protection of Texas's various commercial interests. Although the abolition of slavery primarily concerned many Texans, a fear of Indian attacks that threatened economic security also existed. Texas charged the United States with failing to protect the lives and property of its citizens in the border and frontier regions. The danger from Indian raids was so great that the secession convention remarked that the federal government had rendered the state's condition "more insecure and harassing than it was during the existence of the Republic of Texas." Not only did the U.S. government fail to safeguard the state, but when Texas used its own state resources and capital for protection, the federal government had also refused to reimburse the state for its expenditures. The cost of maintaining the frontier ran anywhere from $35,000 to $150,000 monthly, and the federal government owed Texas a minimum of $800,000. Approximately fourteen thousand copies of the declaration were ordered for printing and distribution to the people, including two thousand in German and two thousand in Spanish.[35]

On February 4, predicting popular support for secession, the convention

33. *Journal of the Secession Convention,* 48–50; Ralph Wooster, *Secession Conventions,* 125, 129–30. The exact details for the popular vote and vote counting were debated and passed in secret secession (see *Journal of the Secession Convention,* 58–59).

34. *Journal of the Secession Convention,* 25. The *Journal of the Secession Convention* lists a Mr. Moore on the committee, but does not clarify which of the three Moores it is; therefore, he has been omitted from the map and county count on representation.

35. "A Declaration of the Causes which Impel the State of Texas to Secede from the Federal Union," in *Journal of the Secession Convention,* 61–66; Day, *Indian Papers,* 4:66; David Paul Smith, *Frontier Defense in the Civil War: Texas' Rangers and Rebels,* 50.

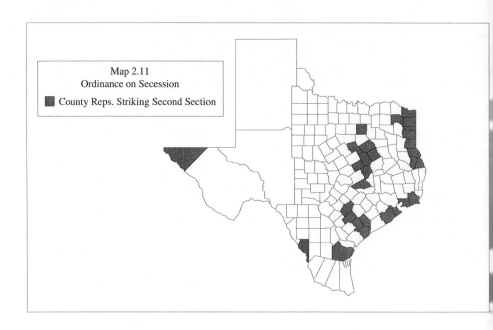

Map 2.11
Ordinance on Secession

County Reps. Striking Second Section

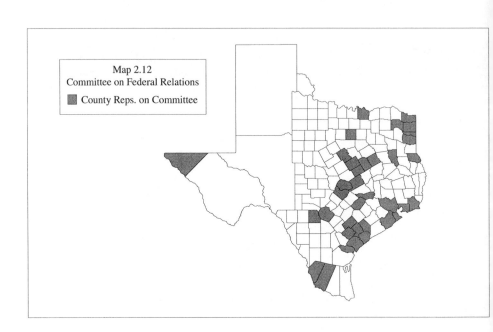

Map 2.12
Committee on Federal Relations

County Reps. on Committee

elected delegates to the Montgomery convention. Some of the most influential men in Texas and the nation were chosen: Louis T. Wigfall, John H. Reagan, John Hemphill, Thomas Neville Waul, John Gregg, Williamson S. Oldham, and William B. Ochiltree. Roberts commissioned these men and admitted them into the convention's secret session.[36]

Texas's commitment to the Confederacy and the Southern cause, however, did not erase the fear and uncertainty, and many politicians continued to question Texas's course of action. On February 6, 1861, opponents of secession wrote and published the "Address to the People of Texas," denouncing the passing of the Ordinance on Secession. They believed it unwise for the people of Texas to support such a measure and that it was best if the South worked to preserve slavery in the Union. The opponents of secession sought to betray the radicalness of the move in an attempt to instill reason in the citizenry. They blamed the "revolutionary movement" on South Carolina. They claimed that South Carolina politicians had acted with the "hottest haste" without regard or preparation for the future. Furthermore, they declared that the South Carolina state government verged on despotism and was "less popular in its form" than other state governments. They further warned the citizenry that secession would result in both higher and more direct taxation, and the real possibility of bloodshed.[37]

In addition, the antisecessionists counseled that any disruption of the Union would inevitably be an agitation and detriment to the institution of slavery. It would be most evident in the driving of slaves from the border-state region, which in turn would unite border states in a common interest with free states. Antisecessionist politicians then played upon the fear of the citizenry by turning the issue of an encroaching government upon its head. They suggested that the secession convention's proposed reconvening in March, after the popular vote on secession, would be a move to take over the whole function of government. They also warned that the assembly would move quickly to change the constitution without popular approval.

---

36. *Journal of the Secession Convention,* 72–80.

37. "Address to the People of Texas, February 6, 1861," *Southern Intelligencer,* Feb. 13, 1861. The address was signed by Senators Martin D. Hart, I. A. Paschal, Emory Rains, and J. W. Throckmorton; by Congressmen M. L. Armstrong, Sam Bogart, L. B. Camp, W. A. Ellett, B. H. Epperson, John Hancock, Jno. L. Haynes, J. E. Henry, T. H. Mundine, A. B. Norton. W. M. Owen, Sam J. Redgate, Robert H. Taylor, and G. W. Whitmore; and by delegates Joshua F. Johnson (Titus), John D. Rains (Wood), A. P. Shuford (Wood), L. H. Williams (Lamar), George W. Wright (Lamar), and William H. Johnson (Lamar).

The "question," they asked, "which lies at the bottom of the whole matter is, how far have you authorized them to act?"[38]

Their appeal to the people, however, mattered little. The state legislature passed an act legalizing the actions of the secession convention, including the passage of the Ordinance on Secession. Furthermore, Sam Houston issued a proclamation ordering a general election on February 23 to ratify or reject the Ordinance on Secession. To counter opponents further, Oran M. Roberts issued an address on February 10 that advocated the adoption of secession.[39]

On February 23, 1861, Texans made their way to the ballot box. The KGC, foreseeing popular approval, held a state convention the prior day, pledging to support the state of Texas in case of turmoil. Approximately 8,000 members showed up, and they were warned to prepare for impending danger at home. By a count of 46,153 to 14,747, Texans voted to leave the Union.[40] After the vote was counted, the hall erupted with joyous cheering. Outside, the Lone Star flag that the ladies from Travis County had presented to the chamber was hoisted atop the dome of the capitol and saluted by artillery fire. Delegates also found that Sam Houston had posted on the southern gate of the grounds a proclamation officially recognizing the popular decision in favor of secession.[41]

Debate over Texas's secession and eventual path centered on the protection of property and commercial interests. The threats of free soil and free labor united Texans behind the liberal tradition of self-interest and property. At its very core, this liberal tradition was based upon the notion of individualism, a division between the public and private spheres. Individualism in this sense was not a notion of egocentrism, but rather a desire to isolate and pursue the rights of life, liberty, and property within the confines of one's own social, economic, and political sphere. Classical liberalism was not a rejection of the public good, but rather saw the public good as something attained through a

38. Ibid.

39. *Journal of the Secession Convention,* 59. The legislature passed its act on Feb. 7; Sam Houston issued his proclamation on Feb. 9 (*Austin Texas State Gazette,* Feb. 16, 1861).

40. Bridges, "The Knights of the Golden Circle," 301; *War of the Rebellion,* 1:624–25; *Journal of the Secession Convention,* 98; Ralph Wooster, *Secession Conventions,* 125, 129–30. The *Journal of the Secession Convention* lists the final vote as being 46,129 to 14,697. Research reveals, however, that the accurate popular vote was 46,153 for and 14,747 against secession. See Joe T. Timmons, "The Referendum in Texas on the Ordinance of Secession, February 23, 1861: The Vote," 12–28.

41. *Journal of the Secession Convention,* 88; *Southern Intelligencer,* Mar. 13, 1861; *Austin Texas State Gazette,* Mar. 9, 1861.

variety of individual interests.[42] Regression analysis of the 1860 census data and the popular vote on secession reveals several significant factors to this end. By examining the relationship between the percentage of support for secession and economic interests, it appears that the move for secession in Texas extended beyond the protection of slavery to encompass the protection of numerous commercial interests (see Appendix 1, "Regression Analysis: Percentage of Support for Secession").

Cotton production in Texas was a critical element in Texas's economy. Texans shipped their cotton to various places, including three of the largest trading centers: Shreveport, Fayetteville, and New Orleans. They also sold their cotton across the Mexican border and in Great Britain. In addition, some growers even sold directly from the field. Cotton producers had no trouble selling their product; the task before them was to sell at the most appropriate place and time to maximize profits. This goal meant producers had to be aware of the market economy and prices, for which they usually relied on the aid of experts called cotton factors. Despite the availability of markets and the reliance on experts to help maximize profits, the threat of abolition potentially served to undermine their economic interests. To protect their commercial interests, cotton producers embraced secession. Regression analysis reveals that those counties that ginned a higher percentage of cotton were more likely to support secession.[43] This tendency holds especially true for the less wealthy landowners. When cotton production and farm value are simultaneously regressed with secession support, statistical analysis reveals that cotton production maintains a significant relationship with secession support, whereas farm value correlates negatively.

The same is also true when considering a county's slaveholding. Residents from higher slaveholding counties more likely supported secession.[44] When the total white population per county and the total slave population per county are simultaneously regressed with secession support, both factors appear significant. White population has a negative correlation, whereas slave population has a positive correlation with secession support.

When simultaneously considering both ginned cotton and slaveholding

42. Joyce Appleby, *Liberalism and Republicanism in the Historical Imagination;* Louis Hartz, *The Liberal Tradition in America: An Interpretation of American Political Thought since the Revolution;* Christopher M. Duncan, *The Anti-Federalists and Early American Political Thought;* Patrick M. Garry, *Liberalism and American Identity.*

43. *Agricultural Census;* Harold D. Woodman, *King Cotton and His Retainers: Financing and Marketing the Cotton Crop of the South, 1800–1925;* Richard Lowe and Randolph Campbell, *Planters and Plainfolk: Agriculture in Antebellum Texas,* 14–19.

44. *Population in 1860.*

within a county, one might initially expect the same finding. When the amount of ginned cotton and the number of slaves held in each county are regressed with secession support, however, both cotton and slavery cease to have a significant relationship with secession. This fact suggests that in Texas's move for secession, the commercial interests associated with slavery are not as vital as many historians have previously believed. What appears to be important, then, is the institution of slavery itself and the wealth tied up in it, not the commercial gains resulting from the product of slave labor. Slavery, apart from its production capacity, was a measure of wealth.[45] On the eve of secession, slave prices in Texas ranged from twelve hundred to two thousand dollars for field hands and one thousand to fifteen hundred dollars for plowboys. Naturally, the more skilled a slave, the higher the price. Slave owners, though, used this labor for their own fields and hired it out.[46] Furthermore, that cotton as a single factor apart from slavery holds a significant relationship with secession further supports the finding that commercial interests separate from slavery were extremely important to Texans considering secession. Maps 2.2 and 2.3, "Slave Population" and "Ginned Cotton x 400 Pounds," respectively, give a visual representation of this fact. Slaveholding was concentrated in the south-central and northeast regions, extending beyond the confines of high cotton-producing counties, and those counties with a higher percentage of slaves did not necessarily gin the most amount of cotton.[47]

It might be assumed, given the importance of cotton and slavery, that landholding too existed as a significant factor in understanding secession. Historians have shown, however, that landholding in antebellum Texas served to unify slaveholders and nonslaveholders in the state. It provided opportunities for ranching, farming, and slave ownership. Given the importance of landholding to both slave owners and non–slave owners in Texas, it seems there is no link between landholding and secession.[48] Statistical analysis supports

45. Research into Virginia slaveholding finds this assertion true. See John O. Allen, "The Wealth of Antebellum Southside Virginia: Tobacco or Slaves?"

46. Elizabeth Silverthorne, *Plantation Life in Texas,* 36; Lowe and Campbell, *Planters and Plainfolk,* 93–94.

47. *Agricultural Census; Population in 1860.* For the historiographical debate concerning the profitability of slavery, see works by Ulrich B. Phillips, Kenneth Stampp, Alfred Conrad and John Meyer, Eugene Genovese, Robert Fogel and Stanley Engerman, and Roger Ransom.

48. Lowe and Campbell, *Planters and Plainfolk,* 190. For other works dealing with landholding, see Ulrich B. Phillips, "The Origin and Growth of the Southern Blackbelts";

this conclusion. In the move for secession, statistical analysis reveals that farm value as a single factor does not have a significant relationship with secession. Thus, wealth in land alone is not an indicator of an individual's support for secession. When landholding is combined with slavery, though, farm value does hold a significant relationship with secession support. In this instance, however, farm value exhibits a negative correlation with secession support, whereas slavery correlates positively. Thus, in those counties where farm value decreased and slaveholding increased, support for secession was stronger. This result reinforces the finding that slaveholding wealth existed as a critical issue for citizens supporting secession.[49]

Previous historians have emphasized that slaveholders and nonslaveholders were united in a market economy by the belief that westward expansion offered non–slave owners the potential to acquire land and unfree labor. Because slavery was not a closed system, all whites could potentially enter the slaveholding ranks. Historians have used this argument to support the notion that whites were united by race more so than class. Although whites were certainly united by race, the emphasis on slavery as the uniting force in a market economy obscures the fact that non–slave owners were capitalists too. The notion of the non–slave owner as a potential capitalist united with other whites in a slave-driven economy is somewhat of a misrepresentation. Multiple factors apart from slavery influenced Texas's move toward secession, exposing the capitalist nature of non–slave owners.[50]

Regression analysis reveals that agricultural interests other than cotton production also had a significant relationship with support for secession, especially wheat and corn production. As single factors, both wheat production and corn production have a significant relationship with secession support. Wheat production, however, has a negative correlation with secession support; those areas that produced less wheat more likely supported secession than large wheat-growing counties. Map 2.4, "Wheat Production, Bushels," reveals two defined regions, the far-west frontier and the black belt, that grew significantly less wheat than the rest of the state. Wheat maintains a significant relationship in this manner when simultaneously regressed with other individual agricultural interests such as corn, rye, and cotton. In these

Frank Owsley, *Plain Folk of the Old South;* and Gavin Wright, *The Political Economy of the Cotton South: Households, Markets, and Wealth in the Nineteenth Century.*

49. *Agriculture in 1860; Population in 1860.*

50. Laurence Shore, *Southern Capitalists: The Ideological Leadership of an Elite, 1832–1885,* 46–47; James Oakes, *The Ruling Race: A History of American Slaveholders,* 228–32.

cases, corn, rye, and cotton also simultaneously hold a significant relationship with secession support. Regression analysis reveals that those counties that grew less wheat yet more corn, rye, and cotton more likely supported secession. These characteristics are most noticeable in the black-belt region of Texas. Nevertheless, when wheat, corn, rye, and ginned cotton are all simultaneously regressed with secession support, only wheat holds a significant relationship, suggesting that in the complex agricultural system, wheat appears to be the most significant factor associated with secession. Wheat also maintains a significant relationship with secession support when regressed with farm value. In this case, farm value also holds a significant relationship with secession support. Thus, those counties with higher farm values that produced less wheat most likely supported secession. In this instance, according to geographical and statistical analysis, the black-belt, Gulf Coast, and east Texas regions most strongly supported secession. This finding, however, is complicated when simultaneously regressing wheat, farm value, rye, corn, and ginned cotton against secession support. In this case, only wheat holds a significant negative relationship with secession support, whereas farm value correlates negatively and rye, corn, and ginned cotton all correlate positively. Thus, in those counties with a decreasing farm value and increasing production of wheat, rye, corn, and cotton, wheat appears to be a significant factor in understanding secession. In this complicated agricultural environment, wheat, not cotton, emerges as the most critical factor in explaining secession between slave owners and non–slave owners.

Commercial interests beyond slavery and agricultural production also existed in Texas's support for secession. For many Texans, the commercial interests associated with ranching were a significant concern related to secession. Ranching was a vital aspect of western commerce. Texans drove their cattle to Kansas City, Chicago, and New Orleans. Livestock could be transported to these sites without a highly developed transportation system, and this migratory wealth could be moved from potential enemy raids. Indians proved to be the greatest threat, not only killing livestock but also stealing it for their own economic interests. For ranchers, failure to protect the frontier had a direct effect on their commercial interests.[51]

51. Myres, "Ranching Frontier"; Jimmy Skaggs, *Prime Cut: Livestock Raising and Meatpacking in the United States, 1607–1983,* 28–30. Many Texans believed that Texas possessed enough cattle to supply the entire Confederate army if needed, and new markets opened for Texas cattle during the Civil War. See *Austin Texas State Gazette,* July 6, 1861.

In Texas's move for disunion, the amount of cattle owned and the value that one received at market for animals slain have a significant relationship with secession support. In this case, both factors have a positive relationship with secession support. Thus, in those counties where cattle holding and the price received at market for all livestock increased, stronger support for secession existed. This fact especially held true in those areas where the total value of livestock owned was decreasing. In other words, as the value of a person's livestock decreased, he was more likely to vote for secession as a means of supporting his commercial interests, especially when he owned a larger amount of cattle and received a greater sum for animals slain. The relationship among cattle holding, livestock value, and the value of animals slain to secession reveals that the commercial interests associated with ranching were intimately tied to secession.

Adding farm value to the equation reinforces these results. When all four factors are considered, the amount of cattle owned, the value of all livestock, and the value of all slain animals hold a significant relationship with secession, whereas farm value appears to be insignificant. Thus, landholding does not appear to be a critical factor in understanding secession, but the commercial interests associated with livestock remain so.

Regression analysis reveals that the road to disunion contained a variety of interests. Agriculture, livestock, and wealth in slaves all existed as significant concerns in considering secession, and the quagmire of threats that Texas faced represented an assault on the state's multifaceted commercial system. Texas was truly geographically and commercially diverse, and many previously documented factors such as ethnocultural ties, religious affiliation, and racial unity influenced an individual's stance for or against secession.[52] Nevertheless, one factor rose above this diversification to unite Texans in their move for secession: the desire for commercial security. The Civil War conflict, therefore, did not represent a manifestation of the battle between the forces of industrialism and agrarianism. Irresponsible politicians and the political system cannot shoulder the blame. In addition, abolitionist threats, the desire to protect slavery, and the ideology behind these sectional differences account for only part of the sectional conflict. Instead, there appears to be a more encompassing determinant. It was not the potential of one day entering the market economy as defined by race that united Texans, but the market economy itself. That both slave owners and non–slave owners partook in a drive to maximize profits through a variety of interests unified whites to the

52. For other factors influencing secession, see Buenger, *Secession and the Union;* Baker and Baum, "Texas Voter"; and Baum, *Shattering of Texas Unionism.*

same degree, if not a greater extent, than race did, revealing the weakness of the race-class dichotomy. For Texas, secession and the resulting Civil War represented a conflict within capitalism.

This conflict and the move to support secession, however, were not a presupposition to joining the Confederacy. The idea of Texas seceding and remaining an independent republic received support. The days of an independent Texas were still fresh in the minds of many Texans, and there stood a real possibility that Texas would return to its former status. The majority of printed and published political speeches, especially before the United States Senate and House of Representatives, all discussed Texas's stance on the crisis and conveyed Texas's concern over the threat to economic security. These speeches also discussed Texas's existence as a separate republic and the state's history of securing its interests. Furthermore, the issue of Texas existing as a separate republic was a critical affair discussed at the secession convention. In its "Address to the People of Texas," the secession convention relayed to the people that the question had been entertained, based upon the Texas Constitution's guarantee that all political power resided in the people and that government was formed by their authority and for their benefit, thus giving citizens the right to alter, reform, or abolish their government for their purpose and advantage.[53]

Moreover, the proposition of returning to an independent republic found popular support. For example, the *Dallas Weekly Herald* often published letters and editorials supporting the proposal. On the same day that the *Weekly Herald* reported a drafting of the Ordinance on Secession, it also ran an editorial questioning the future destiny of Texas. The editorial extolled the virtues of Texas's economic interests. It highlighted Texas's grain, cotton, hemp, sugar, and tobacco production; stressed the availability of salt, granite, limestone, and silver; and emphasized the importance of stock raising. "With all our natural and acquired advantages, shall we not take our place amongst the nations of the earth? At peace with all possible, and no entangling alliance with any." The paper even laid out a blueprint for the political offices of the state, suggesting that the president of Texas hold office for ten years, with a council of five that would have impeachment powers. It also suggested that the legislature receive pay for only one month's session each year. This would lead to political peace and make Texas one of the most desirable countries. The editorial stressed the idea of returning to a separate republic. If Texans could "see this in true light we might behold a star rising from the present gloom which would reveal ourselves and families reclining in the

53. *Journal of the Secession Convention,* 252–53.

shade of our own vines and fig trees, with our servants (slaves) around us, with none to molest or make afraid." Many Texans believed that the only way to procure peace and economic security was to return to a separate republic without an alliance to any other nation. In this way, Texans could enjoy the prosperity of the state and the protection of their economic interests.[54] Even antisecessionists suggested, before and after secession, this course of action. Sam Houston pondered the possibility of how a fledgling nation could protect the interests of his state. In a letter to his Alabama friend R. M. Calhoun, Houston remarked that Texas would have no part of an alliance with other states if it chose to secede. Texas's interests would lead it "to avoid entangling alliances." Texas would rather unfurl its Lone Star banner and return to an independent republic, and "tread the winepress alone," than align itself with a new nation that offered no guarantee of protection. Thus, it was not so much a love for the Union that consumed Houston, but rather a fear of the weakness of a new nation. Houston reminded Calhoun, however, that this was merely his opinion. Calhoun conceded that Texas was indeed in a unique situation, as an "empire within herself" that held great designs for expansion. These were not characteristics of the other Southern states, and he believed that Texas would "not be content to have the path of her destiny clogged."[55]

After secession, former antisecessionists also questioned Texas's course. They raised the issue of Texas joining with other Southern states or remaining independent. "Will you follow the beck and obey the nod of South Carolina," they asked, "or will you not rather prove true to yourselves, and keep your destinies in your own hands?" These men truly feared that seceding and joining the Confederacy would be detrimental to the future of Texas. Many proffered arguments for a separate independence out of fear that the new Confederacy would not be able to provide adequate frontier protection. They implored citizens, therefore, to save the Union. If that was not possible, then "let Texas then choose whether she will stand alone, or unite her destiny with that of others." Above all, they desired that "property be respected." Even if war knocked on the door, they urged Texans to unite like brothers. Despite their outward disapproval of secession, these politicians honorably

---

54. *Dallas Weekly Herald,* Feb. 6, 1861.

55. A. Williams and Barker, *Writings of Sam Houston,* 8:226–31; Williams, *Sam Houston,* 338. Calhoun letter is in *Journal of the Senate, State of Texas, Eighth Legislature (Extra Session),* 31–32. Houston's correspondence with J. M. Calhoun was also printed in the *La Grange True Issue,* Jan. 24, 1861.

supported their constituents by reassuring them that regardless of what lay in the near future, they would stand by their statesmen.[56]

Politicians in other states, however, feared the prospect of Texas returning to its former status. So great was the concern in Louisiana that state commissioner George Williamson addressed the Texas secession convention in Austin on February 11, 1861. Williamson informed Texas politicians of Louisiana's justifications for secession from the Union on January 26, primarily the threat to liberty and property. The people of his state refused to "endanger their liberties and property by submission to the despotism of a single tyrant." He believed further that Northern politicians denied the constitutional equality of Southern states. The Union had failed, he claimed, but not by any fault of Louisiana. Therefore, Louisiana declared itself "a free and independent State."[57]

It was important for Williamson to convince Texas politicians that Louisiana had seceded for these reasons. Behind the rhetoric, fear existed on the part of other states, especially Louisiana, that Texas would chart its own path after secession. Williamson informed the convention that Louisiana looked to the formation of the Confederacy "to preserve the blessings of African slavery," and desired the hearty cooperation of Texas in the establishment of the Confederacy. He stood confident in Texas's ability to maintain a separate existence, and thus was deeply concerned with Texas's ratification of the Ordinance on Secession. Williamson believed it would be a fatal blow to slavery if Texas did not secede and join Louisiana and other Southern states in the formation of the Southern Confederacy. The desire for such cooperation, though, ran deeper than Louisiana's protection of slavery. Williamson made a point of highlighting the similarities of Texas and Louisiana in terms of geography and use of rivers for commercial transport, the staples of sugar and cotton, and banking relations. Williamson claimed that no two states in the Confederacy "are so identified in interest . . . and closely interwoven with each other." Louisiana depended upon Texas's stock and surplus production of wheat and grain, which proved the primary motive behind his remarks. Texas was a vital element in the sustenance of Louisiana's commercial well-being. In hopes of persuading Texas politicians to cast their lot with the Confederacy, Williamson also played on Texas's fear of abolitionist activity by reminding politicians of their recent troubles. Furthermore, he

56. A. Williams and Barker, *Writings of Sam Houston*, 8:226–31; John Hoyt Williams, *Sam Houston: A Biography of the Father of Texas*, 338; Yearns, *The Confederate Governors*, 196.

57. *Journal of the Secession Convention*, 120–23.

reminded them of their border trouble with the Indians and that even under federal protection, the state suffered the consequences of Indian attacks. In Williamson's view, the only way for Texas to secure the liberty of its citizens and the state's commercial interests was to follow in the steps of Louisiana and unite with other Southern states.[58]

Articles from Louisiana appeared in Texas newspapers, expressing the same thoughts as Williamson. The *San Antonio Ledger*, for example, reprinted this article from the *New Orleans Bulletin*, "Texas is an extraordinary State, and her relations to Mexico, in connection with the possible changes that may lie just in the womb of to-morrow, give absorbing interest to us of Louisiana to the movements which she may think proper to make." The commercial ties between Louisiana and Texas invest "the political movements of Texas with so great an interest in the minds of our citizens." Louisiana's fear was that Texas's prospect of remaining independent "would be likely to effect [*sic*] her commercial relations with this State, and New Orleans in particular, and possibly to our lasting injury." The anonymous article went on to say, "[W]e do not attempt to conceal our fears that Texas will cut loose from the other Southern States and again unfurl her Lone Star for good and all." Cajuns realized that Louisiana must do everything possible to thwart independent action on the part of Texas because Mexico would most likely welcome Texas independence. That sentiment, it was held, was most evident in the northern part of Mexico where citizens would welcome a new flag of dominance over the chaotic feuds of Mexican chiefs.[59]

Louisiana's fears, though, were laid to rest as Texas politicians decided not to remain separate, but to join with other Southern states. On March 5, 1861, the secession convention adopted an ordinance uniting Texas with other Southern states. The economic status of the state existed as the primary concern among politicians in considering such a compact. To secure this interest, the secession convention resolved to have U.S. troops in Texas mustered into state service. More important, Texas sent delegates to these bodies in order to secure relations: the Montgomery convention and provisional congress; the authorities in Arizona and New Mexico, "to procure their co-operation"; and the Choctaw, Chickasaw, Creek, and Cherokee Nations.[60]

The immediate concern after secession, though, was Texas's relationship with the Indians. Politicians felt that any uncertainty with their move to the Confederate States would hinder an alliance with the Indian nations. The lack

58. Ibid.
59. *San Antonio Ledger*, Feb. 2, 1861.
60. *Journal of the Secession Convention*, 44, 252–55.

of an alliance would simply heighten the Indian attacks already occurring. The secession convention even debated and passed recommendations seeking the aid of other states in their relations with the Indians. In its "Address to the People of Texas," the convention remarked that any appearance of doubt of Texas joining the Confederacy would possibly stimulate the plundering efforts of the Indians. Texas's association with other Southern states "would give to it additional strength, and promote early success in its negotiations as to peace with the old government—as to the procurement of money—as to recognition by other nations—and as to commercial relations." By joining the Confederacy, Texas hoped to improve its own lot and secure its own place in world economics.[61]

Even by this late date in the crisis, though, opposition could still be found that revealed the uncertainty of Texas's future. Sam Houston, in response to the activity of the secession convention and the noncooperation of either branch of the legislature, refused to take an oath of allegiance. He knew that his stance would cause his seat in the government to be vacated. Houston published his own "Address to the People" in which he denied the power of the convention to speak for the people of Texas. "I PROTEST IN THE NAME OF THE PEOPLE OF TEXAS AGAINST ALL THE ACTS AND DOINGS OF THIS CONVENTION AND DECLARE THEM NULL AND VOID!" Thus, the most that can be said of Sam Houston during this crisis is that he was an honorable man who stood by his convictions, and as a Texas nationalist, he wholeheartedly supported the welfare of the citizenry. As a leader, though, he failed to see the turning tide and was no match for more skilled and fiery politicians such as Wigfall, Reagan, and Roberts. No one can speculate, however, on Houston's influence had he taken the oath and worked with the Texas government instead of against it.[62]

Political speeches and popular support for secession reveal a unified move in Texas, grounded in a liberal tradition, to defend liberty and property. Though fear and insecurity over Texas's future pervaded, and the state remained somewhat divided over the proper course of action, at the heart of this liberal tradition lay Texas's desire to protect its own commercial interests that extended beyond the institution of slavery. Agriculture, livestock, and wealth in slaves all played a significant role in the concern over the state's

61. Ibid., 52, 67, 81, 258–59.
62. *Southern Intelligencer,* Mar. 20, 1861. Some of the citizenry saw Houston's advocation of a separate and independent Texas as a move to disrupt the new Confederacy and not an act of loyalty to the state. See Governors Papers: Sam Houston, Mar. 1861, TSL.

future. This unified activity to secure economic interests impacted Texas's relationship with the Confederacy. Throughout the Civil War period, state politicians and Texas citizens would move beyond defining a separate political and economic identity to clearly establishing a separate identity. This progression became most evident in the beginning stages of the Civil War as Texans battled with Indian tribes to protect their lives and property and would continue as Texans enlisted for military duty in both the Texas state militia and the Confederate army.[63]

63. On Mar. 14, 1861, politicians adopted an ordinance to provide for the continuance of the existing state government (*Journal of the Secession Convention,* 165–66).

PART II

Establishing a
Separate Identity

CHAPTER 3

The Bleeding Frontier

Indian Conflict, 1861–1862

In early 1861, Atascosa County resident Jose A. Navarro wrote a letter to his son revealing the complex situation between Texas and the Indians. "The Indians are aware of our political differences," he said, and view Texas "as much revolutionized and weakened as Mexico." With that belief, Navarro warned, "they will rush, without doubt to redden their spears in human blood, with that ferocity and savageness which they breathe in their blood-shot eyes." Navarro feared that if Texans did not resist the Indians in armed fashion and pursue them into their territory, a "destructive Indian war" would lead to the ruin of Texas. Most Texans viewed the Indians as a ruthless race bent on destruction and death, and believed only the adoption of offensive action could successfully counter the Indian threat.[1]

Scholarship addressing the relationship between Anglo-Americans and Indians during the Civil War has generally focused on the conflict between Indian nations and the Confederacy. Historians have emphasized divisions between slaveholders and non–slaveholders and the Indians' military contribution to the Confederate cause. The examination of Texas's relationship with the Indians, though, reveals tensions within the Confederacy that are more complex than many historians have previously believed.[2]

Texas's trouble with the Indians existed before the days of the republic. Although Indians played a significant role in the development of Texas by

---

1. *Southern Intelligencer,* Mar. 27, 1861. Throughout the chapter I employ the term *Indian* instead of *Native American.* Though some scholars may oppose this term, my work is written from the perspective of nineteenth-century Texas, and this is the term used in the press, personal correspondence, and official correspondence of that era.

2. Thomas, *Confederate Nation;* Annie Heloise Abel, *The American Indian as Slaveholder and Secessionist;* R. Halliburton Jr., *Red over Black: Black Slavery among the Cherokee Indians;* Wilfred Knight, *Red Fox: Stand Watie and the Confederate Indian Nations during the Civil War Years in Indian Territory;* Nancy Hobson, "Samuel Bell Maxey as Confederate Commander of Indian Territory"; John C. Waugh, *Sam Bell Maxey and the Confederate Indians.*

participating in commercial and political relations with Anglos and Hispanics, they also fought to stave off encroachment upon their lands. When Texas became a republic in 1836, relations between Anglos and Indians appeared to improve. Sam Houston, the first president of Texas, attempted to advance peace prospects by enforcing trade laws, removing white trespassers from Indian lands, upholding Indian hunting rights, and negotiating fair treaties. Favorable relations, however, did not last. Under the presidential leadership of Mirabeau B. Lamar, Texas adopted a policy of forced removal. As a result, brutal attacks upon the Indians ensued, and Texas alienated most of the Indian tribes in the region. The Indians did not sit patiently, but sought revenge upon their perpetrators and sacked many towns as far south as Galveston. Sam Houston attempted to remedy the situation when reelected in 1841. On an official level, Houston perhaps succeeded, but skirmishes continued to exist. When the United States annexed Texas in 1845, it assumed the role of frontier protector. Texas-Indian relations fared no better, though, as the United States became preoccupied with the Mexican War. In the 1850s, pressure mounted as white expansion increased, and relations among the Indians, Texas, and the federal government began to deteriorate. Though slavery seized much of the nation's attention, Anglo and Indian atrocities continued to preoccupy the frontier. Prior to the Civil War, a clear pattern of Texas-Indian relations did not exist.[3]

The relationship between Texans and Indians, though, became more fractious with the onset of the Civil War. When U.S. troops evacuated western forts in May 1861, the Indians became alarmed over the confusion. Well aware of the political differences existing between the North and South, the Indians expressed deep concern for their safety and how the outbreak of the Civil War would affect them. Their concern for safety intensified when evacuating federal troops told them of armed Texans "coming to destroy them." As a result of the crisis, the Indians "evinced a boldness and daring never before shown," and Texas citizens blamed the evacuation of federal troops for affording the Indians "a general license to rob and murder at their pleasure." Texas governor Francis Lubbock believed that "the greatest immediate danger we apprehended was from Indian hostilities." The rise in Indian hostility most likely resulted from Anglo expansion that led them to feel threatened. Thus, guerrilla warfare offered one of the few available options to the Indians. In turn, Texas citizens believed that secession and the

---

3. William Banta, *Twenty-seven Years on the Texas Frontier;* W. W. Newcomb Jr., *The Indian of Texas: From Prehistoric to Modern Times;* J. W. Wilbarger, *Indian Depredations in Texas;* Day, *Indian Papers.*

subsequent removal of federal forces placed their region in jeopardy, and that only an offensive war could secure their well-being.[4]

Historically, war and destruction are integral parts of nation building, and those individuals who understand the need for an offensive posture with their enemies truly comprehend the task of defining and building a nation. An offensive approach involves more than armed resistance; it encompasses pursuit both as a reaction to attacks and as a distinctive approach to war. The acceptance of the necessity of offensive posturing, though, as Jose Navarro's letter reveals, reached beyond top military strategists to the ordinary citizen. Unable to rely on previous U.S. or current Confederate assistance regarding the Indians, Texas citizens realized quickly that the Confederate government could offer little to no support. Texans, feeling abandoned by their central government and believing that the Confederate government neglected western interests, forged their own unique relationship with the Indian tribes. A fight for economic survival and growth defined the relationship between Texans and the Indians. Fired by the passion of protecting their lives and property, the relationship between the two races is best characterized by mutual hatred and destruction. Both groups stole the other's property, murdered each other's families, and sought the extinction of the other. For Texas, from 1861 through 1862, a war more serious and defining than the sectional conflict took place on its borders. The offensive posture undertaken against the Indians to protect economic interests contributed to the establishment of a separate identity from that of other Southern states. This process did not occur evenly throughout the state, nor did the political elite impose a separate identity on the common citizen. Instead, at various times throughout 1861 and 1862, different regions and classes all exhibited this separateness, and by 1863, a distinct Texas identity was established in the midst of the Civil War.[5]

The sectional crisis brought fear and insecurity to everyone involved, including the Indians. As wards of the federal government, and as slaveholders, the five organized tribes and smaller bands of Indians west of Arkansas and

4. *Clarksville Standard,* June 22, 1861; *San Antonio Weekly Ledger and Texan,* Apr. 6, 1861; Rains, *Six Decades in Texas,* 337. For a detailed account of federal evacuation from Indian territory, see Dean Trickett, "The Civil War in Indian Territory, 1861" (both articles).

5. Charles Royster, *The Destructive War: William Tecumseh Sherman, Stonewall Jackson, and the Americans.* Samuel J. Watson, in " 'This Thankless . . . Unholy War': Army Officers and Civil-Military Relations in the Second Seminole War," suggests that a primary reason for the failure of the U.S. government to protect citizens from Indian attacks in earlier years was due to the attitude of army officers.

north of Texas were forced to choose sides in the Civil War crisis. Aware of the political crisis and potential threat to their lives and property, the legislatures and general councils of the Cherokee, Chocktaw, Chickasaw, Creek, and Seminole Nations, along with various Comanche tribes, each gathered to deliberate their stance on the crisis.[6]

Stemming from a desire to protect their "tribal and individual" rights, the Chickasaw Nation declared its loyalty to the Confederacy on May 25, 1861. The Chickasaw Nation feared that the war between the states would "surpass the French Revolution in scenes of blood and that of San Domingo in atrocious horrors." As such, the Chickasaws did not view neutrality as the best option. The U.S. government's removal of troops and its reneging on financial payments to the nation further strained relations. Because of U.S. abandonment, the Chickasaw Nation declared itself independent and free to take the necessary steps to secure its own "safety, happiness, and future welfare." In their declaration of support, the nation called upon its citizens to take up arms for the defense of their home, family, country, and property. Warriors were called upon "to form themselves into volunteer companies."[7]

Their move to ready themselves for war in support of the Southern cause, however, did not involve abandoning their own rights and property. Because of their determination to remain free and independent, the Chickasaw Nation sought to retain possession of lands and forts once occupied by the federal government. Texas officials offered their assistance in this pursuit. The Chickasaws acknowledged Texas's offer of assistance, but declined. They did not wish to succumb to a proposition that meant a potential relinquishment of their rights and property. Thus, Texas's relationship with the Indian nations represented a conflict between two distinct groups each in the process of securing its own rights, securing its economic welfare, and defining its own nation.[8]

As with the Chickasaws, the Choctaw Nation viewed the sectional conflict with "deep regret and great solitude," primarily because the crisis threatened aid and protection once furnished them. The Choctaws expressed deep concern for the material well-being of their nation and hoped for a speedy end to the conflict. A desire to protect the institution of slavery embodied much of this concern. Indian agent Douglas Cooper, who sympathized with the South

6. *San Antonio Daily Ledger and Texan,* Mar. 13, 1861; *Galveston Tri-Weekly News,* July 18, 1861.

7. "Resolutions of the Senate and House of Representatives of the Chickasaw Legislature Assembled," in *War of the Rebellion,* 3:585–87; Arrell M. Gipson, *The Chickasaws.*

8. Ibid.

and feared the Republican Party and the threat of abolition to the Indian nations, worked among the tribes to help secure their interest in slavery.[9]

Unlike the Chickasaws, there existed a short-lived division among the Choctaws in siding with the Confederacy. Peter Pitchlynn, an educated, elite member of the nation who had long served the political interests of the tribe, tried to persuade George Hudson, the first principal chief of the nation, to adopt a position of neutrality. Initially, Hudson agreed with Pitchlynn and prepared to address the tribal council with that recommendation. Texas forces, however, thwarted Choctaw neutrality. A vigilance committee from Texas entered Choctaw territory and threatened the life of Pitchlynn. In addition, white men from Texas addressed the tribal council and lobbied for a Confederate alliance, before Hudson had the opportunity to speak, and they called for the hanging of any who opposed a Southern alliance. As a result of Texas's interference and show of force, Hudson ignored Pitchlynn and recommended that the Choctaws join the Confederacy. The Choctaw Nation thus resolved that in case a solution was not afforded, they would side with the Southern states and rely on the Confederacy for the preservation of their "rights of life, liberty, and property." The Indian nations fully understood the sectional conflict and that the political crisis ultimately affected their general welfare. Thus, they moved to establish themselves in an economically advantageous situation.[10]

Therefore, soon after the Choctaws' general council meeting on June 10, 1861, to discuss relations with the United States and the Confederacy, George Hudson proclaimed the Choctaw Nation "free and *independent*." He then ordered all citizens between the ages of eighteen and forty-five to enroll in either the volunteer or the reserve militia and "to hold themselves in readiness to turn out for the defense of the nation at a minutes [*sic*] warning, for the preservation of order and the protection of life and property."[11]

A desire to secure protection from Northern invasion and, more important, a willingness to obtain arms and provisions for tribal security against other

9. Abel, *American Indian*, 42–45. Douglas Cooper was a native of Mississippi, served under Jefferson Davis during the Mexican War, became Indian agent for the Choctaws in 1853, and added the Chickasaw Nation to his charge in 1856 (see Trickett, "Civil War in Indian Territory").

10. "Resolutions Expressing the Feelings and Sentiments of the General Council of the Choctaw Nation in Reference to the Political Disagreement Existing between the Northern and Southern States of the American Union," in *War of the Rebellion*, 1:682; W. David Baird, *The Choctaw People*, 126–28.

11. "Proclamation by the Principal Chief of the Choctaw Nation," in *War of the Rebellion*, 3:593.

Indian tribes bolstered the Choctaws' willingness to support the Confederacy. Well aware of Northern threats and the strife among Indian nations, the Confederate government sought to remedy the situation by supplying arms to the Indians. Tandy Walker, adjutant-general of the army of the Choctaw Nation, urged President Jefferson Davis to make a further call for warriors to "allay a disappointment and rivalry toward the Choctaws, now apparent among the Chickasaws." Behind the veil of unity among the Indian tribes and between the Indians and the Confederacy stood tension and discord with each participating group seeking its own interest.[12]

The Cherokee Nation also stood divided over the issue of neutrality. One group favoring Southern ties formed around the leadership of Stand Watie. Watie, who had served as a delegate to Washington and as a Cherokee council member, opposed the contingent headed by principal chief John Ross that supported neutrality.[13] The split within the Cherokee Nation dated back to the 1835 treaty with the United States. That treaty conveyed all Cherokee land east of the Mississippi River to the United States, and was made against the wishes of John Ross and many Cherokees. As a result, Ross allegedly had many principal men of the treaty party killed. This allegation fueled intense rivalry in the nation that erupted with the sectional crisis. The Confederate government tried to capitalize on the division by offering Watie arms for protection against Ross's contingent. Furthermore, David L. Hubbard, the commissioner of Indian affairs, tried to persuade Ross to join the Southern cause by writing to him with the promise that Cherokee lands, slaves, and nationality would be secure and perpetual. Ross, however, responded to Hubbard that "if our institutions, locality, and long years of neighborly deportment and intercourse do not suffice to assure you of our friendship, no mere instrument of parchment can do it." Ross did not want to bring war down on the Cherokee Nation and remained adamant about staying neutral in the conflict. He further assured Confederate officials of their capability for self-defense in case of Northern invasion, and he declined any offers to have the Confederate government interfere militarily in the Cherokee Nation. Ross did agree, however, to bring the offer of assistance to the attention of the executive council at the next general meeting. Nevertheless, the

12. Tandy to Davis, Aug. 1, 1861, in *War of the Rebellion*, 3:625–26; *San Antonio Weekly Ledger and Texan,* June 1861.

13. Edward Everett Dale and Gaston Litton, *Cherokee Cavaliers: Forty Years of Cherokee History as told in the Correspondence of the Ridge-Watie-Boudinot Family;* Morris L. Wardell, *A Political History of the Cherokee Nation, 1838–1907,* 122; Knight, *Red Fox;* Thomas F. Anderson, "The Indian Territory, 1861–1865"; Alvin M. Josephy Jr., *The Civil War in the American West,* 326; Abel, *American Indian,* 153.

Confederate government did not respect Ross's stance of neutrality. Brig. Gen. Ben McCulloch of Texas wrote a letter to Ross demanding that he allow those Cherokees who supported the Southern cause to form home guards to protect themselves in case of Northern invasion. McCulloch did acknowledge Ross's wish and right to lead his people, but did not respect his right to determine neutrality. There is no doubt that the Indians desired to remain in their territory for the defense of their lives and property, with the full advantage of being supplied by the Confederacy. McCulloch told Secretary of War Leroy Pope Walker that "the Indians are much opposed to marching out of their country. They are willing to organize for its defense, but want to remain in it . . . and I should much fear the censures that would be heaped on our Government by employing them."[14]

Despite McCulloch's insistence, Ross maintained an entrenched neutrality. He knew that more was at stake than protection from hostile forces. In Ross's view, McCulloch's insistence on organizing Indian troops appeared as an assault on the sanctity of his country and its institutions. Ross reminded McCulloch that their country and institutions, regardless of how small and humble, were equivalently sacred and valuable. Ross feared that an alliance with either the North or the South would lead only to the destruction of the Cherokee Nation and Indian rights. McCulloch, however, did not trust the Cherokees and viewed Ross's adamant declaration of neutrality as "a pretext to await the issue of events" and possibly unite with the North. Nevertheless, he hoped for friendly relations with the Indian nations and tried to assure Ross of the Confederacy's desire to protect Indian territory, as both nations shared the same interests and institutions, and a common destiny. This token of assurance, however, simply masked his primary goal of securing Indians to enlist in the Confederate army.[15]

To a certain extent, the Confederacy succeeded in gaining aid from the organized tribes by enlisting several companies. The *Clarksville Standard* reported that "the war excitement among the Indians, has reached the highest pitch. Companies are being rapidly organized in every section, and all seem

14. *War of the Rebellion,* 13:359–61; R. Halliburton, *Red over Black,* 125; John Ross to David Hubbard, June 17, 1861, in *War of the Rebellion,* 13:498–99; John Ross to Ben McCulloch, June 12, 1861, in ibid., 3:591; McCulloch to Ross, June 12, 1861, in ibid., 591–92. For works on Ben McCulloch, see Victor Rose, *Life and Services of Ben McCulloch;* Thomas W. Cutrer, *Ben McCulloch and the Frontier Military Tradition;* and McCulloch to Walker, June 14, 1861, in *War of the Rebellion,* 3:594–95.

15. John Ross to McCulloch, June 17, 1861, in *War of the Rebellion,* 3:596–97; McCulloch to Walker, June 22, 1861, in ibid., 595–96; Ben McCulloch to John Ross, Sept. 1, 1861, in ibid., 690.

anxious to participate in the coming struggle." Those Indians who joined crossed class lines. A majority of the officers were "half breeds, intelligent, and well informed men, and very ardent in the great common cause," whereas others had the ability to express their sentiments only through their native tongue and hand gestures. Indians who sided with the Confederacy often gathered for war dances with great excitement to express their support. In one instance, in August 1861, the Choctaws and Chickasaws gathered to show their support. An elder addressed the warriors of the tribes. He told the young men to emulate the glorious deeds of those Texans "who will lay down their lives in a just cause, and who as yet have never turned their backs to the enemies." The warriors responded with deafening shouts and war cries. "Let not your war path be through your own green corn fields," the elder continued, "but let your knives drink the blood of your enemies in their own towns and villages, side by side with your white brothers, who are fighting for their rights, their own property, and for the protection of the homes of their wives and children." Again the warriors responded with shouts. Just before the Indians broke forth into a war dance, the elder said, "Warriors! we have the same feeling,—we have the same description of property; and need I tell you to look around and see the women and maidens of your race, who have assembled to see the warriors in their paint? Their hands have armed you for the fray, and their hearts will be with you on the field of death." The elder also invoked images of past warriors fighting battles and reminded them that "their blood flows though the veins of the living." The warriors again yelled aloud. The excitement of the gathering was intense as the Choctaws and Chickasaw expressed their support for the Southern cause. More important, the words of the elder reveal that the Indians viewed themselves as a nation with a strong heritage, and that offensive warfare served as a means to strengthen and continue that heritage. The Indians clearly preferred the offensive, understanding the inevitability of destruction in the course of war and the necessity of protecting one's property by taking the battle to the enemy. With both the Indian nations and Texans comprehending this necessity, the struggle between the two groups proved a defining juncture in the process of Texas shaping itself.[16]

In reaction to the Indians' allegiance, and in an attempt to maintain the fidelity of the organized tribes for its own benefit, the Confederate government sought to negotiate treaties with the Indian tribes. President Jefferson Davis commissioned Albert Pike, a man experienced in dealing with the Indian

16. *Clarksville Standard,* July 3, July 20, 1861; *Columbus Colorado Citizen,* Aug. 31, 1861.

tribes, especially in legal matters, and fluent in several Indian languages, for this purpose. Often dressing in traditional Indian wear, his popularity among the tribes helped the Confederacy secure the desired treaties. Between July and August 1861, the Confederate government negotiated treaties with the Creek, Choctaw, Chickasaw, and Cherokee Nations and Comanche tribes that had a direct impact on Texas-Indian relations. These treaties attempted to set boundaries on political and legal rights, and foreign and tribal relations. Analysis of these treaties sheds light on the conflict among Texas, the Indians, and the Confederate government.[17]

Under the guise of "perpetual peace and friendship," the Confederate government established itself as "the protectorate of the several nations and tribes." The Confederacy promised to protect the Indians from domestic strife, hostile invasion from Union forces, and aggression by other Indians. The tension within the Indian tribes kept the Confederacy alert to securing favorable relations. The Confederate government also believed that to ensure such favor and loyalty, it must squelch divisions among the tribes. Most of all, the Confederate government had to guarantee that no harm would come to them from the North. Without the assurance of full protection of their lives and property, the Confederate government stood little chance of persuading the organized tribes to support fully the Southern cause.[18]

The Confederate government endeavored to establish its political authority and legitimacy with the Indian tribes by declaring all laws of the United States that had bound the Indian nations and were contradictory to any terms of the treaties null and void. The government freed the Indian nations from any obligation to the Union, voiding all agreements between the Indians and the Union, unless the Confederate government decided to uphold any agreements previously made, thus attempting to establish themselves as the sole proprietor over the organized tribes.[19]

This protectorship, however, leveled a combination of heavy restrictions and absolute freedom upon the political welfare of the Indian nations. The treaties prohibited any state or territory from passing laws for the Indian nations. Furthermore, territories and individual states could not incorporate

17. *War of the Rebellion,* ser. 4, 1:785; Josephy, *Civil War in the American West,* 323–24; Trickett, "Civil War in Indian Territory" (1939): 324–27; Walter Lee Brown, *A Life of Albert Pike,* 361–81.

18. *War of the Rebellion,* ser. 4, vol. 1: Creek Treaty, 426–43; Choctaw and Chickasaw Treaty, 445–66; Seminole Treaty, 513–27; Comanche Treaties, 542–54; and Cherokee Treaty, 669–87. Hereafter referred to as Creek Treaty, Choctaw and Chickasaw Treaty, Seminole Treaty, Comanche Treaties, and Cherokee Treaty.

19. Choctaw and Chickasaw Treaty, Article 8.

the Indian nations. The Confederate government stipulated in the treaties that political ties existed solely between the organized tribes and the Confederate government. Although this served to simplify political authority, it did restrict the freedom and right of the Indian nations to join with other "political bodies." Second, it kept Texas from taking over any lands by incorporating the Indian nations to further its own expansionist desires. Thus, the Indian nations were restricted from full political negotiations with individual states and foreign powers, unless approved by the Confederate government.[20]

Confederate-Indian treaties contained specific articles regarding the political and legal rights of the Indians. The Confederate government gave general amnesty to all Indians who had violated U.S. or Confederate laws prior to the signing of the treaties. Thus, those Indians charged with an offense received full pardons from the president, and the ones who were imprisoned or held on bail received full discharge. The Confederate government, though, had no power to force individual states to abide by this agreement, and the most Richmond could promise each Indian tribe was its intention and effort to request the state of Texas to grant the same amnesty and pardons from the governor. Thus, from the onset, a division appeared among formal Confederate-Indian-Texas relations.[21]

Confederate treaties with the Comanche Indians dealt thoroughly with Texas-Indian relations, and further exposed the feeble relationship. The Comanche treaties declared that "it is distinctly understood by the said several tribes and bands, that the State of Texas is one of the Confederate States, and joins this Convention, and signs it when the Commissioner signs it, and is bound by it; and that all hostilities and enmities between it and them are now ended and are to be forgotten and forgiven on both sides." Given the presence of Texas forces in Comanche territory, and the tradition of hostility between the two groups, the Confederate government believed it necessary to specifically mention Texas in its treaty with the Comanches. Through such treaty articles, Richmond sought to reassure the Comanches that the entire Confederacy including Texas would support and protect them. This aspect of the treaty greatly pleased Pike, for he knew that any cessation of hostility between Texas and the Indians benefited the South.[22]

20. Creek Treaty; Choctaw and Chickasaw Treaty, Article 10; for Texas expansion, see Frazier, *Blood and Treasure;* and William C. Binkley, *The Expansionist Movement in Texas, 1836–1850.*

21. Choctaw and Chickasaw Treaty, Article 64. The same held true for the state of Arkansas.

22. Comanche Treaties, Articles 10–11; Josephy, *Civil War in the American West,* 328.

The Confederate government also promised the Comanche tribes that all Texas troops in the leased district would withdraw across the Red River and cease to occupy forts or garrisons, except when in Confederate service or on the offense against hostile Indians. Although the Confederate government could force Texas troops out of the territory, it could do little actually to ease the existing hostility. Keenly aware of this fact, Pike strove to bring peace between the Indian tribes and Texans. He believed that peace between the two races could be achieved if Texans retreated from their offensive posture. Pike implored the citizens of Texas not to cross the Red River into Choctaw and Chickasaw territories. He advised Texans that they had no reason or right to be in Comanche territory and that all parties would benefit from their withdrawal and termination of hostilities. In his view, the Indians wanted peace, and the burden for it fell upon Texas citizens. It became their responsibility to keep mounted men and volunteers from interfering in negotiations, regardless of what they believed best.[23]

The Confederate government also sought to control the internal politics of the Indian tribes. For example, the government did not fully trust the Indian nations to deal with law breakers. Confederate authorities required the Indian tribes to turn over anyone who had violated Confederate law. Likewise, the Confederacy agreed to turn over individuals who had violated Indian law. To ensure this outcome, the Confederacy established judicial districts within the Indian nations. This move, however, had an additional twist: any Indian committing a felony against another Indian, their person or property, was required to have a trial in the district court of the Confederate government. Although it may have been an attempt to mute internal strife, it represented a fundamental assault on the right of the Indian nations to settle their differences internally.[24]

The Confederacy also prohibited Choctaw and Chickasaw laws from affecting other tribes, especially the Comanche tribes that leased land from the Choctaws and Chickasaws. The Confederate government reassured the Comanches that the Choctaw and Chickasaw laws held no control over them, especially in terms of interfering with their property rights.[25]

The Confederacy attempted to counter the appearance of subjugating Indian political rights and freedom by promising the organized tribes a

23. Comanche Treaties, Articles 24, 27; *San Antonio Weekly Herald,* Sept. 21, 1861. See also the *McKinney Messenger* and the *Austin Texas State Gazette.*

24. Choctaw and Chickasaw Treaty, Articles 37, 38, 51. For internal strife during the Civil War, see W. W. Newcomb, *Indians of Texas,* 358–59.

25. Comanche Treaties.

political voice in the Confederate government. In order for the Indian nations to "claim their rights and secure their interests without intervention of agents or counsel," the treaties entitled them to a delegate in the Confederate House of Representatives. Each delegate would serve for two years and enjoy the full rights and privileges of delegates from any other territory. The Indian nations had the right to hold an immediate election for their delegate, whereas the Confederate government maintained the right to determine subsequent elections. Furthermore, the Indian treaties also held out the promise of full admittance into the Confederacy. It came, though, with provisions, including the survey of Indian lands and the establishment of lands for education.[26]

The political ties established in the Indian treaties required that the Indian nations be subject to the laws of the Confederate government until they could prove they were "capable of self-government." How or when this was to be proved remained unclear. Thus, the treaty established the Indians as perpetual wards of the Confederacy, for Confederate benefit. It is ironic that the Indian nations moved first through their legitimate and recognized political bodies to establish ties with the Confederacy while at the same time being deemed incapable of self-government. This aspect of the treaty reflected an outright slight of the Indians' political lives and traditions.[27]

When it came to property matters, the Confederate government established specific decrees regarding land, slaves, and livestock. The government granted to all tribes the right to "possess, occupy, and use the reserve allotted to it." The treaties also removed all U.S. restrictions on the sale and disposal of personal property by the Choctaws and Chickasaws. The Confederate government granted the Creek Nation the right to approve land sales by the Seminoles regarding land that the Creek Nation had previously granted to them.[28]

These general statements of usage, however, did not mean total freedom over personal and tribal property. The Indians' right to control their property ended with such generalities and were nullified by specific articles in the

26. Creek Treaty; Choctaw and Chickasaw Treaty, Article 28. The treaties made with the Choctaws and Chickasaws allowed only one delegate, each to be alternatively elected from the Chickasaw and Choctaw Nations, the first being Choctaw.

27. Choctaw and Chickasaw Treaty, Article 12. In 1826, the Choctaws abandoned their native system in favor of a written code of laws. They adopted a constitution and established an executive system of three district chiefs and a national council of representatives. The legislative body met annually to adopt written statutes. See Baird, *The Choctaw People,* 29.

28. Comanche Treaties, Articles 4, 5; Choctaw and Chickasaw Treaty, Articles 8, 25; Creek Treaty.

treaties. The Confederate government restricted unauthorized settling on Indian lands. Violators were subject to Indian law that was not "cruel, unusual or excessive." Furthermore, the treaties forbade the Creeks, Choctaws, and Chickasaws from selling land to any state or foreign power. In such an event, title and control of the land came under the power of the Confederate government. In this manner, the Confederacy could control Unionist and abolitionist movements into the territory and keep the population in the Indian reserves under managed control.[29]

The Confederate government further controlled property by stipulating that a tract of two sections of land in each nation be ceded to the Confederacy under the selection and discretion of the president of the Confederate States of America. The government maintained the right to additional land for building forts, military posts, and necessary roads, even if it meant the destruction of personal property. In such a case, however, Richmond agreed on paper to reimburse such losses. The Confederacy further maintained unrestricted authority to the use of land for railways and telegraph lines. In the event that personal property was destroyed or lost, the treaties required the incorporated company to meet with the Indian council to determine payment. If no agreement could be made, the matter was to be settled by the president of the Confederate States of America. In terms of land control in the agreement between the organized tribes and the Confederate government, Richmond showed little regard for land rights and usage and sought to exert an iron grip over tribal property.[30]

This pattern also surfaced regarding livestock. The organized Indian tribes had a flourishing agricultural economy. They shipped excess foods to U.S. military garrisons and exported cotton to New Orleans. They, especially the Choctaws, also had limited, yet significant, industrial activity, operating grist- and sawmills as well as saltworks and cotton gins. The investment in cattle ranching, though, stood as one of the most vital elements of the Indians' economy. When it came to this aspect of negotiations, the Confederacy desired to protect and support the Indian economy by subsidizing it to control its internal aspects. Richmond prohibited Confederate citizens from pasturing their stock on Indian lands. Citizens, however, could travel through the land with their stock on the way to market, and rest for an appropriate amount of time. This provision revealed a loophole that gave Texas ranchers the freedom to pasture stock on Indian lands, for "an appropriate amount of time" remained completely subjective. Nevertheless, the loophole worked

29. Creek Treaty; Choctaw and Chickasaw Treaty, Articles 9, 32.
30. Creek Treaty; Choctaw and Chickasaw Treaty, Articles 16–18.

both ways because the treaties granted the Indian nations the same privilege while traveling through Confederate territory.[31]

In terms of livestock, the Confederacy sought to mute internal strife and subsidize this element of the Indians' economy rather than restrain it. To control internal hostilities, the Confederate government called for the protection of all horses, cattle, and miscellaneous stock from other tribes. The treaty forbade the Indian nations to "kill, take away or injure any such property of another tribe or band or of any member of any other tribe or band." Richmond declared the stealing of livestock or other articles of property "disgraceful," and demanded that tribal chiefs "discountenance it by every means in their power." In case internal depredations did occur, the Confederate government agreed to give Indians, primarily the Comanche Nation, full indemnity, based upon sufficient proof, for "any horses or any other property that may be killed or stolen from them by any citizen of the Confederate States or by any other Indians."[32]

Subsidizing the economy, the Confederate government bestowed special favoritism on the Comanches. Richmond agreed to "furnish each tribe or band with twenty cows and calves for every fifty persons . . . one bull for every forty cows and calves; and also to furnish to all of said tribes and bands together two hundred and fifty stock hogs." Indian agents determined who received these animals, based upon their ability to care for them. Generally, stock went to responsible Indian farmers who would protect the animals from being "foolishly killed or let to perish by neglect." From an Anglo perspective, the Comanche Nation appeared the least civilized and organized of all the tribes. Thus, Richmond deemed it necessary to take extra measures of favoritism to secure the nation's loyalty. By protecting and subsidizing the economy, the Confederacy attempted to place the Indian nations in a position of unremitting reliance. By accomplishing this feat, the government moved closer to its goal of utilizing the nations as a major resource for food, agricultural products, and materials.[33]

The Confederate government also had a vested interest in protecting the institution of slavery among the Indian tribes. Indians had entered the slave-holding ranks in the late eighteenth century, and the *peculiar institution* continued to thrive amid all the dislocations and disturbances that they had

31. Baird, *The Choctaw People,* 39–42; Creek Treaty; Choctaw and Chickasaw Treaty, Article 33.

32. Comanche Treaties, Articles 8, 10, 12, 13, 21. The Indians also faced restrictions on the ability to "settle, farm or raise stock within the limits of any post or fort of either agency" (Choctaw and Chickasaw Treaty, Article 19).

33. Comanche Treaties, Articles 14, 16.

faced. By the time of the Civil War, slavery existed as a solid institution among the Indian tribes. As with the Southern states, the Indian nations too faced a threat from abolitionists. The Confederate government in its treaties with the organized tribes, therefore, sought to uphold and safeguard slavery. The treaties legalized slavery and declared the existing slave laws binding. They declared "that the institution of slavery in the said nations is legal and has existed from time immemorial; that slaves are taken and deemed to be personal property." Not only did the Confederacy seek to legitimate slavery, but it also wanted to extend legal guarantees to the Indian nations through full rights and privileges of the fugitive-slave act. Richmond called for fair and full return of all slaves on the part of the Confederacy and the Indian nations. Furthermore, the Indian nations had the right to pass on slaves, like any other personal property, to family members in case of death. By protecting the *peculiar institution* in Indian territory, the Confederacy worked to guarantee expansion of its economic institutions.[34]

Richmond's attempt to moderate peace through the treaties, however, mattered little to Texans. They placed no faith in Confederate negotiations with the Indians and believed that hostilities would continue to exist despite treaty negotiations. "You cannot get a fair and favorable contract with a white man while he thinks he holds you in his power," the *Austin Texas State Gazette* reported, "and to suppose that these savages will make and respect treaties favorable to us, while they believe themselves our masters, is absurd."[35]

In this conflict, the Indians were not passive victims, but active participants who sought their own economic security. For the Indians, making war upon Texans did not violate the treaties they had signed with Pike. The Indians viewed whites in the same manner as themselves: one race divided into separate tribes. The Indians looked upon Texans as another "white tribe" in the Confederacy. Therefore, agreements signed with easterners did not necessarily bind the Indians to the same relationship with western whites. As a result, they took advantage of the tumultuous situation and became

34. For the history of slavery in the Creek Nation, see Janet Halliburton, "Black Slavery in the Creek Nation"; Creek Treaty; Choctaw and Chickasaw Treaty, Articles 45, 47. There is no mention of slavery in the Comanche Treaties. Not only did the South take legal measures to safeguard slavery among the Indian nations, but extrapolitical organizations also played a role to this end. The Knights of the Golden Circle were active in the Indian nations, seeking to safeguard slavery there. See Abel, *American Indian,* 22, 68, 86, 166; R. Halliburton, *Red over Black,* 119–20, 125; and Wardell, *History of the Cherokee Nation,* 122.

35. *Austin Texas State Gazette,* Aug. 31, 1861.

"more hostile and bolder than for many years." Texans placed the burden for this consequence on faulty U.S. government relations that the Confederacy continued to uphold. For years, the government had "neither sought to conciliate them [the Indians] by kindness nor chastise them into wholesome fear." Texans believed that the bounty approach of the federal government fostered a belief in the Indians that the white man feared their prowess. This led the Indians to view themselves as "masters of the whole interior region." In turn, the Indians struck out against Texans, marauding throughout the state to secure their own material well-being. The *San Antonio Tri-Weekly Alamo Express* reported that "large parties of bold, bloodthirsty Indians scour the country, committing murder and rapine, being embolden by the withdrawal of the Federal troops." The Indians' worldview combined with a deep-seated belief in self-preservation, therefore, helps explain their sentiment toward Texas. Furthermore, it sheds light on Richmond's ignorance of the hostilities that increased due to the sectional conflict.[36]

During this period, Indian attacks knew no age or gender barrier, and Texas suffered atrocities from the organized Indian nations and "hostile" tribes. The Indians were not passive victims but aggressive perpetrators, and Texans held them in suspect. For example, the *Marshall Texas Republican* reported the story of an attack on two children that occurred in Uvalde County in October 1861. Joseph B. Long, only six years old, was out herding the family's cattle, a half mile from the house, with his brother Andrew. Out of nowhere, five Indians on horseback attacked the two children. They demanded, in plain English, that Joseph give them his clothes, and the little boy complied. Standing there stark naked, the Indians shot an arrow into his side. When Joseph started to run, the Indians launched another arrow into his back. The little boy, wise for his age, fell and feigned death. Thinking the boy dead, the Indians departed and started after his brother Andrew. While chasing him, the Indians came upon Julia Ann, a little girl of eleven years, driving the family horses. The Indians immediately attacked her, pulling her off her horse by her hair and beating her. Her father's quick reaction, though, saved her life. Upon seeing his daughter in the grasp of the Indians, he gave chase, and the Indians let Julia Ann free. The Indians, though, departed with all the family's horses, and Joseph died the next day.[37]

36. *San Antonio Tri-Weekly Alamo Express,* Mar. 13, 1861; Lucy A. Erath, *The Memoirs of Major George B. Erath, 1813–1891,* 22, 98; Trickett, "Civil War in Indian Territory" (1939): 316.

37. Texans referred to the organized Indian nations as the civilized tribes and referred to all other tribes as hostile Indians (*Marshall Texas Republican,* Nov. 23, 1861; *San Antonio Weekly Herald,* Oct. 19, 1861).

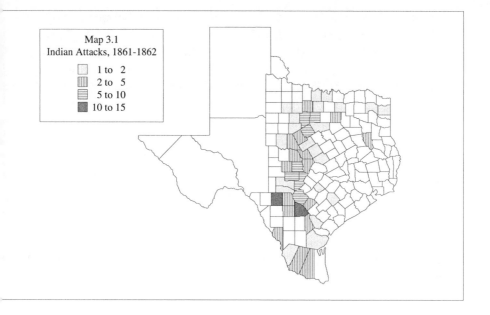

Map 3.1
Indian Attacks, 1861-1862

☐ 1 to 2
▥ 2 to 5
▤ 5 to 10
■ 10 to 15

Throughout 1861 and 1862, such incidents occurred across the state. More than forty Texas counties suffered from Indian attacks. Map 3.1, "Indian Attacks, 1861–1862," reveals that these incursions transcended regional boundaries. "Civilized" Indians crossed the Red River and assaulted northern counties, raids existed all along the western frontier, and hostile Indians crossed from Mexico to invade many south Texas counties. The highest concentration of Indian raids existed along the western frontier, especially in Llano, Blanco, Gillespie, Uvalde, and Atascosa Counties, within close proximity of the capital. The location of these encounters kept Texas politicians aware of the constant danger that Texas citizens faced. Indian raids, however, also extended deep into Texas, beyond the border-frontier regions, and into slaveholding territory. Counties such as Cass, Titus, Cherokee, and Lavaca were among those slaveholding areas that suffered the loss of lives and property. Thus, Indian raids were not a concern solely for frontiersmen, but a serious economic threat that slaveholders and a majority of Texans faced (see the Note on Sources).

Texas's problems with the Indians took on a dual nature. Not only were Indians driven by their desire for the spoils of war to secure their economic well-being, but they were also fueled by the promptings of Northern abolitionists. Abolitionists worked fervently among the Indian tribes to rally support around the Union cause. Several influential Creeks, in fact, changed their loyalty from the Confederacy to the Union. Citizens in Wood County complained in November 1861 that abolitionists were especially strong among the Choctaw Indians. They established friendly relations with many of the Indians and "were doing everything in their power to train the mind of the Choctaw to hate slavery and everything, and every person connected with it, or upholding it." Though frontiersmen had more of a vested interest in livestock and agriculture, their citizenship as Texans joined them, in the minds of Indians, with those linked to slavery. As such, they suffered the consequences of Indian attacks influenced by Northern abolitionists. Furthermore, the effect of abolitionists no doubt inspired the Indians to raid into slaveholding territory where oftentimes slaves suffered death. The Indian tribes did not necessarily heed the abolitionist platform, but rather understood the intensity of the American crisis and took advantage of opportunities to gain financially. Their acceptance of Northern abolitionists remained mixed, and oftentimes they attacked and plundered abolitionist missionaries entering their territories.[38]

Many Texans feared that the Creek, Choctaw, and other Indian nations intended to take over Texas, and the *Galveston Weekly News* reported that this was "no idle boast." Newspapers across Texas gave detailed accounts of the Indian attacks and kept those individuals who did not suffer such hazards keenly aware of the dangers that fellow citizens faced. In their raids upon Texans' property, the Indians primarily sought to steal horses. In virtually every raid made into Texas counties, the Indians succeeded in their quest. Oftentimes, the tribes banded together to maximize their results. To make their raids further successful, they occasionally dressed in Union clothing. They were ingenious in their disguise, and dressing as white men allowed them to move closer without detection. This mode of dress further suggests that Union forces often supported Indian raids into Texas.[39]

Such unified efforts allowed the Indians to capture a significant number of horses. In some cases, they rounded up several hundred horses at a time, virtually depleting counties of their entire horse population. In one instance, hostile Indians stole five hundred horses from Starr County residents, more than 90 percent of the county's entire horse population. Palo Pinto, San Saba,

38. Wardell, *History of the Cherokee Nation,* 120–21; *Marshall Texas Republican,* Nov. 2, 1861; *San Antonio Weekly Ledger and Texan,* June 1, 1861; Abel, *American Indian,* 132; R. Halliburton, *Red over Black,* 93–104.

39. *Galveston Weekly News,* Mar. 26, 1861; *Galveston Weekly Civilian and Gazette,* Jan. 15, 1861; *Marshall Texas Republican,* May 21, 1862.

and Burnet Counties also suffered a high loss of livestock. Map 3.2, "Horses Stolen, 1861–1862," reveals that the majority of horse raids occurred along the western frontier and southern border region. At least twenty-three counties suffered the loss of livestock, which greatly affected the economic well-being of Texas citizens. A family's daily livelihood and commercial success depended in part upon horses. They not only provided the primary means of transportation, but also were necessary for managing cattle. The Indians stole horses both for personal use and for sale at market. Western markets, Mexico, and Northern forces all benefited from the plunder. Stealing horses was a distinct part of their offensive strategy, and also a means to orient further the Indians to the market economy. In their attempt to survive, they partially accommodated themselves to the world against which they struggled.[40]

More devastating than the loss of livestock, however, was the loss of life. No measure can be placed on the cost of lives and the significance of such loss at a time when many counties sent men to war. The calamity of Indian aggressions only compounded the difficulties in each county. At least thirty counties lost men, women, and children due to Indian attacks. Map 3.3, "Lives Lost, 1861–1862," reveals that the loss of life due to Indian attacks was widespread throughout the state. Both frontier and slaveholding counties had citizens killed and injured. Assaults on Texas citizens were often of the most brutal nature. In one instance, Indians attacked and killed a man in Weatherford. "As soon as he fell," reports stated, "he was surrounded by Indians, who commenced torturing him with arrows. . . . When his body was found, his tongue and eyes had been cut out, most probably while still alive. . . . Behind every pine tree in the vicinity was blood." The brutality of the conflict cannot be overemphasized. The Indian tribes undertook an offensive strategy to murder Texas citizens and steal their property. They devastated families and counties for their own personal gain. The brutality of attacks and the loss of life stirred mingled feelings for Texans. Blanco County residents were torn at the loss of a child killed by Indians. The citizens felt "deep pity for the lad, boiling indignation against his brutal murderers, and deep-rooted disgust at the majority of our rulers who have never bestowed a second thought upon frontier protection."[41]

40. *Agriculture in 1860;* T. R. Havins, *Something about Brown: A History of Brown County, Texas,* 22–23; Myres, "Ranching Frontier," 24; Sara Kay Curtis, "A History of Gillespie County, Texas, 1846–1900," 63.
41. *Austin Texas State Gazette,* Oct. 26, 1861; *Marshall Texas Republican,* Feb. 22, 1862.

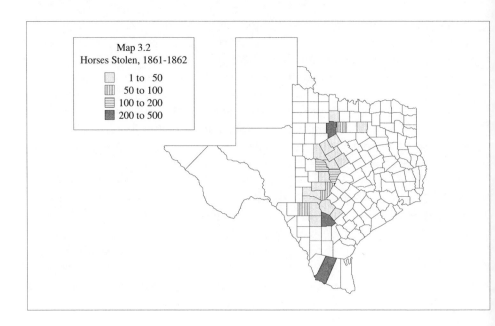

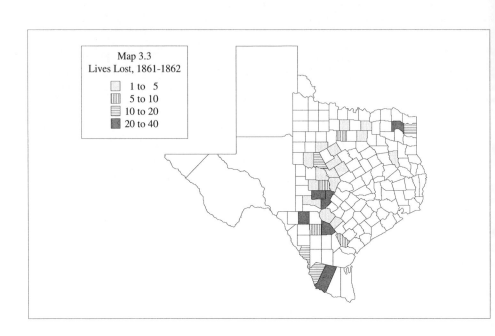

Citizen outrage toward the government in such situations is understandable. Nevertheless, the Texas state government did make an effort to deal with the Indian problem. The Confederate government's delay in ratifying the treaties undermined relations between Texas and the Indians, forcing state politicians to act regarding the safety of Texas citizens. By the end of 1861, the Indian problem emerged foremost in the minds of Texas politicians, and the legislature resolved to have a committee from both houses to "act jointly on measures of frontier defense."[42]

During the political debate that followed over the frontier and Indian problem, Governor Francis Lubbock addressed a joint session of the legislature on November 15, 1861. Texas's relationship with the Indian tribes and the daily occurrence of Indian atrocities concerned him most. He even went so far as to seek advice on the Indian situation from Sam Houston. Houston counseled Lubbock on the Indian problem and told him that he should not allow Texas to be "knocked into a cocked hat," but should look at defending the interests of the state from a multiplicity of threats, including the "savage Indian." Taking Houston's advice, Lubbock told Texas politicians that "our Indian troubles should occupy your attention," for it is "no unfrequent occurrence to hear of murders being committed and property stolen by our Indian enemies." Lubbock also criticized the Confederate government and further remarked that a civilized government could not be expected to make treaties with a "savage foe" that believes it is superior. Lubbock and most Texans fully understood the offensive posture of the Indian tribes and the failure of the Confederate government to handle adequately the situation. The governor did not oppose the Confederate government's attempts to protect, civilize, and support the Indians. However, in the process, the Confederate government had made no attempt to force the Indians to stay on the reserves where they were to be clothed, fed, and protected as wards of the government. Lubbock believed that as long as the Indians were permitted to leave their reserves to hunt and war with other tribes, Texas would hear continually of depredations and come in conflict with them. Because the organized tribes, under the protection of the Confederate government, continued to receive subsidies while simultaneously robbing and murdering Texas citizens, Lubbock placed no faith in the Confederacy's Indian policy. The governor railed against the presence of Indians in Texas territory and told the state legislature to declare that the Indians be deemed and treated as enemies whenever and wherever found on Texas soil. Lubbock believed that too many Texas citizens had been affected in disastrous ways as a result

42. *Senate Journal of the Ninth Legislature Regular Session of the State of Texas,* 43.

of Indian raids and that "it will require years for the people to forget their numerous atrocities."[43]

Due to Richmond's ignorance and neglect of Texas's situation, Lubbock beseeched the state legislature to adopt a meaningful and effective strategy for the protection of Texas. He had in mind the adoption of an offensive strategy and opposed the continued approach of treaty making. "It is my deliberate opinion," he told the legislature, "that we will never have treaties with the Indians on our border, on which we can rely, until they are made to feel the blighting effects of war, visited upon them at their own homes, and around their own firesides." For Lubbock, as for most Texans, adopting an offensive strategy seemed the only means to secure lives and property within Texas's borders.[44]

The hostile relationship with the Indians left most Texas politicians questioning the possibility of peace. The Confederate government's laggard approach in securing a peaceful relationship with the Indian nations contributed to this fear. Treaties signed in mid-1861 did not receive ratification until early 1862, creating a period of flux between Texas and the Indians in which the treaties were not binding. The delay in treaty ratification left the Indian tribes to continue their traditional mode of warfare, harassing Texas citizens. Governor Lubbock knew that Texas had to rely on its own resources to remedy the situation. He understood that the paramount crisis with the Indians required the full attention of the state, both politically and militarily. He believed that Texas needed to mount a full-scale war against the Indian enemy and reminded politicians that Texas would have to rely entirely on the state militia. He believed that citizens would respond promptly to defend Texas soil. Therefore, it stood imperative to revise the militia law.[45]

The Texas legislature heeded Lubbock's words only to a certain extent. On November 19, George B. Erath, chairman of the Committee on Indian Affairs, presented a committee report. The committee found that the Confederate troops on the frontier had done less than an adequate job. The committee criticized the troops for their lack of a full offensive against the Indians, but did, however, acknowledge that the Indians had hampered their duties. Nevertheless, this did not provide a satisfactory excuse for the lack of protection. Due to the Confederate troops' failure, the committee

43. *San Antonio Tri-Weekly Telegraph,* Nov. 5, 1862; *Journal of the House of Representatives of the Ninth Legislature of the State of Texas,* 49–51; *Senate Journal of the Ninth Legislature,* 51–52.

44. *Journal of the House of Representatives of the Ninth Legislature of the State of Texas,* 49–51; *Senate Journal of the Ninth Legislature,* 51–52.

45. Ibid.

suggested that the system of frontier protection be bolstered by men under state authority who would be placed in smaller groups "on the outskirts of the settlements at points so near each other that the distance between any two stations could be traversed every day."[46]

The Texas Senate Committee on Indian Affairs comprised eight individuals from various districts representing fifty counties from across the state. Geographical analysis of the Senate committee reveals that politicians represented counties from every economic region of the state. Both frontier and slaveholding counties had representatives on the Committee on Indian Affairs. The criticism of the Confederate government and the political effort to protect Texas citizens came not only from frontier politicians but also from those politicians representing slaveholding interests, revealing a unified effort to protect the interests of the state and the citizenry.[47]

This unified effort was also apparent in the political activity of state legislators. On November 26, 1861, George B. Erath proposed a bill "making an appropriation for the payment of services of the commissioners sent by the Convention to the various tribes of friendly Indians." The bill was read twice and then referred to the Committee on Claims and Accounts. Two days later, Robert H. Guinn, chairman of the committee, announced the bill and recommended its passage; one week later, the Senate adopted it.[48]

During this period, Texas representatives also debated the important issue of frontier protection. On December 10, 1861, the Texas Senate announced in chamber that the House of Representatives had passed a bill providing for the protection of the frontier, and began debate on the issue the next day. Debate over frontier protection involved several intermingled issues, including questions on the authority over troops, the financing of frontier protection, and the location of troops. In dealing with the mustering of troops, Edwin B. Scarborough from Cameron County proposed to strike a section of the House bill specifically referring to mustering troops from Nueces, Webb,

46. *Senate Journal of the Ninth Legislature,* 88–89. Erath, a native of South Carolina who worked as a farmer and surveyor, represented District 28, which comprised Fall, Coryell, Bosque, McLennan, Comanche, Brown, Hamilton, Ellis, Eastland, Callahan, Coleman, Taylor, Hill, and Runnels Counties, located on the central-Texas frontier.

47. The Committee on Indian Affairs included George B. Erath, Nathan George Shelley, Erastus Reed, Henry C. Cook, Robert H. Guinn, Pryor Lea, Anderson F. Crawford, and John T. Harcourt.

48. *Senate Journal of the Ninth Legislature,* 79, 130, 155. Senate Bill 26 was passed by the House of Representatives in early 1862 (see *Journal of the House of Representatives,* 123–24). Robert H. Guinn, a lawyer from Tennessee, served as president pro tempore of the Texas Senate and represented District 10, which comprised Cherokee County in east Texas, approximately forty miles from present-day Nacogdoches.

Cameron, Starr, Zapata, Goliad, San Patricio, and Goliad Counties. Instead, he proposed that the governor muster companies from any part of the state as he so directed. Scarborough's resolution passed, placing significant power for the control of state troops in the hands of the governor.[49]

The eighth section of the frontier bill dealt with financial responsibility of these proposed troops. The critical aspect of debate revolved around whether the state or the Confederate government had financial responsibility for the troops. Texas politicians hoped to raise troops for frontier protection while placing the burden of financial support on the Confederate government. In addition, they desired that these troops remain on Texas soil, free from Confederate control. Texas politicians did not view this as a contradiction. They believed that the Confederate government had the responsibility for protecting the frontier and could accomplish this goal by financing state troops mustered specifically for this task. The Senate debated these critical issues much of the day, but adjourned without a decision.[50]

The next day, December 12, the Senate entertained again the question of frontier protection. Attempting to bring compromise to the issues of financial responsibility for and state control of the troops, Robert H. Guinn, who served on the Committee on Indian Affairs, offered an amendment "that said regiment shall not become a charge against the State until the Confederate government musters out of service the regiment now stationed upon the frontier or refuses to accept this regiment in lieu thereof." By a vote of eighteen to ten, however, the Senate tabled Guinn's proposal. The majority of Senate members therefore believed that providing for the protection of the frontier took precedence over financial concerns at that moment. The Senate did agree, though, that state troops should not become a charge against the state "until they are mustered into service or placed under orders."[51]

The Senate then sent the amended version of the bill back to the House of Representatives, and politicians there informed the Senate that they agreed to all the changes in the frontier bill except those pertaining to section eight. Politicians believed that the Confederate government should take full responsibility for the proposed troops. As a result, the House appointed a three-man committee to resolve the differences between the two legislative

49. *Senate Journal of the Ninth Legislature,* 117. Scarborough, a Georgia native who worked as a planter and printer, represented District 32, which comprised Cameron, Hidalgo, Starr, Zapata, Webb, Encinal, and Duval Counties, located on the south-Texas–Mexico border.

50. *Senate Journal of the Ninth Legislature,* 124; David Paul Smith, "Frontier Defense in Texas, 1861–1865," 96–98.

51. *Senate Journal of the Ninth Legislature,* 132–33.

branches. On a motion from George B. Erath, the Senate also insisted on its version of the bill and appointed a three-member committee to deal with the differences. On December 17, the Senate passed a resolution dealing with the eighth section "that no portion of said troop shall become a charge against the State until organized as required by the fifth section of this Act and placed under orders." The next day, the House adopted the committee report and this version of the eighth section. The final version of the bill for frontier protection called for a twelve-month enlistment of ten companies. On Governor Lubbock's insistence, the recruited men were to be stationed near their home counties to remain close to their families. In addition, they were to remain on Texas soil. Furthermore, Texas politicians still hoped to place the financial responsibility for the troops on the Confederate government.[52]

The Confederate government, however, refused to accept Texas troops into Confederate service under this agreement. Though the bill came up for debate and passed in the Confederate Congress, President Davis vetoed the bill because it limited executive control and complicated the military administration of the Confederacy. Davis's veto and neglect of Texas's concerns foreshadowed events to come. Due to his veto, the burden for frontier protection fell to the state. Not all Texans were happy with this decision, and many citizens believed the legislature's decision to maintain troops at state expense was "foolish and unconstitutional." Despite minor criticism, Texas politicians did take action toward addressing the Indian issue. Furthermore, the effort of the House and Senate to cast aside differences and settle the critical issue of frontier protection reveals the unity of Texas politicians to secure the welfare of the citizenry and the protection of their lives and property.[53]

In December 1861, the Confederate government deliberated Indian relations when President Davis submitted the Pike treaties to Congress. The ratification process included debate among the Confederate representatives that resulted in several amendments to the treaties. Each of these amendments further restricted the political welfare of the Indian nations and revealed much about the dissemination of political power in the Confederacy.

On December 19, 1861, the Confederate Congress met in executive session and discussed relations with the Indian nations. Mr. Johnson of Arkansas stood before the session and recommended that the treaty with the Choctaws and Chickasaws be ratified with additional amendments. The

52. Ibid., 132–33, 142, 148; D. P. Smith, "Frontier Defense in Texas," 95–97.
53. D. P. Smith, "Frontier Defense in Texas," 98–99; *Austin Texas State Gazette,* Sept. 3, 1862.

first amendment up for debate dealt with Article 27 of the treaty, referring to the right of the Choctaws and Chickasaws to have a delegate in the House of Representatives. As the treaty stood, the Indian delegates were to enjoy "the same rights and privileges as may be enjoyed by Delegates from any Territory of the Confederate States." Johnson sought to have these words stricken from the treaty. Congress debated whether the words should remain, and by a vote of thirteen to zero agreed to strike them. In lieu of this phrase, Johnson sought to have a paragraph inserted that would allow the Indian delegates to "propose and introduce measures for the benefit of said nations," and allow them "to be heard in regard thereto." Any other privileges imparted to the Indian nations were to be determined by the House itself. Robert W. Barnwell of South Carolina, however, moved to have Johnson's amendment reduced to state "such rights and privileges as may be determined by the House of Representatives." Walker Brooke of Mississippi moved to have Barnwell's motion tabled, and his motion prevailed. Congress then debated Johnson's amendment. By a vote of thirteen to zero in the affirmative, Congress passed Johnson's amendment. Regarding Article 27, the first vote prohibited almost full participation of Indian delegates and restricted their political voice, revealing Richmond's disregard for the Indians' political rights. Although the second vote did ensure that the Indian delegates would have the right to present their concerns, some members of Congress fought to further restrict their political representation. Political reason prevailed, however, as the Confederate Congress knew that any further constraints on the Indians' political participation would possibly lead the tribes to reject the treaties. Congress therefore permitted the delegates from the Cherokee, Choctaw, Creek, Seminole, and Chickasaw Nations to voice their concerns, but they did not receive the right to vote.[54]

After deciding on Article 27, Congress deliberated the twenty-eighth article, which dealt with the possible admittance of the Choctaw and Chickasaw Nations into the Confederacy "on equal terms, in all respects, with the original States." By a vote of thirteen to zero, Congress voted to strike out these words and replace them with similar wording with additional restrictions. The passed amendment, by a vote of twelve to zero, gave Congress alone

54. Confederate States of America, *Journal of the Congress of the Confederate States of America, 1861–1865,* 1:590–91; hereafter referred to as *JCCSA.* Thomas B. Alexander and Richard E. Beringer, *The Anatomy of the Confederate Congress: A Study of the Influences of Member Characteristics on Legislative Voting Behavior, 1861–1865,* 13. Born in Georgia, Elias Boudinot, at age twenty-five, representing the Cherokee Nation, was one of the youngest members of the Confederate Congress. Robert Jones of the Choctaw Nation served in both the first and second houses, as did Boudinot.

the power to admit new states into the Union, and "whose consent it is not in the power of the President or of the present Congress to guarantee in advance." Clearly, the Confederacy did not want to uphold the guarantee of statehood in the near or distant future, and Congress balked from its guarantee and offered only a veiled promise to the Indian tribes. The proviso of the article in consideration reveals Richmond's true intent. Confederate politicians were willing to recognize only partially the political voice and interests of the Indians in hopes of maintaining ties in order to secure future interests. By holding out an offer to join the Confederacy, the South would have access to Indian lands and was guaranteed the expansion of economic institutions. Thus, the Confederacy did not so much desire to protect the Indians as it did to carry out the manifest design of conquering the Indians for economic gain.[55]

On December 31, 1861, Congress considered the treaty with the Comanche Indians. Mr. Harris moved to amend Article 13 of the treaty dealing with the release of prisoners. Article 13 read in part, "this article creates no obligation to deliver up Mexicans who may be prisoners." Harris moved that the article instead read, "other prisoners than inhabitants of the Confederate States or Territories thereof." In this way, Indians were not bound to give up Union prisoners of war, thus strategically strengthening their ties with the Confederacy. Harris also moved to have Article 27 completely stricken from the treaty. Striking out Article 27, "that all Texan troops now within the limits of said leased country shall be withdrawn across the Red River," was significant, for it allowed Texans to employ fully an offensive posture against the Indian tribes. All the Texas representatives in Congress, except for William Ochiltree, supported the presence of Texas state troops within Indian territory, regardless of their mission. The inexplicit sanction from Richmond allowing Texas the use of state troops to wage war against the Indians contributed to the establishment of state identity and further reinforced Texas's agenda to pacify or eradicate the Indians for their own economic security. Previous to the ratification of the treaty, though, Texas had already adopted the extralegal position of pursuing the Indians across the Red River. Therefore, the political endorsement from Richmond was essentially of little consequence except to solidify a process already transpiring. It did, however, reveal that Texas representatives in Congress, at this stage in the crisis, had contact with and supported the desires of their constituents.[56]

55. *JCCSA,* 1:591–92; Lary C. Rampp and Donald L. Rampp, *The Civil War in the Indian Territory,* 2.
56. *JCCSA,* 1:632–33.

During the evening session that same day, Congress again took up the Choctaw and Chickasaw Treaty and debated Articles 27, 28, 43, and 44. Articles 43 and 44 established the power of state courts and laws to deal with Indian problems. Though the original version of the treaties stipulated that Indians would receive full rights and representation in court, the amended version left the final decision to individual states. Thus, each state in practice could refuse the Confederate request to abide by the original agreement of Indian representation in the treaties. For Texas, this piece of legislation was significant, enabling it to exercise full political power over foreign individuals. In the face of hostilities, it enabled Texas to take legal measures against the Indians. Still, it was of little consequence because Texas had routinely engaged in extralegal measures to deal with the Indian problem. Frontier ranchers and slave owners constantly had to safeguard their property against all thieves, and the problem with simply arresting individuals was that they were often set free only to continue their raids. This points to the complexity of the threat to lives and property and reveals the effort of individuals to take matters into their own hands instead of relying on the Confederate government. Moreover, Texans did not cease their appeals to the state legislature for aid and protection, thus revealing a continued loyalty to the state and a disregard for Confederate rule. Richmond's political support of state interests came too late for Texas's Indian crisis. Furthermore, Indian hostilities all but nullified Texas's desire to follow Confederate treaties. This grassroots effort at safeguarding lives and property by extralegal maneuvers reveals a fundamental step in the process of establishing a separate identity from that of other Confederate states. Each of these passed amendments were significant pieces of legislation affecting relations between Texas and the Indian tribes. The Indian tribes, however, were not pleased with the amendments, and Pike labored for three days to convince them to accept the amended treaties. Despite his efforts, Congress did not uphold the treaty agreements. Their failure to do so resulted from multiple factors, including a lack of finances, disruptive military campaigns, and a concern for its own continued existence.[57]

Despite Richmond's efforts to secure relations with the Indians, their failure to solve adequately the crisis led Texas citizens to rail against the

57. *Marshall Texas Republican,* Mar. 16, 1861; *JCCSA,* 1:633–34. The Congress also debated the same issues regarding the Creek Treaty (Articles 28, 30, 40), with the same conclusions, and debated the Cherokee Treaty (Articles 35, 44, 33) on Dec. 23, 1861, with the same results; see *JCCSA,* 1:610–11; Josephy, *Civil War in the American West,* 337; and Kenny Franks, "The Implementation of the Confederate Treaties with the Five Civilized Tribes," 33.

Confederate government for its neglect, expressing the same sentiments as their political leaders. Citizens from Coryell County expressed outrage at the Confederate government. Not only did they battle abolitionists and "Reserve Indians," but they also believed they were in a struggle with the Confederate government. They blamed Richmond for purchasing stolen horses from the Indians and paying them in arms and ammunition far superior to any of those owned by Texas citizens. In May 1862, the *Houston Tri-Weekly Telegraph* ran an editorial further criticizing Richmond. Although Texans knew that the Confederate government had to give attention to strategic points in the Confederacy, they complained that the government ignored vital points and interests in Texas. "That we can look for little or no help from the Government is obvious from the fact that the general defense of the whole country demands their exclusive attention to the military strategic points, none of which lie in this State." Texans believed that the economic interests of their state were just as vital as the military interests of the South. Citizens worried that "the strategic" cattle pastures, commercial routes to Mexico, and wheat fields stood "a good chance to be left to the care of old men and boys." Texans believed these economic interests were vital to their destiny and deserved full protection.[58]

Throughout the Civil War, hostilities continued between Texans and the Indians, and citizens complained continually to Governor Lubbock about their troubles. One Palo Pinto resident wrote:

> These Indians are fed by the U. S. Posts at Fort Adams on the Arkansas and Fort Bend and the Indians are paid by the U. S. troops occupying these parts for all the scalps taken from Texas. They are perfectly friendly with the U. S. Troops and in fact with all except Texans. I am satisfied that we will not have any rest from these Indians until we go to their general rendezvous and destroy them, I am satisfied that with a few companies of men great good can be done by an expedition against them.[59]

Requests continually poured into Lubbock's office asking for action against the Indians. Indian attacks became so bad in some areas that open hostility existed between outraged citizens and government troops. Citizens still looked to the state government for protection of lives and property, but they realized increasingly that the responsibility lay in their own hands. This recognition came in part from the failure of the Texas Rangers. Citizens and

58. Zelma Scott, *A History of Coryell County, Texas,* 60; *Houston Tri-Weekly Telegraph,* May 9, 1862.

59. Day, *Indian Papers,* 4:67–68. On Indians being fed, clothed, and given whiskey at various forts, see D. S. Howell, "Along the Frontier during the Civil War," 92–93.

newspapers railed against the poor job of the Rangers, and the *Austin Texas State Gazette* asked, "Where are our Rangers? Wonder if there were not some eight or ten at this place drinking and cutting up worse than Indians during this time: while our citizens are fighting for the recovery of their stolen property."[60]

Despite the criticism and strife, the state legislature did attempt to remedy the Indian problem, but it did not fully succeed. This failure, according to George B. Erath, resulted in part from its little experience in legislating and fully comprehending the task of adopting specific measures necessary to safeguard Texas citizens. The system that it adopted, minutemen, proved more favorable, though, than that of Confederate protection, which accomplished little. Nevertheless, some citizens in the aftermath of attacks complained that the state government failed in its programs and its commitment to protect the lives and property of its citizens. Many Texans believed that the Texas Rangers and the Minute Company system adopted by the legislature failed to protect the Texas frontier.[61]

The Indian problem became so grave that many Texans on the frontier feared to venture from their homes. "The man thus situated," one citizen complained, "dare not go out of the smoke of his own chimney without constant uneasiness and misgiving lest his wife and little ones may be massacred in his absence." Texas citizens, though, believed that the Indians should be hunted down and "killed to the last man." They believed in taking the war to the Indians, to their own hunting grounds, where they would be allowed "no rest nor respite" and "granted no truce or treaty." They held further that the mode of warfare initiated by the Indians was "cowardly as well as cruel, for they attack none but the weak and defenseless." At the very least, they wanted to drive the Indians so far beyond the border that they would cease to cause conflict. Texans expressed severe doubts about the ability of the troops to protect a vast frontier and achieve this goal, and realized the necessity of more localized efforts.[62]

The fact that the Indians held no respect for age or gender only compounded the harsh realities that families faced. Throughout 1861 and 1862, Texans sought to counter the Indians with offensive measures. "Let them be taught that their existence depends on their good conduct," the *Austin Texas State Gazette* reported, "and that their arid plains and mountain vastness will

60. *Marshall Texas Republican,* Feb. 22, 1862; *Austin Texas State Gazette,* Feb. 22, 1862; *San Antonio Weekly Herald,* Mar. 1, 1862.

61. Erath, *Memoirs of Erath,* 95; *Marshall Texas Republican,* Feb. 11, Feb. 22, Mar. 1, 1862.

62. *San Antonio Weekly Herald,* Feb. 1, 1862; *Clarksville Northern Standard,* Mar. 23, 1861.

not protect them from the just vengeance of the Government; and then, and not till then, may we expect such treaties, and such faith in the observance of treaties as will result in continued friendly relations between the two races." Texans did not have faith in Pike's negotiations with the Indian tribes, nor did they agree that they should retreat from their offensive posture. Furthermore, the necessity of combating the Indian problem kept many men and boys from joining the Confederate army. The only effective way to deal with the Indians involved local efforts and incorporating the same tactics used by the Indians. Citizens had no choice but to launch their own offensive measures, and they committed themselves to tracking down the Indians and taking the war to their enemy.[63]

Their offensive posture was not merely a reaction to specific attacks, but a general practice whenever Texans believed Indians lurked in the vicinity. For example, after hearing rumors of Indians present in the area in March 1861, citizens from Webb and Zapata Counties immediately searched the known Indian trails and killed several Indians. A similar situation occurred in February 1862, when Parker County residents tracked down and killed several Indians who had stolen sixty-three horses from local residents. In addition, Texas citizens often pursued the Indians into Choctaw, Chickasaw, and Cherokee territories, where they succeeded in killing a significant number of Indians. In one case, the *Austin Texas State Gazette* reported in February 1862, three hundred Indians were killed in a single battle. In their pursuit of the enemy, Texans had tortured and killed any Indian they happened upon, whether or not he was responsible for raids. Texans acted with vengeance in their objective and often returned with Indian scalps as a show of force and victory.[64]

Map 3.4, "Offensive Measures, 1861–1862," reveals that more than 50 percent of the counties that had suffered from Indian attacks adopted offensive measures. In counties across the state, concerned citizens searched for Indian trails, hoping to catch, torture, and kill the enemy. Oftentimes they left loved ones unprotected for days, a jeopardizing dilemma but a necessary one. In their pursuit, Texans injured and killed a significant number of Indians (Map 3.5). Geographical analysis of the offensive measures and Indians killed reveals that more than 80 percent of the counties succeeded in mounting effectual campaigns of locating, fighting, and killing Indians. Texans were just as brutal and savage as the Indians in their pursuit, and the

---

63. *Austin Texas State Gazette,* Aug. 31, 1861; Theda Purdue, *Nations Remembered: An Oral History of the Five Civilized Tribes, 1865–1907,* 5.

64. *San Antonio Tri-Weekly Alamo Express,* Mar. 18, 1861; *Austin Texas State Gazette,* Feb. 22, 1862; *Marshall Texas Republican,* Mar. 1, 1862.

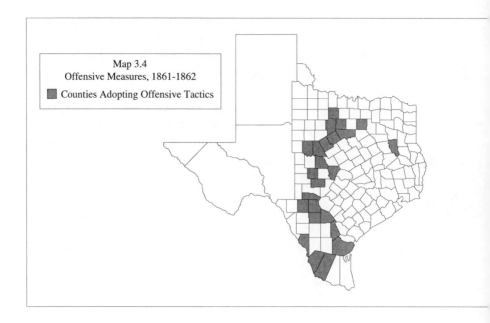

Map 3.4
Offensive Measures, 1861-1862

Counties Adopting Offensive Tactics

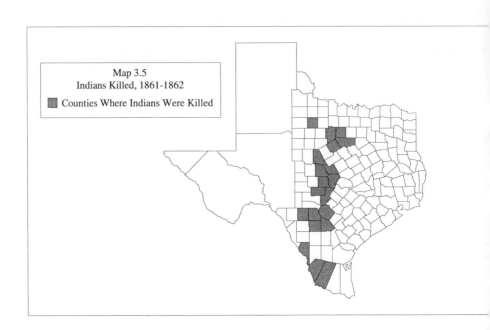

Map 3.5
Indians Killed, 1861-1862

Counties Where Indians Were Killed

offensive posture that united Texans served to establish a separate identity from that of other Confederate states.[65]

Efforts to combat the Indians, however, extended beyond those counties directly affected by atrocities. Throughout this period, citizens turned to other counties for aid to combat the hostility. All Texans were aware of Indian encounters; if their county had not experienced skirmishes in the previous decade, they were at least informed through the press of the hardship that fellow Texans faced. Reports of Indian atrocities were so horrendous and so well known throughout the state that citizens from areas not directly affected gathered to offer support for the afflicted counties. Houston and Galveston stood out as especially generous in their efforts to aid fellow Texans; citizens there often contributed arms and supplies for the frontier. In Seguin, the *Southern Confederacy* reported that "the Indian excitement on the bleeding frontier, has roused the patriotism of some of our gallant citizens," and urged residents to aid frontier citizens. Similar situations occurred across the state, and the frontier countrymen knew that those citizens gave well beyond their means.[66]

Attacked counties, though, were not completely helpless in the struggle. Because Palo Pinto County was "depredated upon almost daily by hostile Indians," Judge W. L. Lasater authorized the county to contract a person to travel to Austin in order to secure powder, lead, and caps, as instructed by the adjutant and inspecting general in November 1862. The 160 families in that county lived in constant fear of Indian attacks, and fear of Northern invasion only surmounted their troubles. Nevertheless, the citizens of that county took it upon themselves to procure the necessities of war to protect their lives and property and recruited men to protect the frontier. In order to recruit men for protection, families gathered in covered wagons at the county seat. Men, accompanied by their wives, filed into the courthouse to draw lots for frontier service. This process was a county effort that involved entire families, bonded together for the protection of their lives and property.[67]

More often than not, though, counties raised their own financial and material support for the aid of frontier defense. Unable to rely on the Confederate or state government for adequate assistance, individual counties collected money, arms, blankets, food, and other basic necessities to aid men willing to brave confrontation with the Indians. The willingness of counties to sacrifice

65. *Marshall Texas Republican,* June 1, 1861.

66. *Dallas Weekly Herald,* Jan. 9, 1861; *San Antonio Tri-Weekly Alamo Express,* Mar. 13, 1861; *Seguin Southern Confederacy,* Mar. 22, 1861.

67. Mary Whatley Clarke, *The Palo Pinto Story,* 52–53.

money and materials for the protection of their citizens' lives and property speaks to the significance of the Indian crisis in daily life, and shows that individual citizens were ready to adopt offensive measures for their own security. Furthermore, the compliance of other counties in assisting their brothers and sisters in the struggle against the Indians reveals a unified state bound in a common struggle. Instead of placing their faith and trust in the government, the Indian problem led most Texans to distrust it, to look to their own defense, and to identify with local as opposed to larger Confederate issues.[68]

Likewise, the Indians could not rely on the Confederate or Texas government. White expansion led to a relationship of hostility and broken promises. Ironically, the Indians' struggle paralleled those of Texas and the Confederacy. The Indians believed that they were assaulted on all sides. They sought to halt encroachment from outsiders and fought to retain their way of life. Struggling against long odds, guerrilla warfare provided an opportunity to attain this goal. In the process, the Indians came to distrust outside forces, which served to unify the Indian tribes and proved a foreshadowing of the embittered conflicts that later surfaced in their quest for survival against invasion and assimilation.[69]

By 1863, Union forces had invaded much of the territory belonging to the Cherokee and Creek Nations, forcing them into Choctaw and Chickasaw territories. The additional presence of Indians along the Red River served to continue the tumultuous relationship as the Indians pressed increasingly upon Texas soil to steal for their own economic gain. In addition, Indian raids continued in south Texas and on the western frontier. Although Texas would become more concerned with its relationship with the Confederate government in 1863, the Indian problems that Texans faced from 1861 through 1862 fostered the establishment of a separate identity for Texas. Military enlistment in the state militia in the beginning stages of the Civil War and throughout the conflict would further establish this separate identity. This in turn directly affected Texas's relationship with the Trans-Mississippi Department and the Confederate government as Texas faced new issues of control and authority that continued to threaten its economic security.[70]

68. *Galveston Weekly News,* Feb. 5, 1861; *San Antonio Weekly Alamo Express,* Mar. 9, 1861; *San Antonio Tri-Weekly Alamo Express,* Mar. 8, 1861.

69. On the Indians after the Civil War, see Frederick E. Hoxie, *A Final Promise: The Campaign to Assimilate the Indians;* Janet A. McDonnell, *The Dispossession of the American Indian, 1887–1934;* and Robert Wooster, *The Military and United States Indian Policy, 1865–1903.*

70. Josephy, *Civil War in the American West,* 375.

CHAPTER 4

Defending the State

Texas Military Enlistment

Looking back upon the Civil War crisis, A. W. Sparks, who served in Ross's Brigade, Texas Cavalry, commented that he had no choice but to fight for Texas. Texas was "the home of my mother, the pride of my father, the guardian of my sister and the home of my boyhood." Therefore, "right or wrong, I fought for Texas, and could see no honorable course for Texas men but to stake their lives, their liberty, their all for Texas." Sparks represented the general sentiment of many Texans who went off to fight during the Civil War crisis.[1]

On April 12, 1861, the American Civil War began with the firing on Fort Sumter, South Carolina. Three days later, Union president Abraham Lincoln called for seventy-five thousand militiamen to enter federal service. Confederate president Jefferson Davis followed by calling for one hundred thousand volunteers. The initial frenzy and excitement of war led many Northern and Southern men to enlist in the Union and Confederate armies. Historians examining military enlistment during the American Civil War generally focus on the actual numbers of men who fought. One century ago, Thomas L. Livermore published the most comprehensive study on the number of men who fought and died in the American Civil War. Livermore estimates that 1,082,119 men were mobilized for Confederate service. Subsequent studies generally rely on or refute to an extent this finding. For example, James McPherson posits that approximately 900,000 men enrolled in Confederate service, and Joseph Harsh has recently argued that the Confederate manpower pool consisted of approximately 1,200,000 men of which 950,000 were mobilized for service. The problem with Livermore's study and subsequent studies, however, is that they do not take into account the numbers of Southern men who often fought for the same "cause" but served instead in state militias. Furthermore, this emphasis on the numbers is rooted

---

1. Sparks, *The War between the States, as I Saw It: Reminiscent, Historical, and Personal,* 11.

in the effect of the "Lost Cause," which stresses that the North overwhelmed the South with superior forces and numbers of men. It reveals little about why men went off to fight and the economic or social concerns they sought to defend.[2]

More recently, though, historians have begun to focus on the social cleavages associated with conscription. For example, Lacy K. Ford argues that South Carolina slaveholders co-opted the upcountry yeomen and small planters into supporting their cause through their involvement in the market economy. Wayne K. Durrill, though, reveals that planters in Washington County, North Carolina, could not "persuade yeoman farmers to join in common cause against the Union." Although it was a rich man's war and a poor man's fight in some instances, there did exist certain situations where poorer individuals often sided with the Union and were not co-opted into the Confederate cause.[3]

The most recent research into military enlistment reveals that men were not co-opted into the Confederate cause, but instead served to defend their material world. Mike Connelly examines the relationship between the initial Essex County, Massachusetts, enlistment in the Union army and railroad construction. He concludes that shoemakers and leather makers were over-represented in the muster rolls by a two-to-one margin. This industry was most affected by the railroad prior to 1860, for rail transportation allowed the industry to ship more than 60 percent of its product to open markets farther south and west. Therefore, as secession threatened shoe markets in the South and West, he argues, shoemakers enlisted in disproportionate numbers to defend those markets. Put another way, those men involved in industries most affected by the railroad economy were most anxious to fight; those least affected, fishermen and farmers, appeared least likely to fight.[4]

John O. Allen reveals in his study on Southside, Virginia, that those men who enlisted in the Confederate cause were not co-opted into the movement.

2. Livermore, *Numbers and Losses in the Civil War in America, 1861–1865;* James M. McPherson, *Battle Cry of Freedom,* 306–7; Joseph Harsh, *Confederate Tide Rising: Robert E. Lee and the Making of Southern Strategy, 1861–1862,* 178–84; William Garrett Piston, *Lee's Tarnished Lieutenant: James Longstreet and His Place in Southern History,* 104–28; Thomas L. Connelly, *The Marble Man: Robert E. Lee and His Image in American Society.*

3. Durrill, *War of Another Kind;* Ford, *Origins of Southern Radicalism: The South Carolina Upcountry, 1800–1860.* See also Eugene D. Genovese, *The Political Economy of Slavery: Studies in the Economy and Society of the Slave South* and *The World the Slaveholders Made.*

4. Michael J. Connelly, "All Points North: Entrepreneurial Politics and Railroad Development in Northern New England, 1830–1860."

Allen reveals that the Virginia tobacco economy was significantly market oriented and market responsive. Slaveholders, he argues, tended to maximize their profits in wealth rather than income. Furthermore, those areas of Virginia that grew tobacco appeared much more proslavery, prosecession, and pro-Confederacy. Allen reveals that those individuals in the tobacco region who did not participate in slavery did not join the Confederate army at the war's onset in anywhere close to the numbers of their slaveholding neighbors. All the above works are significant, for they reveal the intimate relationship between military enlistment and economic concerns. Men fought to safeguard their material world—a world that extended beyond the interest of Southern slavery.[5]

In Texas, men also sought to defend their commercial interests by enlisting in military service. And, as A. W. Sparks's sentiment reveals, these men did so for their own self-interest and the interest of Texas. Earlier studies on military service in Texas focus primarily on regimental history or have examined the conflict inherent in the different conscription laws passed by the state of Texas and the Confederate government. The most recent and comprehensive study dealing with the Texas militia focuses almost exclusively on frontier defense and pays little attention to the relationship between Texas and the Confederate government, or the commercial interests that men defended. Instead, David Paul Smith argues that frontier defenders served as a police force on the frontier from 1861 to 1865. Although these works are valuable, there is still a lack of understanding concerning the local response to war and the economic concerns of these citizens.[6]

An analysis of the local response to state and Confederate conscription reveals the complexity of the relationship between the state and federal governments. The relationship between conscription and commercial interests reveals further to what extent men sought to defend their interest in slaveholding by enlisting in military service. More important, such analysis reveals the degree to which men viewed service in the state militia or Confederate army as the best agency to represent and defend their economic interests in this commercially diverse state. Therefore, in an attempt to illuminate further the inherent conflict within the Confederate States of America, and the process by which Texas established a separate identity, it becomes critical to understand who these men fought for and how this information correlates with the economic interests of the counties they represented. Through

---

5. Allen, "Antebellum Southside Virginia."

6. Ila Mae Myers, "The Relations of Governor Pendleton Murrah, of Texas, with the Confederate Military Authorities," 13–16; D. P. Smith, *Frontier Defense in the Civil War.*

an exhaustive search of the muster rolls, the county residence and year of enlistment are known for approximately 88 percent of the 83,870 men that enlisted in either the Texas state militia or the Confederate army. In an era where men were often bound by the code of honor, being conscripted was viewed as disgraceful. Thus, it is extremely significant to discover with which governmental agency these men enlisted. Over the course of the war, Texans generally enlisted in the state militia rather than the Confederate army. The pattern of military enlistment strengthened the establishment of a separate identity that emerged in the initial stages of war due to the Indian crisis.[7]

At the beginning of the Civil War, men had a choice whether to serve in the state militia or the Confederate army. General enthusiasm existed for enlisting in military service regardless of the type. The enlistment and training of young men for service was a grand social affair. In many areas, local women presented the trainees with hand-sewn flags boldly displaying the Lone Star or county name. In addition, these men were treated to parades and barbecues where politicians and war veterans hoped to stir their emotions through speeches that denounced Republicans and Northern abolitionists. Oftentimes, these social gatherings resulted in many new recruits. Regardless of whether they chose to enter the Texas state militia or the Confederate army, though, all were generally bound by a sense of honor and duty. In their understanding, this meant protecting the family and home both physically and economically. The very threat to their economic security was more than many were willing to submit to.[8]

At the onset of the war, Texans more likely than not chose to enlist in the service of the state rather than the Confederate army to provide this security. Map 4.1, "Number of Men Entering TST, 1861," gives a visual representation of the number of men per county who chose to enter the state militia in 1861. Forty-nine percent of the Texas counties sending men into the Texas State Troops (TST) sent between 1 and 250 men. Twenty-three percent of the counties sent between 250 and 500 men, and 22 percent of the counties sent up to 1,000 men into the state militia. Geographical analysis, though, does not reveal any regional distinctions regarding the actual number of men per county entering state service in 1861 (see Appendix 3, "Regression Analysis: Military Enlistment").

7. Randolph Campbell, "Fighting for the Confederacy: The White Male Population of Harrison County in the Civil War," 27.

8. Ralph Wooster, *Texas and Texans*, 28–29; Carleton Beals, *War within a War: The Confederacy against Itself*, 72–73; W. W. Heartsill, *Fourteen Hundred and 91 Days in the Confederate Army*, 2; M. Jane Johansson, *Peculiar Honor: A History of the 28th Texas Cavalry, 1862–1865*, 4.

Research on individual companies has shown that enlisted men generally reflected the economic circumstances of their home counties. Statistical analysis explicates this and reveals several significant connections between military enlistment and the economic interests of the counties that men represented. When considering the actual number of men per county, there exists a significant relationship with several economic interests. The number of horses, milch cattle, beef cattle, and sheep and the total value of livestock each have a significant relationship to the number of men entering the state militia in 1861. In each case, a positive correlation exists. Thus, in each county where these economic interests were greater, more men were likely to enter state service. The same is also true when considering farm value, wheat production, corn production, and the total number of slaves held per county. In these cases, the relationship with men entering state service also exhibits a positive correlation (see Appendix 2, "County Military Enlistment").[9]

The relationship between men entering state service and county economic interests, however, changes somewhat when several factors are regressed simultaneously. When considering farm value and the amount of ginned cotton, both reveal a significant relationship. Nevertheless, farm value has a positive correlation, whereas ginned cotton has a negative correlation to the number of men per county that entered the state militia. Thus, it was more likely that men who entered state service represented those counties with higher farm values yet lesser amounts of ginned cotton. When ginned cotton and the total number of slaves held per county are simultaneously considered, both have a significant relationship to the number of men who enlisted. Yet, in this instance too, ginned cotton has a negative correlation, whereas slaveholding has a positive correlation. Thus, it was not the product of slave labor as a commercial interest, but rather slaveholding itself that was tied to the number of men per county entering state service in 1861. When farm value and wheat production are simultaneously considered, both have a significant relationship and positive correlation to the number of men entering state service. Thus, those counties with higher farm values and greater amounts of wheat production more likely had men entering the state militia. Statistical analysis reveals, therefore, that the poorer counties did not necessarily send the most men to serve in the state militia in 1861, revealing the misnomer that this was a rich man's war and a poor man's fight.[10]

9. Johansson, *Peculiar Honor,* 20.

10. Campbell, "Fighting for the Confederacy," 36. Campbell reveals that Harrison County men who were slaveholders or from slaveholding families enlisted at a higher proportion than did nonslaveholders.

Although the relationship between county economic characteristics and the actual number of men per county entering the state militia is quite revealing, a slightly different picture emerges when considering the percentage of men from each county that entered state service. Map 4.2, "Percentage of Men Entering TST, 1861," reveals the percentage of men, from ages fifteen to fifty, per county that entered the state militia in 1861. Thirty-one percent of these counties sent up to 25 percent of the available men. Nineteen percent of the counties sent up to 50 percent, and 17 percent of the counties sent as high as 75 percent of the available men in the county. Geographical analysis reveals that four counties, two in the Gulf Coast region and two in the frontier region, had more than 100 percent of the available men entering state service. Having more than 100 percent enter is likely explained by an increase in the population after the 1860 census. It is possible too that some men from surrounding counties joined troops from those counties without correctly identifying the county in which they actually resided. Similar to Map 4.1, there does not appear to exist any regional distinction regarding the percentage of men per county who entered the state militia in 1861 (see Appendix 3 and the Note on Sources).

Statistical analysis, though, does reveal several significant relationships between the percentage of men entering the state militia and the economic characteristics of a county. Here, however, only the number of horses and beef cattle and the total value of livestock have a significant relationship to the percentage of men enlisting. In each case, these factors have a positive correlation with the percentage of men. Thus, those counties that held more horses and beef cattle and had a higher value of all livestock generally sent a greater percentage of the available men into state service. The fact that men representing these wealthier counties more likely entered service provides further evidence that this was not a poor man's fight. To be sure, many prominent politicians and delegates to the secession convention chose to enlist for military duty. Even those politicians that spoke out against secession eagerly joined the ranks of Texas soldiers. James Throckmorton, for example, took the oath of allegiance supporting Texas's secession and organized a group of volunteer soldiers to defend against the Indians and Union invasion by taking over U.S. forts in Indian territory. In addition, even counties such as Lamar and leading individuals such as Samuel Bell Maxey that stood out against secession quickly volunteered and organized county troops to provide protection for the state and its citizens.[11]

11. Elliott, *Leathercoat,* 63–66; Louise Horton, *Samuel Bell Maxey: A Biography,* 17–18.

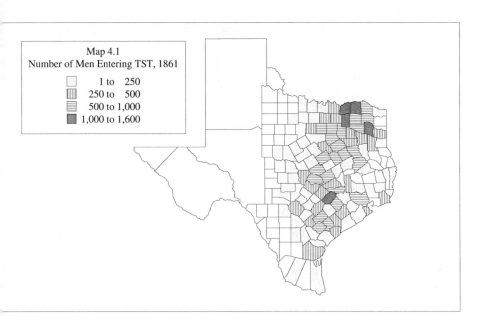

Map 4.1
Number of Men Entering TST, 1861

1 to   250
250 to   500
500 to 1,000
1,000 to 1,600

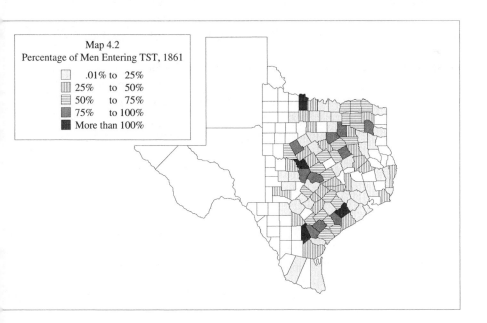

Map 4.2
Percentage of Men Entering TST, 1861

.01% to   25%
25%   to   50%
50%   to   75%
75%   to 100%
More than 100%

Some historians, though, have claimed that enlistment in the state militia was a "method of avoiding Confederate service" and that men chose the militia and frontier protection because it offered less hazards. The problem with this analysis, however, is that many men from the frontier region did join the Confederate army. Furthermore, especially in the initial stages of war, many men were unable to make this type of comparative analysis because they had not experienced war outside of Indian conflict. Instead, men entered the state militia to provide economic security for their families and the state. Even those men not in the frontier region were concerned with providing this security. For example, when Rudolf Coreth traveled to Victoria and enlisted with the Caney Rifles on November 11, 1861, he commented that most of the men were planters who "only wanted to defend the coast of Texas."[12]

Although the vast majority of men in 1861 chose to enlist directly into state service, a good number of men chose instead to enter directly into the Confederate army. Map 4.3, "Number of Men Entering CSA, 1861," reveals the number of men per county that entered Confederate service in 1861. Geographical analysis reveals that men from the northeastern frontier region and the Gulf Coast region more likely entered the Confederate State Army (CSA) than men from other Texas regions. Sixty-seven percent of the counties sending men directly into the Confederate army sent up to 100 men, and 25 percent of the counties sent between 100 and 200.

Statistical analysis also reveals several significant relationships between the number of men per county entering the Confederate army and the economic characteristics of each county. The number of horses, milch cattle, and sheep and the value of livestock each hold a significant relationship with the number of men per county entering Confederate service. In each case, these factors correlate positively with the number of men who enlisted. Likewise, farm value, corn production, and the total number of slaves also have a significant relationship with the number of men entering Confederate service. These too correlate positively. When simultaneously considering the number of slaves and ginned cotton, both have a significant relationship to the number of men entering the Confederate army. In this instance, however, the number of slaves has a positive correlation, whereas ginned cotton has a negative one. This suggests that slaveholding, more so than the production of slave labor, was important in determining the number of men that entered the Confederate army in 1861.

As with the percentage of those who entered into state service, the picture

12. Marten, *Texas Divided,* 97; Minetta Altgelt Goyne, *Lone Star and Double Eagle: Civil War Letters of a German-Texas Family,* 22–23.

changes somewhat when considering the percentage of men per county that entered directly into Confederate service. Map 4.4, "Percentage of Men Entering CSA, 1861," reveals the actual percentage of these men per county. Ninety-eight percent of the counties sending men into Confederate service sent up to 25 percent of the men in the county between the ages of fifteen and fifty. There do not appear to be any regional distinctions, though, regarding the percentage of men entering the Confederate army in 1861. Likewise, statistical analysis reveals no significant relationships between the percentage of men entering Confederate service and the economic interests of a county.

With the onset of war, therefore, a higher number of men and percentage of men per county chose to enter the state militia instead of the Confederate army. Due to Confederate neglect, Texans viewed the state militia as the best vehicle to defend their economic interests. Nevertheless, men in state service often found themselves transferred into Confederate service after a short period. Protection of the frontier, as seen, was a paramount issue for Texans. Not only was frontier protection important due to Indian attacks, but there also did exist some fear that a joining of Union and Indian forces would invade Texas. After all, Texans stood committed to an offensive posture and acted brutally in their expulsion of the Indians from the state, and many feared that the Indians would use this crisis and join with Union forces to exact revenge. Due to the necessity of protecting the frontier, the state often transferred men into Confederate service. This held true even for frontier troops who would remain on Texas soil and defend the state against Indian invasion. The outgoing governor, Edward Clark, spoke on the necessity and practice of raising troops and believed it was necessary to transfer state troops into the Confederate service "to save the state the immense cost of its [own] maintenance."[13]

Map 4.5, "% Entering CSA (Including Transfers), 1861," reveals the percentage of men per county that entered the Confederate army, including those men transferred from the state militia in 1861. Geographical analysis reveals that no regional distinctions existed. Statistical analysis, though, does unveil several significant relationships between the percentage of men entering Confederate service and county economic interests. The number of horses and sheep and farm value each hold a significant relationship with the percentage of men. In addition, in each case, these economic factors correlate positively. Farm value, however, has a significant relationship only when it is simultaneously considered with the amount of ginned cotton per

13. Judith Ann Benner, *Sul Ross: Soldier, Statesman, Educator,* 64; *Senate Journal of the Ninth Legislature,* 22–23.

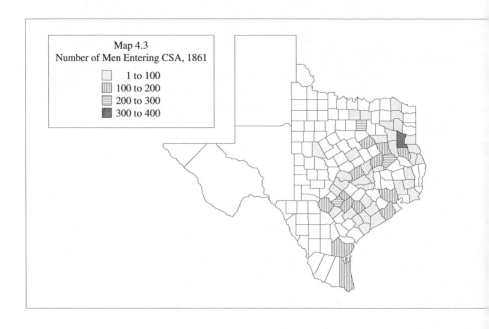

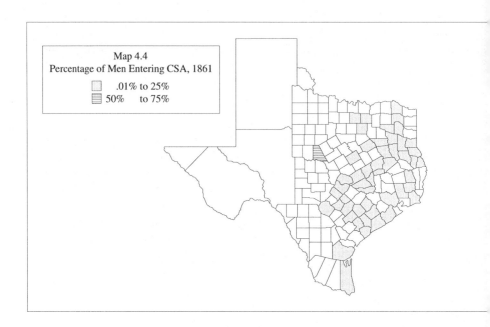

county. In this case, though, analysis reveals that ginned cotton does not have a significant relationship with the percentage of men, and exhibits a negative correlation. Thus, farm value is only significant as cotton production is decreasing, and cotton production does not appear to be a real factor.

These results are important, for they reinforce the finding that in 1861, Texans viewed the state militia as the best vehicle to safeguard their economic interests. In 1861, more men, especially from the northern frontier and Gulf Coast–region counties with higher slave populations and lesser amounts of ginned cotton, entered the state militia. In terms of percentages, though, men representing counties in the central and frontier regions, where the number of horses was higher, and in the central–Gulf Coast region, where the number of beef cattle was higher, sent a greater percentage of men into the state militia. Thus, it does not appear that the poorer counties sent more men to the state militia. Rather, men from every geographic region and economic consideration entered the state militia. This also holds true when considering the number of men per county who entered the Confederate army.[14]

Thus, the general sentiment of Texans was that the state militia provided a more reliable source to protect and provide economic security. This was especially true in the frontier region where, in many counties, men refused to enter Confederate service and opted instead for state service to fight the Indians. For example, in 1861, men from Blanco County stated that they enlisted in the state militia "for the purpose of drilling and defending our Settlement and immediate frontier from the depredations of the Indians or invasion of the Black Republicans." Thus, it was the threat not only to economic security from Indian attacks, but also of Union invasion that concerned Texas citizens. In addition, transferred troops should not be taken as an act of allegiance to the Confederate government. Many Texans choose to enlist in the Texas militia instead of the Confederate army and remained adamant about not being transferred into Confederate service or leaving the state of Texas. For example, when Capt. Richard Sullivan organized the Thirteenth Brigade Cedar Hill Cavalry in 1861, he wrote to the adjutant general and reminded him of the clause in the constitution stating "the Cedar Hill Cavalry being organized as a home guard shall not be taken out of the State of Texas nor marched South or East, except by a two third vote of the company." It should also be kept in mind that many troops did more than defend the economic interests of the state. In some cases, military troops

14. Cattle were a valuable asset, and in many areas the number of cattle actually increased during the war (Will Hale, *Twenty-four Years a Cowboy and Ranchman in Southern Texas and Old Mexico,* 55).

took the offensive to promote and secure commercial interests. Texas had grand expansionist designs, and the state often used military troops for this end. For example, troops led by Lt. John R. Baylor and Maj. Edwin Waller were used to secure parts of New Mexico as part of Texas's expansionist scheme.[15]

The concern to defend commercial interests and keep troops in Texas not only was evident among men enlisting, but also expressed by Texas politicians. On November 7, 1861, newly elected governor Francis Lubbock stood before a joint session of the Texas legislature to deliver his inaugural address. He believed that it was Texans' duty to secure the defense and safety of the state against "the polluted tread of abolition hordes." Frontier security also remained a paramount issue, thus strengthening Lubbock's resolve to have the state readied for self-defense. A week later, Governor Lubbock again addressed the Texas legislature and said that, given the present condition of the country, if Texas were to face any type of invasion, then it would have to rely almost entirely upon the state militia for defense. The Texas State Constitution of 1861 decreed that the legislature would provide for the defense of the state by organizing a state militia. Therefore, believing that Texans would rally to the call, Lubbock suggested to the legislature that it amend the conscription law to subject every male between the ages of seventeen and fifty to military duty. On December 25, 1861, the Texas legislature heeded the governor's call and passed a conscription act subjecting virtually all white males between the ages of eighteen and fifty to military duty. Texas conscription law, though, conflicted directly with Confederate conscription laws.[16]

The conscription law to a large extent, however, did not serve to change the situation of available men entering state service. Map 4.6, "Number of Men Entering TST, 1862," reveals the number of men per county who entered the state militia in 1862. Geographical analysis reveals a much lower number of men entering the state militia than the previous year. Eighty-three percent of the counties sent only as many as 150 men, and 12 percent of the counties sent as many as 300. These lower numbers, of course, are attributed to the high enlistment in 1861 from the initial excitement of war.

Statistical analysis also reveals fewer significant relationships between the number of men entering the state militia and county economic interests.

15. T. R. Havins, "The Frontier Era in Brown County"; Records of the Adjutant General: Muster Roll Collection, Record Group (RG) 401, box 1276, no. 279, 724-3, TSL; Ralph Wooster, *Texas and Texans,* 32. See also Frazier, *Blood and Treasure.*

16. *Senate Journal of the Ninth Legislature,* 16, 52–53; H. P. N. Gammel, comp., *The Laws of Texas, 1822–1897,* 455–65; Myers, "Relations of Governor Murrah," 13.

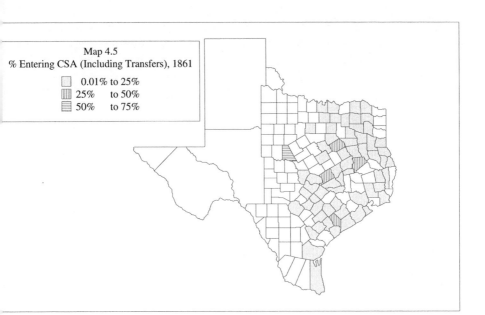

Map 4.5
% Entering CSA (Including Transfers), 1861

☐ 0.01% to 25%
▥ 25% to 50%
▤ 50% to 75%

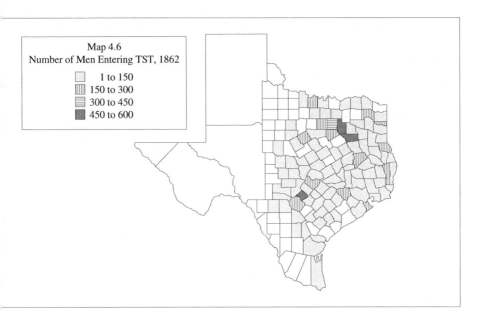

Map 4.6
Number of Men Entering TST, 1862

☐ 1 to 150
▥ 150 to 300
▤ 300 to 450
■ 450 to 600

Nevertheless, when considering the actual number of men entering state service in 1862, the production of wheat does have a significant relationship. In this case, wheat production holds a positive correlation with the number of men entering state service. Thus, those counties that produced more wheat more likely sent men into the state militia in 1862.

When considering the percentage of available men per county entering the state militia in 1862, however, the picture changes. Map 4.7, "Percentage of Men Entering TST, 1862," shows the percentage of men per county entering state service. Fifty-seven percent of the counties sent up to 25 percent of the available men in the county into the state militia, and 10 percent sent as many as 50 percent of the available men. Geographical analysis also reveals that six counties sent more than 100 percent of the available men into the state militia in 1862. Again, this high percentage is most likely due to population increase or a failure of men from outside counties declaring their actual county residency. Statistical analysis also reveals that the number of beef cattle has the only significant relationship with the percentage of men entering the state militia in 1862. In this case, those counties that held fewer beef cattle were more likely than other counties to be represented by men in the state militia.

In March 1862, President Jefferson Davis requested that the Confederate Congress pass legislation for a military draft. It took politicians only two weeks to decide on the act "to Further Provide for the Public Defense" that required all white males between the ages of eighteen and thirty-five to enter Confederate service for a period of three years, or less if the war ended. This conscription law made an impact on the number of men and percentage of available men entering Confederate service. Map 4.8, "Number of Men Entering CSA, 1862," reveals that 95 percent of the Texas counties that men represented sent as many as 250 men directly into the Confederate army, and 4 percent of the counties sent as many as 500 men. Geographical analysis, though, does not reveal any regional characteristics regarding the number of men entering Confederate service in 1862.[17]

Statistical analysis, on the other hand, reveals that a significant relationship exists between the number of available men entering the Confederate army and the number of horses, milch cattle, and sheep and the total value of livestock per county. Furthermore, farm value, wheat production, corn production, and total number of slaves also hold a significant relationship. In all cases, too, each economic factor has a positive correlation. Thus, for

17. *JCCSA*, 2:106; Thomas, *Confederate Nation,* 152–55; Myers, "Relations of Governor Murrah," 14. The act was approved on Apr. 16, 1862.

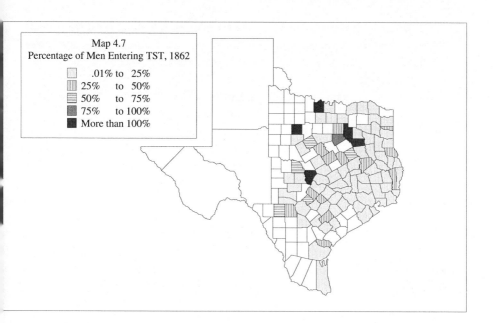

Map 4.7
Percentage of Men Entering TST, 1862

.01% to 25%
25%   to 50%
50%   to 75%
75%   to 100%
More than 100%

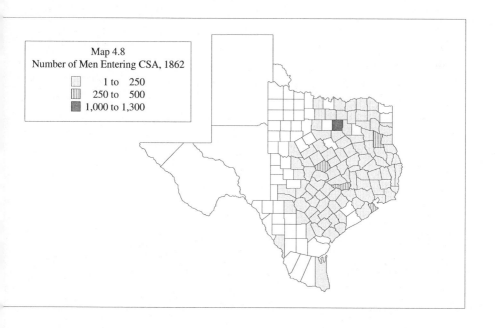

Map 4.8
Number of Men Entering CSA, 1862

1 to   250
250 to   500
1,000 to 1,300

1862, geographical and statistical analyses reveal that there is no simple economic explanation for the number of men that counties sent into Confederate service. The widespread number of enlistments most likely was a reaction to the conscription law.

Map 4.9, "Percentage of Men Entering CSA, 1862," reveals that when considering the actual percentage of men per county, 60 percent of the counties sent up to 25 percent of the available men into the Confederate army. Statistical analysis, however, reveals fewer significant relationships between the percentage of available men that entered Confederate service and county economic characteristics for 1862 than appeared in 1861. In this case, the number of horses and sheep, livestock value, and wheat production are significant with the percentage of men entering Confederate service. Slavery and cotton production as single factors and considered simultaneously do not have significant relationships. These same statistical relationships are also evident when considering the percentage of men, including those transferred from state service, entering Confederate service in 1862. Map 4.10, "% Entering CSA (Including Transfers), 1862," also reveals a higher percentage of men transferred into the Confederate army than the previous year. This was due in part to Governor Lubbock upholding the belief that to secure the financial interest of the state, men should be transferred into Confederate service. Lubbock remarked that the Texas frontier "must also be guarded, at every cost against the ruthless Indian foe; the lives of our men, women and children, preserved from the tomahawk and the scalpknife." By transferring men into Confederate service, the Confederate government then assumed the financial responsibility of the troops. This in turn eased the financial burden of the state.[18]

Men entering military service in both the state militia and the Confederate army in 1862 more likely came from the west-central and north-central frontier regions. These counties generally had more of a vested interest in wheat production, beef cattle, sheep, and horses. In 1862, therefore, it appears that neither slavery nor the product of slave labor existed as a significant factor indicating who went off to war. It is possible that here the scenario of the poorer non–slave owners fighting instead of the wealthy slave owners appears. This scenario, however, would not last, as Texas appeared more willing in 1863 to bolster state defense.

On February 5, 1863, Governor Lubbock delivered a message before the joint houses of the legislature. He touched on many topics, especially conscription. The Texas Supreme Court had recently ruled the Confederate

18. *Senate Journal of the Ninth Legislature*, 16, 22–23.

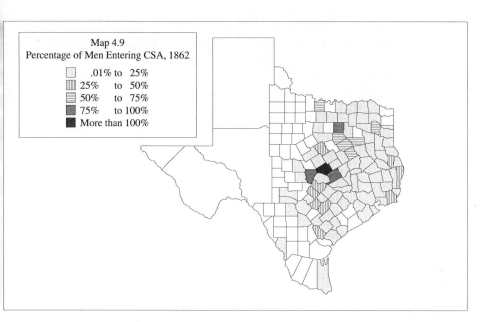

Map 4.9
Percentage of Men Entering CSA, 1862

.01% to 25%
25% to 50%
50% to 75%
75% to 100%
More than 100%

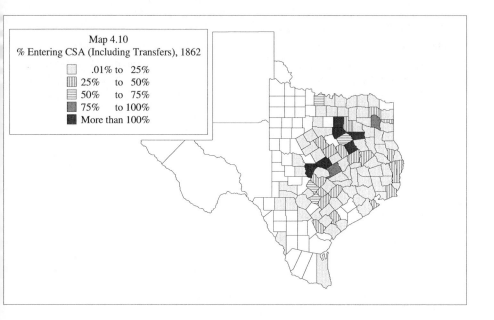

Map 4.10
% Entering CSA (Including Transfers), 1862

.01% to 25%
25% to 50%
50% to 75%
75% to 100%
More than 100%

conscription law constitutional, and Lubbock backed its decision. He told the legislature that it was his aim to cooperate with the Confederate government in the prosecution of the war. His collaboration, though, hinged on the willingness of Confederate authorities to keep adequate troops in the state of Texas for its defense. Lubbock also appeared hesitant in 1863 to call more men into state service. Doing so, he claimed, would cause the Confederate government to justify the removal of its troops from Texas. Thus, Texas would be left alone, dependent on state troops, to defend its borders and interests. These frontier troops under Confederate authority were necessary, for their presence gave frontier settlers a sense of protection and allowed men in the frontier counties to go off to war and leave their loved ones protected. The Confederate government, however, would not promise Lubbock that frontier troops placed into Confederate service would remain on the frontier for protection against the Indians. Although Lubbock acknowledged the need for men to enlist in Confederate service, he confessed that this conflict threw the state militia into a position of disorganization, and he found it difficult at one point to fill a requisition for 5,000 men for state service. By 1863, resistance to military enlistment was very strong in many parts of Texas, especially in Tarrant County. Desertion ran high in many parts of the state, and in many areas new recruits refused to travel outside the state, even to Louisiana.[19]

Furthermore, because Texans believed that the Confederate government had neglected to protect their state, state politicians moved to exert tighter control over state troops. This became apparent on March 6, 1863, when the state legislature passed an act to provide for the defense of the frontier. This act simply restated the position and desire of Texas politicians to have the frontier regiment under the control of the state and financial keep of the Confederate government, yet serve only on the frontier. This legislation allowed the governor to transfer the frontier regiment into Confederate service, but only on the condition that "said regiment shall be retained and remain upon the Indian frontier of the State of Texas, for its protection."[20]

Given the inherent conflict between state and Confederate interests and due to the course of war, Texas would bolster its state militia in 1863 over the manpower needs of the Confederate army. Map 4.11, "Number of Men Entering TST, 1863," reveals that 86 percent of the Texas counties that sent men into the state militia sent up to 150 men, and 10 of the counties sent

19. *House Journal of the Ninth Legislature First Called Session of the State of Texas,* 9, 11, 26–27; Beals, *War within a War,* 72–73.

20. Gammel, *Laws of Texas,* 607–8.

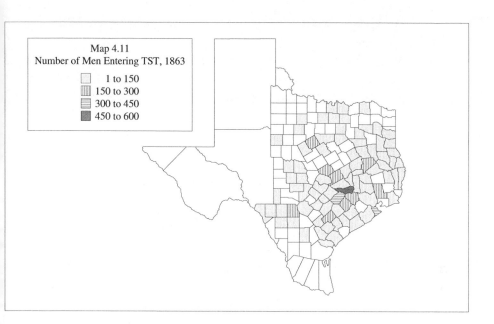

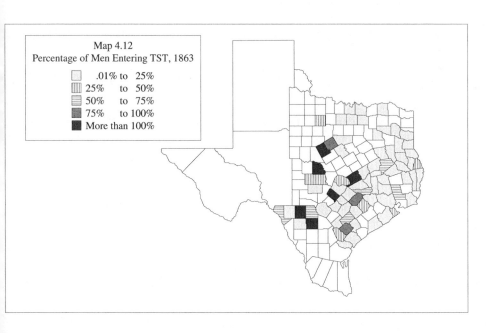

up to 300 (see also Map 4.12). Geographical analysis does not reveal any regional distinctions regarding the number of men per county that entered the state militia in 1863, however.

Statistical analysis reveals that several significant relationships exist between the number of men entering state service in 1863 and the economic characteristics of the counties they represented. The number of horses and milch cattle and livestock value each hold a significant relationship and correlate positively with the number of men entering state service in 1863. Furthermore, farm value, the amount of ginned cotton, and the total number of slaves also have significant relationships and correlate positively. Thus, throughout this tumultuous year, as Union forces made their assault down the Mississippi River and slowly severed the Confederacy, more men per county chose state service as the best agency to protect their economic interests. In fact, statistical analysis reveals that with one exception, no significant relationship exists between the economic interests of a county and the number or percentage of men, including transfers, entering Confederate service for 1863.[21]

Further analysis reveals that only thirteen counties sent men directly into the Confederate army in 1863. Of these, no county sent more than 110 men (Map 4.13). Furthermore, the majority of counties that did send men into the Confederate army that year sent only as many as 25 percent of the available men in the county (Map 4.14). Analysis does reveal, however, that many counties did have men transferred into the Confederate army (Map 4.15). Nevertheless, this did not significantly change the percentage of men per county entering the Confederate army in 1863.

In 1863, similar to 1861, no clear geographical pattern exists concerning the men who enlisted in the state militia. Nevertheless, these men represented primarily the wealthier horse and cattle counties, the wealthier cotton and slaveholding counties, and those counties where farm values tended to be higher. Thus, it cannot be concluded that this was a poor man's fight. Because the general welfare of the state was threatened from the course of war and the mounting Union victories, along with the continual Indian presence, all Texans, not just the poorer ones, sought to safeguard commercial interests through the state militia. When the initial shouts of war rang out, Texans offered themselves to the state militia. When Texas was severed from the Confederacy, Texans again more likely enlisted in the state militia. Thus,

21. The only exception to this is the number of horses and milch cattle held related to the percentage of men, including transfers, entering Confederate service.

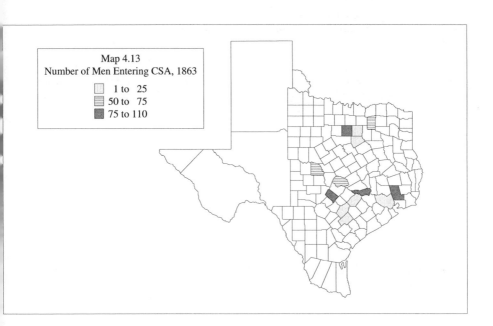

Map 4.13
Number of Men Entering CSA, 1863

1 to 25
50 to 75
75 to 110

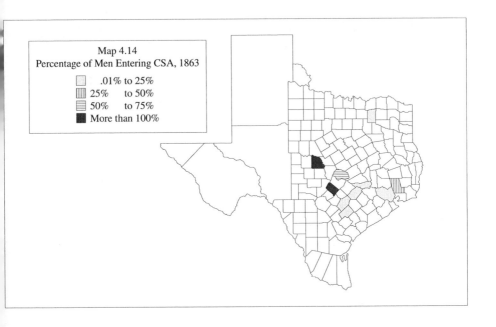

Map 4.14
Percentage of Men Entering CSA, 1863

.01% to 25%
25%   to 50%
50%   to 75%
More than 100%

during this sectional crisis, at its second most critical phase, the majority of Texans stood by the Lone Star State.

By the end 1863, the adjutant and inspector general acknowledged the great number of men in Texas being called into service by the Confederate government and claimed that the Confederate conscription law "has in a great measure destroyed the organization of the State Troops." In fact, there was widespread agreement on this point such that the adjutant and inspector general called for every man above the age of sixteen to be subject to state service, with an end to exemptions and substitutions. As research reveals, however, this sentiment was most likely an overexaggerated fear or a response to the high number and percentage of men entering Confederate service the previous year. Furthermore, at this point in the crisis, Governor Lubbock's view changed somewhat. He held no faith in the ability of the Confederate government to protect the frontier, much less offer adequate aid. In fact, in some cases he exempted men on the frontier from Confederate service so they could remain in the area and protect the frontier.[22]

The year 1863 was a time of transition for the Confederacy and Texas in this crisis. The Union took control of the Mississippi River, severing the Confederacy, and in Texas, Pendleton Murrah replaced Francis Lubbock as governor. In comparison, Governor Murrah was not as cooperative as Governor Lubbock in terms of dealing with the issue of conscripting men into Confederate service or transferring state troops into the Confederate army. Furthermore, in December 1863, the Texas legislature passed an act that gave the governor the power to keep the state militia in state service for another six months after their original time of duty expired. In this manner, many Texas troops were kept out of Confederate service to meet the needs of the state. Even if men were organized and then transferred into Confederate service, they could not leave the state unless specifically permitted by the governor. Governor Murrah would have ultimate power over these troops and could withdraw them from Confederate service or disband them at any time. Thus, the pattern of Texas politics in many cases proved to undermine Confederate needs.[23]

When Governor Murrah came to power, he was upset with the Texas legislature, the previous governor, and Gen. Edmund Kirby Smith over their lack of communication concerning the enlistment of troops. The problem, as

22. *Senate Journal of the Tenth Legislature Regular Session of the State of Texas,* 12–13, 16.

23. Albert Burton Moore, *Conscription and Conflict in the Confederacy,* 246–48; Yearns, *The Confederate Governors,* 208–10; Gammel, *Laws of Texas,* 5:689; Myers, "Relations of Governor Murrah," 16–17.

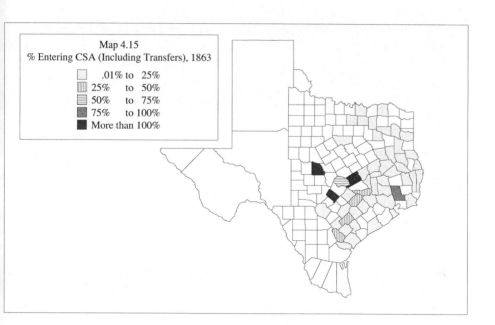

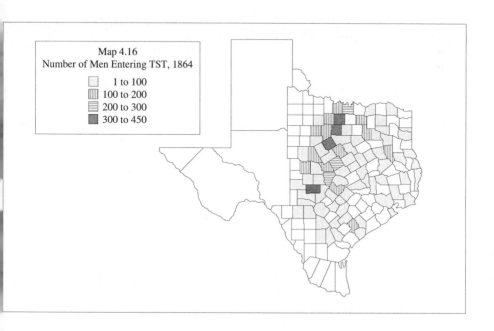

Murrah saw it, was that Texans were confused and upset over Confederate conscription practices. What bothered them is that when their initial stint in the state militia ended, they were often transferred into the Confederate army. This move was made without their consideration, and troops were left without the opportunity to decide whether they wanted to return to state service or actually serve in the Confederate army. In fact, as the war dragged on, there existed increasing incidents where enrolling officers, company captains, and citizens wrote to the governor or adjutant general, reminding them that the troops they raised were strictly for home protection and were not to be transferred into Confederate service or taken out of the state. For example, in 1863, L. Shultze, who had been elected as president of a citizen meeting in Gillespie County, wrote to Governor Lubbock. He reminded the governor that the mounted troops from Gillespie County were raised "for the only purpose of home protection against invasions of the Indians within the limits of Gillespie and contiguous County." He further assured the governor that the county would raise more men on the condition that the governor promise "that this Company shall never be ordered away from its County for any other purpose than home protection against invasions of the Indians." The citizens of Gillespie County believed this necessary "to protect and defend their country as well as the families and property of their fellow citizens of this County."[24]

Murrah, of course, believed that this policy would best serve Texas. He believed the state troops serving on the frontier to protect against Indian invasion would more than adequately protect Texas lives and property, promising "better protection against the peculiar warfare waged upon the frontier by the Indians than any plan heretofore adopted. . . . It seems to harmonize well with the habits, the peculiar interests and pursuits of the people of those counties."[25]

In 1864, as Texans continued to serve in the state militia to protect their material world, a shift occurred such that a larger number of men representing the poorer counties decided to enter the state militia. This shift is due partially to the passage of legislation to protect the frontier. In December 1863, the state legislature passed legislation, which became known as the Frontier Organization, requiring all persons in the frontier counties liable for military duty to be organized for the protection of the border. In January 1864, the

24. *Senate Journal of the Tenth Legislature First Called Session of the State of Texas,* 10; Yearns, *The Confederate Governors,* 210; Records of the Adjutant General: Muster Roll Collection, no. 452-1.
25. *Senate Journal of the Tenth Legislature First Called Session,* 17.

legislature also passed "An Act for the Defense of the State" that allowed Texans to be retained in the state militia. This legislation was a response to the progress of war and the Confederate government's neglect of western interests and was intended to secure the interests of Texas citizens. In turn, Texans gave their allegiance to the state by continuing to enlist in the state militia instead of the Confederate army. Map 4.16, "Number of Men Entering TST, 1864," reveals that counties in the frontier region of Texas more likely sent a larger number of men into the state militia in 1864. Of the counties that sent men into the state militia, 32 percent sent as many as one hundred men, and 15 percent sent as many as two hundred. Map 4.17, "Percentage of Men Entering TST, 1864," further reveals that the majority of frontier counties sent more than 50 percent of the available men in the county. Those counties with lower farm values, less corn production, lower amounts of ginned cotton, and fewer number of slaves more likely sent men directly into the state militia. Thus, as the war waged on and the fear of economic security increased, state service was seen as the best vehicle to protect those economic interests, especially for the less economically advantaged counties.[26]

On February 17, 1864, Confederate conscription policy again changed. This time all men between the ages of seventeen and fifty were subject to military duty. This new conscription law did not, however, have a major impact on the number and percentage of men entering Confederate service. Map 4.18, "Number of Men Entering CSA, 1864," reveals that eight counties sent as few as one to ten men into the Confederate army. The most men that any county sent during this year was no higher than seventy-five, and only three counties sent even that many. Furthermore, according to Map 4.19, "Percentage of Men Entering CSA, 1864," the vast number of counties that sent men into the Confederate army were located in the Gulf Coast region and sent only as many as 25 percent of the available men in the county. Statistical analysis reveals further that those counties that sent fewer and fewer men into Confederate service had more of a vested interest in horses and milch cattle and a higher total of livestock value. This is also true when considering the percentage of men entering the Confederate service and the percentage including transfers into Confederate service (Map 4.20).[27]

In 1864, the counties with a greater investment in horses and cattle sent fewer and fewer men into war. At the same time, a shift occurred such that the poorer counties sent men into the state militia. This holds especially true

26. Ralph Wooster, *Texas and Texans,* 105; David Paul Smith, "Conscription and Conflict on the Texas Frontier, 1863–1865," 251–53.
27. Gammel, *Laws of Texas,* 771–72.

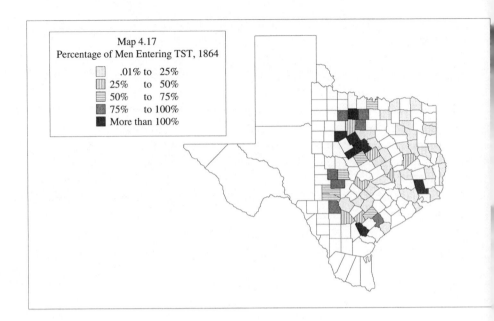

Map 4.17
Percentage of Men Entering TST, 1864

- .01% to 25%
- 25% to 50%
- 50% to 75%
- 75% to 100%
- More than 100%

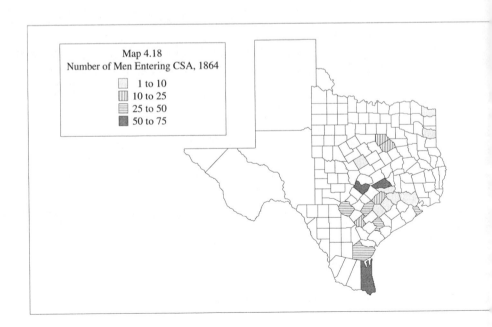

Map 4.18
Number of Men Entering CSA, 1864

- 1 to 10
- 10 to 25
- 25 to 50
- 50 to 75

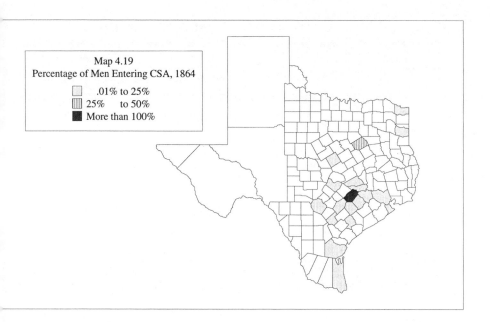

Map 4.19
Percentage of Men Entering CSA, 1864

.01% to 25%
25%   to 50%
More than 100%

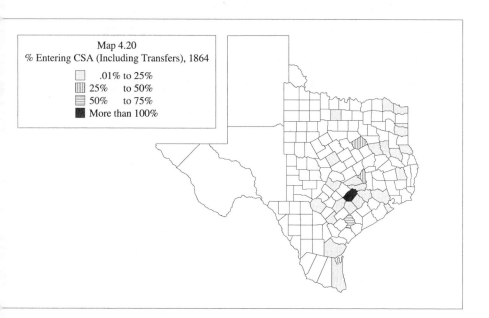

Map 4.20
% Entering CSA (Including Transfers), 1864

.01% to 25%
25%   to 50%
50%   to 75%
More than 100%

for the counties with lower farm values, corn production, cotton production, and numbers of slaves. Thus, for 1864, evidence does suggest that the poorer counties sent more men to fight. Although in some cases this might have been a rich man's war and a poor man's fight, at the most critical stages in 1861 and 1863, it was a unified fight for the Lone Star State. The cords of capitalism tied class lines, commercial interests, and the desire for economic security together.

From the onset of the Civil War, contention existed between Texas and Richmond, especially as Confederate authorities traveled through Texas to raise regiments "without the intervention or cognizance of state authorities." By 1865, opposition to Confederate enlistment was so strong that the Confederate forces in Texas were in a state of disintegration. An analysis of the men going off to fight sheds light on this conflict. Throughout the Civil War, a pattern emerged showing that men chose to enter the state militia instead of the Confederate army. In the initial stages of war, when men had a choice concerning whether to enlist in the service of the state or the Confederacy, men chose state service. They did so to protect their families and provide economic security. Moreover, at the second most critical stage, the severing of the Confederacy by Union forces, men again chose to enter state rather than Confederate service. The pattern of military enlistment and the Indian crisis in Texas jointly served to establish a separate political and economic identity for Texas. These developments clearly did not bode well for the Confederate war effort. This pattern of separation became more evident after 1863 as Texas moved beyond defining and establishing a separate identity. In the face of an encroaching Confederate government, Texas advanced to secure a separate identity by protecting and promoting vital economic interests.[28]

28. *Senate Journal of the Ninth Legislature,* 28. See the Note on Sources regarding 1865 enlistment.

PART III

Securing a
Separate Identity

CHAPTER 5

The Production and Supply of Necessary Material

Texas Institutions, Cloth, Salt, and Iron

On Wednesday, November 4, 1863, Texas governor Francis R. Lubbock stood at the Speaker's stand in the House of Representatives and delivered a message before the joint legislature. "Under the Providence of God," Lubbock told fellow politicians, "our State has been blessed with genial sessions, uninterrupted good health and prosperity." He recounted "the superabundance of our harvests," the "abundance of forage and meat," and the "unparalleled bravery of her noble sons" defending the state. Lubbock believed in the prominence of the Lone Star State and articulated that vision to fellow politicians. As he spoke, however, Lubbock believed that the testing time had arrived. The enemy lurked closer to the border than ever before. Due to the fall of Vicksburg, Texas had to "contend alone against the numerous armies of the enemy," and Lubbock counseled politicians to take all necessary measures for the economic benefit and advancement of the state.[1]

The dilemma politicians confronted revolved around the dissension about securing the financial condition of the state, caring for the needs of Texas citizens, and providing for the interests of the Confederacy. These demands, along with outside pressures, made control of the state penitentiary and its distribution of cloth one of the paramount issues of the tenth legislature. Similarly, debates over the foundry, cap factory, and other material products such as salt and iron are revealing. In these matters, the Texas legislature voted foremost to support the welfare of the citizenry; second, the financial condition of the state; and third, the interests of the Confederacy. The critical issue of state control over institutions and resources reveals that Texas's political allegiance lay firmly with the state for the support of the common citizen. Whereas the needs of both the common man and the Confederate

---

1. *House Journal of the Tenth Legislature Regular Session of the State of Texas,* 8–10.

war effort seemed paramount, Texas politicians cast their loyalty to the citizens of Texas over the Confederacy. By doing so, they worked to secure a separate identity from that of other Southern states. That separate identity conflicted with larger Confederate needs, hindering the South's ability to wage a successful war and undermining the establishment of a separate nation.[2]

In order to ensure the economic founding of this new nation, it became imperative to control the Mississippi River; it was the backbone of the Confederacy. It served as a major pipeline for Confederate trade with England and France, and was militarily important by protecting production. The Union began its assault on this strategic point in 1861 with the goal of capturing Vicksburg and Port Hudson. After two long years of fighting for the Mississippi River, assaults on Vicksburg began in May 1863 under the command of Ulysses S. Grant. The Union's initial assault on Vicksburg, resulting in thousands of casualties, met with failure, forcing the Union to begin a siege on the town. Grant speculated that the siege of Vicksburg would last no longer than one week. Confederate troops, however, put up a valiant defense that extended the conflict. Nevertheless, they could not match Grant's seventy-seven thousand troops, and the Union succeeded in taking Vicksburg on July 4, 1863. The victory gave the Union full control of the Mississippi River, severing the Confederacy.[3]

Many individuals believed that the fall of Vicksburg reflected Richmond's neglect of the western territory, and politicians in the trans-Mississippi West whispered words of secession from the Confederacy. Governor Rector of Arkansas issued a proclamation stating, "Arkansas lost, abandoned, subjugated, is not Arkansas as she entered the Confederate Government. Nor will she remain Arkansas a Confederate State, desolated as a wilderness." Moreover, a real fear existed in some minds at this stage in the crisis that Texas might secede from the Confederacy. Leading politicians pondered Texas's ability to furnish men and material for its own defense and whether the Lone Star State would seek to extend its borders. "The danger," many feared, "is that Texas may seek to make her own terms for their own safety, in a revival of her favorite and ancient idea of separate nationality." Such ruminations caught the attention of Richmond officials who constantly had to be reassured that no sectional or separatist spirit existed in the region.

2. *Senate Journal of the Tenth Legislature Second Called Session of the State of Texas,* 65–66, 72, 90; *House Journal of the Tenth Legislature Second Called Session of the State of Texas,* 140, 142.

3. Samuel Carter III, *The Final Fortress: The Campaign for Vicksburg, 1862–1863;* David G. Martin, *The Vicksburg Campaign;* Rains, *Six Decades in Texas.*

Nevertheless, Richmond considered only one alternative: strengthening the Trans-Mississippi Department.[4]

The Trans-Mississippi Department was officially constituted on May 26, 1862. Initially established as a military authority, command devolved to Brig. Gen. Paul O. Hebert, a Democrat and former governor of Louisiana. Two months later, Maj. Gen. Theophilus H. Holmes succeeded Hebert. Under Hebert and Holmes, the Confederate government constantly shuffled and divided the western states into separate departments, districts, and subdistricts. No formal or distinct structure of government emerged to govern this region separate from Richmond until 1863. When Vicksburg fell into Union hands, cutting communications between Richmond and the West, the Confederacy organized the western states of Missouri, Arkansas, Louisiana, and Texas and the Indian Territory in the Trans-Mississippi Department under the command of Gen. Edmund Kirby Smith. President Davis appointed Kirby Smith, a West Point graduate, Mexican War veteran, and moderate antisecessionist, to lead the department in February 1863. Upon appointment, Kirby Smith established his headquarters at Alexandria, Louisiana. He created several bureaus as an extension of this Confederate military department, including an Ordnance Bureau, Subsistence Bureau, and Quartermaster Bureau. By placing Kirby Smith in charge of all operations in the West and allowing him to locate his government agency in Louisiana, Richmond acknowledged that it could no longer govern the western territory. Kirby Smith's reorganization of the Trans-Mississippi Department signaled the establishment of an official structure for governing the states west of the Mississippi, and he assumed the function of both the president and the cabinet.[5]

Viewing the situation in the trans-Mississippi West as perilous, Kirby Smith believed that only a united political effort could preserve property and independence. The fall of Vicksburg cut the trans-Mississippi off from Richmond with little to no communication getting through, leaving the department "thrown entirely upon its own resources." Kirby Smith told Gen. Samuel Cooper that unless granted extraordinary powers, he would be useless as a department commander. Thus, he could not wait for approval from Richmond and instead called a meeting of western governors, realizing that he needed their support and approval to assume greater responsibility. As

---

4. Letter to Governor H. Flanagin, July 25, 1863, in *War of the Rebellion,* 22:945–46; Thomas C. Reynolds to Hon. James A. Seddon, July 20, 1863, in ibid., 935.

5. Owsley, *State Rights; War of the Rebellion,* 9:713, 15:1, 1005, 22:798; Florence E. Holladay, "The Powers of the Commander of the Confederate Trans-Mississippi Department, 1863–1865," 279.

a result of the isolation and in response to its incorporation into the Trans-Mississippi Department, Texas officials agreed to meet with other leading politicians from Louisiana, Arkansas, and Missouri in Marshall, Texas, for the purpose of making known to President Davis "the true condition of the country." At this August 15, 1863, meeting, Governor Francis Lubbock, Williamson S. Oldham, Pendleton Murrah, and Maj. Guy M. Bryan represented Texas. Col. T. C. Manning, C. J. Merrick, and Albert Voorhies represented Louisiana while Governor Moore remained busy with an impending invasion. Arkansas sent the Honorable Robert W. Johnson, C. B. Mitchell, and W. K. Patterson, and Governor Thomas C. Reynolds represented Missouri. Governor Lubbock served as chairman, and W. K. Patterson served as secretary. At the conference, Kirby Smith first appeared hesitant to assume functions not directly prescribed to him. The desperate conditions and low morale of the western states that talked about secession from the Confederacy, however, forced him to move toward improved organization. He did receive approval from Richmond for the governors' conference, but Richmond's acknowledgment came after he had already organized the gathering.[6]

Texas politicians at the conference discussed the situation of the western Confederacy, and debated placing the control of state resources in the hands of Kirby Smith. The group dealt with additional issues such as the spread of disloyalty, questions of currency and the securing of cotton, foreign relations with French and Mexican officials in Mexico, and arms and supplies. These issues, however, existed as secondary concerns to the overall relationship between the Trans-Mississippi Department and individual states. The conference legitimated Kirby Smith's rule by claiming that the safety of the people necessitated he assume the power and prerogatives of the president and his subordinates. Nevertheless, state politicians voiced concern over the clash between civil and military authority. Therefore, under direction of Governor Lubbock, the conference limited Kirby Smith's authority by stating that it could not exceed the powers of the state. Lubbock's insistence on this matter fell well within the bounds of Confederate law. The Confederate Congress resolved, under suggestion from Texas senator Williamson S. Oldham, that the War Department and military authority be subordinate

6. Circular from Edmund Kirby Smith to the People of Arkansas, Louisiana, and Texas, in *War of the Rebellion,* 22:995, 1005; Edmund Kirby Smith to Gen. S. Cooper, July 28, 1863, in *War of the Rebellion,* 22:949; *Senate Journal of the Tenth Legislature Regular Session,* 8; *House Journal of the Ninth Legislature,* 29–30; J. A. Seddon to Gen. E. Kirby Smith, in *War of the Rebellion,* 22:952–53; Holladay, "Powers of the Commander," 282–83.

to state civil authority. In September 1862, the Confederate Congress ruled that the state's legal system took precedence over military authority. Military authority was virtually powerless to restrict civil-court rulings, and the Confederate Congress declared that commands interfering with the "full exercise of the jurisdiction of such civil judicial tribunals are illegal, unauthorized, and void." Both President Davis and Secretary of War James Seddon acknowledged the difficulty between civil and military authority. Davis told Kirby Smith that he not only had a military problem, but also a political problem involved in his command.[7]

Neither Davis nor Seddon, however, offered Kirby Smith any concrete advice or relayed any specific instructions to deal with the crisis. Seddon suggested only that he "exercise powers of civil administration" by combining both civil and military authority through established bureaus of the Trans-Mississippi Department. However, the governmental structure established under Kirby Smith limited his authority. Furthermore, the Texas legislative Committee on Confederate Relations acknowledged the action of the governors' conference and chose to yield to Governor Lubbock's decision regarding civil authority, and the Texas legislature decided it unnecessary to act further on relations at this point. Although Kirby Smith's appointment received verbal approval from western states and Richmond officials, the governors' conference was not legally binding, and the Texas state government began the process of undermining his authority.[8]

Each state had its needs as did the Trans-Mississippi Department, and the congruity of these needs fostered competition between Texas and the department. Competition eroded relations between these two governmental bodies as each guarded and promoted their own economic interests. Strained relations became apparent when Kirby Smith established the Ordnance, Subsistence, and Quartermaster Bureaus to procure the necessities of war.

The Ordnance Bureau fell under the command of Major Rhett, making him responsible for controlling the location of foundries, contracting with arms manufacturers, and requisitioning from arms and ordnance stores. The bureau's office, however, was located in Marshall, Texas, away from Rhett who served on Kirby Smith's staff in Louisiana. Thus, the critical daily operations, the inspection of returns, and the allocation of money fell under the direction of Maj. Gen. Benjamin Huger who had previously served as chief ordnance officer under Gen. Winfield Scott in the Mexican War.

7. *Senate Journal of the Tenth Legislature Regular Session,* 172–75; *JCCSA,* 2:325–26; *War of the Rebellion,* 22:925–27; Holladay, "Powers of the Commander," 289.

8. Ibid.; *House Journal of the Ninth Legislature,* 30; *Senate Journal of the Tenth Legislature Regular Session,* 173–80.

The Subsistence Bureau was originally located at Shreveport, Louisiana, until May 1864 and then located at Marshall, Texas, under the direction of Maj. W. B. Blair. The Subsistence Bureau was divided into four districts with agents who were given the power of impressment where needed.

The Quartermaster Bureau supplied virtually all the necessities, including supplies, clothing, camp and garrison equipment, horses, fuel, forage, straw, and more. Kirby Smith appointed Lt. Col. L. W. O'Bannon as head quartermaster to oversee these duties. Although authority theoretically rested with Kirby Smith, O'Bannon supervised the main center for all paperwork and details at his headquarters in Marshall.[9]

In the Trans-Mississippi Department, the head quartermaster and field purchasing officers theoretically coordinated efforts to procure the necessities of war. Arkansas, Louisiana, and Texas each had a field officer. Each state, though, worked to secure their own interests, which in turn fostered competition among purchasing officers. Such competition hindered the effectual working of the Trans-Mississippi Department, and Richmond ordered the field officers not to compete with each other over obtaining supplies. Such a directive points to the complexity of the problem. Furthermore, staff members quickly realized that the pattern of Texas politics potentially threatened the interests of the Trans-Mississippi Department. In many cases, staff members circumvented Kirby Smith's authority by appealing directly to Texas officials for the production and supply of necessary material. Such circumvention speaks to the inadequate bureaucratic machinery that Kirby Smith developed and to the necessity of Texas institutions for the success of the Confederacy. Texas politicians, however, were unwilling to comply with the needs of the Trans-Mississippi Department.[10]

To be sure, Texas politicians worked to secure the Lone Star State's interests by supporting state institutions and the development of natural resources through the promotion of manufacturing. Conflict between Texas and the Trans-Mississippi Department appeared most evident in the production and supply of cloth. The production and supply of salt and iron also shed light on this conflict to some extent. Texas politicians directed their attention to the production and distribution of these materials, and the Texas legislature worked to pass legislation to secure the interests of the state and its citizens

9. *War of the Rebellion,* 22:804, 991, 1066; James L. Nichols, "Confederate Quartermaster Operations in the Trans-Mississippi Department," 4–6; Holladay, "Powers of the Commander," 334–35.

10. Nichols, "Confederate Quartermaster Operations," 12; Robert Creuzbaur to Phenis De Cordova, Nov. 16, 1863, Records of the Texas Military Board, RG 2-10/304, TSL.

over the military needs of the Trans-Mississippi Department. Moreover, Texas politicians played the role of mediator in instances of conflict within state institutions and between state institutions and the Trans-Mississippi Department. At times, these issues received intense debate in the legislature that produced political gridlock. Nevertheless, the politicians continually pushed forward to establish a stable policy regarding the production and distribution of these resources. As such, a united political front emerged to provide for the economic security of the citizens and state. This, in turn, secured Texas's separate identity from that of other Southern states.

This process appeared most evident in the strife between the Texas State Penitentiary, the leading producer of cloth west of the Mississippi River, and the Trans-Mississippi Department. Operations for collecting and distributing clothing for the Trans-Mississippi Department fell under the command of Maj. W. H. Haynes as part of the Quartermaster Bureau. Haynes attempted to organize the subdistricts within the department to carry out the operations effectively, thus further extending the department's authority and control. Clothing operations in the Trans-Mississippi Department, though, were hindered from the outset as Texas politicians sought to serve the interests of Texas's indigent families and soldiers' dependents before considering the department's military needs.[11]

The Trans-Mississippi Department relied heavily upon Texas and the state's penitentiary to supply the majority of its clothing needs. The desire of Texas politicians to secure the economic well-being of the Lone Star State and its citizens ahead of the Trans-Mississippi Department, however, became apparent in the protection, operation, and expansion of the Texas State Penitentiary. The penitentiary was created in 1846 in Huntsville, Texas; the same year, funds were collected to erect a public building in the center of the town, ensuring Huntsville as the choice for county seat in Walker County. Construction on the state penitentiary took three years and was completed in October 1849. It operated under the financial direction of John S. Besser.[12]

The Texas State Penitentiary proved vital to Texas's economic welfare, and Governor Lubbock sought to protect the institution from potential hazards. The desire to protect the penitentiary and ensure adequate supply to Texas citizens and soldiers often caused conflict with military authorities in the Trans-Mississippi Department. In 1863, for example, both General Holmes and Kirby Smith requested control of the Texas State Penitentiary.

11. *War of the Rebellion,* 22:870; Nichols, "Confederate Quartermaster Operations," 31–32.
12. Dan Ferguson, "Austin College in Huntsville," 387.

Lubbock gave Holmes control of the quartermasters in Texas, but could not give control of the penitentiary to Holmes or to Kirby Smith. The Texas legislature forbade the governor to undertake such action, exercising full authority over state institutions. Thus, Holmes had to settle for only controlling the distribution of goods to the military instead of exercising full authority over both production and distribution. In another instance, General Magruder approached Governor Lubbock with a request to use the state penitentiary as a place of confinement for prisoners of war. Lubbock agreed on the condition that the use not "impair the material interests of the institution." Soon after, Union prisoners of war arrived, but Lubbock changed his mind and demanded that Brigadier General Scurry remove the prisoners. Five months later, Magruder presented the same request to Lubbock. This time, the governor took a firm stance and objected, refusing to place the sole manufactory of cloth in jeopardy. It was critical that Texas safeguard the state penitentiary, for the gross earnings of the institution from December 1, 1861, to August 31, 1863, totaled $1,174,439.07. From that amount, the state treasury received $800,000. Governor Lubbock remarked that "the penitentiary has been managed with consummate ability and has proved of incalculable benefit to our Army." He stressed the importance of the penitentiary and suggested that the legislature do everything in its power to extend the usefulness of the institution. The governor's decision to protect the state penitentiary reflected a larger dedication of political support for state institutions. At times, this met with challenge, but the determined effort of state politicians to support the citizenry underlay political action to ensure economic and institutional security.[13]

The implementation of such security found expression through legislative action regarding the distribution of cloth from the state penitentiary and protection of the welfare of Texas citizens. These two issues became deeply intertwined in the political process, often resulting in extensive debate. Yet, politicians worked to mediate the best interests of both the penitentiary and the needs of the citizenry. Legislative compromise and the formation of a concrete policy concerning the distribution of cloth and the economic well-being of the citizenry revealed the fundamental values of Texas politicians and society in general. Distributing cloth from the state penitentiary evolved into a paramount issue for Texas politicians. As late as September 1863,

---

13. Lubbock did give Holmes control of the goods from the penitentiary and suggested that Captain Wharton and General Magruder direct their requisitions for goods to him (Records of the Texas State Penitentiary, RG 022-1, TSL; *House Journal of the Ninth Legislature*, 14; *Senate Journal of the Tenth Legislature Regular Session*, 18–19).

the penitentiary did not have a full board of businessmen to direct the institution. It also operated without a set procedure to deposit money into the state treasury or without proper authority to hire additional men for service. Furthermore, counties often requested that Governor Lubbock intervene in the distribution process to aid Confederate soldiers. For example, in August 1863, the chief justice of Washington County wrote to Lubbock requesting a sufficient amount of cloth to clothe each man in the Confederate army from Washington County stationed west of the Mississippi River. Governor Lubbock replied that the institution did not have the capacity to supply the needs of both the army and the community. Lubbock did reassure the chief justice that he would look into whether the quartermasters in the department were supplying Texas troops west of the Mississippi. If they were not, he replied, "I will see that they are to the extent of my ability." When individual requests for cloth came into Lubbock's office, the governor stood by his convictions. He chose not to interfere with the distribution process, and he upheld the power of the penitentiary's officers to distribute cloth to individual counties, keeping in mind the needs of indigent families, dependent families of Texas soldiers, and state troops. Without set procedures, though, it became necessary for the legislature to address guidelines and sales for the penitentiary.[14]

The Texas legislature clearly defined its priority regarding the distribution of cloth. It proposed that the penitentiary distribute cloth to each county that requested it, with each county paying a fixed price. The county then had the responsibility of distributing the cloth and goods to dependents and indigent families. Surplus cloth from the penitentiary would only then be sold to the army at a price not too exorbitant. Officials at the state penitentiary agreed with the proposition. This informal policy, though, was merely a suggestion from the legislature, and in its regular session, the tenth legislature did not officially settle the matter through legislation nor did it establish pricing guidelines for the state institution.[15]

Therefore, without waiting for official legislative approval, penitentiary officials established prices and specific guidelines for distribution. They determined that 150,000 yards of cotton fabric would be furnished semi-annually. This cloth would be apportioned among the counties of the state

14. John S. Besser to Maj. C. R. Johns, Sept. 14, 1863, Records of the Texas State Penitentiary, R 022-1, TSL; Francis Lubbock to Chief Justice of County Commissioners of Washington County, Texas, Aug. 25, 1863, ibid.; Lubbock to A. G. Dickinson, Jan. 24, 1863, ibid.; and Lubbock to N. Kavanaugh, Sept. 5, 1863, ibid.

15. S. B. Hendricks to Pendleton Murrah, Dec. 22, 1863, ibid.; S. B. Hendricks to Pendleton Murrah, Dec. 28, 1863, ibid.

under the direction of the county courts. Indigent families stood at the top of the list to receive cloth. The officials left the duty of determining the number of indigent families to the comptroller. After the comptroller made his report to the penitentiary, the counties had the responsibility of filing for their requisitions of cloth, and orders were processed in the order received.[16]

Penitentiary officials also established set prices for its cloth (per yardage). The institution charged $2.80 for osnaburgs; $3.00 for cotton jeans; $5.50 for white plains; $6.00 for white kersey; and $6.00 for sheep's gray. These prices were dramatically higher than those established before the war. The new pricing policy by the state penitentiary brought an uproar from some counties, especially because the new procedures and prices were deemed retroactive. Galveston County residents and officials wrote to the state penitentiary complaining that the new policy was an injustice to the indigent and dependent families of Texas, and demanded that the penitentiary meet those individual requisitions already filed. In addition, Galveston County officials complained about the inequity in the distribution of cloth, claiming that their county had not received an allotment, whereas Harris County would receive a second shipment shortly. Penitentiary officials replied to Honorable James Pope Cole of Galveston in a most gracious manner, simply outlining the new procedure and prices, requesting that Cole follow proper channels.[17]

Sterling Hendricks, the acting financial agent of the penitentiary, wrote to Governor Pendleton Murrah on the matter and supported the present guidelines and pricing, but also had critical words for the state legislature that had failed to enact any concrete legislation regarding the state penitentiary. Because the legislature had "utterly failed to pass any law on the subject," Hendricks assumed that politicians endorsed the present distribution and pricing guidelines. From Hendricks's perspective, the new policy found satisfaction across the state with the exception of Galveston County. Hendricks did not think it wise to abolish the new guidelines and price structure given Galveston County's complaint and remarked, "It may be right that they [Galveston County] should control this Institution and the State but we have not been able to view it in that light." Hendricks did say that he would comply with new laws if the legislature so enacted, but until that time, he thought it expedient that the present guidelines remain in effect. Complaints about price and procedure were rare, however, and those counties that did

16. S. B. Hendricks to Pendleton Murrah, Jan. 4, 1864, ibid.
17. Circular, Financial Agents Office, Huntsville, Jan. 20, 1864, ibid.; S. B. Hendricks to Hon. J. P. Cole, Mar. 29, May 16, 1864, ibid. Previous prices were $0.80 for osnaburgs, $1.00 for twilled cotton, $2.50 for plain woolens, and $3.00 for twilled woolens and sheep's gray. See ibid., RG 022-4.

complain failed to understand the endeavor to organize and advance state institutions for the benefit of the people. Although not everyone would be satisfied, officials sought the greater good of the state and worked to organize state institutions to operate in the most effective manner.[18]

When the tenth legislature met again in its first called session in May 1864, Governor Murrah had stern words for his fellow politicians regarding operations of the institution. He told the congressmen that the people expected more leadership from them and that they should direct their interests to the welfare of the citizenry and the interests of the state. In ordinary times, he remarked, this might not be such a critical issue. Given the present crisis, however, with both the army and the general population clamoring for fabric and products, there needed to be an established structure of authority and set guidelines for product distribution. For Murrah, this was an especially critical issue because the state penitentiary operated without state financial assistance, and given the financial crisis of the state and the Confederacy, if the state penitentiary could not continue to support itself independently, it would have to decrease or even cease operations.[19]

The Senate and House of Representatives heeded Murrah's words and instructed the respective committees on the penitentiary to consider his message. Immediately thereafter, the House considered a bill to provide for the distribution of cloth manufactured at the penitentiary. The proposed bill gave the penitentiary's financial agent the responsibility for setting aside the entitled amount of cloth for each county and notifying the chief justice of each county when the cloth became ready for distribution. The bill also provided for the adequate clothing of inmates and allowed officers and guards to purchase cloth for themselves at the price sold to the Confederate army, or market value. This stipulation on the price ensured the cheapest cost to them. Furthermore, the bill allowed for the contracting of cloth by private individuals with the financial agent responsible for advertising the reception of sealed bids. Private distributors were required to submit proposals stating the items they intended to furnish, the amount of each item, when they planned to deliver, and the price they would charge. The contract for distribution would go to the lowest bidder who was able to provide sufficient security for distribution. The proceeds from contracting were then to be deposited

18. S. B. Hendricks to Pendleton Murrah, July 4, 1864, ibid., RG 022-1; Hon. J. P. Cole to S. B. Hendricks, Mar. 24, 1864, ibid. Hendricks also served Panola and Harrison Counties in the Ninth Texas Legislature and was a merchant and farmer in Harrison County. Pendleton Murrah replaced Francis Lubbock as governor in Nov. 1863 when Lubbock decided not to run for reelection.

19. *Senate Journal of the Tenth Legislature First Called Session,* 19–21.

into the state treasury once a month. Thus, Texas politicians grappled not only with the issue of cloth, but also with the financial condition of the state, and they worked toward securing financial stability and independence from the Confederacy.[20]

The House adjourned its morning session on May 21 without deciding on the bill. In the afternoon session, Constantine W. Buckley, representing Matagorda, Wharton, and Fort Bend Counties, offered an amendment to the bill requiring county courts to "distribute the cloth to the most needy upon the indigent list of their respective counties in such quantities as their necessities require." Thereafter, the House of Representatives passed the bill "to provide for the distribution of cloth made at the Texas State Penitentiary." The bill was then sent to the Senate where the Finance Committee debated it for one week before the Senate passed it.[21]

The legislation to provide for the distribution of cloth from the state penitentiary coincided with Governor Murrah's desire that an adequate plan exist to support both the state treasury and the indigent families in Texas. Murrah, however, pressed for more action, wanting the legislature to set aside a predetermined amount of cloth to support indigent families and dependents of Texas soldiers. Therefore, intertwined with the issue of proper distribution guidelines lay the critical issue of the citizens' welfare, a matter that the tenth legislature devoted full attention to in each session.[22]

In its regular session, both the Senate and House of Representatives addressed cloth distribution. On November 10, 1863, Washington and Fayette County representative M. W. Baker introduced to the House of Representatives a bill "to regulate the distribution of cloth manufactured at the State Penitentiary among the families of soldiers in the Confederate Army." Baker's bill was referred to the Committee on the Penitentiary. In the interim, the Senate passed a joint resolution concerning the dispersal of cloth at the state penitentiary and informed the House of its action. That same day, December 2, 1863, the House took up the Senate's resolution. The House read the resolution and then referred it to the Committee on the Penitentiary for further deliberation. In the meantime, the Senate informed the House of Representatives that it had taken further action by passing a bill to regulate the distribution of cloth. Though both branches of the legislature

20. Ibid., 38; *House Journal of the Tenth Legislature First Called Session,* 134, 167–70.

21. *Senate Journal of the Tenth Legislature First Called Session,* 64, 71, 172; *House Journal of the Tenth Legislature First Called Session,* 207, 216.

22. *Senate Journal of the Tenth Legislature Second Called Session,* 12–13.

addressed the issue, politicians failed to produce a final measure for cloth distribution.[23]

Thus, as it stood, county courts operated with full legislative authority to distribute cloth to indigent families as they so determined. Governor Lubbock vehemently upheld the power of county courts to determine the distribution of cloth. For example, in February 1863, a fire destroyed the premises of Mr. Wells of Walker County. Wells appealed to Lubbock for cloth from the penitentiary. Lubbock responded by stating that his criteria for cloth did not meet the requirements for indigent families. Lubbock, however, did place the final decision in the hands of county officials. If the county found that Wells's unique situation classified him to receive cloth from the penitentiary, then the county could present its requisition to the penitentiary and it would be filled. By referring such matters back to the county courts, the governor strengthened the power of county officials, which in turn harnessed the loyalty of the citizenry by meeting their needs.[24]

Nevertheless, the state legislature still needed to produce legislation to secure this process. In its first called session, the matter again received legislators' attention. On May 23, 1864, the House of Representatives debated and passed a bill for distributing cloth to the indigent families of Texas. The Senate received notice of the House's action and debated the bill; after one reading, it was referred to the Finance Committee. The bill, however, did not make it out of the committee, and again the legislature adjourned its session without passing effective legislation for distributing cloth to indigent families and the dependents of Texas soldiers.[25]

Governor Murrah called the tenth legislature into session again in October 1864 to deal with this vital issue. By this time in the war, the demand for clothing the army had increased. Richmond officials, Trans-Mississippi Department authorities, and military leaders in Texas all wished to receive supplies from the state penitentiary. Governor Murrah insisted, however, that priority be given first to indigent families, second to dependents of state soldiers, and third to state troops—over the needs of the Trans-Mississippi Department and the remainder of the Confederacy. He appeared unwilling to comply with Confederate needs because the Confederate government already owed Texas a minimum of $1 million for goods sold from the peni-

23. *Senate Journal of the Tenth Legislature Regular Session,* 118; *House Journal of the Tenth Legislature Regular Session,* 80, 198, 204–5, 216–17.

24. Francis Lubbock to the County Court of Walker County, Texas, Feb. 6, 1863, Records of the Texas State Penitentiary, RG 022-1, TSL.

25. *House Journal of the Tenth Legislature First Called Session,* 171, 174; *Senate Journal of the Tenth Legislature First Called Session,* 71, 83.

tentiary. Politicians made efforts to recover the unpaid debt, but Richmond could make only hollow promises. Therefore, the governor instructed the Texas legislature to meet first the needs of its constituents.[26]

In its second called session, the legislature gave substantial attention to the issue of cloth distribution. Of specific concern to politicians was the amount of cloth set aside for distribution to indigent families and soldiers' dependents. On November 5, 1864, the Senate debated specifics of a House bill to regulate the dispersal of cloth and thread. The bill allotted 1 million yards of cloth for distribution to the counties for sale for the purchase of supplies. The state charged $1.80 per yard for cloth, and the bill entitled county courts to levy an additional tax upon this amount, having total discretion over the sale of distributed cloth. Several amendments were offered to substitute this amount, ranging from four hundred thousand to eight hundred thousand yards of cloth. The Senate finally agreed on six hundred thousand yards of cloth. In this debate, the Senate agreed to sell surplus cloth to the Confederate States, with the proceeds going to counties that did not signify a willingness to receive their allotment of cloth. In this way, politicians worked to ensure that the counties of Texas would materially or financially benefit from the productivity of the penitentiary. The Senate legislated further to ensure that those counties that had not been able to receive their quota of cloth did so, and placed this responsibility in the hands of the superintendent and directors of the penitentiary. Their desire to provide adequately for state interests superseded the needs of the Confederacy.[27]

Not all Senate members, however, agreed to this proposition. The Senate Committee on State Affairs gave a long report discouraging passage of the House bill. Pryor Lea, chairman of the committee, reported that the House bill endangered the financial stability of the state. The working assumption of the House bill was that the products of the penitentiary would be specifically divided among the county courts for distribution. The committee disagreed with this plan due to the poor financial condition of the state, suggesting that more attention be given to selling the products, mainly cloth, to the Confederate States, where the proceeds would then go into the state treasury. The committee then offered a substitute bill for regulating the dispersal of cloth from the penitentiary.[28]

Consequently, the Senate again debated various sections of the bill on

26. *Senate Journal of the Tenth Legislature Second Called Session,* 7, 13–14.
27. *House Journal of the Tenth Legislature Second Called Session,* 129–30; *Senate Journal of the Tenth Legislature Second Called Session,* 45–49.
28. *Senate Journal of the Tenth Legislature Second Called Session,* 52–57.

November 9, 1864. Spencer Ford, representing Gonzales, Guadalupe, and Caldwell Counties, offered an amendment to the first four sections of the bill. His amendment stipulated that six hundred thousand yards of cloth be set aside and sold by the financial agent of the penitentiary in the city of Houston. The agent had the responsibility of selling this allotment by auction, to the highest bidder. After paying for transportation costs, the agent was to take the proceeds and directly deposit them into the state treasury. The money was then to be distributed to the county courts for allocation to indigent families and dependents of Texas soldiers. The third section of the bill, so amended by Ford, stipulated that nothing in this process should undermine or interfere with the original amount of cloth so allocated to the counties or the counties' ability to sell that original amount of cloth, provided that the subsistence, material, and labor needs of the state penitentiary were continually met. The amendments offered by Ford were laid on the table by a vote of twelve to ten in order that additional amendments could be offered. Immediately, Edward R. Hord moved to amend Section 1 of the bill so as to allow the county courts to control the distribution process. A move was made to lay this on the table, losing by one vote. A vote was then taken on whether to adopt Hord's amendment, and it lost by a vote of twelve to eleven. After this vote, Mr. Guinn offered to amend the bill to stipulate that "in no case shall the cloth be sold or bartered at less than its market value." A move was made to lay this on the table, yet failed to do so by a vote of twelve to eleven.[29]

The amount of political disagreement over the committee's no-pass recommendation forced the Committee on State Affairs to consider the bill again. This time, the committee suggested that the bill pass with the stipulation that if the chief justice of a county did not notify the financial agent of the penitentiary within ninety days of the county's need for cloth, then that county would not benefit from this act. The Senate passed the bill regulating the distribution of cloth, but voted down distributing cloth directly to proposed beneficiaries, and the House reported that it concurred with the Senate version of the bill.[30]

The House passed the Senate version of the bill on November 13, 1864. The final version of "An Act to Provide More Effectually for the Support and Maintenance of the Indigent Families and Dependents of Texas Soldiers" allotted 600,000 yards of cloth annually for their support, far above the 150,000 yards established by the penitentiary. The penitentiary distributed this cloth to the county, which in turn could keep and distribute the material

29. Ibid., 59–61.
30. Ibid., 90.

or use it to purchase supplies. The comptroller was obligated to provide the financial agent with a list of the indigent families, and responsibility fell to the county courts to obtain the cloth from the financial agent. Those counties that did want cloth had ninety days, as stipulated in "An Act Concerning the Distribution of Cloth from the Penitentiary," for the chief justice of the county to notify the financial agent. The bill also established that excess cloth be sold to the Confederate States, at no less than market value, with the proceeds distributed to various counties. Thus, those counties that did not request cloth potentially still benefited. Furthermore, county officials were prohibited from profiting personally from the sale and distribution of cloth to their said county in order to ensure full assistance to the indigent families and dependents of Texas soldiers.[31]

Legislative support for the families and dependents did not please everyone. During the political debate, discontent emerged from Trans-Mississippi Department officials. Kirby Smith opposed the $1.80-per-yard charge and wrote to the legislature urging politicians to reduce the cost to the Trans-Mississippi Department. The legislature, though, did not comply with his wishes, revealing the determined effort of Texas politicians to care for the needs of the general population above special interests.[32]

The pattern of political support for state and local needs also became evident in the legislature's attempt to expand the state penitentiary through additional labor and machinery. The need for additional labor was paramount to penitentiary officials. Superintendent Thomas Carothers reported to the Board of Directors in late 1863 that the penitentiary operated in fine fashion without any major problems. The only difficulty that he foresaw the institution facing was a decrease in the number of convicts, which would interfere with the daily business operations. Therefore, Carothers reported, additional labor was of absolute necessity. It did not matter if the additional labor was slave, white, or men of poor habits and questionable character. His only concern was the ability to control the laborers, that they work hard and follow specific directions. Without the use of additional labor, Carothers warned, all operations other than manufacturing cloth would have to cease. As such, he requested that penitentiary and state officials work toward an agreement for hiring more labor.[33]

Carothers maintained constant communication with Murrah and relayed

31. Gammel, *The Laws of Texas,* 5:816–18, 819.

32. *House Journal of the Tenth Legislature Regular Session,* 67; Abigail C. Holbrook, "A Glimpse of Life on Antebellum Slave Plantations in Texas," 371–72.

33. Records of the Texas State Penitentiary, RG 022-4, TSL.

to the governor his desire for more labor. When the governor delivered his address before the joint session of the tenth legislature, he pressed the need not only for set guidelines regarding distribution, but also for additional labor and the expansion of the state penitentiary. The need for additional labor and the legislative support in this matter reflected a larger vision of economic growth.[34]

Desiring to keep this invaluable state institution in full operation, the tenth legislature passed "An Act to Provide for the Employment of Additional Labor in the State Penitentiary." This law gave the financial agent of the state penitentiary the authority to hire additional labor, being accountable only to the Board of Directors in this matter. The financial agent received financial liberty and permission to employ both whites and slaves, as many as necessary, for the full working of the institution's machinery. The state penitentiary made a second request from Murrah for more employees in March 1864 and even suggested that the governor take men conscripted into service and send them to the state penitentiary to meet the additional need for labor. By requesting conscripted men, their actions undercut military concerns that were paramount for the Trans-Mississippi Department, further revealing the precedence of economic over military affairs. The request and the legislative compliance reveal the underlying core of concern that permeated throughout the state: a desire for economic security and prosperity.[35]

Not only did the legislature fill the need for additional labor, but it also considered the benefits of expanding the state penitentiary. One avenue involved appropriations for additional machinery to expand cloth production, and the other promoted diversification of production. Joab H. Banton introduced a bill into the House of Representatives on May 24, 1864, that would authorize the purchase of additional machinery for the operations of the state penitentiary and allow for the enlargement of the building. Two days later, the House read the bill a second time, but on motion laid the bill on the table, potentially threatening to kill it. Banton, however, countered this action and motioned to reconsider the bill, whereupon the House voted and passed the measure. On May 27, 1864, the House reported to the Senate that it had passed a bill authorizing the expansion of the state penitentiary and the purchase of additional machinery for its operations. The Senate Finance Committee debated the House bill and reported the next day. Chairman Pryor Lea recommended that the bill be laid on the table. The committee's

34. *Senate Journal of the Tenth Legislature Regular Session,* 67.
35. Thomas Carothers to Pendleton Murrah, Mar. 7, 1864, Records of the Texas State Penitentiary, RG 022-4, TSL; Gammel, *Laws of Texas,* 5:658–59.

justification for not supporting the state penitentiary in this manner was the interest of the general public and the financial straits of the state treasury. The treasury did not have surplus funds to support the expansion. Furthermore, Senate committee members believed that expanding the institution's cloth manufacturing would drive smaller manufacturers in the state out of business. The Finance Committee recommended instead that the penitentiary seek ways to diversify its business. By promoting diversification and the need for more labor, legislators struck a balance between supporting state institutions and the expansion of public entrepreneurship. They exhibited political astuteness by advancing both the public and the private sectors to ensure economic security for the entire state.[36]

The state penitentiary, however, was not without internal and external conflict, and the legislature functioned as both mediator and protector of the institution. This role reflected further the pattern of support for state and local interests over the needs of the Trans-Mississippi Department. The legislature acted on the issue of distribution procedures to ensure that the state institution operated according to proper guidelines. Without proper guidelines and established laws, speculators gained direct access to the penitentiary's cloth, and sold it far above market prices. Such speculation outraged many citizens, who wrote to officials complaining of the practice. It also became necessary to put laws into effect to curb any illegality among penitentiary officers, for the director of the penitentiary oftentimes did not know the full actions of his staff and officers.[37]

Such a dilemma occurred in 1863 when penitentiary officials notified state politicians that financial agent Gen. John S. Besser had been found guilty of impropriety. In 1863, Besser refused to turn over his reports to the Board of Directors, thus inhibiting penitentiary officials from making their biennial report to the legislature. This created a "state of unpleasant feeling" between Besser and the board. Consequently, the officials began to investigate Besser's handling of the penitentiary's finances and his personal conduct. The prison, without adequate storage facilities, purchased cotton from individuals, and allowed the cotton to remain on the seller's property. Though the state placed its cotton purchase in jeopardy of being destroyed by either fire or the enemy, it proved the only affordable solution. The penitentiary had only enough space to hold two hundred bales of cotton, and it

36. *House Journal of the Tenth Legislature First Called Session,* 185, 197; *Senate Journal of the Tenth Legislature First Called Session,* 97, 107.

37. Letter of T. A. Harris, Apr. 9, 1863, Records of the Texas State Penitentiary, RG 022-4, TSL.

fell to the financial agent to determine which cotton should be transported to the facility and when. Besser, however, had long been personally purchasing cotton and storing it at the state penitentiary where it would be safe. He had the cotton he bought on his own account manufactured into cloth, under pretense of it being state cotton, with the proceeds going directly to him. He kept this practice hidden from state and penitentiary officials. Once prison officials became aware of Besser's illegal activities, they requested that Governor Lubbock give his attention to the matter and dismiss Besser. Lubbock, however, strongly supported Besser, believing him to be "a most efficient and able officer." Lubbock's primary concern was not whether Besser was having his cotton manufactured over state cotton, but whether he was guilty of speculation. Lubbock further believed that Besser did not intend to perpetuate a wrong against the state, and that he should be entitled to the profits he had received for his cotton. Nevertheless, the governor yielded to the legislature to make a full investigation and conclude the case.[38]

The legislature established a committee to investigate the affairs of the state penitentiary, and questioned both Besser and other witnesses regarding his illegal practices. He was accused of not only using the state institution for his own purposes, but also employing his son over more qualified individuals, and paying him a questionably high salary. Due to the investigation, Besser tendered his resignation to Governor Murrah on November 28, 1863, which was accepted by comptroller C. R. Johns on December 2, 1863. Sterling Hendricks then replaced John Besser as financial agent. Despite such internal problems and the lack of legislation, the state penitentiary operated as a vital institution for the welfare of the Texas citizenry. As its importance grew in the manufacture of cloth, the legislature concomitantly took measures to steer and safeguard that institution by mediating internal dissension.[39]

The legislature also protected the penitentiary from external conflict. Potential problems for the prison were agreeing to house additional convicts and armed attack. On one hand, additional convicts could prove a solution to the labor problem; on the other, it served as a potential threat to the safety and welfare of the state institution. On November 9, 1863, Colorado County representative William J. Darden introduced to the House of Representatives a bill "to authorize the use of the state penitentiary for the custody of prisoners

38. Letter to Francis Lubbock, Apr. 13, 1863, ibid.; *House Journal of the Tenth Legislature Regular Session,* 19–20.

39. John Easton to Rev. P. Fullenmiser, Apr. 21, 1863, Records of the Texas State Penitentiary, RG 022-4, TSL; reply to John S. Besser, Apr. 22, 1863, ibid.; John S. Besser to Major C. R. Johns, Sept. 14, 1863, ibid.; John S. Besser to Pendleton Murrah, Nov. 28, 1863, ibid.; C. R. Johns to Pendleton Murrah, Dec. 2, 1863, ibid.

of war, deserters, and other offenders against military laws." His bill was referred to the House Committee on the Penitentiary. After three days of deliberation, Joab H. Banton, committee chairman, reported a recommendation for passing the bill to authorize the state penitentiary for use in holding prisoners of war. A minority of the committee, though, dissented from this decision. Those opposing this measure believed that the institution was of such incalculable value that no measure not absolutely necessary should be adopted that would potentially jeopardize its safety. At the center of the debate lay a desire to protect and expand state institutions. The penitentiary needed more convicts for the production of cloth, but politicians also realized that increasing the number of convicts, especially those from outside Texas, potentially threatened the vital institution.[40]

On November 20, 1863, John T. Brady moved to recommit the bill to the House. Given the dissent of opinion, the committee further considered the issue. In the interim, Governor Pendleton Murrah delivered a message to a joint session of the legislature. He pressed politicians to pass legislation for the employment of additional labor and for expanding the state institution. The day after his message, the Committee on the Penitentiary reported to the House that it saw no cause for a change in opinion.[41]

Thus, due to political gridlock, the tenth legislature adjourned its regular session without passing a final measure for housing convicts. It did, though, fully address this critical issue when it met again in its first called session. On May 11, 1864, Joab H. Banton introduced a bill to the House that would permit the penitentiary to confine Confederate army deserters and sentence them to hard labor. After one reading, the House referred the bill to the Committee on the Judiciary. After two days of debate, Alfred W. DeBerry offered an amendment to the bill stipulating that the penitentiary should "not receive said convicts in such number as to exclude convicts by the counties of the state." Marmion H. Bowers then moved to amend the bill further by inserting "duly sentenced by court martial." Amendments such as Bowers's sought to restrict the potential number of Confederate convicts coming into the state penitentiary by ensuring that they were truly convicts and prohibited the state from confining those men only suspected of desertion. By potentially restricting the number of Confederate deserters, state politicians enacted measures to safeguard the state penitentiary. The bill, with amendments, was then taken up for a third reading and passed. On May

40. *House Journal of the Tenth Legislature Regular Session,* 71, 88–89.
41. *Senate Journal of the Tenth Legislature Regular Session,* 103–4, 112–14; *House Journal of the Tenth Legislature Regular Session,* 138, 158–59, 174.

16, 1864, the House informed the Senate that it had passed a bill allowing the penitentiary to be used "for the confinement of deserters from the Army of the Confederate States duly sentenced by court martial." The Senate read the bill twice and then referred it to the State Affairs Committee. The next day, Edward R. Hord recommended that the bill be indefinitely postponed, and the Senate agreed. Again, political gridlock prevented the legislature from passing necessary laws to house convicts.[42]

In its second called session, the legislature again confronted the dilemma of housing additional convicts. Military and government officials continued to request that Texas house prisoners of war and deserters who had been condemned to hard labor. For example, on October 31, 1864, the governor of Louisiana, Henry W. Allen, requested that Governor Murrah recommend to the Texas legislature that it permit the housing of Louisiana convicts. Union forces had destroyed Louisiana's state penitentiary in 1862, forcing the state to discharge more than five hundred prisoners. Due to inadequate facilities, only a fraction of these prisoners were consigned to local jails. The local facilities, argued Governor Allen, were inadequate to ensure their holding and inefficient "to putting in force the labor portion of their punishment." Governor Murrah communicated Governor Allen's message to the Texas Senate and House of Representatives. Murrah's concern remained that the state penitentiary give precedence to Texas prisoners and that all others should be received only upon vacancies. He sought to avoid overcrowding the penitentiary to the point that the institution might become unproductive and hence a burden upon the state. Therefore, Murrah counseled the legislature not to allow for the additional acceptance of prisoners unless it would contribute to the productivity of the institution.[43]

Murrah's action forced the politicians to consider the ability of the state institution to continue to provide for the material and financial interests of the state versus the need to aid sister states in the Confederacy. On November 2, the House bill for the confinement of prisoners from other states was read the first time. Two days later, the House informed the Senate that it had passed a bill authorizing the state penitentiary to confine convicts from the other states within the Trans-Mississippi Department. The Senate read the bill twice and then referred it to the Committee on State Affairs. Ten days later, on November 14, 1864, the Senate passed the bill. The final version

42. *Senate Journal of the Tenth Legislature First Called Session,* 45–46, 57, 132, 136, 140.

43. *Senate Journal of the Tenth Legislature Second Called Session,* 15–16, 28–29, 110–11.

of the bill regarding prisoners, "An Act to Authorize the Use of the Texas Penitentiary for the Confinement of Convicts from the States of Louisiana, Arkansas and Missouri," allowed the state penitentiary to house criminals from the said states. The law strictly prohibited, however, the overcrowding of the institution and stipulated that no outside prisoners were to be received unless open slots existed. Furthermore, the financial burden for these outside prisoners rested primarily with the state in which they were convicted. Texas legislators insisted that the cost associated with transporting and keeping the prisoners should not be a charge against Texas or the prison. This bill was different from that of housing deserters and military prisoners, and Texas agreed to help Louisiana only based upon Governor Allen's assurance that his state would pay for their keep. Thus, meeting outside needs occurred only when it first benefited Texas and was in no sense a direct support of outside governmental needs.[44]

Not only did the legislature have to deal with such dilemmas that potentially threatened the vitality of the penitentiary, but more real and present dangers also existed that required immediate attention. Cloth became such a critical issue that in several instances the penitentiary faced armed threat. On one occasion, troops under the command of Colonel White fired shots into the building at Gen. C. R. Johns, and stormed the penitentiary, carrying away a considerable quantity of goods. Prison officials vehemently complained to the legislature about such threats. Legislators took notice of the situation and immediately passed a bill "to provide for raising a military force to protect the Texas State Penitentiary."[45]

By raising troops to protect state institutions, providing for the needs of the common citizen above those of the Confederacy, and by working to ensure the successful operations of the state penitentiary, Texas politicians cast their loyalty to the citizens of Texas over the Confederacy and helped secure a separate identity based upon the pursuit of economic security.

By 1864, the Clothing Bureau of the Trans-Mississippi Department was virtually hampered or wrecked in its operations, and military leaders resorted to using the press for direct appeals to the people to furnish clothing for troops. Such action reveals the crucial role of the ordinary citizen in

44. *House Journal of the Tenth Legislature Second Called Session,* 127; *Senate Journal of the Tenth Legislature Second Called Session,* 42, 85; Gammel, *Laws of Texas,* 5:820.

45. S. B. Hendricks to Pendleton Murrah, Dec. 6, 1863, Records of the Texas State Penitentiary, RG 022-4, TSL. For additional attacks on the penitentiary, see communication of John S. Besser, Dec. 8, 1863, ibid.; *House Journal of the Tenth Legislature Regular Session,* 218.

wartime. More important, it reveals the inability of the Confederacy to function adequately in a less threatened western theater. Kirby Smith attempted to remedy the problem by placing all responsibilities for supplying order and distributions under Capt. E. Carey in 1864. This, however, created only a bureaucratic muddle and accomplished little to remedy the supply problems of the Trans-Mississippi Department.[46]

Although cloth from the state penitentiary emerged as the most critical, and debated, issue concerning the production and supply of material, secondary issues did arise that also warranted legislative attention. Not only did politicians sustain state institutions for the welfare of Texas over the Confederacy, but they also acted overtly to secure the necessities of war by supporting the manufacturing endeavors of the state foundry and cap factory. Here too a similar pattern emerges wherein Texas politicians exhibited concern primarily for the citizens of the state and thus further worked to secure a separate identity. Part of this effort involved the creation of the Texas State Military Board. The Texas State Military Board was constituted in 1862 by several acts of the Texas legislature. It was established to deal with the poor financial condition of the state and authorized to sell or exchange state bonds for supplies. The board also had the authority to establish ordnance foundries and factories for arms and supplies. The original military board consisted of Governor Francis Lubbock, Comptroller C. R. Johns, and Treasurer Cyrus H. Randolph. Between 1862 and 1864, the military board spent most of its time attempting to procure arms for wartime use by selling state bonds. In 1864, the legislature reorganized the board. The new board was made up of the governor and two appointees, in addition to any necessary clerks to carry out business. Newly elected governor Pendleton Murrah replaced Francis Lubbock and appointed James S. Holman and N. B. Pearce in place of the treasurer and comptroller. The legislature instructed the new board to continue all unfinished business and gave it the authority to control all public works and supplies for the general welfare of the state.[47]

In 1862, the old military board procured a supply of copper and tin from Mexico and established a foundry in Austin for the purpose of supplying the state with cannon. The board also established a percussion-cap factory. Initially, the state foundry did not meet the expectations of officials. In its report to the tenth legislature, the military board noted that the foundry had not operated as successfully as hoped. They pointed to the failed operations

46. Nichols, "Confederate Quartermaster Operations," 40–41.

47. Charles W. Ramsdell, "The Texas State Military Board, 1862–1865," 258–59, 269; Gammel, *Laws of Texas,* 5:680.

of the first furnace in making cannon. Optimistic in outlook, though, Lubbock told the tenth legislature that he expected this situation would soon change. The military board was also optimistic and reported that a new furnace would soon produce the necessary cannon and mentioned that carriages for six guns were near completion. The board reported to the tenth legislature that the cap factory was in full operation and supplied more than the necessary amount of caps for state troops.[48]

Building upon these ventures, the new military board set out to develop manufacturing through state and public endeavors. The new board, seeking the best avenue to continue the existence of manufacturing, turned over the cannon foundry to public enterprise and retained control of the percussion-cap factory. It was not so much the board's manufacturing endeavors that created conflict between Texas and Trans-Mississippi Department officials, but rather legislative support for the board's full-scale efforts to harness resources for Texas's interests, further securing citizens' loyalty, that drove a wedge between state and Confederate authorities.[49]

In order to maintain the cap factory's financial success and aid the citizenry, the legislature permitted the state quartermaster to "dispose of one-tenth of the percussion caps manufactured" to private parties at a price that he deemed proper. Legislation required the state quartermaster to dispose of these caps throughout the state, wherever it was most beneficial to Texas troops and citizens, and dictated that the proceeds would go back into the percussion-cap manufactory in order to support the institution. Thus, much like the state penitentiary, this vital state institution was self-sustaining, and legislators worked to safeguard its vitality and productivity for the benefit of Texas citizens and state troops.[50]

Not only did the cap factory meet Texas's interests, but the foundry had also been instrumental in repairing a great deal of agricultural implements, which in turn kept many of Texas's mills from ceasing operations and thus ending in detriment to the state. The foundry was able to aid greatly the farmers and save Texas's grain crop for that year. Its greatest contribution was to procure the necessary machines for operation in the cap factory. Thus, the foundry was instrumental for Texas; it helped meet the needs of both the military and the ordinary citizen. By August 1863, the foundry operated in good condition with promises of full production and expanded

48. Report of the Texas State Military Board, in *House Journal of the Tenth Legislature Regular Session,* 239–40; Gammel, *Laws of Texas,* 5:688.
49. Ramsdell, "Texas State Military Board," 272.
50. Ibid.

to the building of field batteries. By expanding the operations, the military board ensured that production for the percussion-cap factory would not be interrupted in any way. The foundry was also responsible for making castings for the refining furnace in Texas. As the war progressed, therefore, so did business and manufacturing.[51]

Like the state penitentiary, the needs of the foundry conflicted with the military interests of the Trans-Mississippi Department. Due to the increase in manufacturing, the foundry needed additional labor and sought it at the expense of the army. The factory especially needed a larger workforce for the tedious task of delivering live-oak and musket wood, burning lime for smelting, and working the furnaces. Due to its necessity and success, both the governor and the military board received requests for more labor, often with the suggestion of pulling men from military duty. In May 1863, Superintendent Ralph Hooker requested from Governor Lubbock several men conscripted into various companies. These men would serve as bookkeepers, draftsmen, brick masons, mechanics, and blacksmiths. Hooker did not intend to interfere with the state's military needs and reassured Lubbock that he was "not weakening the army & selecting men that can do the State great service." Given the course of the war and Union occupation of the Mississippi River, it was necessary for Hooker to reassure Lubbock on this matter. The Texas legislature concurred on this need and passed a joint resolution requesting military leaders "to make such details as may be necessary to carry on all manufactories now in operation, or which may hereafter be established, for the purpose of making iron in this State." Such requests undercut the military needs of the Confederacy.[52]

The exigency for additional labor forced the foundry to contract out much of its necessary work. In turn, it was left with only a few men to fulfill Confederate requests. In early 1864, for example, the captain of the Confederate Engineering Department chastised the military board for its handling of the foundry. In one instance, the Engineering Department requested from the foundry a sod cutter and coulter plow to be used in the construction of fortifications. The military board had agreed to the request, but soon after work began, production stopped, despite the Engineering Department supplying

51. *House Journal of the Tenth Legislature Regular Session,* 12–13, 238–39; A. R. Roessler to the Military Board of the State of Texas, Apr. 6, 1863, Records of the Texas Military Board, RG 2-10/304, TSL.

52. Edward P. Turner to Francis Lubbock, Oct. 8, 1863, Records of the Texas Military Board, RG 2-10/304, TSL; William De Ryee to Military Board, Oct. 13, 1863, ibid.; William De Ryee to Military Board, Oct. 23, 1863, ibid.; R. Hooker to Francis Lubbock, May 29, 1863, ibid.; Gammel, *Laws of Texas,* 5:750.

the necessary material and having completed preliminary production. The department criticized the board for its management of state institutions and demanded that work on their requested items begin again at once. Failure to do so would be paramount to disobeying direct military orders. Such threats mattered little to Texas politicians.[53]

Despite full political support of these institutions, cordial relations did not always exist, and the legislature found itself in the role of mediator. In 1863, an argument ensued between William De Ryee, superintendent of the state percussion-cap factory, and Ralph Hooker, superintendent of the state foundry. De Ryee had been occupied with completing a refining furnace and relied on the foundry for completing the job. He complained, however, that he was not receiving due attention from Hooker, who he claimed was wasting time making costly machines, which after waiting in vain for casting were abandoned, thus consuming weeks of the most difficult labor. Hooker, however, claimed that the foundry had always been at De Ryee's disposal and he could have had his work completed if he had only communicated his wishes. De Ryee countered this accusation, denying he had complete access to the institution and claimed that Hooker was too busy with his "pet idea" of casting cannon with copper. Part of the problem revealed in the conflict between the two institutions was the need for labor. Both institutions shared blacksmiths, masons, and pattern makers. The military board worked toward a compromise in which the refining furnace would receive additional attention. The board's mediation between the institutions along with legislative support for additional labor reveal a concerted political effort to move down the path of progress, harnessing competition and productivity for Texas's benefit.[54]

Not only did manufacturing endeavors serve Texas's interests, but the military board's efforts to develop natural resources such as salt and iron also continued the pattern of state self-sufficiency that worked to secure a separate identity. Salt was a primary necessity in the nineteenth century due to the lack of refrigeration, and was in greater demand due to the wartime crisis. Salt was used to preserve such staples as meat, fish, eggs, and butter. It was not limited to human need, but was also vital for animals, especially horses, to prevent foot-and-mouth disease. Furthermore, salt proved necessary for hides. Individuals used horse, mule, hog, and dog hides for leather products such as shoes, and needed a way to preserve the hides before the tanning process began. Before the war, many states imported their salt. With the

53. Rob. Creuzbaur to Phenis De Cordova, Feb. 10, 1864, Records of the Texas Military Board, RG 2-10/304, TSL.

54. William De Ryee to Military Board, Nov. 20, 1863, ibid.

onset of war, though, the price of salt skyrocketed. For example, in Georgia, the price of salt rose from sixty cents to twenty dollars for a 210 pound bag. Such increases forced individual states to explore alternative avenues for salt. The necessity of this vital element was known to all, and during the war the Texas legislature worked to secure the production of salt for the benefit of Texas citizens.[55]

In April 1862, the military board hired Col. A. Bishop of Wise County to examine salines around the state and report on their potential productivity. The ninth legislature, in its extra session, appropriated five thousand dollars for this endeavor. Bishop was sent to report on the number of men needed to mine the salt, the projected amount of salt that could be gathered, who would benefit most from the salt, and the price at which it should be sold.[56]

On September 8, 1863, Bishop reported his findings to the military board. Examining Double Mountain, in the northwest corner of the frontier, Bishop and company found several rivers, creeks, and a lake that contained up to 98 percent salt. Bishop was pleased with the company's findings. He suggested that twenty-five to thirty men could adequately mine salt in that section. He pointed out that beef, flour, and wood were readily accessible in the region to help support the labor and suggested that ordinary citizens be hired to haul supplies in return for salt. As for the amount of salt that could be gathered, Bishop hesitated to conjecture. He noted, though, that Young, Jack, Palo Pinto, Parker, Wise, Montague, Cooke, Denton, Grayson, Collin, and Tarrant Counties stood most likely to profit from such endeavors. His only major concern was the potential threat of Indians. He feared that once the Indians learned of Texas's manufacturing designs in that area, marauding efforts would only grow on their part. As discussed earlier, Indians were already present in that region and known for attack. Such expansion on Texas's part would only exacerbate the situation, and Bishop feared the potential threat to the economic welfare of the state and general population.[57]

The military board's venture into salt production had the full support of the Texas legislature. On Wednesday, December 2, 1863, the Senate announced a joint resolution to authorize the military board to manufacture salt, and after three days of debate, it passed. The joint resolution appropriated fifty thousand dollars to the board, at their discretion, for manufacturing salt. Furthermore, it requested that Governor Murrah secure troops for the protection

55. Ella Lonn, *Salt as a Factor in the Confederacy,* 13–18, 29–31; Charles Ramsdell, *Behind the Lines in the Southern Confederacy,* 19–20.

56. *Senate Journal of the Tenth Legislature Regular Session,* 185.

57. Report of A. Bishop, in *Senate Journal of the Tenth Legislature Regular Session,* 143–49; A. Bishop to Francis Lubbock, Sept. 8, 1863, Records of the Texas Military Board, RG 2-10/304, TSL.

of parties engaged in making salt in the northwestern region of the state. Despite the promise of protection and the occasional presence of troops, the
imminent danger of Indians oftentimes hindered officials from making a full,
detailed report on the operation of the salines. From partial reports, however,
the salines appeared productive and successful. Due to Texas's success in the
salt venture, the Trans-Mississippi Department relied on the state to provide
an adequate supply for its needs. As with cloth, however, Texas politicians
first sought to meet the needs of its indigent families and soldiers' dependents
by selling salt to them at the cheapest price possible, and considered their
needs above those of the Trans-Mississippi Department.[58]

Iron, too, was an essential resource that the Texas legislature sought to
develop. In his address before the tenth legislature, Governor Lubbock remarked that "iron works should be erected as speedily as possible." Due to
the war, the supply of iron was becoming scarce and costly. Thus, to keep
the farming interests from suffering, an increase in the supply of iron was
necessary. Newly elected governor Pendleton Murrah held the same opinion,
and in a message before the joint legislature on November 24, 1863, he stated
that "the development of iron and mineral resources of the State, are [sic] so
obviously necessary that it becomes the duty of the State, so far as she can, to
encourage and stimulate such enterprises by all the legitimate means within
her power." Murrah believed that if the Texas legislature had adopted this
course a few years earlier, the state would be free and independent of foreign
markets. He clearly articulated a vision of separateness and independence,
further warning the legislature that Texas should be prepared to sustain itself,
free from outside support.[59]

Legislators supported the governor's call for iron development, and on
November 28, 1863, the Texas Senate informed the House of Representatives that it had passed a bill authorizing the military board to provide for
the manufacture of iron. Three days later, the House read the Senate bill
for the first time and referred it to the Committee on State Affairs, which
debated the matter for approximately two weeks before finally passing the
bill. Legislation permitted the military board to put into operation one or
more furnaces and forges to manufacture iron. The act also stipulated "that
all iron manufactured by said board, or under their direction, not needed for

58. *Senate Journal of the Tenth Legislature Regular Session,* 121, 125; *Senate Journal
of the Tenth Legislature First Called Session,* 53; Gammel, *Laws of Texas,* 5:752; H. E.
Stevens to Pendleton Murrah, Feb. 2, 1864, Records of the Texas Military Board, RG
2-10/304, TSL; Major Abney to Pendleton Murrah, Jan. 19, 1865, ibid.; Lonn, *Salt as
a Factor,* 29.

59. *Senate Journal of the Tenth Legislature Regular Session,* 13, 103, 107.

the defense of the State or in the performance of their duties, shall be sold to the people . . . and the proceeds of such sales paid into the treasury of the State." The Texas legislature was generous in its financial support for such endeavors and provided the board with up to $1 million for this purpose.[60]

The Texas legislature not only supported manufacturing through the military board, but also sought to promote private enterprise in the production of iron. Governor Murrah believed that "the spirit of public enterprise . . . is not only gratifying but a source of hope and congratulation to the whole state." He believed that capital of every kind, from labor to directors of chartered companies, should be "protected by law against interference or interruption from any and every source." He stood devoted to encouraging public enterprise and told the legislature that it is "the best policy as well as the only one calculated to ensure speedy and certain success, to encourage individual enterprise rather than attempt the accomplishment of these varied, necessary and numerous objects alone through the Capital, agents, employees and management of the State."[61]

The tenth legislature passed legislation that incorporated nine companies for the purpose of manufacturing iron and other metals and established specific guidelines for their operation. Although each company's charter varied in wording, fundamental elements existed in each incorporation. The legislature required each company to elect a board of directors from among the stockholders. In most cases, board members were required to own more than one share of stock. The financial control that the legislature levied on incorporated companies varied from charter to charter. Stock for these companies ranged anywhere from one hundred dollars per share to one thousand dollars per share, with limits on total stock value ranging from a minimum of one hundred thousand dollars to $5 million. Though these values differed with each company, in every case the legislature established clear guidelines on the value of stock and the amount that board members were required to own. Such stipulations were geared toward ensuring a personal stake from entrepreneurs in hopes of securing successful operations.[62]

To make investments more appealing, the legislature in most cases freed officers, agents, superintendents, machinery, tools, land, and slaves from conscription and impressment. Entrepreneurs therefore had the freedom to pursue their business interests without concern for the war. In addition, the

60. *House Journal of the Tenth Legislature Regular Session,* 177, 194, 220; *Senate Journal of the Tenth Legislature Regular Session,* 115; Gammel, *Laws of Texas,* 5:690.

61. *Senate Journal of the Tenth Legislature First Called Session,* 30–31.

62. Gammel, *Laws of Texas,* 5:676–77, 718, 730, 740, 741, 743, 783, 785, 792, 845.

tenth legislature passed "An Act to Encourage the Erection of Certain Machinery by Donations of Land and Otherwise" that encouraged the development of public enterprise. Individuals or companies that successfully erected machinery for the manufacture of iron, salt, and other resources by March 1865 received 320 acres of land for every one thousand dollars worth of machinery in efficient operation. The duty to evaluate progress and success of such ventures fell to the governor and appointed commissioners. The Texas legislature's support for such endeavors was geared not only for wartime interests, but also for the long-term benefit of the state. Iron companies incorporated by the tenth legislature received charters ranging from ten to ninety years, with the majority of the charters set at twenty-five years in length. Thus, Texas politicians were concerned not only with meeting the immediate needs of Texas during the Civil War, but also with securing long-term economic growth for the state.[63]

The production of natural resources was vital to long-range progress, and salt and iron proved only two examples of political support for this goal. By promoting the manufacture of these resources, the legislature balanced the needs between the common citizen and the expansion of private enterprise. Furthermore, Texas politicians confronted the conflict of providing for the general welfare of the state versus the needs of the Confederacy. In doing so, a repeated pattern of political support, protection, and maintenance emerged that served Texas's interests first.

An investigation of the political process reveals a considerable amount of debate regarding necessary material such as cloth, salt, and iron. More important, it reveals the depth to which politicians would go in their struggle to promote and protect the economic security of the state and citizenry. Building on the move to establish a separate identity through conflict and conscription, the Texas legislature secured that separateness through the support of state institutions and manufacturing endeavors. In many ways, the Confederate government aided this process. Richmond authorities and the Confederate Congress treated the Trans-Mississippi Department as a detached and separate entity from the rest of the Confederacy. Richmond's point of view of this region, and its virtual neglect, along with Texas's established course of action, instigated the complete separation of Texas from the Trans-Mississippi Department and the Confederacy. This pattern became even more evident in the wrangling over cotton and the conflict between Texas and Gen. Edmund Kirby Smith's Cotton Bureau.[64]

63. Ibid.
64. Holladay, "Powers of the Commander," 296.

CHAPTER 6

"In Disregard and Defiance"
The Cotton-Trade Controversy

Looking back upon the political conflict within the Confederacy, Texas senator Williamson S. Oldham, an ardent states' right advocate who opposed the
efforts to form a centralized Confederate government, reflected on the root
of Southern discontent. "There was a total want of adaptation," he remarked.
"We must take men as they are, and not as we would have them. If we would
legislate for them as freeman, we must adapt our laws to their sentiments in
order to command their support—if we legislate in disregard and defiance
of their sentiments, they will feel, that they are treated as slaves, and will
rebel against our measures." Born in Franklin County, Tennessee, on June
19, 1813, Williamson S. Oldham grew up on a farm and studied law under
Judge Nathan Green before moving to Arkansas in 1836. There he practiced
law and represented Arkansas in its House of Representatives. In 1844, the
Arkansas legislature elected him associate judge of the Supreme Court, a
position he held until moving to Austin, Texas, for health reasons. In Austin,
he continued his law practice with Judge James Webb. Oldham's astute ob-
servation reflected the prevailing problem of the Confederate government:
it passed legislation contrary to the interests of the general population. In
return, citizens withheld their loyalty, and state governments countered with
measures to protect private property and individual liberty. Such "rebellion,"
Oldham remarked, appeared especially pronounced in Texas.[1]

The political conflict within the Confederacy emerged most significantly
in the wrangling over cotton and the Confederate government's attempt to
regulate private property and free trade. Richmond's pattern of neglecting
western interests contributed to Texas seeking its own economic interests.

1. Oldham, "Memoirs of Williamson Simpson Oldham, Confederate Senator, 1861–
1865," Williamson Simpson Oldham Papers, RG 2R130, Barker Center, 152, 163.
Oldham was a practicing Presbyterian and served as vestryman in the church. As a
states' right Democrat, he won election to the Texas Secession Convention and was later
elected with Louis T. Wigfall to serve in the Confederate Senate (E. Fontaine, "Hon.
Williamson S. Oldham," Oldham Papers, RG 2F164, Barker Center).

Had the Confederacy adopted a stable and consistent policy to secure western interests and encourage state and federal cooperation, conflict and competition over cotton might not have occurred. Nevertheless, by promoting its plan for the purchase of cotton and state manufacturing that conflicted with more immediate demands of the Confederacy, the policy and action of Texas politicians further reflected the effort to secure a separate political and economic identity.

To most Southerners, "King Cotton" served as the lifeline of the Southern economic system. The Confederacy believed that this one staple would force France and England's intervention and official recognition of the Confederacy. Cotton's importance to Southerners in the nineteenth century cannot be overemphasized. Nevertheless, the magnitude of its significance did not always translate to peace within this Southern kingdom. The very importance of cotton as a cash crop led to competition and conflict in the Confederacy. Gen. Edmund Kirby Smith established the Cotton Bureau in 1863 as part of the Trans-Mississippi Department, and it competed directly with the state of Texas for the product and intensified conflict in the western region. As such, Texas citizens and politicians met their own economic needs over those of the Confederacy and Kirby Smith's Trans-Mississippi Department. These three political entities—the Confederate government, the Trans-Mississippi Department, and the state of Texas—passed laws and regulations concerning cotton with the intention of serving their own interests. As such, political turmoil reigned throughout the South.[2]

An investigation of the legislative process regarding cotton issues reveals the steps that both the Texas state and the Confederate governments took in establishing economic policy. It discloses information about the conflict between the two, and reveals the unity of Texas state politicians in forming a stable and concrete cotton policy. Although Texas representatives in Richmond joined ranks to adhere to the demands of their constituents over satisfying the immediate necessities of war, the Confederate government as a whole was unsure of how to deal effectively with the economic aspects of war. The political process further exposes the inconsistency and ignorance of the Confederate government's policy on cotton and Richmond's neglect of western economic interests. The fact that eastern and western interests in the war did not always coincide bolstered this predicament. Furthermore, the political process discloses that the Trans-Mississippi Department often

2. Frank Owsley, *King Cotton Diplomacy: Foreign Relations of the Confederate States of America*, 20–23. See also Robert W. Young, *Senator James Murray Mason: Defender of the Old South.*

operated in contradiction to established law, creating additional competition and conflict over cotton. The failure of the Confederate Congress to produce adequate legislation safeguarding private property and free trade is even more glaring considering that measures affecting commerce and property were not haphazardly passed, but deeply considered and contested.

Theoretically, the rules governing the passage of legislation worked to ensure the passage of productive measures to safeguard the interests of citizens and the Confederacy as a whole. After all, Oldham reflected, the political process was intended to function in such a manner. Clear and concrete rules governed the passage of legislation. Every resolution and bill requiring the concurrent action of both houses of Congress received three readings before taking the questions and voting upon their passage. Furthermore, politicians could not amend a resolution or bill until after the second reading, whereupon they could alter or refer it to a committee. This process was designed to ensure that adequate debate would take place to shape and formulate the wisest policy to govern the interests of the people and the Confederate States of America.[3]

With established procedures for passing legislation, it became incumbent upon legislators to produce measures in the interest of their constituents, even more so during this critical period. When it came to issues of private property and free trade associated with cotton, however, Confederate officials balked. Instead of producing active measures to promote commerce and in turn garner citizen and political support for the war effort, officials adopted a defensive posture in legislation that produced a stranglehold upon the citizens of the Confederacy. Confederate politicians and officials, for the most part, failed to realize the critical connection between offensive legislation and cooperation toward a unified war effort.[4]

Prior to the establishment of Kirby Smith's Cotton Bureau in the Trans-Mississippi Department, political conflict surrounding cotton issues was restricted to a battle between Texas and Richmond. The Confederate Congress passed legislation dealing with the production, export, impressment, and destruction of cotton that affected all Southern states. It passed a majority of the legislation in secret session to avoid stirring discontent among the citizenry. In such cases, official debates over cotton policy did not become public until the actual passage of legislation. Congress held to specific rules regarding the

---

3. Confederate States of America, House of Representatives, *Rules for Conducting Business in the Senate of the Confederate States of America,* sec. 20.

4. Oldham, "Memoirs," 163. I use the term *offensive* to mean favorable legislation that actively promotes the interests of the citizenry.

convening of a secret session. Politicians operated under strict guidelines not to disclose any information discussed behind closed doors, and any officer or politician found guilty of violating guidelines faced expulsion. Legislation debated and passed in secret session was a serious undertaking, especially on matters dealing with cotton that had widespread ramifications for the war effort.[5]

The Provisional Congress of the Confederate States primarily dealt with the issue of cotton exportation and destruction, with the goal of restricting both. Prohibiting cotton from falling into possession of Federal troops became the predominant concern for politicians, and Congress adopted a defensive commercial policy to attain this goal. On May 10, 1861, Mississippi representative William Taylor Sullivan Barry offered a resolution in secret session that the Committee on the Judiciary inquire into a law forbidding shipment of cotton to the United States. Barry graduated from Yale University in 1841, studied law, and served as a member of the Mississippi legislature from 1849 to 1851 and in 1855. As a plantation owner and immediate secessionist who had presided over the Mississippi secession convention, Barry earnestly sought to protect Southern cotton interests. Another strong supporter of defensive commerce was James Alexander Seddon. Seddon was privately educated during his youth before attending the University of Virginia Law School. He was nominated to the Provisional Congress, but lost to William C. Rives by one vote; he later won an appointment due to a vacant seat. Best known as secretary of war for Jefferson Davis, Seddon introduced to the Provisional Congress meeting in secret session a resolution "instructing the Committee on Military Affairs to inquire into the expediency of urging upon the people and providing for the destruction of cotton, tobacco, and naval stores upon the approach of the enemy." Confederate politicians thus sought not only to restrict trade, but also to ensure that any possible Union assaults into Southern territory would not result in the confiscation of cotton to aid the enemy's manufacturing endeavors. To a large extent, the actions of Confederate politicians did have an impact upon Northern industry. The North desperately needed Southern cotton for its factories. Northeastern manufacturers felt the pinch of dwindling cotton supplies, and efforts to grow cotton in Illinois had failed. By June 1862, 3,252,000 of 4,745,750 spindles in the North were motionless. A month later, approximately 75 percent of all Northern spindles ceased to operate.[6]

5. Confederate States of America, *Rules for Conducting Business,* sec. 43, 44.

6. Robert L. Kerby, *Kirby Smith's Confederacy: The Trans-Mississippi South, 1863–1865,* 78; *JCCSA,* 1:205; Ezra J. Warner and Wilfred Buck Yearns, *Biographical Register*

Not only did Confederate politicians seek to disrupt Northern industry, but they also wanted to fully control the cotton business throughout the South. On May 20, 1861, in secret session, the Provisional Congress took up and debated a bill "to prohibit the exportation of cotton from the Confederate States, except through the seaports of said States, and to punish persons offending therein." This measure potentially undermined Texas's entire cotton operation. Texas representative John Hemphill, however, offered an amendment to the bill stipulating that the act would not prohibit the exportation of cotton across the Mexican border. Congress accepted Hemphill's amendment and subsequently passed the bill, and President Davis signed it on May 21, 1861. Thus, from the earliest stages of the conflict, the Confederate government involved itself in attempting to restrict free trade to shape Northern industrial pursuits and control Southern commerce. Due to the action of Texas's representatives, however, these initial efforts did not have an impact on Texas's trade with Mexico. In fact, it actually bolstered the cotton business in the Lone Star State.[7]

Texas's cotton commerce did not escape hazard, though. Beyond the political realm, Confederate military officials actively engaged in interfering with Texas's commerce from the beginning of the Civil War. In 1861, Gen. Paul Octave Hebert issued an order prohibiting the exportation of cotton from Texas, except by those individuals who had obtained a license from Gen. Hamilton Bee. Born in Louisiana, Hebert attended the United States Military Academy and graduated first in his class, ahead of William T. Sherman, in 1840. He also served in the Mexican War, was a sugar planter in Louisiana, and served as governor of that state from 1853 to 1856. Hebert was unpopular among Texas troops and politicians due to his class upbringing, and he himself was not pleased with his command in Texas due to the lack of defense and arms for war. Hamilton Bee was also a well-known individual in Texas. He assisted with the boundary dispute between Texas and Mexico in 1839, served as secretary of the Texas Senate in 1846, fought in the Mexican War, served in the Texas legislature from 1849 to 1859, and was Speaker of the House from 1855 to 1857. Bee enlisted in the Confederate army and earned appointment to brigadier general in 1862. Given his notoriety and power, he was able to place further restrictions on trade. As a prerequisite for obtaining permits, he required that exporters enter into a

---

of the Confederate Congress, 15–16; Ludwell Johnson, *Red River Campaign: Politics and Cotton in the Civil War,* 7–13; Fredericka Meiners, "The Texas Border Cotton Trade," 294–95.

7. *JCCSA,* 1:250–51, 264, 477.

bond to return supplies bought with a portion of the proceeds from the sale of cotton. His actions, however, raised concern among Texas citizens and politicians. Senator Oldham believed Bee's approach impractical because the bonds were illegal and, more important, because many planters could not afford to sacrifice a portion of their cotton due to the enormous prices for supplies. Consequently, few planters contracted with Bee. This in turn led to speculation. Those individuals that did obtain permits from Bee often misrepresented themselves as government agents to the people and demanded the purchase of cotton with the threat of impressment, forcing many planters to sell their cotton.[8]

General Hebert revoked Bee's order after a few months, but little changed because General Holmes, the commander of the department, immediately reissued the order. Gen. John B. Magruder replaced Hebert in September 1862, but Confederate misappropriation did not cease. Magruder, known for his military capacity, attempted to gain full control of all civil and military authority in the trans-Mississippi region. He issued numerous orders aimed at controlling the cotton commerce and even went so far as to use conscripted men to haul cotton to aid in the scheme of monopolizing the cotton trade. Though President Jefferson Davis wrote to Magruder expressing his dissatisfaction, Richmond politicians made no effort to stop such corruption. Although Texas commerce escaped legal Confederate restrictions for the time, extralegal maneuvers had somewhat of an impact on the cotton trade in the Lone Star State. Nevertheless, Texas citizens for the most part prospered from the cotton trade. Texans drove their cotton to Laredo, Brownsville, Rio Grande City, and Eagle Pass. Countless wagons streamed into Mexico with Texas cotton, returning with merchandise and necessary supplies. Trading white gold across the border was big business.[9]

Whereas Confederate political action remained somewhat limited in the first year of the war, these moves foreshadowed the direction of the Confederacy to implement a defensive and restrictive trade policy. This policy ultimately created conflict and instability in the Confederacy. When the Confederate Congress convened its first regular session, it considered specific measures regarding the trade, production, destruction, and impressment of cotton. Military officials also continued their corrupt actions in an attempt

8. Hamilton Bee Papers, Barker Center; Oldham, "Memoirs," 360–62; Meiners, "Texas Border Cotton Trade," 294.

9. Oldham, "Memoirs," 362–64; Ronnie C. Tyler, "Cotton on the Border, 1861–1865," 460–61.

to gain control of the cotton trade in Texas, assaulting on all sides the commercial interests of the Lone Star State.

In its first regular session, Confederate politicians debated the issue of cotton exportation. On March 18, 1862, the Confederate House Ways and Means Committee reported on a bill prohibiting the exportation of cotton and recommended that it not pass. The committee did not have enough time to debate the bill, and when it again came to the floor on March 27, the committee asked for additional time to deliberate. After debating the bill for another two weeks, the committee reported, in secret session, that it had come to an agreement and ordered the bill to be printed. Another two weeks passed before the House of Representatives fully entertained the bill. On April 17, 1862, also in secret session, the House hammered out the details of the bill. The original bill stipulated that no one could export cotton from any Confederate port to any foreign ports unless authorized by the president. Authorization for foreign trade, however, did not include trade with the United States. Authorized agents were required to swear an oath, before any judge or justice of the court, that trade would not be conducted with the United States, and that trade would result only in the obtainment of necessary articles for the prosecution of the war. As it stood then, the original bill would prohibit free trade with Mexico, a move that would profoundly damage Texas's economic interests. Texas representative Peter W. Gray, however, moved to amend the bill to include "that this act shall not apply to the exportation of cotton or tobacco by loyal citizens overland to Mexico, a coterminous neutral country." Born in Virginia in 1819, one of twelve children, Gray moved to Texas in 1838 and studied law with his father in Houston. He also served in the first and fourth Texas legislatures and served as district judge from 1854 to the Civil War. He won a seat in the first regular Congress and became an ardent protector of Texas's economic interests. The House agreed to Gray's amendment, but a move made by Mississippi representative Reuben Davis to postpone consideration of the bill until August passed by a vote of thirty-nine to thirty-seven. Each of Texas's representatives, except Franklin Barlow Sexton who did not vote, agreed to postpone the bill. This respite allowed Texas to continue its trade.[10]

10. *JCCSA,* 5:117, 150, 152, 162, 165, 185, 256–58; Warner and Yearns, *Biographical Register,* 106–7, 217–18. Gray also held nationalist tendencies, and his 1862 suggestion that the Confederacy take absolute control over all railroads, and his support of conscription, caused him to lose reelection in 1863. Sexton was born in Indiana, and moved to Texas at age three. He graduated from Wesleyan College in San Augustine in 1846 and

Richmond politicians, however, primarily concerned themselves at this point with the overall goal of keeping cotton out of Union hands. On March 22, 1862, the Committee on the Judiciary reported on Senate Bill 27, which would prohibit furnishing cotton to the enemy. The bill passed despite contentious debate among representatives, the most serious issue being that the law should not apply to persons or places already in the possession of the enemy. In the meantime, the House of Representatives considered measures to make trade with the enemy illegal. On April 5, 1862, Alabama representative David Clopton offered a resolution into the House for the Committee on the Judiciary to inquire into legislation that would make it a crime for individuals in the Confederate States to sell or exchange cotton with the enemy. Clopton, a descendent of a prominent Virginia planter family who graduated from Randolph Macon College in 1840 with honors, moved to Alabama in 1844. He earned a reputation as a strong prosecessionist and politician who generally supported the centralizing tendencies of President Davis. Whereas Clopton's resolution passed in the House, the Senate remained divided, tabling the bill by a vote of thirteen to ten. Both Oldham and Wigfall agreed to this decision. Despite Richmond's attempt to establish regulations prohibiting trade with the Union, private citizens and public agents often undermined Confederate policy by trading with Union officials. Though the Union enacted a strong blockade against Southern ports to restrict trade, it procured enough cotton for its benefit through clandestine operations.[11]

Not only did the Confederate government seek to restrict trade with the Union through direct legislation, but it also sought to gain control of the Southern cotton supply to further obtain this goal. On January 13, 1863, Tennessee representative Henry Stuart Foote introduced into the House of Representatives a resolution to have the Committee on Ways and Means inquire into the possibility of the Confederate government buying all the cotton in private hands. Foote had defeated Jefferson Davis in the 1853 Mississippi governor's race. Initially a Union man, he was extremely antagonistic toward Davis. Ironically, however, he served as chairman of the Committee on Foreign Affairs and chaired a special committee on illegal impressments. Davis considered Foote his only open assailant in Congress.

---

served as president of the Democratic State Convention in 1860. He ardently supported Texas's interests in Congress but also supported the Confederacy strongly when there appeared no threat to Texas's interests; he was very critical of the Trans-Mississippi Department for draining resources from Texas.

11. *JCCSA*, 2:85, 167, 5:181; Warner and Yearns, *Biographical Register*, 54–55; A. Sellew Roberts, "The Federal Government and Confederate Cotton."

The Confederate government, agreeing to Foote's resolution, attempted to prevent commercial intercourse with the enemy, particularly when it came to cotton trading with the United States because cotton would allow the Union to continue their manufactories and subsequently sustain the government's credit.[12]

While the House entertained legislation to procure the Southern cotton supply, the Senate dealt with restrictions affecting Texas's trade with Mexico. Of primary importance was the clandestine effort of President Davis to interfere with trade relations. Richmond conducted its interference in the cotton trade with a veil of secrecy, and Senator Oldham sought to expose President Davis's conduct and involvement in the matter. On April 11, 1863, Oldham submitted a resolution in the Senate requiring President Davis to inform the legislative branch of all the communications and orders from the War Department to Trans-Mississippi Department officials regarding military restrictions imposed upon the exportation of cotton and general trade across the Rio Grande. Oldham also issued an order for the injunction of secrecy to be removed from the documents. Richmond's involvement in the trans-Mississippi cotton trade created conflict and compelled Texas representatives to take action to protect the interest of their state. Texas representatives endeavored to expose such matters for the benefit of their constituents and to secure their economic well-being. Texas benefited greatly from its trade with Mexico, and state representatives in the Confederate Congress desired to maintain such productivity even if it meant implicating President Davis.[13]

In conjunction with attempting to restrict trade and control the Southern cotton supply, Confederate officials interfered with the personal production of planters. On February 26, 1862, Georgia representative Hines Holt, a strong nationalist who called for unqualified support of President Davis, offered a resolution in the Senate requiring the Committee on Ways and Means to inquire into a law restricting the production of cotton in the Confederacy, and permitting the Confederate government to control all cotton on hand and to be grown in the states during the war. The Senate sent Holt's resolution to the Committee on Ways and Means for debate. In the meantime, South Carolina representative William Waters Boyce offered a resolution in the House to recommend to planters that they refrain from cultivating cotton and instead devote their energy to raising provisions. The House agreed to Boyce's resolution, but the Senate rejected it on March 13. The next

12. *JCCSA*, 6:8–9; Warner and Yearns, *Biographical Register,* 86–87; Oldham, "Memoirs," 352–53.
13. *JCCSA*, 3:277, 333.

day, however, the Senate passed a resolution asking the House to resubmit Boyce's resolution to them, and the House complied. After minimal debate, the Senate informed the House that it had agreed to and passed Boyce's resolution.[14]

Resolutions passed by Congress, however, did not carry the full weight of law. Thus, citizens continued to plant and cultivate cotton. In an attempt to gain a stronger hold on Southern commerce to uphold its original goal of impeding trade with the Union, Richmond now moved to allow for the destruction of cotton. On February 25, 1862, Tennessee representative Henry Foote introduced a bill for the destruction of cotton in certain cases. The House read the bill twice and referred it to the Committee on Military Affairs. While the House of Representatives considered the destruction of cotton, the Senate resolved in open session to instruct the committee to inquire into the possibility of the Confederate government taking control of all the cotton within the limits of the Confederate States "with a view to the destruction of said products." Whenever Union forces potentially stood the chance of capturing an area, the planters' cotton would immediately be subject to destruction without their consent. This measure coincided with Richmond's desire to fully interfere with Union attempts to gain control of Confederate cotton. More important, though, it reflects the government's attempt to regulate private property and interfere with individual economic interests. On February 26, 1862, Louisiana representative Edward Sparrow, chairman of the Committee on Military Affairs, asked that the committee be discharged from considering the resolution, and suggested that the Committee on Finance take up the matter.[15]

Sparrow's action reveals that some anxiety existed regarding the economic impact of destroying cotton, but not enough concern to avoid Senate defeat of his suggestion. While the Senate continued to wrangle over the issue of destruction, the House committee reported on Foote's proposed bill with a recommendation for passage. The bill would allow military officials to destroy all cotton potentially falling into the hands of the enemy, with just compensation given to owners. The House passed the bill with minor amendments on March 6, 1862. All of Texas's representatives cast votes in favor of passing the bill, except William Bacon Wright who did not vote. Texas representatives could justify their support for such legislation because

14. *JCCSA*, 5:29, 76, 94, 98–99, 106; Warner and Yearns, *Biographical Register*, 125–26.

15. *JCCSA*, 2:20, 24, 5:27; Warner and Yearns, *Biographical Register*, 230. Sparrow was born in Ireland and emigrated to Louisiana in 1831 where he studied law and won election to the secession convention as an immediate secessionist.

their state did not face any real threat from the enemy, and the destruction of cotton in other Southern states would bolster Texas's cotton trade.[16]

Although Texas planters had little to fear from the actual destruction of their cotton by military authorities, they did not fully escape the manacles of Confederate law. By far, the most disturbing legislation for Texans passed by the Confederate Congress dealt with the impressment of cotton. On January 30, 1863, Virginia representative James P. Holcombe, an expert in business and commercial law, introduced a bill "to authorize and regulate impressments of private property." Holcombe was a strong believer in states' rights, and though he supported government and military control of production and transportation, he sought to protect private property from arbitrary laws. His bill made it to a second reading and was ordered for printing. After several failed attempts to bring the bill up for debate, the House finally considered it on February 12. The bill specifically stated that any commanding officer of the Confederate States may authorize the impressment of private property to obtain necessary supplies. The only items exempted from impressment were "grain, forage, slaves, or other property necessary for the use of his plantation." If owners did not agree to the impressment, they had little recourse. The bill clearly stated that in case of discrepancy over the amount of remuneration, a committee of local citizens would determine the fair value of impressed property. Though Holcombe viewed impressment as necessary for the war effort, his move to place some authority in local hands was an attempt to protect property rights. Despite his attempt to strike a balance between national and local interests, Holcombe's bill received criticism from fellow Virginia representative James Lyons who offered to amend the bill entirely. Lyons, a radical secessionist who generally opposed state and local interests during the war, wanted more clarification on the allowance of impressment, and his version stipulated that commanding officers could impress property only after making full attempts to gain supplies by the proper quartermaster and commissary stores. In addition, Lyons's amended version of the bill provided for the impressment of slaves. After offering his amended version, the House agreed to print the bill and then adjourned for the day. Over the next several days, the House amended several portions of the bill, but these

16. *JCCSA*, 5:55, 63; Warner and Yearns, *Biographical Register*, 180–81, 264. Wright was born in Georgia and moved to Texas in 1854 where he practiced law. He was an ineffective politician and lost his seat in Congress in 1863 to Simpson H. Morgan. Morgan was born in Tennessee and moved to Texas in 1844. He generally supported a more centralized government for war purposes. He was a prominent businessman who held land in several Texas counties and was involved in the railroad industry. For the effect of destroying cotton on relations, see Owsley, *King Cotton Diplomacy*.

sections primarily dealt with the issue of slave impressment and did not affect the right of military officers to impress private property, including cotton. On February 16, 1863, the House read the bill a third time and passed it by a vote of fifty-two to seven. All of Texas's representatives voted to pass the bill, except for William B. Wright who again did not vote.[17]

After passing the bill, the House sent it to the Senate where on February 23, 1863, Georgia representative Benjamin Harvey Hill, a proponent of strong centralized government, from the Committee on the Judiciary recommended that the bill be printed without amendment. When it came up again on the Senate floor three days later, Landon Carter Haynes from Tennessee moved to amend the bill by striking out most of it. Haynes, a lawyer, preacher, farmer, and politician, walked a fine line between state and federal rights. He supported impressment on the grounds that the Confederate government pay market prices. Furthermore, he supported the destruction of private property, but held the belief that the government should not interfere with a farmer's choice of production. Haynes's amended version was significant, for it placed greater control over impressment in the hands of quartermaster and commissary agents instead of military commanders in the field. His version stipulated that only field commanders had the authority to impress property, after having received written authorization from a bonded quartermaster or commissary. The Senate, though, postponed any further action on the bill until March 4. Thereupon, Alabama representative William Lowndes Yancey, a radical secessionist who had long supported the Southern Confederacy, amended the bill further, requiring that Confederate officials publicly advertise the necessities of the army and offer payment to any willing seller before moving toward impressment. Yancey's amendment, however, lost, and Haynes countered by offering another version only slightly different, but not affecting the process of impressment that he had originally suggested. Yancey, however, countered back by proposing a separate section to the bill stating "that no impressment of private property shall be made except in cases where the public peril or danger is imminent and immediate, or the military necessity so urgent as not to admit of delay." Thus, instead of changing the procedure of who could impress property and under what authority, Yancey attempted to change the circumstances under which private property could be impressed. His amendment lost by a vote of fourteen to nine. Due to the heated debate surrounding the impressment bill, the Senate opted to move into secret session on March 10 to discuss the issue further. There, the Senate

17. *JCCSA,* 6:61, 100–103, 105–7; Warner and Yearns, *Biographical Register,* 122–23.

amended the bill and provided any officer of the Confederate States with the authority to impress property without public notification of supplies needed or written permission. The Senate passed this amended version of House Bill 9 by a vote of seventeen to five, with both Oldham and Wigfall supporting its passage, and informed the House of its action.[18]

The amended version, however, did not please many House members, and Virginia representative James Holcombe immediately moved to vote on whether to accept the Senate version. The House disagreed with the Senate's version by a vote of forty-one to thirty-four. Afterward, the House moved to appoint a three-member committee to resolve the difference between the two branches. The House committee consisted of Holcombe, Alabama representative William Paris Chilton, and Augustus Hill Garland from Arkansas. Although the Senate responded by insisting upon its version of the bill, it acquiesced by also forming its own committee to meet with House members, and selected Haynes, Louis T. Wigfall, and Allen Taylor Caperton of Virginia to mediate the conflict. After some debate, the two committees agreed to a new version to the impressment bill. Section 1 of the bill, pertaining to the authorization and instance for impressment, was more vague than any previous version offered. "Whenever the exigencies of any army in the field are such as to make impressments of forage, articles of subsistence, or other property absolutely necessary, then such impressment may be made by the officer or officers whose duties it is to furnish such forage, articles of subsistence, or other property for such army." President Davis agreed to the legislative compromise and signed House Bill 9 on March 26, 1863.[19]

By 1863 then, Confederate law permitted Texans to trade their cotton across the Rio Grande. The Confederate government, however, did not fully ensure the protection of private commercial interests. Political pressure from Congress to cultivate crops other than cotton, along with the potential destruction of cotton, threatened farmers' economic interests. Furthermore, although the Confederate government attempted to impose guidelines and restrictions on impressments, their legislative efforts proved to be failures. The vagueness of the bill regarding the authority and instances for impressment left room for complete violation of personal-property rights. Some

18. Warner and Yearns, *Biographical Register,* 113–14, 118–19. Although Hill personally opposed conscription, he nevertheless defended it before the Georgia legislature (*JCCSA,* 3:90, 102–3, 123–24, 133–34, 147–48, 264–65, 6:178).

19. *JCCSA,* 3:173, 189, 216, 6:178–79, 186, 216–17. Chilton, a lawyer, Whig politician, and state senator, supported the exemption of farmers from military service. Garland was a strong proponent of personal rights. Caperton, a Yale graduate, generally opposed impressment and supported the rights of farmers.

politicians believed that military officials did not regard the law as one imposing restriction, but rather conceived it as a confirmation of their claimed and exercised power. Thus, military officials continued to impress cotton regardless of the rules and laws proscribed by the government. The ineffective legislation passed by the Confederate Congress caused citizens to rail not only against military officials, but also against Congress, revealing the politicians' ignorance of the vital link between effective offensive legislation and support for the war effort.[20]

Texas's cotton troubles, though, did not end with the Confederate government in Richmond. When Union occupation of the Mississippi River forced Richmond to establish the Trans-Mississippi Department as its official political organ for governing territory west of the Mississippi River, matters became more complicated. On August 3, 1863, Gen. Edmund Kirby Smith overstepped the boundary of authority and through illegal general orders established the Cotton Bureau to supervise the purchase, collection, and sale of cotton within the Trans-Mississippi Department. Richmond authorities, despite acknowledging its illegality, did not dissuade or order Kirby Smith to dismantle the bureau. Kirby Smith placed Col. W. A. Broadwell in charge of the Cotton Bureau and ordered all government purchasing agents to report to him. The bureau operated with the goal of controlling the cotton trade in the trans-Mississippi region. Due to the illegality of the bureau and his hidden agenda, Kirby Smith sought to win support of western politicians at the 1863 governors' conference in Marshall, Texas. Designated committees at the conference discussed many critical issues, including cotton. Senator Oldham, Louisiana chief justice C. J. Merrick, Arkansas politician C. B. Mitchell, Missouri governor Thomas C. Reynolds, and Texas governor Francis R. Lubbock constituted the committee on cotton issues. They concurred that Kirby Smith had the authority to purchase and impress cotton. With western politicians giving verbal approval to his authority over cotton, Smith began his move to control the cotton trade in the trans-Mississippi region.[21]

Competition for cotton was intense. Kirby Smith located the main office of the Cotton Bureau in Shreveport, Louisiana, a point too distant to maintain any type of control or authority over trade in Texas. Due to military demand, he attempted to remedy the situation in late 1863 by establishing branch offices in Houston and in Monticello, Arkansas. Kirby Smith's goal

---

20. Oldham, "Memoirs," 156–57, 161–62.

21. Kerby, *Kirby Smith's Confederacy,* 138; Agnes Louise Lambie, "Confederate Control of Cotton in the Trans-Mississippi Department," 32; *House Journal of the Tenth Legislature Regular Session,* 254–63.

regarding the Houston branch was to place Texans in control of the office to gain the trust of Texas planters. He gave orders for the Houston office to obtain, through either purchase or impressment, all cotton necessary to meet the demands of the army, and required all agents to report to Col. William J. Hutchins. Kirby Smith's authority to establish the Houston office and appoint Hutchins came from a directive by Confederate officials. According to General Orders 198, he held the authority to obtain from planters, by sale or impressment, all cotton necessary for the purchase of supplies to meet departmental needs. Agents desiring contracts for transporting and selling cotton were required to obtain their permits through Hutchins. Driven by his desire to control western commerce, Kirby Smith opposed the promotion of private enterprise and refused individual requests to exempt cotton for personal trade on the grounds that the Trans-Mississippi Department had a greater need and was more proficient in trade than the individual planter. Kirby Smith's actions received backing from official Confederate orders allowing for the full impressment of cotton. He even had approval to use all military assistance necessary to execute impressment.[22]

Backed by vague Confederate laws that virtually allowed for indiscriminate impressment and with an inordinate amount of power, Hutchins potentially held free reign over the control of cotton in Texas. However, he met with difficulty in gaining cotton from Texas planters and in December 1863 issued an open letter to the press appealing for their support. The lack of supply, he complained, has not been the fault of the planters. Rather, the difficulty in obtaining cotton resulted from the various and conflicting orders issued by Kirby Smith and the government, the numerous government agents engaged in acquiring cotton, and the exorbitant rates stemming from the intense competition. Hutchins stressed to Texas planters that Kirby Smith and the Cotton Bureau maintained full authority to purchase, and impress if necessary, all Texas cotton. He formulated a strategy to gain access to Texas cotton that he believed would be "liberal and just" to Texas planters. His plan involved the purchase of one-half of a planter's cotton. Upon delivery of that cotton to a government depot, the planter would receive an exemption from impressment for an equal amount of cotton. The owner then had freedom to export the remaining cotton. In addition, the seller would receive "certificates at its specie value, to be paid for in cotton bonds or such other equivalent as Congress may provide." Hutchins told Texas planters that Senator Oldham backed this idea and even assured Trans-Mississippi

22. Lambie, "Confederate Control," 36, 42–44; *War of the Rebellion,* 26:437–38.

Department officials that he would work to secure favorable legislation to this end. He further stressed that the army stood in the greatest need, and as a result individual wants would have to wait, and he forbade planters from removing any cotton from the state until they had delivered half their crops to the nearest government depot. Hutchins warned that any planter attempting to remove his cotton from the region without a permit faced the risk of having all his cotton impressed by the government. Furthermore, anyone interfering with the cotton trade or transportation of cotton by attempting to forestall the hiring of teams, or by offering or giving a higher rate of freight than the terms proposed by the Houston office, jeopardized any benefits or exemptions they might receive for selling cotton.[23]

Hutchins's letter to Texas planters sounded more threatening than appealing and garnered little support from the citizenry. Furthermore, his plan only added to the chaos as conflict reigned throughout the Trans-Mississippi Department over the control of cotton. To make matters worse, Confederate military officials in the department often issued contradictory orders regarding Texas's cotton trade. For example, in December 1863, General Magruder issued orders restricting all cotton trade across the Rio Grande. Magruder had the responsibility of controlling the cotton trade in the Trans-Mississippi Department before the establishment of the Houston office. Either slighted by his loss of authority or unaware that the Cotton Bureau operated independently and was not under military authority, Magruder continued to issue orders affecting the cotton trade, often conflicting with Kirby Smith's orders and Hutchins's plan. Ironically, Kirby Smith, despite reprimanding Magruder for these orders, soon followed the latter's lead by prohibiting all government and private cotton trade from Texas across the Rio Grande.[24]

Due to the tumultuous situation, the Confederate government often failed to procure enough cotton for the purchase of goods and military supplies. In the summer of 1863, for example, General Bee did not have enough cotton to purchase items that had arrived at the port in Brownsville. Consequently, he asked for Magruder's advice on the matter; in turn, Magruder sought Kirby Smith's council. Kirby Smith told Magruder that in all circumstances, he had the right to impress cotton, according to guidelines, without first seeking approval from headquarters. Thus, word filtered to Bee to impress cotton, but only for the amount needed for the purchase of goods. Bee, however, resorted to old practices. He levied a 20 percent contribution stipulation on all cotton in Brownsville. Once the owner turned his cotton over to the government,

23. *War of the Rebellion,* 26:480–82.
24. Lambie, "Confederate Control," 49–54; *War of the Rebellion,* 53:184.

he received a certain price in Confederate Treasury notes. It was well known that General Bee had unmitigated power and could exempt whomsoever he pleased from this contribution or other imposed regulations. He often exempted his loyal contractors, who had previously received his permits, but imposed regulations on all other individuals. In more instances than not, military officials disregarded Confederate law prescribing the mode of impressment, and often confiscated cotton from individuals without proper remuneration and without proper evidence for claims.[25]

Kirby Smith did not support such overt illegality and issued his strategy to secure Texas cotton. His plan involved issuing specie certificates to vendors for one-half the amount of their cotton. The selling price ranged from ten to fifteen cents per pound, depending on the quality of the cotton. The vendors' other half remained exempt from impressment, and they were free to sell it elsewhere or could obtain a permit from the Cotton Bureau for exportation. Kirby Smith's system operated on the assumption that vendors could afford to spare at least half their cotton supply at low prices. According to Senator Oldham, however, Kirby Smith's practice of issuing specie certificates was illegal and done without authority. Furthermore, the certificates themselves became subject to speculation that greatly affected the price and trade of cotton. In the spring of 1864, cotton covered by permits was worth fifteen cents a pound and only eight cents per pound without the permit. Moreover, Kirby Smith's plan only complicated matters as military and Cotton Bureau officials all operated under their own legal and extralegal guidelines.[26]

By 1864, the Trans-Mississippi Department was in utter chaos. Kirby Smith became distraught over the situation. "Everything (officially) has gone wrong," he told his wife. "I am miserable, discontented, unhappy." The Cotton Bureau, however, continued to issue permits, and Magruder and Bee persisted in their endeavors to monopolize the cotton trade, which only served to inflame Texas citizens. As most Texans understood, there was to be no military interference with Texas's free trade across the Rio Grande, and the *Austin Texas State Gazette* railed against this infringement and the Confederate government's failure to control its military leaders. Furthermore, Texas politicians in Richmond condemned military interference. Senator Oldham remarked of the situation, "Bee sat at the gate of the Rio Grande, and Magruder at those of the ports of the Gulf[.] What a Field for

25. Kerby, *Kirby Smith's Confederacy,* 173–74; Oldham, "Memoirs," 351, 365; *War of the Rebellion,* 26:78, 184.

26. *Senate Journal of the Tenth Legislature First Called Session,* 23–24; Oldham, "Memoirs," 370.

corruption!!" Although Oldham criticized such illegality, he did not place the blame for corruption on the shoulders of the western officials; instead, he found fault with Confederate politicians in Richmond who had surrendered the Trans-Mississippi Department to its fate. Such disregard was a "gross and palpable outrage" upon the rights of the citizens. Confederate political and military interference, therefore, sparked the outrage of Texas citizens and politicians, and the Lone Star State stood in direct opposition to the Confederate government.[27]

Texas planters and politicians faced and opposed the barrage of inconsistency over the cotton policy of Confederate officials in Richmond and the Trans-Mississippi Department. Though the Committee on Cotton at the governors' conference gave Kirby Smith verbal approval to control cotton in the region, the conference itself held no legal standing. Thus, verbal approval did not bind Texas or other western states to any dictates issued by Kirby Smith's illegal Cotton Bureau and allowed western states to formulate their own cotton policies, which often contradicted Kirby Smith's desire to control western cotton. As such, Texas politicians railed against Confederate policy and took direct measures to counter any negative effects on Texas's economic welfare, seeking to protect trade and production. Under Governor Pendleton Murrah, the Lone Star State formulated a design to procure cotton. The main features of Murrah's plan included the vendor transferring his cotton to the state. At his own expense and risk, yet under authority of the state, the vendor had permission to transport the cotton to the Rio Grande. The vendor would be allowed to retain half the amount of his cotton supply for personal use, and he could opt to transport it under state authority with the rest of the cotton and sell it in Mexico. The Texas government paid vendors from nine to eleven cents per pound in the form of state bonds. The advantage one had in selling to the state included the assurance of personal trade with Mexico under state authority and the freedom from having the entire amount of cotton impressed by Confederate officials. Furthermore, state bonds yielded approximately 8 percent per annum. The Cotton Bureau of the Trans-Mississippi Department could not guarantee Texas citizens these benefits. Murrah's plan found favor among Texas planters. Their acceptance created conflict and a cotton shortage for the Trans-Mississippi Department

27. Edmund Kirby Smith Papers, Barker Center; *Austin Texas State Gazette,* Aug. 11, Sept. 16, 1863; Oldham, "Memoirs," 371–73; Frank Vandiver, *Ploughshares into Swords: Josiah Gorgas and Confederate Ordnance,* 98; Kerby, *Kirby Smith's Confederacy,* 160–61.

whereby Hutchins urged Kirby Smith to impress as much Texas cotton as possible.[28]

Not only did Governor Murrah seek to safeguard Texas's commercial interests, but representatives in the Texas legislature sought to defend Texas's trade against Confederate encroachment as well. On November 13, 1863, Marmion Henry Bowers introduced a resolution to the Texas House of Representatives calling for the Committee on Military Affairs to investigate Confederate restrictions on the cotton trade in Texas. Bowers, a devout Baptist and Mason hailing from Travis County, was born in Indiana and received a law degree from Indiana University before moving to Austin in 1853 where he practiced law. During the Civil War, he served in Flournoy's regiment from Travis County and held the rank of captain, and afterward he won election to the tenth legislature. Bowers and other politicians were concerned with whether Confederate restrictions uniformly applied to all citizens, and whether some individuals received special privileges. Texas politicians knew that Confederate military leaders on the border conspired to monopolize the cotton trade, they worried how Confederate restrictions tended to affect the interests of Texans, and they wondered whether the government interfered with their citizens' economic welfare. Thus, in a move to remedy the corruptive practices of Magruder and Bee, Caldwell County representative Spencer Ford introduced a bill on November 30 to punish the speculation of permits to export cotton. Ford's bill made it to a second reading before politicians referred it to the Judiciary Committee. Furthermore, Lavaca County representative W. H. Howard, a member of the Committee on State Affairs, reported on the prevention of cotton trading on the western frontier. The committee recommended that the bill not pass. The House took up the committee report on November 27, 1863. Liberty County representative Frederick F. Foscue motioned that the committee report be tabled, and the House concurred. By laying the report on the table, the House theoretically abided by the committee report, but also left the issue open for future debate. Texas politicians' desire to continue open trade with Mexico coincided with the wishes of Governor Murrah, who believed trading cotton with Mexico for necessary supplies was vital to the continual maintenance of machinery in Texas's institutions. Murrah told the legislature that it was

28. Oldham, "Memoirs," 369; *House Journal of the Tenth Legislature Regular Session,* 254–63; Kerby, *Kirby Smith's Confederacy,* 142; *War of the Rebellion,* 26:535–38, 53:979–80; *Senate Journal of the Tenth Legislature First Called Session,* 25–26; James W. Daddysman, *The Matamoros Trade: Confederate Commerce, Diplomacy, and Intrigue,* 128–29.

absolutely necessary that it establish laws allowing for the continuance of free trade.[29]

Not only did Texas politicians deal with trade issues, but they also dealt with cotton production. Cotton production, though, did not require heavy debate. The matter was simple; Texas's trade with Mexico was too lucrative to limit cotton production. Texas existed as Mexico's major source of cotton, a fact that even Northern manufacturers recognized. As Northern mills continuously ceased operations due to the lack of cotton, Northern attention focused more closely on Texas's cash crop. Northern newspapers commented that Texas stood out as the sole source and hope to restart their faltering manufactories. On November 17, 1863, the Committee on Agricultural Affairs reported on a bill regulating the cultivation of cotton in Texas. Smith County representative Lovick P. Butler, chairman of the committee, reported that after debate on the matter, the committee had recommended that the bill not pass, and the House of Representatives accepted the report. Thus, in the face of Confederate law and Cotton Bureau illegality, Texas sought to carve its own niche in the cotton trade and secure the general welfare of itself and its citizens, regardless of Confederate need.[30]

By 1864, the independent path of Texas contributed to Confederate troubles. The conflict over cotton created discontent among Confederate politicians in Richmond, who exhibited listless apathy regarding important legislation. As despondency and despair set in, many politicians began to denounce President Davis and his cabinet. Oldham claimed that many politicians seemed paralyzed due to the crisis of the Confederacy. Yet, some politicians remained patriotic and zealous, and continued to work in the interest of the Confederacy.[31]

For the most part, the Confederate government remained disconnected from reality. Only a few politicians, such as Texas senator Williamson S. Oldham, truly understood the correlation between western interests and the greater good of the Confederacy. In a speech before the Senate on December 23, 1863, Oldham addressed the status of Confederate finances. In that

29. *House Journal of the Tenth Legislature Regular Session,* 97, 130, 174; *Senate Journal of the Tenth Legislature Regular Session,* 118; *Senate Journal of the Tenth Legislature First Called Session,* 21. Ford also represented Gonzales and Guadalupe Counties; Foscue also represented Jefferson, Chambers, and Orange Counties.

30. *House Journal of the Tenth Legislature Regular Session,* 115, 160; L. Johnson, *Red River Campaign,* 13–14. For Texas's cotton trade with Mexico, see Daddysman, *Matamoros Trade.*

31. Oldham, "Last Days of the Confederacy," Oldham Papers, RG 2R131, Barker Center, 3.

speech, he railed against military control of the cotton trade in Texas, arguing that it was one reason for the disparity between the supply and demand of currency. He argued that Texas should be permitted to trade its cotton supply without interference from the Confederate government. By allowing Texans to profit from such commerce, in turn the Confederacy would also profit.[32]

Despite Oldham's arguments, Confederate politicians continued striving to gain control over all aspects of cotton production and trade. On May 21, 1864, the Confederate Senate considered Senate Bill 20 to establish the Bureau of Foreign Supplies. The Bureau of Foreign Supplies was charged with purchasing cotton for export to procure the necessities of war, and was allowed to hire agents for the purpose. The bill specifically stipulated that an office of the bureau be set up west of the Mississippi River to compete for cotton. Furthermore, the office was granted the power to establish depots at its discretion to control trade across the Rio Grande. Kirby Smith's Cotton Bureau would be subordinate to and subsumed by the new agency. The Confederate government finally appeared willing to recognize the instability of western commerce created from competition and corrupt practices, and the inability of the Cotton Bureau to adequately control the trade in Texas. Despite the Trans-Mississippi Department's cotton supply being depleted due to trade with the Union and the policy of destruction, Kirby Smith did not appear willing to relinquish any authority or what little control he wielded over the cotton trade. He again took measures into his hands, well beyond the legal limits. On June 1, 1864, he ordered the impressment of one-half of all cotton in the trans-Mississippi region, reaffirming a practice that had begun at the onset of the war.[33]

Texas politicians, however, continually countered impressment attempts. On May 14, 1864, the Texas Senate voted and passed a bill "to define and punish the unlawful interference with the exportation and transportation of cotton or other articles." Grimes County representative David C. Dickson offered an amendment to the bill regarding citizen trade with the Trans-Mississippi Department. This amendment stipulated that the bill not be enacted retroactively. Thus, those individuals who had contracted with agents of the Trans-Mississippi Department escaped any negative effects of the bill. Engaging in cotton trade with the Trans-Mississippi Department instead of the state did not equate to interference with Texas's cotton trade. The amend-

32. Oldham, *Speech of Hon. W. S. Oldham, of Texas, on the Subject of Finances, Senate, December 23, 1863,* 3.

33. *JCCSA,* 4:70–71; Kerby, *Kirby Smith's Confederacy,* 161; *War of the Rebellion,* 26:78.

ment therefore served to protect the planter and thus laid the foundation for future trading with the state over Confederate authorities. Twelve days later, the Senate received a message from the House that it had passed the Senate bill, and two days afterward, the legislature presented the bill to Governor Murrah for his approval.[34]

By March 1864, approximately one-half of all baled cotton in Texas was sold to state officers. Kirby Smith appeared distraught over the situation and the lack of available cotton resulting from Murrah's plan. In July 1864, he invited Murrah to meet in Hempstead, Texas, to discuss the problem. He persuaded Murrah to relent from his state plan. After the meeting, Murrah issued an open letter to Texas citizens, requesting that they send their cotton to the army in return for whatever payments were offered. The governor also ceased to offer protection. In many ways, the Hempstead meeting and Murrah's actions were meaningless. Too much resentment persisted among Texas citizens, and politicians continued in their efforts to counter Kirby Smith's and the Confederate military's efforts to gain cotton. Only two weeks after the meeting, the secretary of war ordered Kirby Smith to surrender all control of the cotton trade to the Trans-Mississippi Treasury Agency created to oversee the cotton business in Texas.[35]

Texas politicians stood united in their effort to promote the economic interests of Texas and actively participated in legislation toward that end. Such political action was not a radical states' right line but rather a moderate course aimed at securing the overall economic good for the citizens and the state. The majority of legislation dealing with cotton issues came to a vote during the first called session of the tenth legislature. Analysis of the Senate roll-call votes on bills dealing with cotton interests reveals a unified political effort to protect and promote Texas's cotton commerce. The majority of Texas senators actively participated in cotton legislation by casting votes from 70 to 100 percent of the time.[36]

Though participation on cotton legislation was extremely high, support for Texas's interests did appear somewhat divided in the Senate. Nevertheless, such division on cotton matters did not translate into a clean regional split between high-producing and low-producing cotton regions. State interests

34. *Senate Journal of the Tenth Legislature First Called Session,* 42, 47, 49, 86, 100. Dickson also represented Montgomery and Walker Counties.

35. Kerby, *Kirby Smith's Confederacy,* 201–3, 293; Yearns, *The Confederate Governors,* 212–13.

36. See Owsley, *State Rights,* for the states' rights argument. For a challenge to Owsley's argument, see Beringer, *Elements of Confederate Defeat.* Roll-call votes in the first called session of the House of Representatives are not listed in the House journal.

overshadowed counties and economic-entity regions. Map 6.1, "Voting Support for Texas Cotton Issues," reveals that 76 to 100 percent of all political support for Texas cotton interests came from both high- and low-cotton-producing regions. Senators in the heart of Texas's black belt actively supported Texas's cotton interests, as did those senators in the southern border region where cotton trading across the Rio Grande remained extremely active. Furthermore, high support existed among those politicians representing the northwestern frontier region of the state, an area better known for its cattle holding and noncotton agricultural pursuits. Considering that the majority of all Texas senators cast favorable votes at least 76 percent of the time, a more unified political picture emerges. To be sure, geographical analysis reveals that senators from only two small regions in south and east Texas cast favorable votes less than 51 percent of the time. In addition, regression analysis of the roll-call votes from the Senate's first called session and the amount of ginned cotton in each county reveals that no significant relationship existed between the amount of cotton ginned in each county and whether that county's representative voted to support Texas's cotton interests. It is thus inaccurate to assume that only those politicians from high-cotton-producing counties voted to protect and promote Texas's cotton interests.[37]

Despite such unification, Texas still had to confront the problem of Confederate policy that changed with the wind. This inconsistency was most apparent in the Confederate policy on trading cotton. On November 17, 1864, the Confederate Senate agreed in secret session to a resolution submitted by Alabama representative Richard Wilde Walker that the Committee on Commerce investigate the possibility of establishing a law that would allow for the exportation of cotton to points within the enemy's lines, in payment for army supplies. This move was a direct contradiction to previous legislation and reveals Richmond's inconsistent cotton policy that wreaked confusion and havoc for the western theater. Though the official Confederate policy was to burn cotton and keep it out of the hands of Union officials, Confederate leaders such as John Magruder acknowledged that clandestine trade was already under way and necessary to procure some necessities of war. He worried and admitted, though, that open trade with the Union would demoralize the people and wished that such practice in the Trans-Mississippi Department remained a secret. Magruder further stressed that if such trade did occur, it

---

37. *Senate Journal of the Tenth Legislature First Called Session; Agricultural Census.* At a 95 percent confidence level, regression analysis of political support for Texas cotton and ginned cotton produces a p-value of .289 (r-sq 0.7 percent), with a negative relationship of 74.1–.0005.

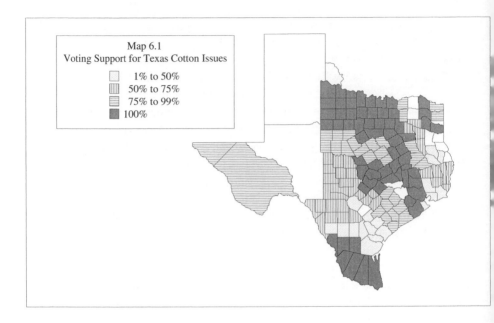

Map 6.1
Voting Support for Texas Cotton Issues

☐ 1% to 50%
▥ 50% to 75%
▤ 75% to 99%
■ 100%

should be conducted in the most efficient manner, for the greatest need facing the army was adequate clothing, especially since the Texas State Penitentiary served Texas citizens over the army. On the other hand, Magruder feared that the policy of burning cotton would instill fear in the citizenry that the Union troops might be close at hand and aiming at an invasion of the region. His sentiments clearly express the quandary of the Confederate government. Richmond politicians knew that the Confederacy was in trouble. Instead of promoting public confidence and support through free trade and protection of private property, however, the government waffled by passing inconsistent legislation.[38]

While debating the issue over trade with the Union, the Confederate government upheld its policy of impressment. On May 28, 1864, the Senate read Senate Bill 51, "to provide supplies for the army and to prescribe the mode of making impressments," twice ordering it placed on the calendar and printed. On June 1, the Senate took up the bill for a third reading, and it passed. The next day, the House read Senate Bill 51 twice with an order for its printing. The bill reaffirmed military necessity and the legal right of impressment. This piece of legislation was significant, however, for it reflected a stronger interest in protecting private property. Section 2 of the bill stipulated that

38. *JCCSA*, 4:270; *War of the Rebellion*, 41:1025–26, 1099.

the supplies necessary to support cotton producers and their families should be exempt from undue impressment. Nevertheless, this was still an arbitrary statement open to abuse by officials.[39]

The ever changing cotton-trade policy of the Confederate government also wreaked havoc on officials' ability to procure the necessities of war. In January 1863, for example, when the Confederate government issued orders allowing cotton exportation across the Rio Grande without full assurance of the return of supplies, cotton prices rose from twenty-five cents to as high as sixty cents. Such high prices were not affordable for the Confederate government, and Simeon Hart requested that he be allowed to impress cotton to meet his obligations. Hart, however, was also hampered by Kirby Smith's unwillingness to turn over money to him for fear that it would interfere with the needs of the Trans-Mississippi Department. Hart's difficulties were further compounded by Texas's purchases of large amounts of cotton. Some Confederate officials such as Magruder wished to counter such state initiatives by having the Confederate government buy all the cotton in Texas. How such a plan could be enacted without serious pitfalls is unimaginable, considering that Magruder knew that even the impressment of Texas cotton would create mounting dissatisfaction and serious trouble. As such, Hart received authorization to impress cotton, but was forbidden to impress any cotton belonging to the state of Texas.[40]

The Confederate policy of exporting cotton in 1864 stipulated that no cotton could be exported except by an individual state or the Confederate States of America. Confederate officials on the Rio Grande received orders in October 1864 to prohibit all cotton trade with Mexico unless vendors had proper permits issued by the Cotton Bureau. Violators ran the risk of having their wagons, cotton, and teams seized by military officials. Kirby Smith, however, confided in Governor Murrah that this policy by Richmond was abominable, for Richmond did not thoroughly understand the needs of the trans-Mississippi region. Kirby Smith did not intend to abide by Confederate law and told Murrah that he would not change his previous trading practices. He reassured the governor that he would continue to give his approval to those who applied for applications under the law, and asked Murrah to unite with him in addressing the president on this matter. Kirby Smith believed it his duty and within his power to override the president's decision to restrict trade across the Mexican border. His cooperative spirit with Murrah, how-

39. Confederate States of America, Senate, *A Bill to Provide for the Army and to Prescribe the Mode of Making Impressments,* copy in Barker Center.

40. *War of the Rebellion,* 26:62–63, 172; Meiners, "Texas Border Cotton Trade," 299.

ever, was only a veiled attempt to win western favor to continue his illegal activities.[41]

Despite Richmond's move to ensure undue impressment of private property and Kirby Smith's conciliation toward Texas interests, Texas politicians continued to oppose Richmond's cotton policy. In response to Confederate efforts to regulate Texas trade and impress citizens' property, the Texas legislature passed an act "to define and punish the unlawful interference with the exportation and transportation of cotton, or other articles, and the unlawful impressment of property." Texas politicians endeavored to safeguard their legally sanctioned trade from Confederate authorities and labored to protect the ordinary citizen. Officials guilty of breaking the law would receive fines not to exceed the amount of cotton with which they interfered. If officials unjustly impressed cotton from the ordinary citizen, they received fines double the amount of property taken unless they could prove just compensation to the property holder. Both offenses carried potential terms of imprisonment for up to one year with the additional possibility of a civil suit.[42]

The Texas legislature remained firm in its stance against Confederate trade interference. Geographical analysis of Senate opposition to impressment reveals that the majority of Texas senators opposed Confederate attempts to regulate free trade by impressing cotton. Map 6.2, "Political Opposition to Confederate Impressment," depicts a unified political effort to promote Texas's economic interests and free trade over the interests of the Confederacy. The vast majority of Texas senators opposed Confederate impressment, casting favorable votes for Texas's interests 90 to 100 percent of the time. Opposition to Confederate law ran high in Texas, and representatives in the Senate displayed a unified political effort to protect the economic welfare of their constituency.

To safeguard Texas's interests further, the state legislature resolved that Governor Murrah communicate Texas law to Confederate authorities. In a further resolution passed by the tenth legislature concerning Richmond's attempt to impose an export duty on cotton, Texas politicians were more direct in their criticism of Confederate policy. They railed against Confederate involvement in regulating the cotton trade and criticized President Davis and the Confederate Congress for their ever changing policies. They claimed that Confederate policy undermined legitimate trade, depreciated the value of all property, and interfered with property owners' business endeavors. More striking, they blamed Confederate officials for undermining the war effort.

41. *War of the Rebellion,* 41:972, 1082–84.
42. Gammel, *Laws of Texas,* 770–71.

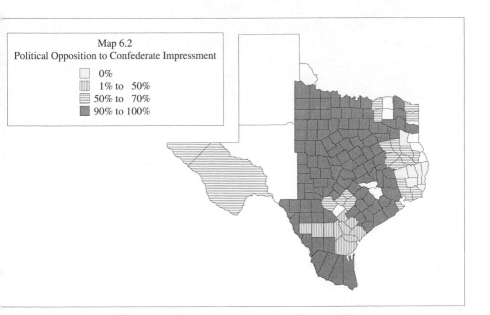

Map 6.2
Political Opposition to Confederate Impressment

☐ 0%
▥ 1% to 50%
▤ 50% to 70%
■ 90% to 100%

Confederate attempts to regulate trade, the Texas politicians claimed, caused Confederate officers to neglect their military duties by forcing them to pay more attention to commerce. Thus, the policy was a threat to not only Texas's economic interests, but also the entire economic interests of the South and the war effort overall. Because of the government's interference, the ordinary citizen became discouraged and shied away from directly selling his cotton to government officials. "The result is unprofitable, as always happens when a government enters the market."[43]

By this, though, the state legislature referred solely to the federal government and not the state government's involvement in commercial activity. Politicians and plain folk identified more with local and state interests and saw no conflict with state involvement in commerce. The commitment to Texas's economic security was reflected not only in the legislation against Confederate interference with trade, but also in the political dedication to economic growth and the welfare of the state through legislation to promote industrial progress in the cotton industry. From 1863 through 1864, the Texas legislature incorporated nineteen companies to promote the manufacturing of cotton and cotton products. These industries engaged in producing cotton

43. Ibid., 830. For the importance of cotton to the ordinary citizen, see Ramsdell, *Behind the Lines.*

and woolen fabrics, cotton yarns, spinning jennies, spinning wheels, looms, reels, cotton cards, and cotton-seed oil. The legislature also supported each company's efforts to trade and export cotton. It advocated such industry throughout the state, especially in the Gulf Coast and eastern and central Texas counties, but primarily throughout the Cotton Belt. Production ranged from 0 to 31,342 bales of cotton across the state, and those counties where cotton manufacturing companies existed produced from 0 to 23,221 bales of cotton. When considering the mean production of cotton, however, those counties with incorporated companies produced 5,050 bales of cotton, much higher than the state's mean of 3,480 bales. Although the tenth legislature did not promote cotton manufacturing in several of the counties with the highest cotton production, as a whole those counties produced more than the state average. In most cases, the legislature also permitted these companies to expand their operations to other parts of the state if they proved successful in their manufacturing endeavors. Statistical analysis reveals, however, that no significant relationship existed between county cotton production and the location of cotton manufacturing sites, suggesting an ulterior motive other than production for the placement of manufacturing sites.[44]

Furthermore, the state legislature strove to ensure the success of such manufacturing endeavors through strict stipulations and generous benefits. In all cases, the state government stipulated the limit of stock the company could not exceed and set the amount for each share of stock. Stock limits ranged from two hundred thousand dollars to five million, and individual shares ranged anywhere from one hundred to one thousand dollars. Such stipulations ensured that more well-to-do individuals would have a personal stake in such endeavors. The legislature further required that companies first sell a certain amount of stock and that the board of directors of each company own a specific amount of stock before operations began. In this manner, the government sought to promote the safe progress of manufacturing by avoiding bust endeavors and ensuring that individuals associated with the company had a personal stake in the company's success. Furthermore, it stipulated in most cases that it held the right to alter and amend the company charters at any time in the future to safeguard the interests of the state and the company. Many of these companies received benefits from the state, such as land grants as provided by the 1863 law. Benefits to chartered companies, however, not only affected investors but also extended to the ordinary citizen. In most company charters, the legislature exempted all company employees from military service and forbade the impressment

44. *Agricultural Census.*

of any property, including wagons, livestock, machines, and slaves. Such exemptions reinforced county-court decisions. County courts held a great deal of authority over exemptions and released numerous individuals, such as wagon makers, millers, mill engineers, and blacksmiths, from service. Thus, both state and local politics coincided to protect and promote manufacturing endeavors.[45]

By protecting the ordinary laborer and his property as well as company assets, manufacturing endeavors not only promoted the general welfare of the state, but also served to protect the economic prosperity of citizens. This concern was not a short-term goal for Texas politicians, but rather an effort to promote long-term economic growth. Accordingly, the legislature granted nine of the companies twenty-year charters and seven of them twenty-five-year charters, and three had no limit. The liberal economic worldview of Texas politicians ensured that Texas's interests superceded those of the Confederacy, thus securing a separate political and economic identity.[46]

By 1865, Texas representatives in Richmond began to act more overtly to protect and promote Texas cotton. In addition, the corruption that pervaded the Trans-Mississippi Department finally aroused the ire of Confederate politicians. As a result, they turned their attention to bringing suit against the department, allowing for proper claims and remuneration, and continued to deal with cotton production.

Kirby Smith's practice of purchasing cotton on promise of payment and not remunerating citizens finally received the attention of representatives in Richmond, and Missouri representative George Graham Vest, who had the ignominious distinction of being the sole member of Congress to be publicly horsewhipped, introduced a resolution into the House of Representatives requiring President Davis to have the Military Department inform the House of all cotton transactions made with the Trans-Mississippi Department. The House agreed to Vest's resolution, but western representatives remained unsatisfied and pushed for further action. Outraged over the Cotton Bureau's impressment of cotton and failed promises of remuneration, Texas representative Caleb Claiborne Herbert called for an investigation into Kirby Smith's trading and purchasing practices. Herbert served in the Texas Senate from 1857 to 1859. As a radical states' rights advocate, he had voted for calling the secession convention. In the Confederate Congress, he sought to protect

45. Orders and Circulars, Records of the Trans-Mississippi Department, 1861–1865, RG 109, General Orders 13, National Archives; *War of the Rebellion,* 26:126; Moore, *Conscription and Conflict,* 185.

46. Gammel, *Laws of Texas,* 720, 734, 737, 740, 745, 786, 787, 788, 793, 794, 795, 796, 838, 842, 844.

Texas's cotton industry and commerce more than any other politician. Herbert also was known for supporting Texas's withdrawal from the Confederacy. On December 2, 1864, he offered a resolution into the House, which was adopted, requiring the Committee on Claims to investigate Kirby Smith's purchase of cotton from Texas citizens. In addition, Texas representative Stephen Heard Darden offered a resolution requesting that President Davis inform the House "with such official information relative to the transactions of the office, or 'Cotton Bureau,' established in Texas by the commander of the Trans-Mississippi Department for the purpose of purchasing and exporting cotton." Darden was born in Fayette County, Mississippi, and moved to Texas in 1841. As a landholder in Gonzales County, he represented that county in the House of Representatives before the war. He initially opposed secession, but joined with the majority, and won election to the Confederate Congress in 1864 where he became known for his opposition to a centralized government. A Texas landholder, Darden was concerned with any impropriety between Davis and Trans-Mississippi officials that affected Texas's commerce. Building on Vest's move, Darden's resolution sought to get to the crux of illegality by narrowing the scope of inquiry.[47]

Thus, in the span of one month, Texas representatives joined by other western politicians in the Confederate Congress launched a full offensive intended to disclose the corruption; it was an attempt to finally remedy the conflict affecting Texas's cotton trade. President Davis took his time in responding to these legislative resolutions. Nevertheless, he had no option and eventually complied with all the requests by February 1865.[48]

Despite Davis's quasi-cooperation, congressional representatives still clamored for more information and action to resolve problems in the West. Louisiana representative Lucius J. Dupre offered a resolution requiring President Davis to turn over all communications and orders from the secretary of war to Kirby Smith that pertained to the latter's civil and military administrations, maintenance of the Cotton Bureau, and cotton-trading activity. Kirby Smith's illegal practices had been officially revealed during a court-martial in Louisiana the previous year, and politicians sought to fully uncover any impropriety, including whether he had ever had the authority to establish the Cotton Bureau. At the court-martial, Kirby Smith was asked whether he was authorized to assume such broad powers and control of

---

47. *JCCSA,* 7:283, 318, 354; Warner and Yearns, *Biographical Register,* 117–18, 254–56; Rable, *Confederate Republic,* 155. Vest supported state control over troops and was a harsh critic of Jefferson Davis.

48. *JCCSA,* 7:376, 551.

government agents. He replied that he believed, according to instructions from the secretary of war, he had the authority to assume widespread control for the maintenance of the department to support the armies in the field. He acknowledged, though, that even without direct instructions, he believed he held the authority to pursue such action. By his own admission, Kirby Smith had transcended legal limits and authority in establishing the Cotton Bureau. He acted on his own initiative without regard to Confederate law.[49]

Consequently, politicians moved to bring suit against Kirby Smith and the Cotton Bureau. On January 20, 1865, Texas representative Caleb C. Herbert reported a bill that required suits to be brought against persons connected with the Cotton Bureau. The bill called for suits to be brought against any person who, under government authority, financially gained from the acquisition of cotton through impressment, from the selling of exportation permits, and from any other improper means. Politicians sought to end the prohibition on trade and the government's threat and practice of illegal impressments. Texas representatives in Richmond could no longer tolerate the commercial threat to Texas citizens. Herbert found support from other Texas politicians. Senator Oldham remarked that every man "whose hands were soiled by the touch of that cotton" was obligated to make a complete disclosure of his transactions for judgment. On January 20, 1865, the House considered Herbert's bill and after a second reading referred it to the Committee on the Judiciary. On March 2, 1865, the committee reported with an amendment and ordered a printing of the bill. A week later, the House informed the Senate that it had passed H.R. 341 by a vote of thirty to twenty-seven. Texas representatives, though, were not thoroughly satisfied with the bill due to the potential implication of Texans, and all representatives except Herbert voted against passage of the bill. Herbert remedied the problem by pushing for an amendment that changed the wording of the bill, taking out *Texas* and inserting *Trans-Mississippi Department*. The House then asked the Senate to concur on the bill. The Senate referred the bill to the Committee on the Judiciary and then passed it without amendment on March 13, 1865. The Senate further ensured that no suit would be brought against Texans by placing Senator Oldham in charge of nominating the committee to investigate the Trans-Mississippi Department's activity. Two days later, Jefferson Davis signed the bill.[50]

49. Ibid., 7:403.
50. Confederate States of America, House of Representatives, *A Bill Requiring Suit to Be Brought against Persons Connected with the Cotton Bureau and Cotton Office in Texas,* copy in Barker Center; Oldham, "Memoirs," 376; *JCCSA,* 4: 685–786, 701, 708,

Not only did Confederate politicians move to bring suit against Kirby Smith and his cohorts, but House and Senate politicians also attempted to aid citizens in the recovery of money owed by the Trans-Mississippi Department. In January 1865, Herbert introduced a bill into the Confederate House of Representatives to provide for the auditing of the Cotton Bureau, and the Senate also entertained bills calling for the auditing of and payment of claims by the bureau. On March 2, the Confederate House of Representatives passed a bill "providing for the auditing and payment of properly authenticated claims against the Cotton Bureau in the Trans-Mississippi Department." All of Texas's representatives, except Sexton and Morgan who did not vote, voted to pass the bill. The House then passed the matter on to the Senate where it concurred with no amendments offered. Confederate politicians finally appeared united in an effort to correct injustices that had occurred throughout the war.[51]

More important for Texas citizens, their representatives had finally sought to counter Confederate law by promoting the production of cotton in the trans-Mississippi region. In January 1865, Senator Louis T. Wigfall introduced Senate Bill 174 calling for the encouragement of the production of cotton in the Trans-Mississippi Department. Herbert made the same move in the House, in secret session. The House of Representatives referred Herbert's bill to the Committee on Ways and Means. The committee, however, was slow in reporting on the bill, and so on February 25, Herbert again introduced a bill to encourage the production of cotton. The bill made it to a second reading upon which Herbert moved to suspend the rule requiring the bill to be referred to a committee. His motion lost, and again the Ways and Means Committee considered the bill. Finally, on March 1, the committee recommended that the bill not pass. Herbert immediately called for a vote on the matter, and the House voted thirty-five to twenty-eight to accept the committee's recommendation. Each of Texas's representatives, except Morgan who did not vote, voted against the committee's recommendation. In the Senate, Wigfall's bill fared no better. The Senate Committee on Finance debated Senate Bill 174 for more than a month and on March 9 requested that it be discharged from further consideration of the bill. Thus, although Confederate politicians appeared willing to correct injustices and stem illegal activities, they still did not waver from their effort to control the cotton business in the South, and Texas's representatives could do little to alter the

---

7:469, 676, 733–34, 757, 781. Senator Oldham selected Henry D. Ogden, Clement R. Johns, and John D. Morris for the investigating committee.

51. *JCCSA,* 4:507, 594, 7:469, 648, 650, 682, 709.

situation. The split between the Texas state government and the Confederate government now matured into a clear division between eastern and western Confederate politicians.[52]

The political effort by Confederate representatives to remedy western conflict, however, appeared too little, too late. Texas pursued its own economic interests, which conflicted with Confederate needs. A cooperative scenario, however, could have come to full fruition only if the Confederate government had initially moved to protect trade and private property in all aspects. Instead, it and Trans-Mississippi Department officials had launched a full assault, fraught with illegality, on free trade and private property. "Had there been no illegal interference with the people, in the exercise of their legal right to export their cotton," remarked Senator Oldham, "all the wants of the country would have been supplied with those articles of necessity and common use, usually obtained from abroad. In addition, the wants of the soldiers in the army would have, in most cases been relieved, by the contribution of comforts from parents, brothers, sisters and friends." Confederate politicians and military officials failed to realize from the beginning of the conflict the critical link between promotion of the rights of citizens and citizens' support for the war effort. In addition, the course pursued by Texas politicians on matters of economic security, especially regarding cloth and cotton interests, secured a separate political and economic identity for Texas. Furthermore, there was possibly little that the Confederate government could have accomplished because Texas politicians, through unbridled support for economic security and social welfare, strove to implement the foundation of a separate identity throughout the Civil War crisis.[53]

52. Ibid., 4:507, 676, 7:497, 652, 672.
53. Oldham, "Memoirs," 354.

PART IV

Implementing a Separate Identity

CHAPTER 7

"Her Present and Proud Condition"

Railroads, Education, Mutual-Aid Societies, and Asylums

On November 15, 1861, Texas governor Francis Lubbock stood before a joint session of the state legislature and compelled politicians to "sustain the State in her present and proud condition." Lubbock believed that secession from the government of the United States "was not only a right possessed, but a great political necessity." Texans, he declared, "determined that they would never submit to have their own rights, or the rights of the State government, absorbed by a fanatical Government, fast drifting to centralism." Lubbock further told his fellow politicians that Texans worried about their security, and he urged the legislators to provide for the welfare of the citizenry. The fear of centralization combined with a desire to promote economic security and social welfare pervaded Texas politicians, and the legislature worked to secure the economic and social well-being of the state and its citizens.[1]

Entering the Civil War, many Texans loosely held to a Jacksonian ideology that included a belief that it was "wrong for internal improvements within the states to be financed by the federal government." Consequently, the state legislature undertook efforts to safeguard and promote the economic well-being of the state. The move to secure railroads, education, mutual-aid societies, and state welfare institutions reflected to the citizens a concerted political effort to promote economic security and social welfare. Whether this endeavor immediately succeeded in many ways was irrelevant. The effort by the state was more than the Confederate government could begin to offer, and this bolstered the perception, if not the reality, that Texas could exist on its own in the Confederacy. This concerted political effort to promote economic security and social welfare throughout the Civil War paved the

1. *Senate Journal of the Ninth Legislature,* 48–50.

way for citizens' support of the state and symbolized the implementation of a separate political and economic identity.[2]

One of the primary modes of promoting economic security came in the political effort to sustain and promote the railroad system in Texas. Railroads were vital to consolidation in the nation. Transportation was necessary for progress, especially in an agricultural society. At the time of the Civil War, a vast railway system existed in the South. Robert C. Black III, however, points out that "everywhere through Dixie railroads were stretching iron fingers toward one another, but not yet everywhere had they joined hands." Though both Texas and the Confederacy progressed in rail growth, the South still lacked juncture points that would have linked the nation. The South was "still in an infancy stage in regards to industrial unification." Texas was extremely isolated in these regards, and remained so even after the Civil War. For example, Austin, the capital of Texas, was fourteen hundred miles from the Confederate capital in Richmond and during the war would remain beyond the reach of both railroad and telegraph.[3]

In Texas, Houston existed as the central point of the rail system. This was due in part to the consequence of war. Houston established itself as a major center for trade and business as merchants shifted their facilities from Galveston. General trade and blockade running were big business, and individuals sought to protect their trade at all costs. The transference of business from the island to Houston spurred rail growth. The Civil War was the first conflict in which railroads played an important part, and historians who have criticized the South for its lack of control over the railroad system have failed to look at the state level for such regulation. The efforts, therefore, to secure the railroad industry at this point predominately emerged as an individual state effort. For Texas, then, the Civil War became a critical period for the support of railroads.[4]

Texas politicians sought to sustain railroads not only for the economic benefit, but also for its connection to the general school fund. State policy connected the railroad system and the school system, and if one suffered

2. Buenger, *Secession and the Union,* 26.

3. Black, *The Railroads of the Confederacy,* 9, 76; David C. Humphrey, "A 'Very Muddy and Conflicting' View: The Civil War as Seen from Austin, Texas," 369. See also Charles W. Ramsdell, "The Confederate Government and the Railroads"; and James Arthur Irby, "Confederate Austin, 1861–1865."

4. Earl Wesley Fornell, *The Galveston Era: The Texas Crescent on the Eve of Secession,* 11. See also Frank Vandiver, *Confederate Blockade Running through Bermuda, 1861–1865;* Paul Levengood, "In the Absence of Scarcity: The Civil War Prosperity of Houston, Texas"; and John Stover, *American Railroads.*

neglect, then both would possibly fail. Governor Murrah urged politicians to sustain and foster both systems. The idea was that as the railways prospered they would be responsible for payment, from their profits, to the state treasury for aiding and supporting the school system. This policy also existed in Georgia where the state was able at one point to rely upon the rail companies for the support of a tax-free school system.[5]

Though the actual mileage of rail in Texas remained relatively low compared to other Southern states, Texas ranked third behind Louisiana and Virginia in terms of capital investment in railroads, spending $31,186 per mile of track. More than that, Texas politicians during the Civil War remained committed to sustaining incorporated rail companies, a move that symbolized their vision for economic security and internal improvement. Texas's ninth legislature entertained several bills during its meeting that incorporated rail companies. The primary issue confronting politicians was to sustain the incorporated companies financially and to prevent forfeiture of company charters. The impact of war upon Texas railroads often made it difficult for rail companies to complete the required sections of track. In addition, railroads spent a great deal of time carrying soldiers and prisoners of war to various camps and outposts in Texas. This in turn led to financial difficulty because rail companies were slow to receive revenue from general operations. Companies thus had a troublesome time paying the interest due on bonds and loans from the general school fund. Therefore, politicians intervened and bolstered the finances of incorporated rail companies in the state. The mode of relief came in the form of payment extensions. The legislature passed numerous bills for the relief of rail companies that provided for the extension of payments of all interest on bonds and loans from the school fund until 1864, or six months after the close of the war. Politicians thus permitted rail companies to continue their operations and building with less financial burden. Believing the war to be a short-term obstacle, politicians supported the maintenance and growth of the railways at the expense of the state's financial stability.[6]

Not only did the ninth legislature ease payment requirements, but it also relaxed the provisions requiring companies to complete the stipulated miles of track. Charters for incorporated rail companies contained specific provisions detailing the initial amount of track each company was required to lay

5. *Senate Journal of the Tenth Legislature Regular Session,* 106. See also Peter Wallenstein, *From Slave South to New South: Public Policy in Nineteenth-Century Georgia.*

6. Gammel, *Laws of Texas,* 481; Frank MacD. Spindler, "The History of Hempstead and the Formation of Waller County, Texas," 415.

to prevent forfeiture of their charter. An act passed by the ninth legislature, however, stated that "the failure of any chartered Railroad Company in this State to complete any section or fraction of a section of its road, as required by the existing laws, shall not operate as a forfeiture of its charter." In the case of the Eastern Texas Railroad Company, the legislature granted it a reprieve from completing the first fifty miles of its road until one year after the termination of the war. Thus, incorporated rail companies received political assurance for their continued operations during this period of difficulty. Furthermore, the legislature acknowledged that oftentimes the basic operations of the company became hindered. War affected the rail companies in the sense that members of their boards of directors and their principal investors were often conscripted into service. This made it difficult for railroad companies to make their annual reports to the legislature as required by law. Failure to make an annual report violated the charter agreement and potentially threatened the security of the company. In some instances, companies were unable to make their annual report, and the legislature proved lenient, granting rail companies additional time to make their report without forfeiting their charter. The legislature acknowledged that the war impeded rail growth, but holding to its vision and commitment of economic security, politicians worked to ensure the safety of such corporations to meet the desired goals.[7]

Not only did the state subsidize railroad companies, but politicians also sought to foster rail growth through enticements to chartered companies. These enticements came in the form of land grants and additional loans. The legislature urged railroad companies to complete the required sections of track stipulated in their charters. To promote rail growth, companies that completed twenty-five miles of road became entitled to state grants of sixteen sections of land for every mile of road constructed, with the possibility of more land under special provisions. These grants gave the railroad companies alternate sections of land per mile with other alternate sections retained by the state for donation to the general school fund. Texas's land-grant policy to railroad companies followed the alternate-section principle established by the federal government in earlier years. In certain cases, the legislature also enticed rail companies to finish sections of track with the promise of additional loans. In 1861, for example, the legislature promised the Eastern Texas Railroad Company a thirty thousand–dollar loan from the school fund if it completed an additional five consecutive miles of track, beyond the

7. Gammel, *Laws of Texas,* 490–91, 528, 565; Southern Pacific Railroad Company, Railroad Commission Records, RG 4-3/448, TSL.

completed twenty-five, or if it connected their track with that of the Texas and New Orleans Railroad. In the case of the Southern Pacific Railroad, the legislature approved the section of its track running from Jonesville in Harrison County eastward to the Louisiana border as part of the section of twenty-five consecutive miles in addition to the twenty-five miles already completed. This entitled the company to a loan of six thousand dollars per mile under the provisions of the 1856 act "to provide for the investment of the special school fund, in the bonds of Railroad companies, incorporated by the State."[8]

Along with sustaining rail companies and urging continued rail growth, the legislature sought to remedy the predicament of connecting the various lines in the state. The primary weakness of the southern rail system was the lack of connections due to different gauge systems. Texas politicians sought to remedy this during the war. In certain cases, charters bound companies to connect with existing rail lines using the same gauges. For example, when the legislature revived the Galveston and Houston Junction Railroad Company in 1863, it required the rail company to connect with the Galveston, Houston and Henderson, and Texas Central Railroads using similar gauges and complete the construction before 1864.[9]

Thus, realizing the effect of war on internal construction and improvements, politicians worked to keep railroad companies operating during the war. Their efforts reveal that although the amount of track laid during this period was less than pre- and postwar periods, railroad companies continued to operate, and the economic security of the state was maintained. Thus, the critical period for railroads in Texas came not after the war but during the war as politicians sought to sustain the operation of such vital corporations. While the war effort may have hampered the building of railways, it in no way deterred politicians from promoting economic security in the state.

The ninth legislature's voting participation and support for railroad issues reflect this commitment. Analysis reveals that politicians throughout the state actively partook in debating and casting votes on legislation pertinent to Texas railroads. The most active political participation came from those politicians representing the southernmost region of Texas and from politicians representing counties in the heart of Texas's black-belt and southwestern border-frontier regions. Politicians from those two regions voted on

8. Gammel, *Laws of Texas,* 490–91, 542, 549–50; Ralph N. Traxler Jr., "The Texas and Pacific Land Grants: A Comparison of Land Grant Policies of the United States and Texas," 361–62.
    9. Gammel, *Laws of Texas,* 635–36; Black, *Railroads of the Confederacy,* 76.

every issue that came before the Senate and House of Representatives, and represented 27 percent of Texas's counties. In addition, strong voting participation came from politicians representing the majority of Texas counties. Politicians representing 48 percent of Texas's counties, seventy-seven counties throughout the state, participated in voting on railroad issues 75 to 100 percent of the time.

Voting participation, though, appeared relatively higher than actual voting support on railroad issues. Geographical analysis of voting support for railroad issues reveals that the strongest support came from those politicians who exhibited the highest degree of participation. Map 7.1, "Ninth Legislature Voting Support—Railroad Issues," reveals that those politicians from the same two regions, Texas's black-belt and southwestern border-frontier areas, strongly supported railroad issues by casting votes in support of legislation to sustain and promote railroad companies. Politicians from these regions, representing 12 percent of all Texas's counties, cast favorable votes 100 percent of the time. This pattern of support, though, did not hold true for the rest of Texas's politicians, and the vast majority of those who actively participated in railroad issues cast their votes against supporting them. In fact, politicians representing 41 percent of Texas's counties supported railroad issues less than 50 percent of the time (see Appendix 6, "Legislative Participation and Support").[10]

Nevertheless, the percentage of nonsupport did not outweigh the overall support for Texas railroads, enabling politicians to pass legislation favoring the railroad industry. Statistical analysis explicates the difference between political participation and support for railroad issues, and sheds light on the regional interests that politicians represented in their support for Texas's railroads. Land, ranching, and manufacturing interests along with population characteristics each appear to have a significant relationship with political support for railroads. Geographical and statistical analysis reveals that those politicians representing counties in the black belt evinced strong support for railroads. It is not the actual number of slaves held that appears significant with railroad support, but rather slave density. Politicians representing counties with a higher slave density showed stronger support for railroads. In addition, politicians representing counties with significantly higher farm values were more likely to support railroads. Nevertheless, it should not be assumed that these politicians represented the interests of the slaveholding

10. Favorable and nonfavorable votes do not necessarily correspond with "yea" and "nay" votes. Votes were analyzed in regard to the best interest of the rail company and economic growth and coded into the database appropriately.

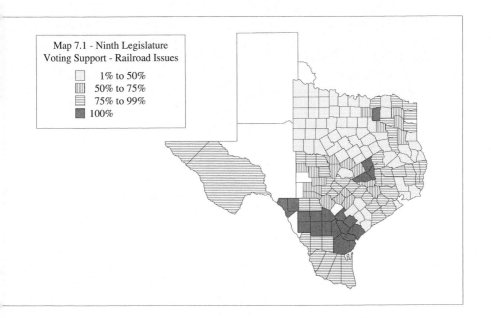

Map 7.1 - Ninth Legislature
Voting Support - Railroad Issues

- 1% to 50%
- 50% to 75%
- 75% to 99%
- 100%

elite. Strong support for railroad companies also came from those politicians representing counties that had a higher total capital investment in manufacturing endeavors, especially in lumber. More important, those politicians representing counties with larger cattle holdings also evinced strong support for railroads; the higher a county's cattle holding, the more likely their representative voted to support railroad issues. In addition, in those counties where the value of livestock increased and the value of animals sold for slaughter decreased, their representative more likely voted for railroad support. This suggests that significant political support came from those regions that needed and desired direct market access. Sustaining railroad companies and urging continual growth ensured better access to markets, especially in those regions where livestock existed as a valuable asset (see Appendix 4, "Regression Analysis: Ninth Legislature").

Each of these factors having a significant relationship with railroad voting support reveals that politicians from the more economically advantaged counties in the state supported railroads. It was not just the rich landholder, cattle rancher, or slave owner, though, who benefited from such support. Labor also was a critical issue, and maintaining the railroads meant employment for a vast number of people. At the beginning of war, for example, the Southern Pacific Railroad employed approximately 473 people, 400 of whom worked as general-construction hands. Thus, political support for

Texas's railroads, while it came from politicians representing the more economically prosperous counties, benefited all classes of citizens.[11]

The support for Texas's railroads was also intimately tied to the general interest in education because profits from the rail companies were to be paid into the general school fund from issued loans and bonds. Even during the Civil War, Texans kept education a high priority. Education during the Civil War was not restricted to elite members of society; even the poorest families in Texas found ways to educate their children, through either public or private schools and tutors. Generous benefactors and teachers, in many cases, waived tuition fees for dependents of soldiers. The political support for education went far beyond these ties to include the incorporation of schools and endowments for professorships. In the ninth legislature of Texas, participation on educational issues appeared extremely high and widespread throughout the entire state. Legislators representing 60 percent of all Texas counties cast votes on 100 percent of all bills entertained. Nevertheless, politicians representing those counties that ginned lesser amounts of cotton yet had a higher value of farmland were more likely to vote on education issues than fellow representatives.[12]

One of the critical issues that legislators participated in involved the incorporation of schools in the state. In 1860, there existed 1,218 common schools with 1,274 teachers and 34,611 pupils. In addition, there were 97 academies with 236 teachers and 5,916 pupils. During the Civil War, the Texas legislature expanded upon the educational system of Texas and incorporated additional schools and academies, placing special emphasis on female education. It incorporated 4 additional academies and institutions during its session. These additional schools were located not in the heart of the black belt or more highly populated counties, but rather in the northern frontier and the central and Gulf Coast border regions.[13]

Geographical analysis of legislative voting behavior reveals that the strongest support for education during the ninth legislature came from politicians representing the Gulf Coast, southwestern frontier, and central-midwestern frontier regions. Map 7.2, "Ninth Legislature Voting Support— Education Issues," reveals that politicians representing forty-five counties, 28 percent, cast favorable votes supporting education 100 percent of the time. The counties whose representatives strongly supported education through

11. Railroad Commission Records, Southern Pacific Railroad Company, RG 4-3/448, TSL.

12. Frank Vandiver, "Notes and Documents: Letters from the Confederate Medical Service in Texas, 1863–1865," 382; Levengood, "Absence of Scarcity," 30.

13. Michael Allen White, "History of Education in Texas, 1860–1884," 128; Anita Louis White, "The Teacher in Texas, 1836–1879."

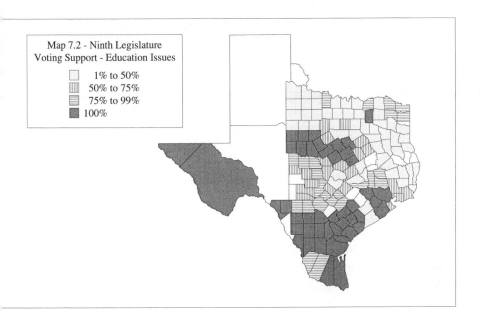

Map 7.2 - Ninth Legislature
Voting Support - Education Issues
☐ 1% to 50%
▥ 50% to 75%
▤ 75% to 99%
■ 100%

the incorporation of academies and institutions generally had higher farm values than other counties. In addition, the counties that these politicians represented had a significantly lower white population than other counties. Furthermore, politicians representing counties with higher cattle holdings more likely voted to support education. It was not just cattle holding, but also livestock value and the value of animals slaughtered for market that held a significant relationship with educational voting support. In those counties where livestock value increased and the value received for slain animals decreased, political support appeared high. This suggests that those politicians who more strongly supported education came from those regions that had a vested interest in cattle yet limited access to markets. These factors suggest that the support for education did not appear to be predominately an urban issue. Instead, it came from the lesser-populated regions that had a stake in farming apart from cotton production. Thus, the political support for education during the ninth legislature did not come from the wealthier cotton-producing regions but rather from those politicians representing counties that had higher farm values and lower production of ginned cotton. The interest and support for education did not merely exist among the slaveholding elite, but was something that the ordinary citizen valued as well and understood its necessity for success. As seen, such political action garnered the support of the citizenry.

Texas politicians not only concerned themselves with protecting the economic well-being of citizens and the state through railroads and education, but they also maintained it through the incorporation of mutual-aid societies and the continued support for state institutions. Mutual-aid societies, though performing many of the same functions, were fundamentally different from the mutual-benefit societies, fraternities, and secret societies that arose in the nineteenth century. Whereas fraternal organizations represented a form of masculine solidarity and promoted the concept of manhood and masculinity, and secret societies such as the Knights of the Golden Circle existed as vehicles to influence the political and economic sphere on a grand scale, mutual-aid societies existed first to aid the poor and dependents of soldiers, and second to profit economically. Mutual-aid societies functioned with the purpose of conducting and managing general mercantile business. The structure of mutual-aid societies resembled that of general corporations. They held the right to own and sell property, to sue and be sued. Furthermore, such societies sold shares of stock to investors. In most cases, though, the legislature placed a limit on the capital stock of the societies and stipulated the specific dollar amount for individual shares, usually in amounts less than one hundred dollars per share. The merchant class in Texas, consisting in part of those individuals who organized such societies, played a dominant role in shaping Texas's economy and aiding the general citizen. The primary goal of mutual-aid societies was to sell supplies and goods to needy persons and families of soldiers. The societies, however, were not to benefit financially from their benevolence, and the legislature specifically mandated in company charters that goods were to be sold at cost to these burdened individuals. Once the needs of the poor and soldiers' families were met, these societies had the right to earn their profits through general business.[14]

Political participation on bills to incorporate mutual-aid societies varied throughout the state. Politicians representing 32 percent of all Texas counties participated 100 percent of the time on bills for incorporating mutual-aid societies. Furthermore, politicians representing eighty-six Texas counties, 54 percent of all counties, participated at least 75 percent of the time. The highest degree of participation came from politicians representing counties in the Gulf Coast and western-frontier regions of the state, with high participation also scattered throughout the state.

14. Gammel, *Laws of Texas,* 642, 645–47; Susanne L. Summers, "Persistence and Change among the Merchant Community in Houston and Galveston, Texas, 1836–1880s." See also Mary Ann Clawson, *Constructing Brotherhood: Class, Gender, and Fraternalism;* and Carnes, *Secret Ritual.*

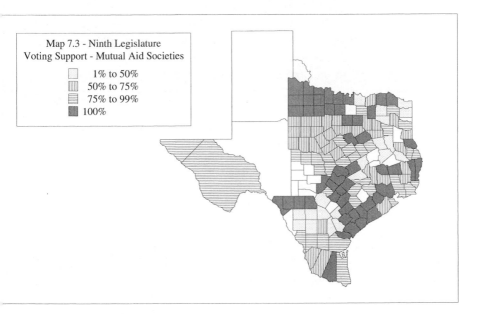

Map 7.3 - Ninth Legislature
Voting Support - Mutual Aid Societies
    1% to 50%
    50% to 75%
    75% to 99%
    100%

Map 7.3, "Ninth Legislature Voting Support—Mutual Aid Societies," reveals that these politicians also exhibited a high degree of support for incorporation. The legislature incorporated societies in six central and Gulf Coast counties. Those politicians that strongly supported mutual-aid incorporation represented counties with larger cattle holdings. Furthermore, as in the case with educational support, those counties where livestock value increased and the value of animals slaughtered decreased, their representatives evinced a stronger support for mercantilist activity and support for the poor and dependents. These results suggest that a stronger political concern for economic security and social welfare existed among those representatives whose counties had limited access to markets. It did not come from politicians representing the interests of the slaveholding elite, but rather from those legislators who represented counties with more of a vested interest in livestock and cattle ranching. Thus, by incorporating mutual-aid societies to protect against speculators and extortioners for the benefit of the poor and families of soldiers, Texas politicians worked to promote a policy of economic security and social welfare that benefited Texas citizens.

Not only did politicians seek to harness the loyalty of citizens and offer security through mutual-aid societies, but they also sought to meet the extraordinary needs of citizens' welfare by maintaining various asylums. To garner the support of the citizenry, it became incumbent upon politicians to concern themselves with and legislate for the welfare of even the most destitute citizens of the state. Incorporated before the war, the Lunatic Asylum, the Institute for the Deaf and Dumb, and the Asylum for the Blind all received attention from the Texas legislature. During the war period, the legislature was careful to attend to the needs of the various asylums and oftentimes appointed committees to check on the conditions and wants of the institutions. Due to the failure of the Confederate government to offer aid or coordination for such institutions, the legislature's primary goal was to bring these asylums under financial control.[15]

On August 28, 1856, the Texas legislature founded the Lunatic Asylum of Texas, currently the Austin State Hospital. Politicians appropriated fifty thousand dollars for the construction of the institution, and the governor appointed a three-member commission to select a site for the building and a superintendent to oversee all responsibilities in the asylum. The legislature reserved one hundred acres for the asylum, and the commission chose a site within two miles of the state capital in Austin. The construction and location of the asylum followed the plans of Dr. Thomas Kirkbride, superintendent of the Pennsylvania Hospital's Department of the Insane. His book *On the Construction, Organization, and General Arrangements of Hospitals for the Insane* became the standard for most asylums in the nineteenth century. The Lunatic Asylum opened its doors on May 11, 1861, with twelve patients.[16]

The asylum operated under the control of a superintendent and a matron, generally the superintendent's wife, and additional staff members. The superintendent of the asylum served as the chief executive and medical officer of the institution. He took charge of all patients, staff, finances, and the physical grounds. Unlike asylums in other states, Texas's institutions did not experience the physical effects of war, and the grounds of the asylum were a beautiful spectacle that caught most Austinites' eyes. The grounds were "most tastefully arranged with walks, shade trees, shrubbery, and flowers," and the orchards of the asylum were well maintained. The superintendent's primary responsibility, though, revolved around the medical, moral, and dietetic treatment of the patients. There existed many widespread beliefs regarding insanity, from the effect of an increasingly complex society to the taxing of mental powers due to insatiable greed or from the failure to

15. *House Journal of the Ninth Legislature,* 120. Though these terms may be offensive to some, I have chosen to use the terms *asylum* and *patient* because that was the language used during this period.

16. Chris Brownson, *From Curer to Custodian: A History of the Texas State Lunatic Asylum, 1857–1880,* 4–5, 12; Hogg Foundation, *Know Your Texas State Hospitals and Special Schools.*

strengthen the brain with study and discipline. Most superintendents during this period adhered to a "cult of curability" and believed that cure was most possible if patients received treatment during the first year of insanity "attacks." As such, the state asylum gave preference to those who had less than a year's insanity, then attended "the most refractory and dangerous, rather than the inoffensive idiot and hopeless epileptic." The matron's duties involved care of the female patients in the asylum. She controlled the kitchen and laundry and made sure that the cooking, washing, sewing, and ironing were completed properly.[17]

Patients admitted into the asylum fell into one of two categories: public patients or private patients. Public patients were those admitted by the county at the cost of two dollars per week, paid quarterly. Private patients were those admitted by family members or friends at the cost of the family and charged five dollars per week, paid semiannually. Patients entered the asylum for numerous reasons, from dementia to melancholia to suicidal tendencies. Records reveal that a variety of causes labeled one for admission into the Lunatic Asylum. Most individuals admitted into the asylum suffered from some form of monomania. All admitted patients were "made perfectly clean, and free from vermin, or any contagious disease." In addition, all patients received sufficient clothing, but the institution made efforts to have family members send clothing if possible. Once admitted into the asylum, patients adhered to a strict daily schedule of exercise, meals, and work. Each patient worked at an assigned job, which served to instill regularity and the learning of socially acceptable actions, and aided the staff as a means of social control. The daily exercise routines became an essential means to divert patients from their illness, loneliness, and boredom. Staff members kept the asylum as clean as possible, and both patients and staff were required to be respectful to one another.[18]

Politicians had a moral responsibility to the social welfare of the citizenry, and because the legislature could not restructure society, the alternative to aiding the insane involved the creation and maintenance of asylums to control a patient's environment. Although Texas politicians succeeded in the first part of their responsibility, erecting an institution, it has been a general

17. Peter McCandless, *Moonlight, Magnolias, and Madness: Insanity in South Carolina from the Colonial Period to the Progressive Era;* Austin State Hospital, *By-Laws, Rules, and Regulations for the Government of the Texas State Lunatic Asylum, Austin,* 3, 7; Brownson, *From Curer to Custodian,* 16–18, 23; *Report of the Superintendent and Managers of the State Lunatic Asylum for the Year 1866,* 4, 9.

18. *Report of the Lunatic Asylum,* 15; Austin State Hospital, *By-Laws,* 15–18; *House Journal of the Ninth Legislature,* 32; Brownson, *From Curer to Custodian,* 20–21.

assumption that politicians failed in the second part, to maintain such institutions. The ninth legislature, however, was deeply concerned with the maintenance of state institutions. In November 1861, Governor Francis Lubbock told the Senate and House of Representatives that the Lunatic Asylum as well as other welfare institutions should merit their attention. "They have, doubtless, accomplished much good, and if properly managed in the future, will confer great benefits on a large number of our unfortunate people, and reflect great credit on the State." Lubbock urged politicians to place such institutions on better footing and offered his full cooperation in the matter. The legislature acknowledged the governor's wishes and in January 1861 appropriated a maximum of twenty-four thousand dollars for the Lunatic Asylum's 1862–1863 operations.[19]

In addition, the legislature involved itself in the internal operations of the Lunatic Asylum to ensure its proper functioning and service. In some instances, the legislature even intervened and required the asylum to admit patients. One such case involved declared lunatic Margaret Needham from Travis County. Officials for some obscure reason wished not to admit Needham. Most likely it was due to the question of financial ability on the part of the institution or the county. Nevertheless, the legislature ordered the chief justice of Travis County to admit Needham into the Lunatic Asylum and make all the necessary provisions for her support and maintenance. In other cases, the legislature ruled that it was the financial responsibility of the family or guardian or both to provide adequate financial support and maintenance. For example, the legislature ordered the Lunatic Asylum to admit Minerva J. Fannin in 1862 and demanded that her guardian, Thomas F. McKinney, provide for her financial support for the duration of her life. Under no circumstance was Fannin to be a charge against the state, and the legislature declared that any part of Fannin's personal estate, including inheritances, were to be turned over to the asylum for her keeping. Thus, in some cases, the state sought to have the institution free from state support; in this way, politicians could keep the costs of the institution in check while maintaining a commitment to patients' welfare.[20]

Similar to many of the state institutions, questions regarding fiscal responsibility often arose. In one instance, the legislature instructed the Senate Committee on Retrenchment and Reform to investigate the internal finances

19. Brownson, *From Curer to Custodian,* 9, 55; *Senate Journal of the Ninth Legislature,* 55; Gammel, *Laws of Texas,* 491–93.

20. Gammel, *Laws of Texas,* 559–60, 569–70; *Senate Journal of the Ninth Legislature,* 142, 216.

of the Lunatic Asylum. The committee found in early 1862 that the institution operated according to procedures and believed there to be no reason to alter or reduce the number of staff or pay for asylum employees. A minority report from the committee, however, suggested that any board member or staff employee who boarded family members at the institution (not for official purposes) be financially responsible for them instead of charging their expenses to the state. By appropriating the necessary operating expenses, intervening in the admission of patients, and working to ensure fiscal responsibility, the ninth legislature worked to maintain the operation of this vital institution during the initial stages of the war. By 1863, the Lunatic Asylum operated in fine condition, fulfilling its mission of mercy. Though Governor Lubbock wished that the legislature would increase the rate of board charged to the county for public patients, the legislature found that superintendent Dr. J. M. Steiner had done all in his power to ensure the successful operation of the asylum and found no need for an increase.[21]

The Institution for the Deaf and Dumb also operated successfully, and served the means of educating a number of unfortunates who would otherwise have "grown up in ignorance and made them blessings instead of curses to society." The Institute for the Deaf and Dumb was created by an act of the legislature in 1856 and opened its doors in 1857 with three students. Joseph Van Nostrand served as superintendent, James Wells as teacher, and Josephine Snydor as matron. Van Nostrand graduated with a theological degree from the University of the City of New York and was a senior professor at the New York Institution for the Deaf and Dumb. He appeared well qualified to take the position of superintendent. He was responsible to the Board of Trustees, selected by the legislature, for all matters. Van Nostrand operated the institute in an excellent manner, and the Senate legislative committee inquiring into the institution remarked, "[W]e cannot commend this institution and its management too strongly to the Legislature and the people of the state." As a result, in January 1862, the ninth legislature appropriated a maximum of seventeen thousand dollars for the institution's 1862–1863 operations.[22]

Similar to the Lunatic Asylum, politicians held a cooperative relationship with the superintendent of the Institute for the Deaf and Dumb. Van Nostrand often requested that politicians examine the pupils and in one case had

21. *Senate Journal of the Ninth Legislature,* 208; *House Journal of the Ninth Legislature,* 32, 192.

22. *House Journal of the Ninth Legislature,* 192; Gammel, *Laws of Texas,* 491–93; William W. Blackburn, "Evolution of the State School for the Deaf from an Asylum to an Accredited School," 10.

legislators gather in House chambers for an examination of the students' progress. Before a packed house of politicians and ordinary citizens, Nostrand allowed the audience to test the students to see how much they had learned. Audience members gave the students words and instructed them to construct sentences. In one instance, an audience member gave a young lady the word *rebel,* and she responded by writing, "The Southern rebels have a right to disobey Lincoln." Citizens and politicians appeared well pleased with the institution, the students' learning, and Van Nostrand's management.[23]

As with the Lunatic Asylum and the Institute for the Deaf and Dumb, the Asylum for the Blind operated under the direction of a superintendent, with the aid of a matron and teaching staff. The superintendent taught courses in science and maintained general control over the institution, including teachers, pupils, and all other connected personnel; he received $500 per month for his duties. The asylum also hired a matron who cared for the physical welfare of the students, kept their clothing clean and in good repair, and gave out general supplies as needed. For her services, she received a monthly salary of $250 dollars. The music teacher also aided in teaching science along with vocal and instrumental music, and earned $250 per month.[24]

The state Asylum for the Blind, however, did not appear as successful as the other state institutions. This resulted from internal problems, not political neglect or financial difficulty. The ninth legislature closely monitored the Asylum for the Blind, as it had the other institutions, and appropriated a maximum of $32,000 for its 1862–1863 operations. Nor were the institution's difficulties due to the inability of the students to learn or a poor curriculum, for the Board of Directors met with the students and monitored their studies in January 1861 and were satisfied with the management of the institution and the students' progress.[25]

Instead, personal misconduct undermined successful operations of the Asylum for the Blind. In August 1861, a female member of the institution, Miss Caffey, charged acting superintendent Dr. Haynie with improper liberties. The Board of Directors investigated the matter and after a thorough evaluation of the matter unanimously declared Haynie not guilty of the charges against him. The rumors and charges of sexual misconduct, though, came to the attention of several legislators and Governor Lubbock. When Miss Caffey again brought charges against Dr. Haynie in December 1861, Governor

23. *Senate Journal of the Ninth Legislature,* 60–61; *Austin Texas State Gazette,* Nov. 23, 1861; Blackburn, "School for the Deaf," 11.

24. Minutes of the Board of Trustees, Texas School for the Blind, 1856–1919, RG 771, TSL.

25. Gammel, *Laws of Texas,* 491–93.

Lubbock requested that the directors of the asylum take all necessary action to remedy the situation. This time Lubbock informed the Board of Trustees, forcing the Board of Directors to spend more time investigating the matter. The second investigation found other students willing to substantiate Miss Caffey's charges. As a result of the investigation and charges, Dr. Haynie tendered his resignation in December 1861. The Board of Directors, though finding Haynie a suitable person to run the asylum and who believed that the institution would suffer without his leadership, unanimously agreed to accept his resignation, effective January 1, 1862.[26]

Governor Lubbock also called the matter to the attention of the legislature on January 1, 1862. He relayed to politicians that although the Board of Trustees could not sustain the charges against Dr. Haynie, they had unanimously agreed that it would be in the best interest of the asylum for the superintendent to resign. In addition, though, all but one of the trustees had also resigned, suggesting that whatever impropriety occurred either went further than just the actions of Dr. Haynie or the trustees sought to avoid any public disgrace by their association with the asylum. When Lubbock visited the asylum, after the resignations, he found only two students remaining, an old man from Comal County who had little hope of being educated, and a fifteen-year-old girl, Amelia Bailey, from Calhoun County who appeared "positively idiotic" and most likely would have benefited more from the Lunatic Asylum. Governor Lubbock appeared to be at a loss to explain how either the students or those in charge could abandon the institution. He regretted "that an institution calculated to do so much good could have been thus far of so little benefit to those for whose benefit it was established." He then left the decision whether to continue the asylum's operations up to his fellow politicians.[27]

Lubbock, however, did not wait for the legislature to make a decision on the fate of the asylum. Instead, he appointed a board of trustees to monitor the institution and instructed the Board of Directors to advertise in the paper for a suitable superintendent. Several individuals applied for the position, and the board settled on hiring the Reverend W. A. Smith in March 1862.[28]

Despite hiring a new superintendent, the good condition of the asylum buildings, the hiring of staff, and sufficient appropriations, the Board of Directors reported to Governor Lubbock and the legislature that the asylum

26. *Senate Journal of the Ninth Legislature*, 284; Minutes of the Board of Trustees, Texas School for the Blind, TSL.
27. *Senate Journal of the Ninth Legislature*, 284–85.
28. Minutes of the Board of Trustees, Texas School for the Blind, TSL.

stood in poor condition. The board urged the legislature to give its full attention to the asylum, for it was important that it be revived to fulfill its mission. The lack of students proved the primary problem. The board believed, though, it was only a matter of time before either new students enrolled or the former students returned. With their positive outlook and the future of the asylum in jeopardy, the board advertised in the paper for the reception of students.[29]

The reorganization of the asylum did result in the admittance of several new students. As with prior procedures, the financial and material responsibility, especially for clothing, for patients in the asylum fell to family members. In cases where a family could not afford the cost, they were required upon application to provide a certificate from the chief justice of the county in which they were declared indigent stating to what extent the county would financially or materially aid the hospitalized individual.

Once reorganized, the asylum continued with its daily operations. Students woke well before sunrise to the ringing of the asylum's bells and gathered outside for morning exercise. After one hour of exercise, all students met in the music room for prayer. Breakfast was served after morning prayers, followed by another round of physical exercise. Then, from half past seven until noon, students received their academic instructions. Their study hours were strenuous and conducted in complete silence. After lunch the boys met in the factory and worked for two hours while the girls spent time knitting, sewing, and practicing the piano. Around sunset, the students again gathered outside for afternoon exercises. Staff members did not tolerate any disruptions or quarreling and made sure that students maintained the regimented schedule. In addition, male and female students could commingle only if supervised by staff members. Students who did not abide by the rules were subject to expulsion, and in several cases, the board did find that action necessary. The regiment of the asylum not only served as a means of social control for the staff, but worked to the benefit of the students as well. As a result of the rigid schedule and teachings, the asylum propelled the students toward self-reliance in every way possible.[30]

The number of new arrivals, though, did not offset rising expenses, and a financial crisis ensued. Therefore, on June 30, 1862, the Board of Trustees met and decided to close the Asylum for the Blind. They justified their decision based upon the number of students and the "distracted state of our Country." They resolved to close the doors of the asylum on July 31, 1862.

29. Ibid.
30. Ibid.

Governor Lubbock, however, did not approve of this decision. To resolve the matter, he met with Superintendent W. A. Smith and the Board of Directors. He advised them to develop a plan that would bring the financial situation of the asylum under control. After deliberating the matter, the board resolved to change the rate of pay for Smith, the matron, and the music teacher. Under the new agreement, Smith received twenty dollars a month for every student in instruction, and the music teacher received five dollars per month for every student in instruction who was able to prove his or her musical talent. This temporary measure served to bring the asylum under financial control for its continued existence. By September 1863, the Asylum for the Blind was full to capacity and operating in fine condition. Therefore, the Board of Directors sought to restore the old salary agreements to the superintendent and teachers.[31]

The ninth legislature succeeded in promoting economic security and social welfare during its tenure. As the war dragged on, and Texas faced an encroaching Confederate government with greater needs, it remained to be seen how Texas politicians would handle the new challenges and if they would retain their commitment to economic security and social welfare.

Railroad maintenance and support did not receive the same degree of attention by the tenth legislature as it had in the previous legislative session. With guidelines for construction and financial support already in place, politicians now concerned themselves only with the reception of bond payments from the incorporated companies. Consequently, the voting turnout among politicians appeared lower in comparison to the ninth legislature. Politicians from only 56 percent of the counties partook in roll-call votes dealing with railroad issues during the session, and politicians from 43 percent of the counties abstained from voting. Those politicians who did participate represented a total of eighty-nine counties located primarily in Texas's black belt and the central and southern border-frontier regions. These politicians represented counties that had a significantly higher white and slave population and that ginned more cotton (see Appendix 5, "Regression Analysis: Tenth Legislature").

In terms of support for railroad issues during the session, however, the actual percentage of support appeared higher than that from the ninth legislature. Map 7.4, "Tenth Legislature Voting Support—Railroad Issues," reveals that politicians representing 36 percent of the counties cast favorable votes 100 percent of the time, compared to the 27 percent from the ninth legislature. These politicians represented counties in the Gulf Coast, central-, and

31. Ibid.

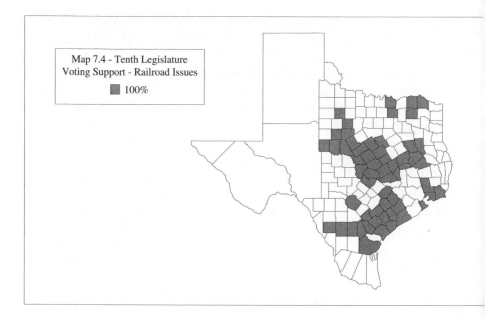

Map 7.4 - Tenth Legislature
Voting Support - Railroad Issues

██ 100%

western-frontier regions of the state. Nevertheless, the tenth legislature also exhibited a higher percentage of abstaining votes, 43 percent, as compared to the 5 percent from the ninth legislature. The distinctly low political participation and voting support on railroad bills during this session, though, is most likely attributed to the fact that politicians in the ninth legislative session settled the critical issues of support and financing for railroad companies, and bills in the tenth session allowing the state comptroller to receive payments on bonds did not garner nearly the amount of attention from legislators as previous debates. Nevertheless, geographical and statistical analysis reveals those areas where railroads were most critical and received the strongest political support.

Those politicians in the tenth legislature who supported railroad issues represented counties with substantially higher farm values, especially where the amount of ginned cotton decreased. This suggests that politicians supporting Texas railroads did not necessarily represent the slaveholding elite's interests. Furthermore, however, it was not just politicians from the wealthy landowning counties, but also those regions with a vested interest in livestock, especially from those counties where land value decreased and livestock value increased, who supported railroads. As in the previous session, it appears that political support came from politicians representing the regions with limited access to markets, for political support came from the areas where livestock value increased and the value of slaughtered animals decreased. Despite the diverse economic regions and concerns of the state, a degree of political unification emerged to secure the interests of the citizenry.

The political effort to sustain and promote rail growth in Texas during the Civil War not only represented an attempt to safeguard and promote the economic well-being of the state and its citizens, but was also an attempt to promote democratic institutions and combat monopolizing tendencies. To be sure, in its attempts to sustain the various incorporated railroad companies, the Texas legislature sought to safeguard the rights of citizens who invested in railroad ventures. In dealing with the companies, the legislature forbade companies to sell out stockholders. In cases where companies were sold and exchanged hands, as in the instance of the Texas Central Railroad being sold to W. J. Hutchings in 1861, the legislature demanded that the rights and interests of the original stockholders be secured. Furthermore, any effort by the owners of any railroad company to deny the rights of its stockholders prohibited a company from receiving potential land grants and loans from the school fund.[32]

Though the ninth legislature answered the financial questions surrounding railroad support, the tenth legislature still heeded the question of continuing their support for education. The consensus on Texas's education system during this period is that the legislature neglected education and stripped the general school fund bare for wartime priorities. The poor financial condition of the school fund was also attributable to failed interest payments from railroad companies on bonds issued from the school fund. According to Governor Murrah, in November 1863, the amount due to the general school fund from bonds of the railroad companies amounted to $345,317.60. The annual accumulation of interest for the bonds stood at approximately $106,858,80. The condition of the school fund and the railroad system was a serious issue for Texas politicians, and Murrah reminded the legislature that the two were intimately connected through legislation. Although previous attention has generally focused on the financial condition of the general school fund and the financial dilemma of Texas's education system, it is also important to note that politicians continued to support and extend education in Texas as the war progressed. They worked to incorporate additional educational institutions and schools, continuing with their effort to provide education for both male and female students.[33]

32. Gammel, *Laws of Texas,* 487–88, 490–91.
33. *Senate Journal of the Tenth Legislature Regular Session,* 106.

During its meeting, the tenth legislature incorporated additional academies and institutions, including seven located predominately in central Texas. In conjunction with the educational institutions incorporated by the ninth legislature, it appears that politicians did not favor any one region of the state but rather incorporated institutions across Texas. Furthermore, analysis reveals widespread voting participation on education issues among legislators across the state. Texas legislators representing ninety-six counties, 60 percent, participated 100 percent of the time on all education bills (Map 7.5). It was also quite a departure from the ninth legislative session, in which politicians representing a mere 28 percent of Texas counties supported educational issues 100 percent of the time. Though the war dragged on, the political commitment to education did not wane. Politicians continued to support and expand education through the establishment of academic institutions.

The tenth legislature also retained the commitment to the economic welfare of Texas citizens, and support for the incorporation of mutual-aid societies increased during the war period. Texas governor Pendleton Murrah believed that caring for indigent citizens and dependents of soldiers was one of the leading duties of the state government and "an obligation which she cannot neglect." It was absolutely necessary, he told the legislature, to provide for Texas citizens. As a result, the tenth legislature continued to support the incorporation of mutual-aid societies and upheld their general purpose to furnish necessities for members, families, dependents of soldiers, and the general market.[34]

Map 7.6, "Tenth Legislature Voting Support—Mutual Aid Societies," reveals that political participation and support for mutual-aid societies appeared markedly higher in the tenth legislature than the ninth legislature, with the vast majority of Texas county representatives supporting incorporation. The legislature incorporated societies in three additional central south-Texas counties. Politicians representing sixty-nine counties, 43 percent, cast favorable votes 100 percent of the time to incorporate mutual-aid societies, as compared to the 32 percent in the ninth legislature.

Geographical and statistical analysis reveals that high voting participation and support for the incorporation of mutual-aid societies came from politicians representing all economic regions in the state. Politicians representing counties where farm values tended to be lower generally supported mutual-aid societies more. In addition, politicians from those counties that

---

34. *Senate Journal of the Tenth Legislature Second Called Session,* 8; Gammel, *Laws of Texas,* 731.

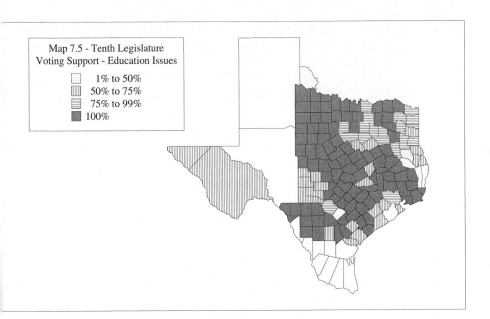

Map 7.5 - Tenth Legislature
Voting Support - Education Issues
1% to 50%
50% to 75%
75% to 99%
100%

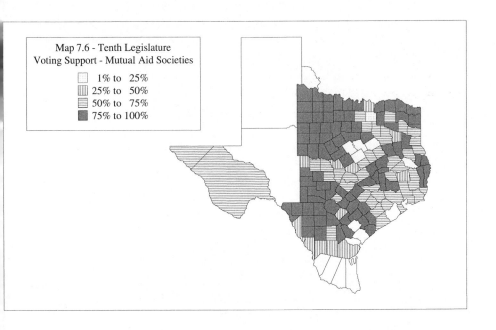

Map 7.6 - Tenth Legislature
Voting Support - Mutual Aid Societies
1% to 25%
25% to 50%
50% to 75%
75% to 100%

had lower cattle holdings and total value of livestock appeared to exhibit strong support for the incorporation of mutual-aid societies. Furthermore, though strong support did exist among politicians representing larger slave-holding counties, it was those politicians representing counties with a lower capital investment in cotton manufacturing that significantly supported the societies. Nevertheless, politicians representing the counties with a higher amount of ginned cotton, especially where farm values decreased, more likely supported the incorporation of mutual-aid societies than other politicians. As the war progressed and financial strain became more pronounced, especially through speculation from a scarcity of goods, political support to safeguard citizens' economic well-being also increased. Furthermore, the general interest in supporting mercantilist activity, especially from politicians representing counties with a vested interest in cotton production, increased during the Civil War. In this one instance then, it does appear that the politicians representing the slaveholding elite had more of an active support in politics than the previous legislative session, but not to the degree that it outweighed political support on all issues from other regions. Thus, throughout the Civil War, Texas politicians committed themselves to providing for the welfare of the citizenry and in doing so garnered their support. Not only did the citizens identify with local as opposed to larger Confederate issues, but state politicians exhibited the same concern and outlook as well.

The commitment to state asylums also remained strong among politicians. The effort to sustain the various state asylums not only reflected the trend toward institutionalization, but also revealed a pervasive concern for the state and welfare of the citizenry. After all, Governor Murrah believed that even in war it did matter how the state treated and cared for its citizens. As a result, the legislature increased appropriations for each of the state asylums. Governor Murrah also mandated that the state penitentiary do a better job of supplying the asylums with goods and cloth. He believed it was "very poor economy and very lame financing" to appropriate money for the purchase of supplies whenever the state was in a situation where one institution could benefit another. He argued that the asylums should receive, at a fixed price, whatever products they needed from the state prison.[35]

Murrah believed the Lunatic Asylum operated in excellent condition, and also urged the legislature to adopt measures that would extend the usefulness of the asylum. The legislature, acknowledging the Lunatic Asylum's vitality to the welfare of the citizenry and the state, raised appropriations from $24,000 to $100,000 for 1864–1865, and later increased this amount

35. *Senate Journal of the Tenth Legislature First Called Session,* 21.

to $150,000 in May 1864. Politicians deemed the additional appropriation necessary because the Lunatic Asylum operated at full capacity and appeared successful in its mission to cure the insane.[36]

By the end of the war, the superintendent, Dr. B. Graham, operated the institution with success. The asylum maintained its strict schedule throughout the Civil War and even introduced religion, dancing, and music as additional means of therapy. During this period, 35 percent of the patients received discharge from the asylum, 25 percent of whom were diagnosed as being fully recovered. By the end of the war, the Lunatic Asylum was filled to capacity, and, with an excellent management report and a large percentage of cures, the superintendent continually received requests from persons across the state seeking admission. Dr. Graham believed that at least six hundred "lunatics and idiots" existed in the state by the end of 1865, and he trusted that the legislature would provide all necessities to meet the increase in demand for admission into the asylum.[37]

The Institution for the Deaf and Dumb also continued to operate in good condition, and Governor Lubbock believed the institution to be on a prosperous course. The tenth legislature also increased its appropriations for the institution to $8,000. During this period, the school enrolled approximately sixty students. Though the appropriations for the institution appeared adequate, the school strove to be self-reliant in all possible means, as a way both to ensure financial stability and to teach self-sufficiency to the students. Josephine Snydor often taught the younger girls to shear sheep and taught the older girls to make it into clothing that the institution used. In addition, the institution grew much of its food, and the boys were responsible for the upkeep of the garden. The Institution for the Deaf and Dumb prospered to the point that it needed additional teachers, and in 1864, Emily Lewis was hired. A former student of the school, Lewis spent time teaching the valuable lessons she had learned. Much of the education those students received revolved around academic and moral training; vocational training did not come until years later.[38]

Political support for the Asylum for the Blind also continued with the tenth legislature. Politicians approved of the operations of the asylum and increased appropriations to a maximum of $32,000 for 1864–1865. The

36. *House Journal of the Tenth Legislature Regular Session,* 26; David J. Rothman, *The Discovery of the Asylum: Social Order and Disorder in the New Republic,* 237–38; Gammel, *Laws of Texas,* 696, 768; *Report of the Lunatic Asylum,* 4.

37. *Report of the Lunatic Asylum,* 4, 8–9, 14.

38. *Senate Journal of the Tenth Legislature Regular Session,* 25; Gammel, *Laws of Texas,* 696; Blackburn, "School for the Deaf," 12–13.

Board of Directors and the superintendent, though, desired that the institution operate as independently as possible. Therefore, the asylum engaged in producing any and all goods, such as candles and brooms, that they might use. The asylum aimed at producing the products for personal and institutional use, or possible sale, instead of draining their finances by purchasing all necessary materials. In addition, the asylum relied on the state penitentiary for cloth for its sheets and pillowcases.[39]

By 1864, the Asylum for the Blind operated at full capacity and confronted the need for additional labor and salary increases to maintain successful operations. The Board of Directors agreed in March 1864 to hire three additional employees: a male, a female, and a child. The asylum also continued with its daily schedule, including lessons in mechanical arts, and hired a music teacher to live at the asylum and teach music lessons to students twice a week. The institution upheld its commitment to the welfare of its students, and Governor Murrah believed the Asylum for the Blind was a vital institution and urged the legislature's continued support. By 1865, the asylum continued to progress and grow. As a result, the Board of Directors agreed with the superintendent's request to hire an additional teacher. Furthermore, the board decided to raise the salaries of the superintendent, matron, and music teacher.[40]

On June 7, 1865, however, the board and superintendent considered it necessary to close the school due to the poor financial condition of the state and the usefulness of treasury warrants, a direct effect of the war. Thus, the Asylum for the Blind became a temporary casualty, a product of war, not state neglect. Nevertheless, it reopened its doors in 1866 under Texas governor James Throckmorton.[41]

The tenth legislature retained the commitment to economic security and social welfare evinced in the ninth legislature. Except for the railroad issues that politicians had settled during the ninth legislative session, political support for education, mutual-aid societies, and state asylums increased through the war. As the war dragged on, politicians' concern and commitment to protecting the economic security and social welfare of the citizenry increased. Their political activities reflected the general interests of their counties, and they passed legislation to benefit the state in its entirety. Furthermore, political support for economic security and social welfare transcended the

39. Minutes of the Board of Trustees, Texas School for the Blind, TSL.
40. *House Journal of the Tenth Legislature Regular Session,* 27; Minutes of the Board of Trustees, Texas School for the Blind, TSL.
41. Minutes of Board of Trustees, Texas School for the Blind, TSL.

interests of Texas's slaveholding elite. More important, legislative activity represented the implementation of a separate political and economic identity. It did not matter if their endeavors fully succeeded; what mattered is that the citizens, even the most destitute of the state, realized the political effort of their representatives to sustain Texas in its present and proud condition.

Conclusion

Historians concentrating on the formation of central state authority and the creation of a Southern nation have posited that the adoption of a constitution, the organizational structures of the Confederacy, and the centralizing tendencies to conduct a war all point to the formation and at least temporary success of a new nation. They have often assumed, however, that citizens automatically looked to the Confederate government for the protection of their rights and liberties. When closely examining the local response to war and the intricate process of nation building, the pattern of Texas politics and the actions of citizens from the Lone Star State reveal that Texas defined, established, secured, and implemented a political and economic identity separate from that of other Confederate states. This development transpired out of the desire for economic security.

The definition of a separate identity emerged in the secession crisis as politicians and ordinary citizens defined their economic interests through political action. Political speeches from pro- and antisecessionist politicians provided the fundamental basis for defining a separate political and economic identity based upon the desire for economic security. Political necessity forced politicians to base their arguments on a constitutional foundation. They quickly moved to provide a social and economic justification for and against secession. Prosecessionist politicians also discussed the fear of abolition and a right to slavery, and railed against the Republican Party and an encroaching federal government. Political arguments also relied on Texas's history as a separate republic and accepted annexation into the United States for economic security. Antisecessionists, though more cautious of the ramifications of secession, expressed similar issues and fears as prosecessionists. They did not necessarily support the Union per se, so much as the commercial interests of the state. Taken together, political speeches not only reflected the ordinary values of the citizenry, but also revealed a deep concern for material well-being.

The definition of a separate identity rested not only on the shoulders of Texas politicians, but also on the actions of Texas citizens. Extrapolitical activity in the form of fraternal organizations, specifically the Knights of the Golden Circle, represented the outgrowth of fear and concern and also depicted popular support for secession and the striving for economic security. In addition, Texans supported calling a secession convention and overwhelmingly endorsed secession at the ballot box. Statistical analysis reveals several significant economic interests associated with the support for secession. Cattle holding, cotton production, wheat production, and slaveholding each had a significant relationship to the support for secession. These economic interests were the ones that politicians spoke about protecting and citizens sought to safeguard. Taken together, political rhetoric and citizen action defined a separate political and economic identity based upon the desire for economic security.

Once Texas seceded from the Union, citizens and politicians moved beyond defining to establishing a separate identity. The decision to join the Confederacy and support the Southern cause, however, did not erase the fear or threats to economic security. The burdens that Texas faced differed somewhat from the affairs of other states in the Confederacy. Texans were concerned not only with the abolition of slavery, but also with protecting a vast frontier from Indian atrocities, their stake in cotton and livestock, and state institutions. From the onset of crisis, Texas viewed itself as unique, and the actions to defend the lives of its families and to protect its commercial interests represented the establishment of a separate identity. Immediately after secession, Texans faced the dilemma of dealing with the Indian tribes on its border. They protected their lives and property against Indian atrocities on a daily basis, a conflict that other Southern states did not face, fully understand, or support. Texas had always experienced trouble with the Indians. Nevertheless, the Civil War further fractured relations between Texans and the Indians and revealed that tensions also included the Confederate government. From the onset, the Confederate government attempted to negotiate peace with the Indians and protect Texas citizens. On both counts, however, the government failed. Though it promised both sides that hostilities would cease, they did not, and Texans believed that Richmond had neglected them and their interests. Consequently, Texas politicians and citizens railed against the Confederate government. The state legislature attempted to remedy the situation by bolstering frontier protection, but its efforts too met with little success. Thus, Texans adopted an offensive strategy to deal with the Indians to protect their lives and economic well-being.

While Texans were dealing with the Indian problem, they also faced the concern of military enlistment in the Civil War. At the beginning of the conflict, men had a choice of whether to enlist in the Texas State Militia or the Confederate army. Of the men whose county residence is known, 81 percent of the men who went off to fight entered the Texas militia, whereas only 19 percent directly entered the Confederate army. When counting the number of men who transferred into Confederate service, only 33 percent of the men who went off to fight served in the Confederate army, still far short of the 81 percent that entered the Texas militia. Men from the less wealthy counties were not co-opted into the Southern cause. Instead, at the beginning of the war, it was more likely that the wealthier counties sent men into war. It was not until 1863 that individuals from the poorer counties of Texas more likely enlisted in military service. Previous research has shown that enlisted men reflect the general economic characteristics of their county residence. An examination of the county economic characteristics reveals that commercial interests beyond slavery were tied to enlistment. Men who entered military service represented a wide range of economic interests, including horses, cattle, wheat, corn, cotton, and slavery. Furthermore, it appears that the same economic interests are generally associated with both state and Confederate enlistment. Therefore, it did matter where these men served, and research reveals that Texans preferred service in the state militia. In dealing with the threat of Indian invasion and military enlistment, it becomes clear that citizens identified more with state and local interests than with a larger Confederate cause, and in doing so established a separate identity.

Although the actions of citizens and politicians that affect lives, liberty, and property are an integral part of the nation-building process, another essential component involves the testing of this identity between official governing bodies. Texans believed that the fall of Vicksburg further reflected Richmond's neglect of western interests. As a result, Richmond placed Edmund Kirby Smith in control of the Trans-Mississippi Department. Texans believed that this new authoritative structure threatened their economic well-being. Consequently, Texas politicians, despite occurrences of political gridlock, began to secure a separate identity by uniting to protect state and local interests. Through an examination of the production and supply of necessary materials, such as cloth, salt, and iron, evidence suggests that Texas politicians worked to promote the economic security of the citizens and the state. The Texas State Penitentiary proved one of the most useful institutions west of the Mississippi River. As the leading producer of cloth, it met the clothing needs of Texas citizens, troops, and the Confederacy. Moreover, it was directly responsible for meeting the clothing needs of other state institutions, and the legislature met its obligation to care for the state and citizens by supporting the prison. In addition, the legislature played an active role in maintaining general operations and providing security for the Texas State Penitentiary. In addition, Texas politicians supported the development of resources and the incorporation of companies for salt and iron production. Here too the pattern of Texas politics reveals that legislators met the needs of the citizenry ahead of the Confederate government and army. Texas politicians were unwilling to comply with Confederate requests for the necessities of war. In the conflict among Texas, the Trans-Mississippi Department, and Richmond, Texas politicians met first the needs of the citizens, second the needs of the state, and third the needs of the Confederacy. To make matters worse, the Confederate government allowed Kirby Smith complete control over the western states and did little to aid him in obtaining the necessary materials for war.

This conflict, and the securement of a separate political and economic identity, became more apparent in the wrangling over cotton. Confederate legislation had little effect on the Texas cotton trade before 1863. Once Kirby Smith established the Cotton Bureau as part of the Trans-Mississippi Department, however, conflict started to erupt. He attempted to gain control of Texas's cotton trade for the department's benefit, a threat to the economic interests of Texans. To make matters worse, the Confederate government began passing legislation that directly impacted the cotton trade in the West. Richmond passed restrictive legislation dealing with the production, export, impressment, and destruction of cotton that not only interfered with Kirby Smith's designs but also potentially threatened to undermine the entire cotton trade in Texas. Chaos reigned throughout the West as the Confederate government failed to realize the vital link between supportive legislation and garnering the allegiance of citizens for the war effort. Their failure to realize this and to fully understand western interests led Richmond to produce conflicting policies regarding cotton. In addition, the Confederate government could not control military officials such as Hamilton Bee and John Magruder who took it upon themselves to interfere in the cotton trade of Texas with the intention of monopolizing it for the Southern cause. Kirby Smith, exercising the powers and prerogatives of the president and Congress, also tried to take control of the cotton trade in the West and attempted to financially gain through illegal trade with the Union. As the war dragged on, and the military needs of the Confederacy became more pressing, Texas politicians stood firm in their commitment to the economic security of the state. At every turn, however, Texas politicians countered the Confederacy by opposing impressments, formulating its own plan for the purchase of cotton that benefited citizens and the state, and bringing suit against Kirby

Smith and the Cotton Bureau. The pattern of Texas politics symbolized the securement of a separate political and economic identity.

Could there have been less turmoil, less conflict between Richmond and western states? Possibly. Nevertheless, Richmond would have been hard pressed to accomplish this because the pattern of Texas politics supported the citizenry, even the most destitute, and strove to promote the economic security of the citizenry and the state throughout the war period. During the Civil War, the legislature supported the maintenance of the railroad system, extended educational facilities, incorporated mutual-aid societies, and maintained state asylums. Both the ninth and the tenth legislatures evinced strong political participation and support for these issues. Through these endeavors, the legislature did more than the Confederacy could ever hope to achieve. As a result, the legislature implemented a separate political and economic identity that garnered the support of the citizenry.

The Confederacy, from its genesis, conglomerated many local interests; the only true link existed from a united proslavery posture. Could a group of locals with little national identity effectively create a nation with the ability to fight a total war? In the Confederacy's case, no. The attempts at centralization through increased federal power caused by the perceived necessities of war resulted in substantial disaffection. Support grew tepid when the threat to economic security began to strike home. Could the Confederate government have done better? Perhaps. Their own localism and the presence of war at their doorstep, however, hindered politicians in Richmond. Some legislation, especially impressment, seemed imperative. The inability, however, to correctly envision a Confederacy that worked doomed the Rebel domestic policy and increased local disaffection, which contributed to Southern defeat. Texans chartered their own course as pragmatic individuals believing in the doctrine, efficacy, and prosperity available through liberal laws, property rights, and practical rules allowing the development of self-interest. Richmond and Kirby Smith never understood; Texas accomplished more for itself than anything the Confederacy could offer.

The process of nation building reveals that from 1861 to 1865, Texas existed on its own in the Confederacy. This development, and the likelihood of this existence pertaining to other states, helps to explain the violent reaction to carpetbaggers and forced Republican rule until 1877. Furthermore, it sheds light on the legacy of Jim Crow and the Southern insistence on evading constitutional law. In the Southern mind and in Southern practice, the struggle to maintain economic, social, and political institutions continued after military defeat. The South continued the struggle, unsatisfied with its ability to create a southern nation, and unsatisfied with military defeat. From this perspective, it becomes apparent that the process of nation building, and understanding the Civil War through this lens, not only leads to a deeper understanding of the past, but also sheds light on the present as our society continues to define, establish, secure, and implement its identity both within and outside its geographical borders.

Regression Analysis

Support for Secession

Dependent Variable: Percentage of Support for Secession

Constant	White Males	Total White	Total Slave	R-Sq.
.78	-.000 (.772)			0.1%
.77		-.000 (.817)		0.0%
.71			.000 (.003)	7.1%
.76		-.000 (.028)	.000 (.000)	10.9%

Const.	Horses	Sheep	Wool	Milch Cattle	Other Cattle	Livstck Value	Value Slain Animal	R-Sq.
.78	-.000 (.612)							0.2%
.78		-.000 (.446)						0.5%
.79				-.000 (.025)	.000 (.107)			4.8%
.76						.000 (.959)		0.0%
.73							.000 (.146)	1.8%
.76						-.000 (.251)	.000 (.065)	2.9%
.78			-.000 (.409)					0.6%
.78		-.000 (.935)	-.000 (.744)					0.6%
.81				-.000 (.076)				2.6%
.75					.000 (.396)			0.6%
.77	.000 (.489)	-.000 (.915)		-.000 (.058)	.000 (.030)	-.000 (.137)	.000 (.005)	12.3%
.76	-.000 (.937)	-.000 (.494)		-.000 (.017)	.000 (.113)		.000 (.008)	10.6%

Const.	Farm Value	Wheat	Rye	Corn	Ginned Cotton	R-Sq.
.74	.000 (.215)					1.3%
.79		-.000 (.004)				6.9%
.75			.000 (.103)			2.2%
.74		-.000 (.001)		.000 (.007)		12.6%
.74	.000 (.983)	-.000 (.001)		.000 (.068)		12.6%
.72				.000 (.03)		3.9%
.74		-.000 (.000)	.000 (.102)	.000 (.03)		14.6%
.72					.000 (.002)	7.6%
.74	-.000 (.204)				.000 (.002)	8.9%
.74	.000 (.807)	-.000 (.000)	.000 (.10)	.000 (.199)		14.7%
.74		-.000 (.003)	.000 (.08)	.000 (.62)	.000 (.21)	15.8%
.74	-.000 (.723)	-.000 (.008)	.000 (.09)	.000 (.553)	.000 (.202)	15.9%

Constant	Farm Value	Livstck Value	Total Slave	Ginned Cotton	Wheat	Rye	Corn	R-Sq.
.71			.000 (.431)	.000 (.270)				8.1%
.77	.000 (.077)	-.000 (.205)						2.6%
.73	-.000 (.032)		.000 (.001)					10.7%
.74		-.000 (.954)			-.000 (.001)	.000 (.103)	.000 (.058)	14.6%
.76	.000 (.045)				-.000 (.001)			10.1%
.73	-.000 (.579)						.000 (.063)	4.2%
.76		-.000 (.054)	.000 (.000)					10.1%
.75	-.000 (.213)	-.000 (.408)	.000 (.001)					11.3%
.74	-.000 (.294)	.000 (.908)	.000 (.082)	.000 (.515)	-.000 (.048)			15.2%

Regression Analysis
Military Enlistment

Dependent Variable: Number of Men Entering State Militia, 1861

Constant	Horses	Milch Cattle	Other Cattle	Sheep	Livestk Value	Value Slain An	R-Sq.
117.38	.063 (.000)						23.6%
138		.03 (.000)					13.3%
194			.004 (.003)				7.2%
167				.019 (.000)			16.8%
29.8					.000 (.000)		28.7%
124.8						.003 (.000)	21.9%
110.37		.001 (.025)	.101 (.002)				15.2%
102.94	.05 (.011)	.003 (.685)	-.000 (.587)	.008 (.079)			26.0%

Constant	Farm Value	Wheat	Rye	Corn	Ginned Cotton	Total Slaves	R-Sq.
178.48	.000 (.000)						12.5%
229.39		.004 (.000)					14.7%
265.17			.021 (.135)				1.8%
175.27				.000 (.000)			13.9%
257.83					.007 (.155)		1.7%
183.41						.064 (.000)	10.7%
177.10	.000 (.000)				-.014 (.042)		15.4%
186.91					-.023 (.011)	.121 (.000)	14.0%
135.39	.000 (.184)	.003 (.006)	-.005 (.687)	.000 (.007)	-.014 (.081)		27.0%
154.92	.000 (.001)	.003 (.000)					22.0%

Dependent Variable: Percentage of Men Entering State Militia, 1861

Constant	Horses	Milch Cattle	Other Cattle	Sheep	Livestk Value	Value Slain An	R-Sq.
21.87	.003 (.000)						10.0%
27.41		.000 (.172)					1.5%
22.1			.000 (.000)				9.9%
27.85				.000 (.08)			2.5%
20.97					.000 (.005)		6.3%
30.53						.000 (.564)	0.3%
22.00		.000 (.966)	.000 (.001)				9.9%
22.79	.004 (.038)	-.001 (.183)	.000 (.152)	-.000 (.71)			13.5%

Constant	Farm Value	Wheat	Rye	Corn	Ginned Cotton	Total Slaves	R-Sq.
30.75	.000 (.614)						0.2%
30.32		.000 (.160)					1.6%
32.48			-.000 (.71)				0.1%
32.31				-.000 (.912)			0.0%
33.45					-.000 (.42)		0.5%
30.91						.000 (.918)	0.0%
30.66	.000 (.127)				-.001 (.099)		2.5%
31.94					-.001 (.241)	.002 (.383)	1.2%
29.89	.000 (.852)	.000 (.187)					1.7%
30.59	.000 (.3370	.000 (.439)	-.000 (.586)	-.000 (.981)	-.000 (.314)		3.1%

Dependent Variable: Number of Men Entering Confederate Army, 1861

Constant	Horses	Milch Cattle	Other Cattle	Sheep	Livestk Value	Value Slain An	R-Sq.
16.94	.007 (.001)						8.1%
14.44		.004 (.002)					7.6%
26.45			.000 (.108)				2.1%
24.47				.001 (.021)			4.3%
6.8					.000 (.000)		9.9%
11.32						.000 (.000)	13.7%
12.78		.004 (.007)	.000 (.626)				7.8%
12.65	.004 (.266)	.002 (.237)	-.000 (.690)	.000 (.665)			9.6%

Constant	Farm Value	Wheat	Rye	Corn	Ginned Cotton	Total Slaves	R-Sq.
19.47	.000 (.001)						8.0%
32.4		.000 (.157)					1.6%
32.41			.004 (.151)				1.7%
19.33				.000 (.001)			8.5%
29.04					.002 (.055)		3.0%
17.42						.011 (.000)	9.9%
19.41	.000 (.01)				-.000 (.659)		8.1%
18.48					-.002 (.15)	.018 (.002)	10.2%
15.31	.000 (.2)	.000 (.811)	.000 (.682)	.000 (.144)	-.001 (.394)		10.6%
18.52	.000 (.003)	.000 (.463)					8.4%

Dependent Variable: Percentage of Men Entering Confederate Army, 1861

Constant	Horses	Milch Cattle	Other Cattle	Sheep	Livestk Value	Value Slain An	R-Sq.
2.93	.000 (.203)						1.3%
3.13		.000 (.397)					0.6%
3.27			.000 (.429)				0.5%
3.37				.000 (.44)			0.5%
2.88					.000 (.327)		0.8%
3.31						.000 (.468)	0.4%
2.97	.003 (.475)	-.000 (.962)	-.000 (.957)	-.000 (.979)			1.3%
2.92		.000 (.556)	.000 (.614)				0.8%

Constant	Farm Value	Wheat	Rye	Corn	Ginned Cotton	Total Slaves	R-Sq.
3.1	.000 (.241)						1.1%
3.9		-.000 (.743)					0.1%
3.87			-.000 (.825)				0.0%
3.51				.000 (.618)			0.2%
3.36					.000 (.287)		0.9%
2.89						.000 (.184)	1.4%
3.11	.000 (.554)				.000 (.74)		1.2%
3.27					.000 (.682)	.000 (.82)	1.0%
3.36	.000 (.341)	-.000 (.716)	-.000 (.881)	-.000 (.527)	.000 (.707)		1.9%
3.20	.000 (.2)	-.000 (.537)					1.4%

Dependent Variable:
Percentage of Men Entering Confederate Army (Including Transfers), 1861

Constant	Horses	Milch Cattle	Other Cattle	Sheep	Livestk Value	Value Slain An	R-Sq.
4.02	.000 (.015)						4.8%
4.6		.000 (.143)					1.8%
4.51			.000 (.064)				1.8%
4.55				.000 (.032)			3.8%
3.07					.000 (.009)		5.5%
4.7						.000 (.114)	2.1%
3.94		.000 (.408)	.000 (.161)				3.4%
3.80	.000 (.412)	-.000 (.812)	.000 (.656)	.000 (.381)			5.5%

Constant	Farm Value	Wheat	Rye	Corn	Ginned Cotton	Total Slaves	R-Sq.
4.82	.000 (.1)						2.2%
5.48		.000 (.133)					1.9%
5.81			.000 (.587)				0.2%
5.35				.000 (.359)			0.7%
5.83					.000 (.739)		0.1%
4.79						.000 (.17)	1.5%
4.81	.000 (.047)				-.000 (.239)		3.3%
5.24					-.000 (.416)	.001 (.227)	1.3%
4.67	.000 (.171)	.000 (.488)	.000 (.846)	-.000 (.87)	-.000 (.54)		3.8%
4.62	.000 (.181)	.000 (.247)					3.3%

Dependent Variable:
Number of Men Entering State Militia, 1862

Constant	Horses	Milch Cattle	Other Cattle	Sheep	Livestk Value	Value Slain An	R-Sq.
65.63	.002 (.458)						0.5%
51.59		.004 (.053)					3.0%
76.87			-.000 (.642)				0.2%
72.02				.000 (.943)			0.0%
55.6					.000 (.188)		1.4%
61.23						.000 (.221)	1.2%
58.70		.000 (.022)	-.000 (.187)				4.4%
60.60	.001 (.82)	.005 (.068)	-.000 (.273)	-.001 (.517)			4.8%

Constant	Farm Value	Wheat	Rye	Corn	Ginned Cotton	Total Slaves	R-Sq.
66.31	.000 (.443)						0.5%
63.86		.000 (.024)					4.1%
70.13			.002 (.528)				0.3%
69.2				.000 (.672)			0.1%
74					-.000 (.801)		0.1%
63.9						.003 (.436)	0.5%
66.06	.000 (.181)				-.002 (.26)		1.5%
67.89					-.003 (.29)	.01 (.268)	1.1%
61.98	.000 (.7)	.000 (.084)	.001 (.828)	-.000 (.91)	-.000 (.844)		4.2%
61.94	.000 (.793)	.000 (.034)					4.1%

Dependent Variable:
Percentage of Men Entering State Militia, 1862

Constant	Horses	Milch Cattle	Other Cattle	Sheep	Livestk Value	Value Slain An	R-Sq.
-8.97	-.003 (.832)						0.0%
-32.78		.003 (.711)					0.1%
75.95			-.004 (.01)				5.4%
-33.97				.002 (.574)			0.3%
10.04					-.000 (.598)		0.2%
-31.07						.000 (.7)	0.1%
30.03		.013 (.134)	-.005 (.003)				7.2%
27.94	.024 (.36)	.004 (.736)	-.006 (.002)	.003 (.6)			8.7%

Constant	Farm Value	Wheat	Rye	Corn	Ginned Cotton	Total Slaves	R-Sq.
-.41	-.000 (.693)						0.1%
-24.3		.000 (.63)					0.2%
-23.6			.007 (.66)				0.2%
-26.2				.000 (.767)			0.1%
-18.9					.000 (.927)		0.0%
-19.3						.001 (.949)	0.0%
-3.76	-.000 (.517)				.004 (.6)		0.4%
-17.75					.001 (.926)	-.001 (.959)	0.0%
-19.54	-.000 (.268)	.001 (.461)	.003 (.856)	.000 (.603)	.005 (.617)		1.4%
-8.97	-.000 (.604)	.000 (.557)					0.4%

Dependent Variable:
Number of Men Entering Confederate Army, 1862

Constant	Horses	Milch Cattle	Other Cattle	Sheep	Livestk Value	Value Slain An	R-Sq.
27.91	.015 (.002)						7.8%
32.13		.007 (.017)					4.6%
55.6			.000 (.345)				0.7%
34.43				.005 (.002)			7.9%
-6.1					.000 (.000)		14.2%
19.98						.001 (.000)	11.4%
31.83		.007 (.029)	.000 (.966)				4.6%
28.47	.014 (.109)	.000 (.887)	-.000 (.21)	.003 (.145)			11.1%

Constant	Farm Value	Wheat	Rye	Corn	Ginned Cotton	Total Slaves	R-Sq.
25.12	.000 (.000)						11.8%
33.74		.002 (.000)					32.6%
57.5			.011 (.058)				2.9%
37.4				.000 (.005)			6.2%
54.46					.003 (.09)		2.3%
32.5						.022 (.001)	7.9%
24.70	.000 (.000)				-.004 (.135)		13.4%
34.40					-.004 (.193)	.034 (.006)	8.2%
9.35	.000 (.263)	.002 (.000)	.002 (.622)	-.000 (.476)	.004 (.143)		38.6%
9.32	.000 (.003)	.002 (.000)					37.3%

Dependent Variable:
Percentage of Men Entering Confederate Army, 1862

Constant	Horses	Milch Cattle	Other Cattle	Sheep	Livestk Value	Value Slain An	R-Sq.
5.96	.002 (.007)						5.9%
7.02		.001 (.057)					3.0%
10.86			.000 (.586)				0.2%
8.06				.000 (.032)			3.7%
3.42					.000 (.006)		6.2%
7.93						.000 (.068)	2.7%
7.28		.001 (.067)	-.000 (.844)				3.0%
7.42	.003 (.046)	-.000 (.904)	-.000 (.123)	.000 (.67)			8.0%

Constant	Farm Value	Wheat	Rye	Corn	Ginned Cotton	Total Slaves	R-Sq.
9.03	.000 (.125)						1.9%
9.17		.000 (.002)					7.6%
11.02			.001 (.261)				1.0%
10.02				.000 (.293)			0.9%
11.32					.000 (.577)		0.3%
8.77						.001 (.13)	1.8%
8.99	.000 (.108)				-.000 (.455)		2.4%
9.52					-.000 (.437)	.003 (.188)	1.7%
7.55	.000 (.733)	.000 (.008)	.000 (.614)	-.000 (.663)	.000 (.551)		8.7%
7.60	.000 (.378)	.000 (.005)					8.2%

Dependent Variable:
Percentage of Men Entering Confederate Army (Including Transfers), 1862

Constant	Horses	Milch Cattle	Other Cattle	Sheep	Livestk Value	Value Slain An	R-Sq.
8.41	.003 (.003)						7.1%
11.14		.001 (.063)					2.8%
16.17			.000 (.468)				0.4%
12.94				.000 (.046)			3.3%
4.34					.000 (.003)		7.3%
11.03						.000 (.028)	4.0%
11.09		.001 (.088)	.000 (.983)				2.8%
11.83	.006 (.013)	-.000 (.654)	-.000 (.105)	.000 (.977)			9.2%

Constant	Farm Value	Wheat	Rye	Corn	Ginned Cotton	Total Slaves	R-Sq.
14.69	.000 (.193)						1.4%
14.01		.000 (.001)					8.3%
16.1			.002 (.077)				2.6%
14.83				.000 (.2)			1.4%
17.78					.000 (.677)		0.1%
13.28						.003 (.102)	2.1%
14.65	.000 (.155)				-.000 (.475)		1.8%
14.20					-.001 (.229)	.006 (.083)	2.6%
11.33	-.000 (.915)	.000 (.007)	.001 (.305)	.000 (.972)	.000 (.655)		9.8%
12.39	.000 (.545)	.000 (.003)					8.6%

Dependent Variable:
Number of Men Entering State Militia, 1863

Constant	Horses	Milch Cattle	Other Cattle	Sheep	Livestk Value	Value Slain An	R-Sq.
36.64	.006 (.028)						3.9%
20.6		.007 (.000)					10.2%
39			.000 (.053)				3.0%
47.13				.001 (.269)			1.0%
15.58					.000 (.000)		9.5%
30.4						.000 (.003)	7.2%
17.59		.006 (.002)	.000 (.512)				10.5%
17.56	-.004 (.469)	.008 (.003)	.000 (.302)	-.000 (.826)			11.2%

Constant	Farm Value	Wheat	Rye	Corn	Ginned Cotton	Total Slaves	R-Sq.
25.62	.000 (.000)						13.2%
54.9		-.000 (.963)					0.0%
55			-.000 (.929)				0.0%
36.53				.000 (.009)			5.4%
36.3					.005 (.000)		11.1%
26.48						.018 (.000)	12.7%
25.85	.000 (.034)				.002 (.204)		14.4%
30.38					.002 (.264)	.01 (.196)	12.3%
30.46	.000 (.016)	-.000 (.773)	-.000 (.666)	-.000 (.262)	.003 (.173)		16.0%
27.47	.000 (.000)	-.000 (.282)					14.1%

Dependent Variable:
Percentage of Men Entering State Militia, 1863

Constant	Horses	Milch Cattle	Other Cattle	Sheep	Livestk Value	Value Slain An	R-Sq.
29.01	-.003 (.174)						1.5%
7.86		.002 (.198)					1.4%
19.28			-.000 (.964)				0.0%
24.1				-.000 (.397)			0.6%
28.1					-.000 (.368)		0.7%
24.8						-.000 (.429)	0.5%
10.38		.002 (.159)	-.000 (.56)				1.6%
8.12	-.016 (.002)	.008 (.001)	.000 (.120)	.000 (.905)			11.2%

Constant	Farm Value	Wheat	Rye	Corn	Ginned Cotton	Total Slaves	R-Sq.
22.19	-.000 (.616)						0.2%
23.47		-.000 (.144)					1.8%
22.93			-.004 (.196)				1.4%
23.8				-.000 (.444)			0.5%
19.63					-.000 (.879)		0.0%
25.05						-.002 (.520)	0.3%
22.23	-.000 (.578)				.000 (.775)		0.3%
21.99					.000 (.721)	-.004 (.592)	0.3%
26.90	.000 (.799)	-.000 (.26)	-.003 (.388)	-.000 (.778)	-.000 (.932)		2.7%
24.78	-.000 (.864)	-.000 (.168)					1.8%

Dependent Variable:
Number of Men Entering Confederate Army, 1863

Constant	Horses	Milch Cattle	Other Cattle	Sheep	Livestk Value	Value Slain An	R-Sq.
.98	.001 (.08)						2.5%
.255		.000 (.057)					2.9%
2.29			.000 (.355)				0.7%
1.68				.000 (.116)			2.0%
.118					.000 (.096)		2.3%
2.22						.000 (.333)	0.8%
.054		.000 (.096)	.000 (.825)				3.0%
-.18	.000 (.804)	.000 (.359)	-.000 (.931)	.000 (.542)			3.5%

Constant	Farm Value	Wheat	Rye	Corn	Ginned Cotton	Total Slaves	R-Sq.
1.62	.000 (.125)						1.9%
3.29		.000 (.509)					0.4%
3.92			-.000 (.776)				0.1%
2.61				.000 (.402)			0.6%
2.65					.000 (.251)		1.1%
2.42						.001 (.176)	1.4%
1.63	.000 (.309)				.000 (.927)		1.9%
1.76					-.000 (.884)	.001 (.34)	1.8%
1.91	.000 (.393)	.000 (.576)	-.000 (.630)	-.000 (.635)	.000 (.627)		2.6%
1.51	.000 (.158)	.000 (.752)					2.0%

Dependent Variable
Percentage of Men Entering Confederate Army, 1863

Constant	Horses	Milch Cattle	Other Cattle	Sheep	Livestk Value	Value Slain An	R-Sq.
2.45	.000 (.559)						0.3%
2.62		.000 (.657)					0.2%
4.32			-.000 (.859)				0.0%
3.85				.000 (.984)			0.0%
4.87					-.000 (.771)		0.1%
6.21						-.000 (.343)	0.7%
3.16		.000 (.581)	-.000 (.707)				0.3%
3.71	.001 (.373)	-.000 (.974)	-.000 (.433)	-.000 (.6)			1.0%

Constant	Farm Value	Wheat	Rye	Corn	Ginned Cotton	Total Slaves	R-Sq.
5.48	-.000 (.456)						0.5%
4.01		-.000 (.905)					0.0%
4.56			-.000 (.513)				0.4%
5.77				-.000 (.372)			0.7%
4.94					-.000 (.481)		0.4%
4.73						-.000 (.554)	0.3%
5.47	-.000 (.729)				-.000 (.801)		0.5%
5.19					-.000 (.798)	-.000 (.866)	0.4%
5.99	-.000 (.897)	.000 (.938)	-.000 (.676)	-.000 (.767)	-.000 (.962)		0.8%
5.45	-.000 (.463)	.000 (.957)					0.5%

Dependent Variable:
Percentage of Men Entering Confederate Army (Including Transfers), 1863

Constant	Horses	Milch Cattle	Other Cattle	Sheep	Livestk Value	Value Slain An	R-Sq.
9.92	-.001 (.393)						0.6%
1.17		.001 (.217)					1.3%
6.37			.000 (.939)				0.0%
8.48				-.000 (.563)			0.3%
9.98					-.000 (.528)		0.3%
8.08						-.000 (.708)	0.1%
2.12		.001 (.193)	-.000 (.668)				1.4%
1.31	-.006 (.02)	.003 (.008)	.000 (.243)	.000 (.977)			7.0%

Constant	Farm Value	Wheat	Rye	Corn	Ginned Cotton	Total Slaves	R-Sq.
7.63	-.000 (.769)						0.1%
9.00		-.000 (.141)					1.8%
8.38			-.001 (.28)				1.0%
7.35				-.000 (.832)			0.0%
6.48					.000 (.941)		0.0%
5.64						.000 (.83)	0.0%
7.66	-.000 (.626)				.000 (.692)		0.2%
6.27					-.000 (.972)	.000 (.927)	0.0%
9.34	.000 (.939)	-.000 (.214)	-.001 (.393)	.000 (.756)	-.000 (.782)		2.4%
8.86	.000 (.963)	-.000 (.151)					1.8%

Dependent Variable:
Number of Men Entering State Militia, 1864

Constant	Horses	Milch Cattle	Other Cattle	Sheep	Livestk Value	Value Slain An	R-Sq.
61.03	-.002 (.362)						0.7%
50.06		.000 (.676)					0.1%
66.12			-.000 (.111)				2.1%
59.75				-.000 (.367)			0.7%
69.95					-.000 (.137)		1.8%
69.42						-.000 (.044)	3.3%
58.68		.002 (.263)	-.000 (.058)				3.1%
59.82	-.001 (.731)	.003 (.191)	-.000 (.227)	-.000 (.538)			3.8%

Constant	Farm Value	Wheat	Rye	Corn	Ginned Cotton	Total Slaves	R-Sq.
74.53	-.000 (.002)						7.5%
52.61		.000 (.698)					0.1%
58.26			-.004 (.176)				1.5%
72.37				-.000 (.005)			6.3%
68.75					-.004 (.001)		8.2%
66.66						-.011 (.005)	5.9%
74.27	-.000 (.247)				-.002 (.135)		9.2%
73.49					-.002 (.34)	-.008 (.284)	9.0%
74.95	-.000 (.244)	.000 (.454)	-.003 (.355)	-.000 (.989)	-.002 (.373)		10.2%
72.59	-.001 (.001)	.000 (.246)					8.5%

Dependent Variable:
Percentage of Men Entering State Militia, 1864

Constant	Horses	Milch Cattle	Other Cattle	Sheep	Livestk Value	Value Slain An	R-Sq.
22.2	-.011 (.104)						2.2%
20.6		-.005 (.186)					1.4%
-9.19			.000 (.942)				0.0%
5.4				-.000 (.385)			0.6%
2.08					-.000 (.698)		0.1%
-9.0						.000 (.953)	0.0%
13.83		-.007 (.145)	.000 (.531)				1.8%
9.36	-.021 (.105)	-.000 (.923)	.001 (.134)	.001 (.719)			4.1%

Constant	Farm Value	Wheat	Rye	Corn	Ginned Cotton	Total Slaves	R-Sq.
-10.96	.000 (.848)						0.0%
2.68		-.000 (.174)					1.5%
-8.8			.001 (.9)				0.0%
-15.33				.000 (.639)			0.2%
-12.79					.001 (.661)		0.2%
-12.1						.003 (.73)	0.1%
-10.81	-.000 (.866)				.001 (.668)		0.2%
-12.87					.001 (.81)	.000 (.994)	0.2%
-8.62	.000 (.815)	-.001 (.142)	.001 (.847)	.000 (.606)	-.002 (.662)		2.1%
-4.99	.000 (.603)	-.000 (.15)					1.7%

Dependent Variable:
Number of Men Entering Confederate Army, 1864

Constant	Horses	Milch Cattle	Other Cattle	Sheep	Livestk Value	Value Slain An	R-Sq.
-1.08	.001 (.000)						14.3%
-.7		.000 (.001)					9.0%
.29			.000 (.002)				7.7%
.85				.000 (.002)			7.7%
-1.43					.000 (.001)		8.6%
3.72						.000 (.91)	0.0%
58.68		.002 (.263)	-.000 (.058)				3.1%
59.82	-.001 (.731)	.003 (.191)	-.000 (.227)	-.000 (.538)			3.8%

Constant	Farm Value	Wheat	Rye	Corn	Ginned Cotton	Total Slaves	R-Sq.
2.66	.000 (.247)						1.1%
3.92		-.000 (.887)					0.0%
3.95			-.000 (.835)				0.0%
4.19				-.000 (.738)			0.1%
4.21					-.000 (.615)		0.2%
3.07						.000 (.549)	0.3%
74.27	-.000 (.247)				-.002 (.135)		9.2%
73.49					-.002 (.34)	-.008 (.284)	9.0%
74.95	-.000 (.244)	.000 (.454)	-.003 (.355)	-.000 (.989)	-.002 (.373)		10.2%
72.59	-.000 (.001)	.000 (.246)					8.5%

Dependent Variable:
Percentage of Men Entering Confederate Army, 1864

Constant	Horses	Milch Cattle	Other Cattle	Sheep	Livestk Value	Value Slain An	R-Sq.
-14.9	.01 (.024)						4.1%
-32.8		.009 (.001)					8.4%
-5.2			.000 (.144)				1.8%
2.1				.001 (.309)			0.9%
-28.1					.000 (.015)		4.8%
-6.92						.000 (.113)	2.1%
-34.68		.008 (.004)	.001 (.788)				8.4%
-32.97	.001 (.908)	.009 (.02)	.000 (.815)	-.001 (.618)			8.6%

Constant	Farm Value	Wheat	Rye	Corn	Ginned Cotton	Total Slaves	R-Sq.
-6.3	.000 (.079)						2.5%
14.13		-.000 (.724)					0.1%
10.52			.001 (.724)				0.1%
-0.74				.000 (.211)			1.3%
-0.02					.003 (.093)		2.3%
-1.65						.009 (.142)	1.7%
-.17					.003 (.354)	.000 (.983)	2.3%
-6.1	.000 (.421)				.001 (.535)		2.8%
-4.15	.000 (.06)	-.000 (.432)					3.0%
-3.83	.000 (.305)	-.000 (.59)	.001 (.807)	-.000 (.725)	.001 (.674)		3.2%

Dependent Variable:
Percentage of Men Entering Confederate Army (Including Transfers), 1864

Constant	Horses	Milch Cattle	Other Cattle	Sheep	Livestk Value	Value Slain An	R-Sq.
-13.9	.01 (.025)						4.1%
-31.51		.009 (.001)					8.2%
-4.23			.000 (.146)				1.7%
3.43				.001 (.332)			0.8%
-27.41					.000 (.015)		4.8%
-6.12						.000 (.112)	2.1%
-33.4		.000 (.004)	.000 (.782)				8.3%
-31.49	.001 (.88)	.009 (.022)	.000 (.821)	-.001 (.582)			8.5%

Constant	Farm Value	Wheat	Rye	Corn	Ginned Cotton	Total Slaves	R-Sq.
-5.56	.000 (.077)						2.6%
15.14		-.000 (.703)					0.1%
11.37			.001 (.722)				0.1%
-0.12				.000 (.20)			1.3%
.82					.003 (.093)		2.3%
-1.03						.009 (.137)	1.7%
-5.43	.000 (.412)				.001 (.541)		2.9%
.50					.003 (.363)	.000 (.964)	2.3%
-3.12	.000 (.298)	-.000 (.56)	.001 (.807)	-.000 (.749)	.001 (.701)		3.3%
-3.35	.000 (.057)	-.000 (.413)					3.1%

County Military Enlistment

TST = Texas State Troop Enlistment
CSA = Confederate Enlistment, Excluding Transfers
TR = Men Transferred to CSA

County	1861			1862			1863			1864		
	TST	CSA	TR	TST	CSA	TR	TST	CSA	TR	TST	CSA	TR
Anderson	623	110	94	82	93	22	1	0	1	97	0	64
Angelina	0	0	0	75	8	75	93	0	13	0	0	0
Archer	0	0	0	0	0	0	0	0	0	0	0	0
Atascosa	103	0	0	12	49	11	0	0	0	93	0	0
Austin	97	0	0	190	119	184	177	0	10	0	2	0
Bandera	0	0	0	13	1	0	0	0	0	64	0	0
Bastrop	354	0	1	72	138	0	83	0	83	26	0	0
Baylor	0	0	0	0	0	0	0	0	0	0	0	0
Bee	193	0	1	0	12	0	5	0	5	36	0	0
Bell	715	0	0	42	289	39	185	0	131	14	0	14
Bexar	388	128	0	241	75	103	68	0	2	26	36	26
Blanco	104	0	0	63	69	21	63	0	63	63	0	0
Bosque	99	0	0	110	104	0	4	0	0	129	0	0
Bowie	91	0	0	0	0	0	0	0	0	0	3	0
Brazoria	75	100	0	26	51	0	65	0	0	0	0	0
Brazos	0	40	0	110	13	0	4	0	4	82	0	82
Brown	52	37	0	0	1	0	0	0	0	199	0	0

County	1861			1862			1863			1864		
	TST	CSA	TR	TST	CSA	TR	TST	CSA	TR	TST	CSA	TR
Buchanan	0	0	0	121	0	0	100	0	0	122	0	0
Burleson	307	65	0	73	21	124	91	0	0	15	72	0
Burnet	418	0	2	112	88	32	0	0	0	241	0	0
Caldwell	231	119	1	122	31	132	27	0	0	19	0	0
Calhoun	391	42	1	0	25	0	0	0	0	17	0	0
Callahan	0	0	0	0	0	0	0	0	0	0	0	0
Cameron	215	159	3	28	13	2	0	0	0	0	65	0
Cass	0	0	0	43	0	43	0	0	0	0	0	0
Chamber	0	0	0	14	8	11	0	0	0	0	0	0
Cherokee	195	78	95	58	99	58	2	0	2	102	0	102
Clay	99	0	0	65	0	0	0	0	0	0	0	0
Coleman	158	0	0	49	0	0	0	0	0	93	0	0
Collin	441	5	197	149	98	97	145	0	66	107	0	0
Colorado	756	40	0	4	65	2	182	0	61	0	7	0
Comal	7	0	0	545	2	70	0	0	0	0	0	0
Comanche	142	0	0	2	0	2	71	0	0	67	0	0
Concho	0	0	0	0	0	0	0	0	0	0	0	0
Cooke	187	0	165	90	0	90	81	0	0	276	0	0
Coryell	190	0	0	13	2	13	0	0	0	230	3	0
Dallas	516	237	69	337	1285	337	71	7	71	0	0	0
Dawson	0	0	0	0	0	0	6	0	0	0	0	0
Denton	281	90	103	59	96	94	3	0	3	0	0	0
Dewitt	524	5	3	107	25	0	155	1	93	74	0	0
Dimmit	0	0	0	0	0	0	0	0	0	0	0	0
Duval	0	0	0	0	0	0	0	0	0	0	0	0
Eastland	0	0	0	1	0	0	0	0	0	44	0	0
Edwards	0	0	0	0	0	0	6	0	0	0	0	0

County	1861			1862			1863			1864		
	TST	CSA	TR	TST	CSA	TR	TST	CSA	TR	TST	CSA	TR
El Paso	0	0	0	0	0	0	0	0	0	0	0	0
Ellis	967	0	258	178	93	178	75	1	75	28	24	0
Encinal	0	0	0	0	0	0	0	0	0	0	0	0
Erath	18	0	0	293	0	62	219	0	0	311	0	0
Falls	0	0	0	0	2	0	0	0	0	38	0	0
Fannin	1294	0	0	81	55	77	0	0	0	20	0	0
Fayette	1497	0	0	61	135	9	371	1	119	0	14	0
Fort Bend	68	0	0	33	39	0	0	0	0	0	0	0
Freestone	736	0	96	96	79	96	31	0	0	12	0	0
Frio	0	0	0	0	0	0	55	0	0	0	0	0
Galveston	329	0	90	207	320	178	434	0	236	84	36	0
Gillespie	111	0	0	39	0	0	73	0	0	318	0	0
Goliad	538	0	4	26	3	0	90	0	23	0	0	0
Gonzales	469	126	0	12	195	7	107	7	0	37	30	0
Grayson	286	0	174	0	75	0	106	0	106	0	0	0
Greer	0	0	0	0	0	0	0	0	0	0	0	0
Grimes	467	0	0	25	6	25	91	0	77	35	0	0
Guadalupe	221	200	0	12	156	123	27	0	0	15	0	0
Hamilton	40	0	0	0	1	0	0	0	0	93	0	0
Hardeman	0	0	0	0	0	0	0	0	0	0	0	0
Hardin	0	44	0	2	1	0	0	0	0	0	0	0
Harris	512	174	0	119	170	48	102	5	5	1	8	1
Harrison	371	0	0	60	197	60	59	0	59	28	1	28
Haskell	0	0	0	0	0	0	0	0	0	0	0	0
Hays	187	6	7	50	77	9	134	87	4	35	0	0
Henderson	473	91	0	455	217	308	83	0	2	0	0	0
Hidalgo	0	0	0	0	0	0	0	0	0	0	0	0

County	1861			1862			1863			1864		
	TST	CSA	TR	TST	CSA	TR	TST	CSA	TR	TST	CSA	TR
Hill	362	0	125	0	0	0	0	0	0	91	0	0
Hopkins	826	0	99	0	136	0	0	0	0	66	0	0
Houston	566	264	118	245	60	134	153	0	37	25	0	0
Hunt	1013	0	96	0	4	0	0	50	0	0	0	0
Jack	130	0	0	0	0	0	0	0	0	180	0	0
Jackson	421	6	125	84	1	0	22	0	22	22	0	0
Jasper	110	0	39	165	3	165	8	0	3	0	0	0
Jefferson	255	1	0	59	80	57	8	0	7	11	0	0
Johnson	227	0	0	67	88	17	50	0	50	91	0	0
Jones	0	0	0	0	0	0	0	0	0	0	0	0
Karnes	286	0	0	11	50	6	36	0	1	72	23	0
Kaufman	666	0	0	522	3	74	0	0	0	188	0	0
Kendall	0	0	0	0	1	0	65	0	26	65	0	0
Kerr	65	0	0	32	8	0	0	0	0	57	0	0
Kimble	0	0	0	0	0	0	0	0	0	20	0	0
Kinney	0	0	0	0	0	0	9	0	0	0	0	0
Knox	0	0	0	0	0	0	0	0	0	0	0	0
La Salle	0	0	0	0	0	0	0	0	0	0	0	0
Lamar	1179	0	189	1	63	1	3	0	3	0	0	0
Lampassas	249	0	0	43	3	42	0	0	0	128	0	0
Lavacca	169	146	11	116	86	3	88	0	77	0	7	0
Leon	38	166	0	97	180	97	77	0	37	0	0	0
Liberty	76	83	0	102	42	63	207	77	207	28	0	0
Limestone	545	0	0	96	16	96	0	0	0	58	0	0
Live Oak	167	0	0	2	7	0	0	0	0	80	0	0
Llano	67	0	0	37	14	0	77	0	0	56	0	0
Madison	0	33	0	62	16	62	37	0	10	0	0	0

County	1861			1862			1863			1864		
	TST	CSA	TR	TST	CSA	TR	TST	CSA	TR	TST	CSA	TR
Marion	0	0	0	173	1	173	0	0	0	4	0	4
Mason	30	0	0	28	0	0	70	0	0	73	0	0
Matagorda	178	63	0	0	0	0	30	0	9	0	0	0
Maverick	0	0	0	0	0	0	0	0	0	0	0	0
McCullock	0	0	0	66	0	0	40	0	0	105	0	0
McLennan	592	81	0	110	1	110	0	0	0	83	0	0
Mcmulle	50	0	0	8	0	6	89	0	0	17	0	0
Medina	91	0	0	95	3	7	160	0	0	93	0	0
Menard	0	0	0	0	0	0	0	0	0	0	0	0
Milam	512	182	74	4	229	4	173	0	76	0	0	0
Montague	77	0	0	188	90	0	0	0	0	113	0	0
Montgomery	126	0	0	25	16	25	49	0	11	0	0	0
Nacogdoches	0	112	0	3	111	3	135	0	6	1	0	1
Navarro	801	117	172	0	137	0	0	0	0	0	24	0
Newton	221	0	0	1	77	1	2	0	2	31	0	0
Nueces	347	139	0	26	0	0	0	0	0	0	37	0
Orange	66	0	0	93	1	66	0	0	0	0	0	0
Palo Pinto	0	0	0	0	0	0	0	0	0	158	0	0
Panola	0	15	0	140	131	45	138	0	0	0	0	0
Parker	310	0	100	0	92	0	0	0	0	412	0	0
Polk	0	0	0	56	38	46	0	0	0	0	0	0
Presidio	0	0	0	0	0	0	0	0	0	0	0	0
Red River	967	47	115	76	1	76	0	0	0	1	0	1
Refugio	201	0	0	0	1	0	33	0	33	0	0	0
Robertson	68	84	68	70	83	1	3	0	3	31	0	0
Runnels	0	0	0	0	0	0	0	0	0	0	0	0
Rusk	271	352	0	96	289	95	74	0	74	0	0	0

County	1861			1862			1863			1864		
	TST	CSA	TR	TST	CSA	TR	TST	CSA	TR	TST	CSA	TR
Sabine	0	78	0	1	75	0	64	0	1	16	0	0
San Augustine	0	65	0	5	153	5	68	0	0	0	0	0
San Patricio	38	0	0	34	0	0	8	0	8	0	0	0
San Saba	82	0	0	71	2	0	89	50	0	99	0	0
Shackleford	0	0	0	0	0	0	0	0	0	0	0	0
Shelby	0	80	0	218	6	112	89	0	1	91	0	91
Smith	322	4	0	9	144	9	0	0	0	95	0	0
Starr	40	0	0	0	0	0	0	0	0	0	0	0
Tarrant	706	0	87	155	0	154	0	88	0	34	0	34
Taylor	0	0	0	0	0	0	2	0	2	0	0	0
Throckmorton	0	0	0	0	0	0	0	0	0	0	0	0
Titus	903	86	122	176	132	176	0	0	0	0	0	0
Travis	336	60	82	182	249	1	66	0	0	139	58	0
Trinity	229	0	0	56	95	6	2	0	2	0	0	0
Tyler	118	41	0	63	5	1	5	0	5	68	0	1
Upshur	1520	53	84	29	142	29	6	0	6	0	0	0
Uvalde	0	0	0	130	0	3	127	0	0	55	0	0
Van Zandt	321	0	96	48	0	48	34	0	8	28	0	0
Victoria	526	7	58	55	35	53	32	0	32	132	27	71
Walker	0	0	0	69	7	57	70	0	67	18	0	0
Washington	544	80	0	117	311	29	593	105	168	0	1	0
Webb	0	0	0	0	80	0	0	0	0	0	0	0
Wharton	327	1	0	0	0	0	43	0	21	0	0	0
Wichita	0	0	0	0	0	0	0	0	0	0	0	0
Wilbarger	0	0	0	0	0	0	0	0	0	0	0	0
Williamson	735	36	0	7	22	5	35	72	0	78	0	0
Wilson	86	69	0	0	23	0	0	0	0	0	0	0

County	1861			1862			1863			1864		
	TST	CSA	TR	TST	CSA	TR	TST	CSA	TR	TST	CSA	TR
Wise	82	0	0	140	1	70	67	0	0	425	0	2
Wood	589	89	0	2	45	2	3	0	3	4	0	0
Young	1	0	0	0	0	0	67	0	0	83	0	0
Zapata	0	0	0	0	0	0	0	0	0	0	0	0
Zavala	0	0	0	0	0	0	1	0	0	0	0	0

Regression Analysis

Ninth Legislature

Dependent Variable: Railroad Voting Support

Constant	White Males	White Females	Total White Population	Total Slave Population	R-sq
58.21	-.0006 (.749)				0.1%
58.83		-.0011 (.597)			0.2%
58.66			-.0004 (.643)		0.2%
54.25				.0021 (.160)	1.5%
58.08			-.0019 (.117)	.0037 (.041)	3.3%

Ninth Legislature
Regression Analysis
Dependent Variable: Railroad Voting Support

Constant	Manuf. Estab.	Total Capital	Lumber Capital	Cotton Capital	Agriculture Capital	Livestock Capital	Cost Labor	Product Value	R-sq
51.49	.144 (.601)								0.4%
49.37		.0000 (.029)							6.0%
50.03			.0001 (.034)						5.7%
53.14				-.0004 (.565)					0.4%
52.41					.0000 (.813)				0.1%
52.05						.0002 (.498)			0.6%
49.29							.0856 (.195)		2.2%

Constant	Manuf. Estab.	Total Capital	Lumber Capital	Cotton Capital	Agriculture Capital	Livestock Capital	Cost Labor	Product Value	R-sq
65.14								.0000 (.658)	0.3%
49.17		.0000 (.062)					.0000 (.916)		6.0%
49.03		.0000 (.279)						.0000 (.839)	6.1%
49.45	-.127 (.609)							.0000 (.059)	4.9%
49.4	.002 (.994)	.0000 (.035)							6.0%
50.64	-.097 (.744)						0002 (.301)		1.8%
49.23	-.047 (.881)	.0000 (.346)					.0000 (.938)	.0000 (.832)	6.1%

Ninth Legislature
Regression Analysis
Dependent Variable: Railroad Voting Support

Const.	Farm Value	Milch Cow	Oxen	Cattle	Livestk Value	Wheat	Rye	Corn	Gin Cotton	Value Slain Animals	R-sq
52.39	.000 (.048)										3.2%
51.30		-.000 (.950)	-.000 (.943)	.000 (.027)							4.5%
52.61					.000 (.235)						1.2%
56.14						-.000 (.095)	-.000 (.822)	.0000 (.208)			3.3%

Const.	Farm Value	Milch Cow	Oxen	Cattle	Livestk Value	Wheat	Rye	Corn	Gin Cotton	Value Slain Animals	R-sq
54.43									.0007 (.110)		2.1%
57.38										-.000 (.883)	0.0%
52.41	.000 (.230)								.000 (.776)		3.2%
53.60	.000 (.102)				-.000 (.678)						3.3%
50.85				.000 (.018)							4.5%
53.0					.000 (.09)					-.000 (.221)	2.4%
52.3	.000 (.315)	.001 (.331)	-.001 (.832)	.000 (.120)	-.000 (.459)	-.000 (.734)	.001 (.409)	.000 (.088)	-.000 (.982)	-.000 (.061)	13.4%

Ninth Legislature
Regression Analysis
Dependent Variable: Education Voting Support

Constant	White Males	White Females	Total White Population	Total Slave Population	R-sq
65.92	-.0047 (.033)				3.4%
66.52		-.006 (.018)			4.2%
66.25			-.0026 (.024)		3.8%
61.97				-.003 (.09)	2.2%
66.42			-.0022 (.119)	-.001 (.617)	4.0%

Ninth Legislature
Regression Analysis
Dependent Variable: Education Voting Support

Constant	Manuf. Estab.	Total Capital	Lumber Capital	Cotton Capital	Agriculture Capital	Livestock Capital	Cost Labor	Product Value	R-sq
51.88	-.168 (.542)								0.5%
51.44		-.0000 (.427)							0.8%
50.06			-.0000 (.876)						0.0%
50.62				-.0015 (.097)					3.5%
46.99					.0002 (.292)				1.4%
48.84						-.0001 (.737)			0.1%
47.76							.0001 (.511)		0.6%

Constant	Manuf. Estab.	Total Capital	Lumber Capital	Cotton Capital	Agriculture Capital	Livestock Capital	Cost Labor	Product Value	R-sq
50.96								-.0000 (.69)	0.2%
50.49		-.0000 .(416)						+.0000 (.658)	1.1%
52.02	-.151 (.638)							-.0000 (.918)	0.5%
52.74	-.123 (.666)	-.0000 (.507)							1.1%
50.4	-.546 (.146)						.0004 (.141)		3.3%
51.57	-.671 (.096)	-.0000 (.234)					.0006 (.069)	.0000 (.708)	6.3%
48.62		-.0000 (.208)					.0002 (.239)		2.6%

Ninth Legislature
Regression Analysis
Dependent Variable: Education Voting Support

Const.	Farm Value	Milch Cow	Oxen	Cattle	Livestk Value	Wheat	Rye	Corn	Gin Cotton	Value Slain Animals	R-sq
58.32	-.000 (.586)										0.2%
51.99		.0012 (.257)	-.01 (.009)	.0005 (.00)							15%
54.5					.0000 (.602)						0.2%
63.59						-.000 (.373)	.0002 (.85)	-.000 (.04)			4.7%

Const.	Farm Value	Milch Cow	Oxen	Cattle	Livestk Value	Wheat	Rye	Corn	Gin Cotton	Value Slain Animals	R-sq
60.2									-.0009 (.075)		2.6%
65.18										-.0002 (.007)	5.8%
86.4	.0000 (.009)								-.0012 (.061)		5.4%
53.49	-.000 (.164)				.0000 (.167)						1.8%
46.2				.0004 (.00)							9.5%
55.98					.0000 (.002)					-.0003 (.00)	13%
54.42	.0000 (.529)	.0014 (.264)	-.005 (.461)	.0006 (.03)	-.0000 (.679)	-.000 (.859)	.0017 (.253)	.0000 (.287)	-.0009 (.315)	-.0003 (.077)	21%

Ninth Legislature
Regression Analysis
Dependent Variable: Mutual Aid Society Voting Support

Constant	White Males	White Females	Total White Population	Total Slave Population	R-sq
70.3	-.0009 (.668)				0.1%
70.41		-.0011 (.642)			0.2%
70.7			-.0006 (.595)		0.2%
67.93				.0005 (.755)	0.1%
70.44			-.0012 (.385)	.0016 (.45)	0.7%

Ninth Legislature
Regression Analysis
Dependent Variable: Mutual Aid Society Voting Support

Constant	Manuf. Estab.	Total Capital	Lumber Capital	Cotton Capital	Agriculture Capital	Livestock Capital	Cost Labor	Product Value	R-sq
71.04	-.358 (.244)								1.8%
65.17		.0000 (.54)							.05%
65.98			.0000 (.752)						0.1%
67.41				-.0014 (.143)					2.8%
62.83					.0003 (.206)				2.1%
66.53						.0000 (.975)			0.0%
67.25							-.0000 (.85)		0.0%
65.14								.0000 (.658)	0.3%
65.42		.0000 (.665)						-.0000 (.916)	0.5%

Constant	Manuf. Estab.	Total Capital	Lumber Capital	Cotton Capital	Agriculture Capital	Livestock Capital	Cost Labor	Product Value	R-sq
69.20	-.576 (.107)							.0000 (.228)	3.6%
69.71	-.427 (.178)	.0000 (.357)							2.9%
70.1	-.596 (.158)						.0002 (.407)		2.6%
66.63		.0000 (.427)					-.0001 (.586)		0.9%
69.12	-.667 (.144)	-.0000 (.858)					.0001 (.773)	.0000 (.488)	3.8%

Ninth Legislature
Regression Analysis
Dependent Variable: Mutual Aid Society Voting Support

Const	Farm Value	Milch Cow	Oxen	Cattle	Livestck Value	Wheat	Rye	Corn	Gin Cotton	Value Slain Animals	R-sq
66.61	.0000 (.416)										0.5%
61.7		.0006 (.591)	-.002 (.631)	.0003 (.043)							4.4%
62.43					.0000 (.14)						1.8%
70.21						.0000 (.484)	-.0007 (.655)	-.0000 (.56)			0.9%
68.71									.0000 (.936)		0.0%
71.67										-.0000 (.37)	0.7%
66.56	.0000 (.285)								-.0005 (.483)		0.9%

Const	Farm Value	Milch Cow	Oxen	Cattle	Livestck Value	Wheat	Rye	Corn	Gin Cotton	Value Slain Animals	R-sq
62.13	-.0000 (.677)				-.0000 (.678)						3.3%
61.9				.0003 (.024)							4.1%
63.3					.0000 (.006)					-.0002 (.012)	6.7%
63.04	.0000 (.982)	.0007 (.576)	.0001 (.798)	.0000 (.586)	.0000 (.688)	.0001 (.440)	.0002 (.893)	.0000 (.647)	.0006 (.506)	-.0003 (.128)	7.9%

Regression Analysis
Tenth Legislature

Dependent Variable: Railroad Voting Participation

Constant	White Males	White Females	Total White Population	Total Slave Population	R-sq
50.09	.0067 (.036)				3.3%
50.63			.0034 (.043)		3.1%
54.45				.0052 (.042)	3.1%
50.12			.0021 (.296)	.0033 (.283)	3.9%
49.95		.0081 (.028)			3.6%

Tenth Legislature
Regression Analysis
Dependent Variable: Railroad Voting Support

Constant	White Males	White Females	Total White Population	Total Slave Population	R-sq
35.95	.0017 (.596)				0.2%
35.93			.0007 (.661)		0.1%
39.89				-.001 (.675)	0.1%
36.33			.0017 (.407)	-.0026 (.412)	0.7%
35.07		.0022 (.544)			0.3%

Tenth Legislature
Regression Analysis
Dependent Variable: Railroad Voting Support

Constant	Manuf. Estab.	Total Capital	Lumber Capital	Cotton Capital	Agriculture Capital	Livestock Capital	Cost Labor	Product Value	R-sq
39.16	-.401 (.338)								1.2%
31.21		.0000 (.347)							1.1%
36.82			-.0001 (.315)						1.3%
34.62				-.0008 (.556)					0.5%
35.99						-.0005 (.455)			0.7%
34.81							-.0000 (.893)		0.0%
32.63								.0000 (.729)	0.2%
32.5					.0001 (.680)				0.2%
33.62		.0000 (.256)					-.0002 (.509)		1.7%

Constant	Manuf. Estab.	Total Capital	Lumber Capital	Cotton Capital	Agriculture Capital	Livestock Capital	Cost Labor	Product Value	R-sq
33.62		.0001 (.253)						-.0000 (.457)	1.9%
37.14	-.64 (.189)							.0000 (.332)	2.4%
36.8	-.525 (.222)	.0000 (.228)							3.1%
38.04	-.679 (.238)						.0003 (.477)		1.9%
36.71	-.578 (.351)	.0000 (.487)					.0001 (.822)	-.0000 (.902)	3.2%

Tenth Legislature
Regression Analysis
Dependent Variable: Railroad Voting Support

Const.	Farm Value	Milch Cow	Oxen	Cattle	Livestck Value	Wheat	Rye	Corn	Gin Cotton	Value Slain Animals	R-sq
39.13	.0000 (.774)										0.1%
30.67		-.000 (.913)	-.004 (.535)	.0007 (.002)							8.1%
29.49					.0000 (.097)						2.2%
27.97	-.000 (.157)				.0000 (.031)						3.9%
44.66						.0000 (.728)	-.002 (.303)	-.000 (.501)			1.7%
43.95									-.001 (.203)		1.3%
43.1										-.0000 (.555)	0.3%
38.9	.0000 (.09)								-.0024 (.036)		3.6%
26.4				.0006 (.002)							7.3%

Const.	Farm Value	Milch Cow	Oxen	Cattle	Livestck Value	Wheat	Rye	Corn	Gin Cotton	Value Slain Animals	R-sq
30.71					.0000 (.006)					-.0003 (.025)	6.2%
28.82	-.000 (.317)			.0007 (.002)							8.1%
32.09	.0000 (.711)	-.002 (.283)	.0002 (.987)	.0002 (.596)	.0000 (.367)	-.000 (.299)	-.003 (.206)	-.000 (.467)	-.0019 (.176)	.0001 (.577)	12.3%

Tenth Legislature
Regression Analysis
Dependent Variable: Education Voting Support

Constant	White Males	White Females	Total White Population	Total Slave Population	R-sq
77.28	.001 (.620)				0.2%
76.75		.0016 (.506)			0.3%
77.21			.0005 (.601)		0.2%
77.9				.0008 (.612)	0.2%
77.13			.0003 (.778)	.0005 (.802)	0.3%

Tenth Legislature
Regression Analysis
Dependent Variable: Education Voting Support

Constant	Manuf. Estab.	Total Capital	Lumber Capital	Cotton Capital	Agriculture Capital	Livestock Capital	Cost Labor	Product Value	R-sq
82.38	-.119 (.616)								0.3%
79.26		.0000 (.363)							1.1%
78.38			.0001 (.091)						3.7%
82.14				-.0022 (.003)					10.8%
79.81					.0000 (.639)				0.3%
80.49						.0001 (.772)			0.1%
81.93							-.0000 (.699)		0.2%
80.12								.0000 (.758)	0.1%

Tenth Legislature
Regression Analysis
Dependent Variable: Education Voting Support

Const.	Farm Value	Milch Cow	Oxen	Cattle	Livestck Value	Wheat	Rye	Corn	Gin Cotton	Value Slain Animals	R-sq
80.24	-.000 (.793)										0.1%
74.95		.0008 (.457)	.0024 (.540)	-.000 (.377)							2.8%
75.67					.0000 (.340)						0.7%
78.83						.0000 (.438)	-.001 (.471)	.0000 (.795)			0.8%
80.16									-.0001 (.735)		0.1%
80.22	-.000 (.974)								-.0001 (.830)		0.1%
78.03										.0000 (.602)	0.2%
79.6	-.000 (.420)					.0001 (.358)	-.001 (.412)	.0000 (.439)			1.4%

Tenth Legislature
Regression Analysis
Dependent Variable: Mutual Aid Society Voting Support

Constant	White Males	White Females	Total White Population	Total Slave Population	R-sq
77.87	-.0039 (.062)				2.6%
77.53			-.002 (.072)		2.4%
73.55				-.0017 (.30)	.08%
77.53			-.002 (.144)	-.0000 (.994)	2.4%
76.94		-.004 (.096)			2.1%

Tenth Legislature
Regression Analysis
Dependent Variable: Mutual Aid Society Voting Support

Constant	Manuf. Estab.	Total Capital	Lumber Capital	Cotton Capital	Agriculture Capital	Livestock Capital	Cost Labor	Product Value	R-sq
75.71	-.346 (.161)								2.5%
72.77		-.0000 (.463)							0.7%
70.57			.0000 (.598)						0.4%
72.57				-.0021 (.009)					8.6%
72.31						-.0002 (.527)			0.5%
74.3							-.0001 (.298)		1.4%
72.99								-.0000 (.545)	0.5%
74.6					-.0002 (.184)				2.3%
74.47		-.0000 (.786)					-.0001 (.434)		1.5%

Constant	Manuf. Estab.	Total Capital	Lumber Capital	Cotton Capital	Agriculture Capital	Livestock Capital	Cost Labor	Product Value	R-sq
72.86		-.0000 (.68)						-.0000 (.997)	0.7%
75.56	-.364 (.207)							.0000 (.904)	2.6%
76.19	-.321 (.209)	-.0000 (.679)							2.8%
75.8	-.319 (.348)						-.0000 (.905)		2.6%
75.84	-.442 (.228)	-.0000 (.357)					-.0000 (.889)	.0000 (.393)	3.7%

Tenth Legislature
Regression Analysis
Dependent Variable: Mutual Aid Society Voting Support

Const.	Farm Value	Milch Cow	Oxen	Cattle	Livestck Value	Wheat	Rye	Corn	Gin Cotton	Value Slain Animals	R-sq
76.51	-.000 (.022)										4.3%
79.82		.0009 (.407)	-.004 (.36)	-.000 (.006)							8.0%
82.5					-.0000 (.004)						6.7%
75.59						-.000 (.176)	-.000 (.776)	-.000 (.272)			3.5%
70.22									.0000 (.918)		0.0%
75.56										-.0001 (.089)	2.3%
82.33	-.000 (.806)				-.0000 (.076)						6.7%
76.68	-.000 (.001)								.0018 (.012)		9.1%
79.42				-.000 (.002)							7.3%

Const.	Farm Value	Milch Cow	Oxen	Cattle	Livestck Value	Wheat	Rye	Corn	Gin Cotton	Value Slain Animals	R-sq
82.42				-.000 (.019)						.0000 (.813)	6.7%
81.92	-.000 (.233)			-.000 (.02)							8.2%
80.46	-.000 (.145)	.0005 (.702)	.0018 (.771)	-.000 (.116)	.0000 (.705)	-.000 (.675)	-.001 (.613)	-.000 (.671)	.0018 (.048)	-.0000 (.649)	14.4%

Legislative Participation and Support

Ninth Legislature

	0% vote	1% to 50% vote	50% to 75% vote	75% to 100% vote	100% vote
Railroad Participation	% of counties: 5% total number: 8	3% 5	15% 24	48% 77	27% 44
Railroad Support	5% 8	41% 65	12% 20	29% 46	12% 19
Education Participation	5% 8	3% 5	8% 13	22% 36	60% 96
Education Support	9% 15	33% 53	13% 21	15% 24	28% 45
Mutual Aid Society Participation	12% 19	12% 20	20% 33	22% 35	32% 51
Mutual Aid Society Support	12% 19	12% 20	20% 33	22% 35	32% 51

Tenth Legislature

	0% vote	1% to 50% vote	50% to 75% vote	75% to 100% vote	100% vote
Railroad Participation	% of counties: 43% total number: 69				56% 89
Railroad Support	63% 101				36% 57
Education Participation	10% 17	0% 1	15% 25	12% 19	60% 96
Education Support	10% 17	0% 1	15% 25	12% 19	60% 96
Mutual Aid Society Participation	10% 16	6% 11	27% 44	9% 15	45% 72
Mutual Aid Society Support	10% 16	8% 13	27% 43	10% 17	43% 69

Note on Sources

In Chapter 3, the data for Indian attacks, horses stolen, lives lost, offensive measures, and Indians killed are based on an exhaustive search of the entire newspaper collection from 1861 through 1862 at the Barker Center for American History, University of Texas at Austin. All accounts appearing in newspapers were compared to ensure accuracy. There is no doubt, however, that many more attacks occurred during this period than are accounted for here.

The analysis of Chapter 4 is based on the complete muster-roll collection at the Texas State Library, Archives Division, Austin. Although the best effort was made to determine county residence for enlisted men, several difficulties did exist. Oftentimes, a muster roll listed only one county for all the men. It is quite possible, however, that in many cases some of the men listed did not reside in the said county, but instead hailed from a surrounding county. In some cases, a muster roll listed only the state of nativity. Other muster rolls listed only the camp where men enlisted. In these cases, even though the county location of the camp is known, the number of men were not included in the analysis because there was not a definite assurance of where these men came from. In still other instances, when the county where men resided is known, yet no date is given for their enlistment, these too were excluded from the analysis. There also existed a few instances where the city instead of the county was listed. In these cases, an attempt was made to identify correctly the county. Nevertheless, due to duplicate city names in several counties, there were instances where men were not included in the analysis. At any point where there appeared a discrepancy among several muster rolls for the same company, names and numbers of men were cross-referenced to obtain the most accurate count. Sadly, there are numerous muster rolls in such poor shape that they are completely incomprehensible. An exhaustive search of the muster-roll collection reveals that approximately 83,870 men went off to fight in either the state militia or the Confederate army. Due to the illegibility of many muster rolls, there is no doubt that this number falls short of the actual number of men who fought from 1861 to 1865. In the maps that document the numbers and percentages of men who enlisted in the state militia and Confederate service, the counties shaded white are an indication that, based upon the findings, no mappable data exist.

Analysis for the percentage of men enlisted is based upon census data listing the number of white males between fifteen and fifty years old. Even though the initial conscription law covered men between the ages of eighteen and thirty-five, numerous muster rolls reveal that men as young as fourteen and as old as sixty-five enlisted in both the state militia and the Confederate army. For the years 1862–1864, the number of available men for each year is based upon the number of men between eighteen and fifty minus the number previously enlisted in the state militia and the Confederate army. Furthermore, Texans did enter both the state militia and the Confederate army in 1865. Nevertheless, the numbers are too low to warrant a geographical or statistical analysis. According to the muster rolls, only three Texas counties sent men into the state militia in 1865, and all of these men were transferred into the Confederate army. The muster rolls do not reveal any men entering the Confederate army directly.

Bibliography

Manuscript Collections

Barker Center for American History, University of Texas at Austin
   Hamilton Bee Papers
   Davenport Collection
   Benjamin H. Good Papers
   Washington Daniel Miller Papers
   Williamson Simpson Oldham Papers
   John H. Reagan Papers
   Edmund Kirby Smith Papers
   Louis T. Wigfall Papers
National Archives, Washington, D.C.
   George Bickley Papers
   Records of the Trans-Mississippi Department
Rice University Microfilm Collection
Texas State Library, Archives Division, Austin
   Executive Record Book: Sam Houston
   Governor's Papers: Sam Houston
   Military Papers
   Railroad Commission Records
   Records of the Adjutant General: Muster Roll Collection
   Records of the Texas Military Board
   Records of the Texas State Penitentiary
   Texas School for the Blind

Newspapers

Austin Texas State Gazette
Austin Tri-Weekly State Gazette
Bellville Countryman
Brenham Enquirer
Clarksville Northern Standard
Clarksville Standard
Columbia Democrat and Planter
Columbus Colorado Citizen
Confederacy

Corpus Christi Ranchero
Corsicana Navarro Express
Crockett Printer
Dallas Weekly Herald
Fort Lancaster Western Pioneer
Galveston Daily Civilian
Galveston Tri-Weekly News
Galveston Weekly Civilian and Gazette
Galveston Weekly News
Harrison Flag
Houston Telegraph
Houston Tri-Weekly Telegraph
Houston Weekly Telegraph
Indianola Courier
Jefferson Confederate News
Jefferson Herald and Gazette
La Grange True Issue
Marshall Texas Republican
McKinney Messenger
Red Land Express
San Antonio Daily Herald
San Antonio Daily Ledger and Texan
San Antonio Herald
San Antonio Ledger
San Antonio Semi-Weekly News
San Antonio Tri-Weekly Alamo Express
San Antonio Tri-Weekly Telegraph
San Antonio Weekly Alamo Express
San Antonio Weekly Herald
San Antonio Weekly Ledger and Texan
Seguin Southern Confederacy
Southern Intelligencer
State Rights Democrat
Texas Baptist
Tyler Reporter
Waco South West-Quarter Sheet

Other Sources

Abel, Annie Heloise. *The American Indian as Slaveholder and Secessionist.* 1915. Reprint, Lincoln: University of Nebraska Press, 1992.

Agriculture of the United States in 1860, Compiled from the Original Returns of the Eighth Census. Washington, D.C.: U.S. Government Printing Office, 1864.

Alexander, Thomas B., and Richard E. Beringer. *The Anatomy of the Confederate Congress: A Study of the Influences of Member Characteristics on Legislative Voting Behavior, 1861–1865.* Nashville: Vanderbilt University Press, 1972.

Allen, John O. "The Wealth of Antebellum Southside Virginia: Tobacco or Slaves?" Ph.D. diss., Catholic University of America, 2002.

Anderson, Charles. *Speech of Charles Anderson, ESQ., on the State of the Country, at a Meeting of the People of Bexar County, at San Antonia, Texas, November 24, 1860.* Washington, D.C.: Lemuel Towers, 1860.

Anderson, Thomas F. "The Indian Territory, 1861–1865." *Confederate Veteran* 4 (1896): 85–87.

Appleby, Joyce. *Liberalism and Republicanism in the Historical Imagination.* Cambridge: Harvard University Press, 1992.

Austin State Hospital. *By-Laws, Rules, and Regulations for the Government of the Texas State Lunatic Asylum, Austin.* Austin: Daily Republican Office, 1868.

Bailey, Lelia. "The Life and Public Career of O. M. Roberts, 1815–1883." Ph.D. diss., University of Texas, 1932.

Baird, W. David. *The Choctaw People.* Phoenix: Indian Tribal Series, 1973.

Baker, Robin E., and Dale Baum. "The Texas Voter and the Crisis of the Union, 1859–1861." *Journal of Southern History* 53 (Aug. 1987): 395–420.

Banta, William. *Twenty-seven Years on the Texas Frontier.* 1893. Reprint, Council, Okla.: L. G. Park, 1933.

Barfoot, Jessie L. *A History of McCulloch County, Texas.* Master's thesis, University of Texas, 1937.

Barkley, Mary Starr. *History of Travis County and Austin, 1839–1899.* Waco: Texian Press, 1963.

Barney, William L. *The Secessionist Impulse: Alabama and Mississippi in 1860.* Princeton: Princeton University Press, 1974.

Baum, Dale. *The Shattering of Texas Unionism: Politics in the Lone Star State during the Civil War Era.* Baton Rouge: Louisiana State University Press, 1998.

Beals, Carleton. *War within a War: The Confederacy against Itself.* New York: Chilton Books, 1965.

Beam, Harold. *A History of Collin County, Texas.* Master's thesis, University of Texas, 1951.

Beckwith, Arthur. "Texas Letter from John Hemphill to His Brother, James, in Tennessee." *Southwestern Historical Quarterly* 57 (Oct. 1953): 222–24.

Bell, James Hall. *Speech of Hon. James H. Bell, of the Texas Supreme Court, Delivered at the Capitol on Saturday, Dec. 1st, 1860.* Austin: Intelligencer Book Office, 1860.

Benner, Judith Ann. *Sul Ross: Soldier, Statesman, Educator.* College Station: Texas A&M University, 1983.

Bensel, Richard. *Yankee Leviathan: The Origins of Central State Authority in America, 1859–1877.* Cambridge: Cambridge University Press, 1990.

Beringer, Richard. *The Elements of Confederate Defeat: Nationalism, War Aims, and Religion.* Athens: University of Georgia Press, 1988.

Binkley, William C. *The Expansionist Movement in Texas, 1836–1850.* New York: DeCapo Press, 1970.

Black, Robert, III. *The Railroads of the Confederacy.* Chapel Hill: University of North Carolina Press, 1952.

Blackburn, William W. "Evolution of the State School for the Deaf from an Asylum to an Accredited School." Master's thesis, University of Texas, 1958.

Bledsoe, Albert Taylor. *Is Davis a Traitor?* Richmond: Hermitage Press, 1907.

Boritt, Gabor S., ed. *Why the Confederacy Lost.* New York: Oxford University Press, 1992.

Bowden, M. G. *History of Burnet County.* Master's thesis, University of Texas, 1940.

Bowen, Nancy Head. "A Political Labyrinth: Texas in the Civil War—Questions in Continuity." Ph.D. diss., Rice University, 1974.

Bridges, C. A. "The Knights of the Golden Circle: A Filibustering Fantasy." *Southwestern Historical Quarterly* 44 (Jan. 1941): 287–302.

Brown, Walter Lee. *A Life of Albert Pike.* Fayetteville: University of Arkansas Press, 1997.

Brownson, Chris. *From Curer to Custodian: A History of the Texas State Lunatic Asylum, 1857–1880.* Austin: [University of Texas?], 1992.

Buenger, Walter. *Secession and the Union in Texas.* Austin: University of Texas Press, 1984.

———. "Secession Revisited: The Texas Experience." *Civil War History* 30 (winter 1984): 293–305.

———. "Texas and the Riddle of Secession." *Southwestern Historical Quarterly* 87 (Oct. 1983): 151–82.

By-Laws of the San Antonio Castle, "K.G.C.," Approved June 15, 1861. San Antonio: Ledger and Texan Office, 1861.

Campbell, Randolph. *An Empire for Slavery: The Peculiar Institution in Texas, 1821–1865.* Baton Rouge: Louisiana State University Press, 1989.

———. "Fighting for the Confederacy: The White Male Population of Harrison County in the Civil War." *Southwestern Historical Quarterly* 104 (July 2000): 23–40.

Campbell, Randolph, and Richard G. Lowe. *Wealth and Power in Antebellum Texas.* College Station: Texas A&M University Press, 1977.

Cantrell, Greg. "Whither Sam Houston?" *Southwestern Historical Quarterly* 97 (Oct. 1993): 345–57.

Carnes, Mark. *Secret Ritual and Manhood in Victorian America.* New Haven: Yale University Press, 1989.

Carter, Samuel, III. *The Final Fortress: The Campaign for Vicksburg, 1862–1863.* New York: St. Martin's Press, 1980.

Channing, Steven A. *Crisis of Fear: Secession in South Carolina.* New York: Simon and Schuster, 1970.

Clarke, Mary Whatley. *The Palo Pinto Story.* Fort Worth: Manney, 1956.

Clawson, Mary Ann. *Constructing Brotherhood: Class, Gender, and Fraternalism.* Princeton: Princeton University Press, 1989.

Confederate States of America. House of Representatives. *A Bill Requiring Suit to Be Brought against Persons Connected with the Cotton Bureau and Cotton Office in Texas.* 1865.

———. *Rules for Conducting Business in the Senate of the Confederate States of America.* Richmond: R. M. Smith, 1864.

———. Senate. *A Bill to Provide for the Army and to Prescribe the Mode of Making Impressments.* 1864.

Connelly, Michael J. "All Points North: Entrepreneurial Politics and Railroad Development in Northern New England, 1830–1860." Ph.D. diss., Catholic University of America, 2000.

Connelly, Thomas L. *The Marble Man: Robert E. Lee and His Image in American Society.* New York: Alfred A. Knopf, 1977.

Craven, Avery O. *The Growth of Southern Nationalism, 1848–1861.* Baton Rouge: Louisiana State University Press, 1953.

Creighton, James A. *A Narrative History of Brazoria County.* Waco: Brazoria County Historical Commission, 1975.

Crenshaw, Ollinger. "The Knights of the Golden Circle: The Career of George Bickley." *American Historical Review* 47 (Oct. 1941): 23–50.

Curtis, Sara Kay. "A History of Gillespie County, Texas, 1846–1900." Master's thesis, University of Texas, 1943.

Cutrer, Thomas W. *Ben McCulloch and the Frontier Military Tradition.* Chapel Hill: University of North Carolina Press, 1993.

Dabney, Robert L. *A Defense of Virginia.* New York: E. J. Hale and Son, 1867.

Daddysman, James W. *The Matamoros Trade: Confederate Commerce, Diplomacy, and Intrigue.* Newark: University of Delaware Press, 1984.

Dale, Edward Everett, and Gaston Litton. *Cherokee Cavaliers: Forty Years of Cherokee History as Told in the Correspondence of the Ridge-Watie-Boudinot Family.* Norman: University of Oklahoma Press, 1938.

Davenport, Harbert. *History of the Supreme Court of Texas.* Austin: Southern Law Book, 1917.

Day, James M., ed. *The Indian Papers of Texas and the Southwest, 1825–1916.* 5 vols. Austin: Texas State Historical Association, 1995.

DeLeon, Arnoldo. *The Tejano Community, 1836–1900.* Albuquerque: University of New Mexico Press, 1982.

———. *They Called Them Greasers: Anglo Attitudes toward Mexicans in Texas, 1821–1900.* Austin: University of Texas Press, 1983.

Deutsch, Karl. *Nationalism and Social Communication: An Inquiry into the Foundations of Nationality.* Cambridge: MIT Press, 1966.

Donnell, Guy Renfro. *The History of Montague County, Texas.* Master's thesis, University of Texas, 1940.

Duncan, Christopher M. *The Anti-Federalists and Early American Political Thought.* DeKalb: Northern Illinois University Press, 1995.

Dunn, Roy Sylvan. "The K.G.C. in Texas, 1860–1861." *Southwestern Historical Quarterly* 70 (Apr. 1967): 543–73.

Durant, A. R. *Constitution and Laws of the Choctaw Nation.* Dallas: John F. Worley, 1894.

Durrill, Wayne K. *War of Another Kind: A Southern Community in the Great Rebellion.* New York: Oxford University Press, 1990.

Eilers, Kathryn. *A History of Mason County, Texas.* Master's thesis, University of Texas, 1939.

Elliott, Claude. *Leathercoat: The Life History of a Texas Patriot.* San Antonio: Standard Printing, 1938.

———. "Union Sentiment in Texas, 1861–1865." *Southwestern Historical Quarterly* 50 (July 1947): 449–77.

Eoff, Vallie. *A History of Erath County, Texas.* Master's thesis, University of Texas, 1937.

Erath, Lucy A. *The Memoirs of Major George B. Erath, 1813–1891.* Austin: Texas State Historical Association, 1923.

Escott, Paul. *After Secession: Jefferson Davis and the Failure of Confederate Nationalism.* Baton Rouge: Louisiana State University Press, 1978.

Ezell, Camp. *Historical Story of Bee County, Texas.* Beeville, Texas: Beeville Publishing, 1973.

Ferguson, Dan. "Austin College in Huntsville." *Southwestern Historical Quarterly* 53 (Apr. 1950): 386–403.

Foner, Eric. *Free Soil, Free Labor, Free Men: The Ideology of the Republican Party before the Civil War.* New York: Oxford University Press, 1970.

Ford, Lacy K. *Origins of Southern Radicalism: The South Carolina Upcountry, 1800–1860.* New York: Oxford University Press, 1988.

Fornell, Earl Wesley. *The Galveston Era: The Texas Crescent on the Eve of Secession.* Austin: University of Texas Press, 1961.

Foster, Gaines M. *Ghosts of the Confederacy: Defeat, the Lost Cause, and the Emergence of the New South, 1865–1913.* New York: Oxford University Press, 1987.

Foster, Morris W. *Being Comanche: A Social History of an American Indian Community.* Tuscon: University of Arizona Press, 1991.

Franks, Kenny. "The Implementation of the Confederate Treaties with the Five Civilized Tribes." *Chronicles of Oklahoma* 51 (1973): 21–33.

Frazier, Donald S. *Blood and Treasure: Confederate Empire in the Southwest.* College Station: Texas A&M University Press, 1995.

Gammel, H. P. N., comp. *The Laws of Texas, 1822–1897.* 10 vols. Austin, 1898.

Garry, Patrick M. *Liberalism and American Identity.* Kent, Ohio: Kent State University Press, 1992.

Gellner, Ernest. *Nations and Nationalism.* Ithaca: Cornell University Press, 1983.

Genovese, Eugene D. *The Political Economy of Slavery: Studies in the Economy and Society of the Slave South.* New York: Pantheon Books, 1965.

———. *The World the Slaveholders Made.* New York: Pantheon Books, 1969.

Gienapp, William. *The Origins of the Republican Party, 1852–1856.* New York: Oxford University Press, 1987.

Gipson, Arrell M. *The Chickasaws.* Norman: University of Oklahoma Press, 1971.

Goyne, Minetta Altgelt. *Lone Star and Double Eagle: Civil War Letters of a German-Texas Family.* Fort Worth: Texas Christian University Press, 1982.

Green, Fletcher M. "Democracy in the Old South." *Journal of Southern History* 12 (Feb. 1946): 3–23.

Hale, Will. *Twenty-four Years a Cowboy and Ranchman in Southern Texas and Old Mexico.* Norman: University of Oklahoma Press, 1959.

Halliburton, Janet. "Black Slavery in the Creek Nation." *Chronicles of Oklahoma* 56 (1978): 298–314.

Halliburton, R., Jr. *Red over Black: Black Slavery among the Cherokee Indians.* Westport, Conn.: Greenwood Press, 1977.

Hamilton, Andrew Jackson. *Speech of Hon. Andrew J. Hamilton, of Texas, on the State of the Union, Delivered in the House of Representatives of the United States, February 1, 1861.* Washington, D.C.: Lemuel Towers, 1861.

Harsh, Joseph. *Confederate Tide Rising: Robert E. Lee and the Making of Southern Strategy, 1861–1862.* Kent, Ohio: Kent State University Press, 1998.

Hartz, Louis. *The Liberal Tradition in America: An Interpretation of American Political Thought since the Revolution.* New York: Harcourt, Brace, 1955.

Havins, T. R. "The Frontier Era in Brown County." *West Texas Historical Association Journal* 13 (Oct. 1937): 64–81.

———. *Something about Brown: A History of Brown County, Texas.* Brownwood, Texas: Banner Printing, 1958.

Heartsill, W. W. *Fourteen Hundred and 91 Days in the Confederate Army.* Ed. Bell Irvin Wiley. Wilmington, N.C.: Broadfoot Publishing, 1987.

Heleniak, Roman J., and Lawrence L. Hewitt, eds. *Leadership during the Civil War: Themes in Honor of T. Harry Williams.* Shippensburg, Pa.: White Mane Publishing, 1992.

Hemphill, John. *Speech of Hon. John Hemphill, of Texas on the State of the Union, Delivered in the Senate of the United States, January 28, 1861.* Washington, D.C.: Lemuel Towers, 1861.

Hicks, Jimmie. "Some Letters Concerning the Knights of the Golden Circle in Texas, 1860–1861." *Southwestern Historical Quarterly* 65 (July 1961): 80–86.

Hietala, Thomas R. *Manifest Design: Anxious Aggrandizement in Late Jacksonian America.* Ithaca: Cornell University Press, 1985.

Hobsbawm, Eric. *Nations and Nationalism since 1780: Programme, Myth, Reality.* New York: Cambridge University Press, 1990.

Hobson, Nancy. "Samuel Bell Maxey as Confederate Commander of Indian Territory." *Journal of the West* 12 (July 1973): 424–38.

Hogg Foundation. *Know Your Texas State Hospitals and Special Schools.* Austin: Hogg Foundation for Mental Hygiene, 1954.

Holbrook, Abigail C. "A Glimpse of Life on Antebellum Slave Plantations in Texas." *Southwestern Historical Quarterly* 76 (Apr. 1973): 361–83.

Holladay, Florence E. "The Powers of the Commander of the Confederate Trans-Mississippi Department, 1863–1865." *Southwestern Historical Quarterly* 21 (1918): 279–98, 333–59.

Horton, Louise. *Samuel Bell Maxey: A Biography.* Austin: University of Texas Press, 1974.

House Journal of the Ninth Legislature First Called Session of the State of Texas. Ed. James M. Day. Austin: Texas State Library, 1963.

House Journal of the Tenth Legislature First Called Session of the State of Texas. Ed. James M. Day. Austin: Texas State Library, 1965.

House Journal of the Tenth Legislature Regular Session of the State of Texas. Ed. James M. Day. Austin: Texas State Library, 1965.

House Journal of the Tenth Legislature Second Called Session of the State of Texas. Ed. James M. Day. Austin: Texas State Library, 1966.

Howell, D. S. "Along the Frontier during the Civil War." *West Texas Historical Association Journal* 13 (Oct. 1937): 82–95.

Hoxie, Frederick E. *A Final Promise: The Campaign to Assimilate the Indians.* Lincoln: University of Nebraska Press, 1991.

Humphrey, David C. "A 'Very Muddy and Conflicting' View: The Civil War as Seen from Austin, Texas." *Southwestern Historical Quarterly* 94 (Jan. 1991): 369–414.

Irby, James Arthur. "Confederate Austin, 1861–1865." Master's thesis, University of Texas, 1953.

Jewett, Clayton E. "Establishing a Separate Identity: Texas' Offensive Struggle with the Indian Nations, 1861–1862." In *The Southern Albatross: Race and Ethnicity in the American South,* ed. Philip D. Dillard and Randal L. Hall, 51–82. Macon, Ga.: Mercer University Press, 1999.

———. "Louis T. Wigfall." In *Leaders of the American Civil War: A Biographical and Historiographical Dictionary,* ed. Charles F. Ritter and Jon L. Wakelyn, 434–42. Westport, Conn.: Greenwood Press, 1998.

Johansson, M. Jane. *Peculiar Honor: A History of the 28th Texas Cavalry, 1862–1865.* Fayetteville: University of Arkansas Press, 1998.

Johnson, Francis White. *A History of Texas and Texans.* Chicago: American Historical Society, 1914.

Johnson, Ludwell. *Red River Campaign: Politics and Cotton in the Civil War.* Baltimore: Johns Hopkins University Press, 1958.

Johnson, Michael P. *Toward a Patriarchal Republic: The Secession of Georgia.* Baton Rouge: Louisiana State University Press, 1977.

Jordan, Terry. *German Seed in Texas Soil: Immigrant Farmers in Nineteenth-Century Texas.* Austin: University of Texas Press, 1966.

Josephy, Alvin M., Jr. *The Civil War in the American West.* New York: Random House, 1991.

Journal of the Congress of the Confederate States of America, 1861–1865. 7 vols. Washington, D.C.: U.S. Government Printing Office, 1904; reprint, New York: Kraus Reprint, 1968.

Journal of the House of Representatives of the Ninth Legislature of the State of Texas. Ed. James M. Day. Austin: Texas State Library, 1963.

Journal of the Secession Convention of Texas, 1861. Ed. E. W. Winkler. Austin, 1912.

Journal of the Senate, State of Texas, Eighth Legislature (Extra Session). Austin: John Marshall, 1861.

Kerby, Robert L. *Kirby Smith's Confederacy: The Trans-Mississippi South, 1863–1865.* New York: Columbia University Press, 1972.

KGC. *A Full Exposure of the Southern Traitors: The Knights of the Golden Circle, Their Startling Schemes Frustrated.* Boston: E. H. Bullard, n.d.

King, Alvy L. *Louis T. Wigfall: Southern Fire-Eater.* Baton Rouge: Louisiana State University Press, 1970.

Klement, Frank. *Dark Lanterns.* Baton Rouge: Louisiana State University Press, 1984.

Knight, Wilfred. *Red Fox: Stand Watie and the Confederate Indian Nations during the Civil War Years in Indian Territory.* Glendale, Calif.: Arthur H. Clark, 1988.

Kohn, Hans. *American Nationalism: An Interpretive Essay.* New York: Macmillan, 1957.

Lambie, Agnes Louise. "Confederate Control of Cotton in the Trans-Mississippi Department." Master's thesis, University of Texas, 1915.

Ledbetter, Billy D. "The Election of Louis T. Wigfall." *Southwestern Historical Quarterly* 77 (Oct. 1973): 241–54.

———. "Slavery, Fear, and Disunion in the Lone Star State: Texans' Attitudes toward Secession and the Union, 1846–1861." Ph.D. diss., North Texas State University, 1972.

Levengood, Paul. "In the Absence of Scarcity: The Civil War Prosperity of Houston, Texas." *Southwestern Historical Quarterly* 101 (Apr. 1998): 401–28.

Livermore, Thomas L. *Numbers and Losses in the Civil War in America, 1861–1865.* Boston: Houghton Mifflin, 1901.

Lonn, Ella. *Salt as a Factor in the Confederacy.* University: University of Alabama Press, 1965.

Lord, Clyde W. "Ante-Bellum Career of Louis Trezevant Wigfall." Master's thesis, University of Texas, 1925.

Lowe, Richard, and Randolph Campbell. *Planters and Plainfolk: Agriculture in Antebellum Texas.* Dallas: Southern Methodist University Press, 1987.

Madray, I. C. *A History of Bee County with Some Brief Sketches about Men and Events in Adjoining Counties.* Beeville, Texas: Bee-Picayune, 1934.

Manufactures of the United States in 1860; Compiled from the Original Returns of the Eighth Census. Washington, D.C.: U.S. Government Printing Office, 1865.

Marten, James. *Texas Divided: Loyalty and Dissent in the Lone Star State, 1856–1874.* Lexington: University Press of Kentucky, 1990.

Martin, David G. *The Vicksburg Campaign.* New York: Gallery Books, 1990.

McCandless, Peter. *Moonlight, Magnolias, and Madness: Insanity in South Carolina from the Colonial Period to the Progressive Era.* Chapel Hill: University of North Carolina Press, 1996.

McCaslin, Richard. *Tainted Breeze: The Great Hanging at Gainesville, Texas, 1862.* Baton Rouge: Louisiana State University Press, 1994.

McDonnell, Janet A. *The Dispossession of the American Indian, 1887–1934.* Bloomington: Indiana University Press, 1991.

McPherson, James M. *Battle Cry of Freedom.* New York: Oxford University Press, 1988.

Meiners, Fredericka. "The Texas Border Cotton Trade." *Civil War History* 23 (Dec. 1977): 293–307.

Member of the Order. *An Authentic Exposition of the "K.G.C." "Knights of the Golden Circle"; or, A History of Secession from 1834 to 1861.* Indianapolis: C. O. Perrine, 1861.

Montejano, David. *Anglos and Mexicans in the Making of Texas, 1836–1900.* Austin: University of Texas Press, 1987.

Moore, Albert Burton. *Conscription and Conflict in the Confederacy.* New York: Hillary House, 1963.

Myers, Ila Mae. "The Relations of Governor Pendleton Murrah, of Texas, with the Confederate Military Authorities." Master's thesis, University of Texas, 1929.

Myres, Sandra L. "The Ranching Frontier: Spanish Institutional Backgrounds of the Plains Cattle Industry." In *Essays on the American West,* ed. Harold M. Hollingsworth and Sandra L. Myres, 19–39. Austin: University of Texas Press, 1969.

Newcomb, James P. *Sketch of Secession Times in Texas and Journal of Travel from Texas through Mexico to California, Including a History of the "Box Colony."* San Francisco, 1863.

Newcomb, W. W., Jr. *The Indians of Texas: From Prehistoric to Modern Times.* Austin: University of Texas Press, 1961.

Nichols, James L. "Confederate Quartermaster Operations in the Trans-Mississippi Department." Master's thesis, University of Texas, 1947.

Niven, John, ed. *The Salmon P. Chase Papers.* Vol. 1, *Journals, 1829–1872.* Kent, Ohio: Kent State University Press, 1993.

Nunn, W. C., ed. *Ten More Texans in Gray.* Hillsboro, Texas: Hill Junior College Press, 1980.

Oakes, James. *The Ruling Race: A History of American Slaveholders.* New York: Alfred A. Knopf, 1982.

Oldham, Williamson Simpson. *Speech of Hon. W. S. Oldham of Texas, on the Subject of Finances, Senate, December 23, 1863.* Richmond, 1863.

Osterweis, Rollin G. *Romanticism and Nationalism in the Old South.* New Haven: Yale University Press, 1949.

Owsley, Frank. *King Cotton Diplomacy: Foreign Relations of the Confederate States of America.* Chicago: University of Chicago Press, 1931.

Parks, Joseph H. *General Edmund Kirby Smith, C.S.A.* Baton Rouge: Louisiana State University Press, 1954.

———. *Plain Folk of the Old South.* Baton Rouge: Louisiana State University Press, 1949.

———. *State Rights in the Confederacy.* Chicago: University of Chicago Press, 1931.

Phillips, Ulrich B. *American Negro Slavery: A Survey of the Supply, Employment, and Control of Negro Labor as Determined by the Plantation Regime.* 1918. Reprint, Baton Rouge: Louisiana State University Press, 1989.

———. *Life and Labor in the Old South.* Boston: Little, Brown, 1965.

———. "The Origin and Growth of the Southern Blackbelts." *American Historical Review* 11 (July 1906): 798–816.

Pickering, David, and Judy Falls. *Brush Men and Vigilantes: Civil War Dissent in Texas.* College Station: Texas A&M University Press, 2000.

Piston, William Garrett. *Lee's Tarnished Lieutenant: James Longstreet and His Place in Southern History.* Athens: University of Georgia Press, 1987.

Pollard, Edward. *The Lost Cause: A New Southern History of the War of the Confederates.* New York: E. B. Treat, 1866.

Pool, Oran. *A History of Hamilton County.* Master's thesis, University of Texas, 1954.

Poos, Larry R., and Clayton E. Jewett. "Digitizing History: GIS Aids Historical Research." *GIS World* (May 1995): 48–51.

Population of the United States in 1860, Compiled from the Original Returns of the Eighth Census. Washington, D.C.: U.S. Government Printing Office, 1864.

Potter, David M. *The South and the Sectional Conflict.* Baton Rouge: Louisiana State University Press, 1968.

Proctor, Ben. *Not without Honor: The Life of John H. Reagan.* Austin: University of Texas Press, 1962.

Purdue, Theda. *Nations Remembered: An Oral History of the Five Civilized Tribes, 1865–1907.* Westport, Conn.: Greenwood Press, 1980.

Rable, George C. *The Confederate Republic: A Revolution against Politics.* Chapel Hill: University of North Carolina Press, 1994.

Rains, C. W., ed. *Six Decades in Texas; or, Memoirs of Francis Richard Lubbock, Governor of Texas in War-Time, 1861–1863.* Austin: Ben C. Jones, 1900.

Rampp, Lary C., and Donald L. Rampp. *The Civil War in the Indian Territory.* Austin: Presidial Press, 1975.

Ramsdell, Charles W. *Behind the Lines in the Southern Confederacy.* Baton Rouge: Louisiana State University Press, 1944.

———. "The Confederate Government and the Railroads." *American Historical Review* 22 (1917): 794–810.

———. "The Frontier and Secession." *Studies in Southern History and Politics* (1914): 63–79.

———. "Some Problems Involved in Writing the History of the Confederacy." *Journal of Southern History* 2 (Feb. 1936): 133–47.

———. "The Texas State Military Board, 1862–1865." *Southwestern Historical Quarterly* 27 (1924): 253–75.

Reagan, John. *State of the Union Speech of the Hon. John H. Reagan of Texas, Delivered in the House of Representatives, January 15, 1861.* Washington, D.C.: W. H. Moore, 1861.

Real, Matilda. *A History of Kerr County, Texas.* Master's thesis, University of Texas, 1942.

Report of Superintendent and Managers of the State Lunatic Asylum for the Year 1866. Austin: State Gazette Office, 1866.

Roberts, A. Sellew. "The Federal Government and Confederate Cotton." *American Historical Review* 32 (1927): 262–75.

Roberts, Oran Milo. "Speech of Judge Oran Milo Roberts of the Supreme Court of Texas, at the Capitol, on the 1st December, 1860, upon the 'Impending Crisis.'" N.p., n.d.

Rose, Victor. *Life and Services of Ben McCulloch.* Austin: Steck, 1958.

Rothman, David J. *The Discovery of the Asylum: Social Order and Disorder in the New Republic.* Boston: Little, Brown, 1971.

Rountree, Joseph G., III. *History of Bee County, Texas.* Beeville, Texas: n.p., 1960.

Royster, Charles. *The Destructive War: William Tecumseh Sherman, Stonewall Jackson, and the Americans.* New York: Random House, 1993.

Sandbo, Irene. "The First Session of the Secession Convention of Texas." *Southwestern Historical Quarterly* 18 (Oct. 1914): 162–94.

Scott, Zelma. *A History of Coryell County, Texas.* Austin: Texas State Historical Association, 1965.

Senate Journal of the Ninth Legislature Regular Session of the State of Texas. Ed. James M. Day. Austin: Texas State Library, 1963.

Senate Journal of the Tenth Legislature First Called Session of the State of Texas. Ed. James M. Day. Austin: Texas State Library, 1965.

Senate Journal of the Tenth Legislature Regular Session of the State of Texas. Ed. James M. Day. Austin: Texas State Library, 1964.

Senate Journal of the Tenth Legislature Second Called Session of the State of Texas. Ed. James M. Day. Austin: Texas State Library, 1966.

Shore, Lawrence. *Southern Capitalists: The Ideological Leadership of an Elite, 1832–1885.* Chapel Hill: University of North Carolina Press, 1986.

Silverthorne, Elizabeth. *Plantation Life in Texas.* College Station: Texas A&M University Press, 1986.

Skaggs, Jimmy. *Prime Cut: Livestock Raising and Meatpacking in the United States, 1607–1983.* College Station: Texas A&M University Press, 1986.

Smith, Anthony D. *Theories of Nationalism.* London: Duckworth Press, 1971.

Smith, David Paul. "Conscription and Conflict on the Texas Frontier, 1863–1865." *Civil War History* 36 (Sept. 1990): 250–61.

———. "Frontier Defense in Texas, 1861–1865." Ph.D. diss., North Texas State University, 1987.

———. *Frontier Defense in the Civil War: Texas' Rangers and Rebels.* College Station: Texas A&M University Press, 1992.

Smyrl, Frank H. "Unionism in Texas, 1861–1865." *Southwestern Historical Quarterly* 68 (Oct. 1964): 172–95.

Sparks, A. W. *The War between the States, as I Saw It: Reminiscent, Historical, and Personal.* 1901. Reprint, Longview, Texas: D and D Publishing, 1987.

Spindler, Frank MacD. "The History of Hempstead and the Formation of

Waller County, Texas." *Southwestern Historical Quarterly* 63 (Jan. 1960): 404–27.

Sprague, John T. *The Treachery in Texas, the Secession in Texas, and the Arrest of the United States Officers and Soldiers Serving in Texas.* New York, 1862.

Stambaugh, J. Lee, and Lillian J. Stambaugh. *A History of Collin County, Texas.* Austin: Texas State Historical Association, 1958.

Stephens, Alexander. *A Constitutional View of the Late War between the States.* New York: Appleton Press, 1872.

Stover, John. *American Railroads.* Chicago: University of Chicago Press, 1961.

Summers, Susanne L. "Persistence and Change among the Merchant Community in Houston and Galveston, Texas, 1836–1880s." Paper presented at the Rice University Symposium on Southern History, Houston, May 1997.

Thomas, Emory. *The Confederate Nation, 1861–1865.* New York: Harper and Row, 1979.

Thompson, Jerry D., ed. *Juan Cortina and the Texas-Mexico Frontier, 1859–1877.* El Paso: Texas Western Press, 1994.

Thornton, J. Mills, III. *Politics and Power in a Slave Society: Alabama, 1800–1860.* Baton Rouge: Louisiana State University Press, 1978.

Timmons, Joe T. "The Referendum in Texas on the Ordinance of Secession, February 23, 1861: The Vote." *East Texas Historical Journal* 11 (fall 1973): 12–28.

Timrod, Henry. *Poems of Henry Timrod.* New York: E. J. Hale, 1873.

Traxler, Ralph N., Jr. "The Texas and Pacific Land Grants: A Comparison of Land Grant Policies of the United States and Texas." *Southwestern Historical Quarterly* 61 (Jan. 1958): 359–70.

Trickett, Dean. "The Civil War in Indian Territory, 1861." *Chronicles of Oklahoma* 17 (1939): 315–27.

———. "The Civil War in Indian Territory, 1861." *Chronicles of Oklahoma* 18 (1940): 142–53.

Tyler, Ronnie C. "Cotton on the Border, 1861–1865." *Southwestern Historical Quarterly* 73 (Apr. 1970): 456–77.

Vandiver, Frank. *Confederate Blockade Running through Bermuda, 1861–1865.* Austin: University of Texas Press, 1947.

———. "Notes and Documents: Letters from the Confederate Medical Service in Texas, 1863–1865." *Southwestern Historical Quarterly* 55 (Jan. 1952): 378–93.

――――. *Ploughshares into Swords: Josiah Gorgas and Confederate Ordnance.* Austin: University of Texas Press, 1952.

――――. *Rebel Brass: The Confederate Command System.* Baton Rouge: Louisiana State University Press, 1956.

――――. "Some Problems Involved in Writing Confederate History." *Journal of Southern History* 36 (Aug. 1970): 400–410.

――――. *Their Tattered Flags: The Epic of the Confederacy.* New York: Harper's Magazine Press, 1970.

Wakelyn, Jon L. *Biographical Dictionary of the Confederacy.* Westport, Conn.: Greenwood Press, 1977.

――――. *Southern Pamphlets on Secession, November 1860–April 1861.* Chapel Hill: University of North Carolina Press, 1996.

――――. *Southern Unionist Pamphlets and the Civil War.* Columbia: University of Missouri Press, 1999.

――――. "The Speakers of the State Legislatures' Failure as Confederate Leaders." In *Leadership during the Civil War: Themes in Honor of T. Harry Williams,* ed. Roman J. Heleniak and Lawrence L. Hewitt, 153–70. Shippensburg, Pa.: White Mane Publishing, 1992.

Wallenstein, Peter. *From Slave South to New South: Public Policy in Nineteenth-Century Georgia.* Chapel Hill: University of North Carolina Press, 1987.

Wardell, Morris L. *A Political History of the Cherokee Nation, 1838–1907.* Norman: University of Oklahoma Press, 1938.

Warner, Ezra J., and Wilfred Buck Yearns. *Biographical Register of the Confederate Congress.* Baton Rouge: Louisiana State University Press, 1975.

War of the Rebellion: Official Records of the Union and Confederate Armies. Washington, D.C.: U.S. Government Printing Office, 1883.

Watkins, Clara. *Kerr County, Texas, 1856–1976.* Hill Country Preservation Society, 1975.

Watson, Samuel J. " 'This Thankless . . . Unholy War': Army Officers and Civil-Military Relations in the Second Seminole War." In *The Southern Albatross: Race and Ethnicity in the American South,* ed. Philip D. Dillard and Randal L. Hall, 9–49. Macon, Ga.: Mercer University Press, 1999.

Waugh, John C. *Sam Bell Maxey and the Confederate Indians.* Fort Worth: Ryan Place, 1995.

White, Anita Louis. "The Teacher in Texas, 1836–1879." Ph.D. diss., Baylor University, 1972.

White, Michael Allen. "History of Education in Texas, 1860–1884." Ph.D. diss., Baylor University, 1969.

Wigfall, Louis T. *Speech of Hon. Louis T. Wigfall of Texas, in Reply to Mr. Douglas, and on Mr. Powell's Resolution, Delivered in the Senate of the United States, December 11th and 12th, 1860.* Washington, D.C.: Lemuel Towers, 1860.

———. *Speech of Louis T. Wigfall, on the Pending Political Issues, Delivered at Tyler, Smith County, Texas, September 3, 1860.* Washington, D.C.: Lemuel Towers, 1860.

Wilbarger, J. W. *Indian Depredations in Texas.* Austin: Hutchings Printing House, 1889.

Williams, Amelia, and Eugene C. Barker, eds. *The Writings of Sam Houston.* 8 vols. Austin: University of Texas Press, 1941.

Williams, John Hoyt. *Sam Houston: A Bibliography of the Father of Texas.* New York: Simon and Schuster, 1993.

Woodman, Harold D. *King Cotton and His Retainers: Financing and Marketing the Cotton Crop of the South, 1800–1925.* Lexington: University Press of Kentucky, 1968.

Wooster, Ralph. "Ben H. Epperson: East Texas Lawyer, Legislator, and Civil Leader." *East Texas Historical Journal* 5 (Mar. 1967): 29–42.

———. *The Secession Conventions of the South.* Princeton: Princeton University Press, 1962.

———. *Texas and Texans in the Civil War.* Austin, Texas: Eakin Press, 1995.

Wooster, Robert. *The Military and United States Indian Policy, 1865–1903.* New Haven: Yale University Press, 1988.

Wooten, Dudley G., ed. *A Comprehensive History of Texas, 1685–1897.* Austin: Texas State Historical Association, 1986.

Wright, Gavin. *The Political Economy of the Cotton South: Households, Markets, and Wealth in the Nineteenth Century.* New York: W. W. Norton, 1978.

Wyatt-Brown, Bertram. *Southern Honor: Ethics and Behavior in the Old South.* New York: Oxford University Press, 1982.

Yearns, Wilfred Buck, ed. *The Confederate Governors.* Athens: University of Georgia Press, 1985.

Young, Robert W. *Senator James Murray Mason: Defender of the Old South.* Knoxville: University of Tennessee Press, 1998.

Index